ENGAGING STUDENTS IN ACADEMIC LITERACIES

The Common Core State Standards require schools to include writing in a variety of genres across the disciplines. *Engaging Students in Academic Literacies* provides specific information to plan and carry out genre-based writing instruction in English for K–5 students within various content areas. Informed by systemic functional linguistics—a theory of language IN USE in particular ways for particular audiences and social purposes—it guides teachers in developing students' ability to construct texts using structural and linguistic features of the written language. This approach to teaching writing and academic language is valuable in addressing the persistent achievement gap between ELLs and "mainstream" students, especially in the context of current reforms in the U.S.

Rooted in the experiences of urban classroom teachers and their students, this text transforms systemic functional linguistics and genre theory into concrete classroom tools for designing, implementing, and reflecting on instruction and provides essential scaffolding for teachers to build their own knowledge of its essential elements applied to teaching. Lessons anchored on theory include strategies for apprenticing students to writing in all genres, features of elementary students' writing, and examples of practice in elementary school across English language arts, social studies, math, and science. The implicit argument developed throughout is that knowledge of how texts work will enhance teachers' ability to support students in their literacy development.

The ideas and data in this timely and important text have been tested for six years in pre-service teacher education courses and in-service teacher preparation. Making systemic functional linguistics and genre theory accessible and offering careful guidance in applying it, *Engaging Students in Academic Literacies* equips pre- and in-service teachers to be well prepared to implement the Common Core Standards and provides the tools for elementary schools to plan and carry out their writing curriculum.

María Estela Brisk is Professor, Boston College, USA.

ENGAGING STUDENTS IN ACADEMIC LITERACIES

Genre-based Pedagogy for K–5 Classrooms

María Estela Brisk

NEW YORK AND LONDON

First published 2015
by Routledge
711 Third Avenue, New York, NY 10017

and by Routledge
2 Park Square, Milton Park, Abingdon, Oxon OX14 4RN

Routledge is an imprint of the Taylor & Francis Group, an informa business

Library of Congress Cataloging-in-Publication Data
Brisk, María Estela, 1940–
Engaging students in academic literacies : genre-based pedagogy for K–5 classrooms / María Estela Brisk.
pages cm
Includes bibliographical references and index.
1. Education, Bilingual—United States. 2. Functionalism (Linguistics) 3. Systemic grammar. 4. Language arts (Elementary)—Standards—United States. I. Title.
LC3731.B683 2014
370.117'50973—dc23
2014009604

ISBN: 978-0-415-73703-6 (hbk)
ISBN: 978-0-415-73704-3 (pbk)
ISBN: 978-1-317-81616-4 (ebk)

Typeset in Bembo
by Apex CoVantage, LLC

To all the teachers and their students who taught me so much,
especially my friend and colleague Elizabeth MacDonald.

CONTENTS

PREFACE

The introduction of the Common Core State Standards (CCSS) in 2010, adopted by 45 states, the District of Columbia, four territories, and the Department of Defense Education Activity, has put more emphasis on writing and on literacy across the curriculum. This book supports these new demands on school districts and schools by providing explicit ways to approach writing instruction within the English language arts, science, and social studies curricula.

The purpose of *Engaging Students in Academic Literacies* is to provide teachers with an approach to teaching writing grounded on systemic functional linguistics that will expand students' knowledge of a variety of genres useful in various disciplinary contexts. This approach guides teachers in developing students' ability to construct texts using structural and linguistic features of the written language. Lessons are anchored on theory, features of elementary students' writing, and suggestions for practice. The content of the book draws on work in two urban schools carried out over 5 years. The whole staff participated in professional development, analysis of student work, and implementation of units. Their work is featured throughout the book. Their names have been used with their permission because they are important contributors to the development of this book's content (One teacher allowed me to use only her first name). Both native speakers of English and linguistically and culturally diverse students were enrolled in these schools. Because of the flexibility of the approach, teachers have been able to adjust the content to a variety of students' background and levels of development.

Overview

The book is organized in nine chapters and a conclusion. Chapters 3–9 open with a chapter map for easy reference of their content. Part I, chapters 1–3, provides the background knowledge needed to implement instructional strategies covered in chapters 4–9.

Chapter 1 briefly describes systemic functional linguistic (SFL) theory and the teaching and learning cycle (TLC). Both support the content and approach to teaching writing recommended in this book. It also explains how this approach compares with current practices and the CCSS. A description of children's writing development helps situate the possibilities of writing instruction.

Chapter 2 proposes how a school can organize its writing curriculum and how teachers can implement writing units based on the experience working with schools over the years. Chapter 3 explains aspects of language and challenges of second language (L2) writers that teacher candidates and teachers implementing the ideas in the genre chapters will need to know.

In Part II, chapters 4–9 present ways to create units of writing for various genres: Procedure (chapter 4), Recounts and Historical Genres (chapter 5), Reports (chapter 6), Explanations (chapter 7), Arguments (chapter 8), and Fictional Narratives (chapter 9). Each chapter contains suggestions for unit preparation and teaching of purpose, stages of the genre (text structure), and aspects of language that would be most helpful to develop in order for children to write in that particular genre. Each aspect is explained and illustrated with examples of students' performance (student names are pseudonyms) and followed by suggestions for lessons. Lessons are not fully developed in the interest of saving space and to allow teacher flexibility. A number of resources at the end of each chapter support implementation, such as forms to analyze student work, graphic organizers, children's literature useful to model the genre, and others.

A concluding chapter, Part III, describes the purpose of the book and the place of English academic literacy learning in the wider context of the variety of language and literacy experiences that children attending elementary schools have. It also gives suggestions on how it can be used to map a writing program in an elementary school.

Because this work and the resulting book were developed to enhance what was happening in actual schools it does not cover response to literature genre or teaching of spelling and mechanics. Most schools cover those two skills as writing instruction. The recommendations in this book expand that concept of writing to include a greater variety of genres with a strong emphasis on language as meaning-making resource.

Background

The content of this book has been piloted for a number of years in both pre-service and in-service preparation. An important goal of this preparation has been to change the way teacher candidates and teachers see text, both published and student produced. When reading, most teachers extract content from published text. This book aims at teaching how authors structure text when writing in different genres, and how they use language to write what they mean. Being able to read as a writer allows teachers to help students learn ways of writing sanctioned by the culture, especially in academic settings. Similarly, scrutinizing student texts with focus on text structure and language helps teachers plan instruction that is specific to enhancing students' ability to organize text that makes sense and appropriate the language that they need to mean in academic contexts.

Depending on the age/grade level of the students and English language ability of the children, those using the book may want to carry out lessons to greater depth and breadth. It is always important to cover the purpose and stages or structure of the genre so that students have a sense of whole text and what they can accomplish by writing in that genre. The specifics of language can be covered over the grades as students become more proficient in the language of writing. However, it does need to be addressed if children are going to excel in academic writing.

One fundamental principle reflected in this book is that the role of the teacher is indeed to teach by interacting with students around texts and language in the context of interesting content that enhances students' knowledge. This instruction on how written English works helps students gain confidence in their ability to express ideas and share their writing with audiences.

ACKNOWLEDGMENTS

This book is the result of many years of study and collaborations. I would like to thank Mary Schleppegrell for introducing me to systemic functional linguistics through her copious writings and to my Australian colleagues whose work and intellectual generosity helped me navigate the intricacies of the theory and practice, particularly Jim Martin, Sally Humphrey, Beverly Derewianka, David Rose, Frances Christie, and Pauline Jones. I am grateful to the school leaders, especially Tamara Blake-Canty and Caitlin Keeton, who facilitated and supported my work in the schools. I am deeply indebted to my doctoral students who helped me collect and make sense of the data, especially Margarita Zisselsberger, Liz Harris, Tracy Hodgson-Drysdale, Frank Daniello, Christina Pavlak, Catherine Michener, Marla DeRosa, and Meredith Moore, and to my undergraduate research assistants who spent hours entering data and keeping it straight.

Without courageous and bright teachers ready to learn and try new things the book would have never come to be. They and their students have taught most of what I know.

I would also like to thank the reviewers—Meg Gebhard, University of Massachusetts Amherst, USA; Sally Humphrey, Australian Catholic University Australia; and Joy Janzen, Stony Brook University, USA—whose comments highly enhanced the original manuscript.

PART I
Content and Pedagogy

1

PRINCIPLES FOR PRACTICE

This chapter addresses the theories that inform this book, makes connections with the dominant approach to writing both nationally and internationally and to the Common Core State Standards (CCSS), and briefly explains children's writing development. Systemic functional linguistics (SFL) and genre pedagogy inform the content, units, and lessons proposed in this book. SFL is a theory of language developed by Michael Halliday (Halliday, 1985; 1994; Halliday & Matthiessen, 2004). According to this theory, texts exist in context. Language users' choices impact and are constrained by the social context. SFL has been applied to the study of texts and genres by James Martin and by other scholars (Martin & Rose, 2008). Through experiences in the school, the notion of the Teaching and Learning Cycle emerged and was refined over time (Rothery, 1996).

To help educators position the content of this book in past and current contexts of teaching writing, this chapter makes the connection between the pedagogy proposed in this book and process writing, the dominant theory in schools in the United States and in other parts of the world. In addition, the genres developed in this book are compared with the text types proposed in the CCSS. These standards have been recently issued in the United States and have been adopted by 45 states, the District of Columbia, four territories, and the Department of Defense Education Activity. Implementation, however, is still in its infancy.

The chapter concludes with an overview of children's writing development. Throughout the chapter, topics are related to bilingual children writing in English as a second or additional language. These students populate many classrooms in the English-speaking world, particularly urban centers in the United States.

Systemic Functional Linguistics and Genre Pedagogy

SFL is rooted in Halliday's (1985) scholarship on social semiotics, which can be defined as the relationship between text and context. SFL is "a very useful descriptive and interpretive framework for viewing language as a strategic, meaning-making resource" (Eggins, 2004, p. 2). SFL is helpful for teachers because it gives them a concrete way to guide their students in the use of language, especially in academic contexts. Learning all of the contextual and linguistic elements that come together to create a text allows teachers to discuss them with students and help identify them in texts they read and write.

Other linguists and educators applied SFL to education, including the practices of reading and writing (Derewianka & Jones, 2012; Humphrey, Droga, & Feez, 2012; Rose & Martin, 2012). In the United States, SFL caught the interest of educators, especially those working with bilingual populations (Brisk, 2012; Brisk & Zisselsberger, 2011; Bunch, 2013; De Oliveira & Iddings, forthcoming; Fang & Schleppegrell, 2008; Gebhard, Chen, & Britton, in press; Schleppegrell, 2004). Research on and practice of literacy in elementary and secondary contexts in connection to a variety of disciplines has emerged from this work.

Language Metafunctions

Most definitions of language include the notion that language is a system of communication (Harris & Hodges, 1995). SFL theory argues that language has three metafunctions: ideational (which includes the experiential and the logical functions), interpersonal, and textual. The experiential function involves the language used to represent experiences or content, that is, language used to express ideas. In written language, this occurs through the expression of meaning through clauses and their components: processes (verb groups), participants (noun groups), and circumstances (adverbials). When these clauses combine to form clause complexes, the logical function is present expressing logical relations between multiple ideas, that is, the language used to connect ideas.

The interpersonal function enables language users to interact with each other. These interactions are between the composer of the text (speaker or writer) and the audience (listener or reader). When writing, the authors choose language with awareness of their audience and the voice or identity they want to reflect.

Language also functions to create a cohesive oral, written, or multimodal message, the textual function. In written language, this includes the flow of the text facilitated by a variety of lexical and grammatical features. In written language, it also includes components of the writing system, such as spelling and mechanics (Christie, 2012; Derewianka, 2011; Halliday & Matthiessen, 2004).

Language Levels

There are three levels or strata of language resources available to users to accomplish the functions introduced earlier: semantic, lexicogrammatical, and expressive. These levels function in close interrelation (Butt, Fahey, Feez, Spinks, & Yallop, 2000; Christie, 2012). When writing, authors express meaning through words and grammar, which in turn are represented using the writing system of the language. For example, to write the clause "Snakes have only one shape," writers need to tap into their semantic resources to consider how they map on to lexical items, such as *snakes* and *shape.* They also need to know how to order the words to reflect that they are talking about snakes having only one shape, talking about snakes collectively and generally by adding the plural marker, and describing how things are by using the timeless present tense. They also need to know how to form the letters, use capitalization, and use commas to encode comprehensible ideas.

Therefore, one of the functions of schooling is to develop students' proficiency in language at these three levels in order to become accomplished writers. For writing, it is essential to focus on the meanings related to the various disciplines in school, the vocabulary of the discipline, the grammar of written language, and the features of the writing system that will make their text comprehensible.

Bilinguals have these resources available in both languages. Depending on proficiency, the lexical representation of concepts may be stronger in one language (Kroll & Stewart, 1994; Leider, Proctor, & Silverman, in review). Linguistic resources from the stronger language are relied upon when writing in the weaker language (what is known as transfer). For example, a 3rd grader new to English did not use the subject pronoun with a verb as it is done in Spanish, writing, *And then hatch* instead of "And then it hatched." However, when she learned she needed to use subject pronouns with a verb in English, she started using them in both languages (Brisk, 2012). Bilinguals may switch to a different language (code-switch) for specific reasons. For example, in her 2013 autobiography *My Beloved World,* U.S. Supreme Court Justice Sonia Sotomayor uses Spanish to express family experiences. She refers to her *abuela* when talking about her grandmother and describes poems and songs from her childhood in the womb of a Puerto Rican community. Thus, when teaching in students' second language, teachers must be aware that children have linguistic resources that they can tap into in the process of developing English.

Context of Culture: Genres

An essential premise of SFL is that language is conceived as whole text rather than as isolated words or sentences. These texts exist in the immediate context of the situation, which in turn is nested in the larger context of culture (Butt et al., 2000; Christie, 2012). The writing practices of a culture are characterized by recurrent forms of texts used for specific purposes with specific discourse organization and language features. These are called *genres* (Martin & Rose, 2008). The most common writing genres in elementary school include different types of recounts, fictional narratives, procedures, reports, explanations, and expositions (in this book, expositions will be referred to as arguments) (See Table 1.1). Recounts relate a series of events based on personal experience (personal recounts), an observed incident, or observations of phenomena (procedural recounts); they can also record historical events (autobiography, biography, and historical recounts) (Coffin, 2006). In addition, students may be asked to write in character (empathetic autobiography) as a way to understand a person or time in history (Christie & Derewianka, 2008). By contrast, fictional narratives tell an imaginative story consisting of a problem that leads to a crisis followed by a resolution. Fictional narratives are meant to entertain and to teach cultural values (Martin & Rothery, 1986). Procedures provide instructions for how something is done, whether general or scientific. A report is a factual text used to organize and store information clearly and succinctly (Schleppegrell, 2004). Explanations, like reports, are factual texts that explain how or why things happened. Finally, expositions or arguments persuade people to a particular point of view, with reasons introduced and supported with evidence. Discussions present both sides of the argument (Butt et al., 2000; Dewsbury, 1994). There are a variety of responses to literature genres: personal comment, character analysis, and thematic analysis (Christie & Derewianka, 2008). Often, students must respond to prompts on reading tests with an argumentative stance, where they need to prove a point through inferencing and supporting a claim with textual evidence.

Traditionally, schools have categorized all of these genres in large generic categories of fiction and non-fiction. Lessons specifically on non-fiction writing sometimes follow personal recounts (often called personal narratives), suggesting

TABLE 1.1 Genres of Elementary School

General Purpose	*Genre*	*Type of Organization*
Storytelling	Personal Recounts Procedural Recounts Autobiographies Empathetic Autobiographies Biographies Historical Recounts Fictional Narratives	Chronological
Giving instructions	Procedures	
Organizing information	Reports Explanations	Rhetorical
Persuading	Expositions or Arguments Discussions	

that personal recounts are not non-fiction or factual. Although for young children it may be useful to stress the difference between fiction and non-fiction, a better distinction to support writing development is determining whether a text requires a chronological or rhetorical organization. All forms of recounts and procedures are organized chronologically, a more natural organization for young students. On the other hand, reports, explanations, and arguments are organized by subtopics based on content and purpose. Decisions for grouping the material require an ability to categorize and abstract, a task that can be quite difficult for elementary students.

The purpose of each genre differs and is achieved through the stages and language used. For example, the book *Slinky Scaly Slithery Snakes* (See Figure 1.1) is written as a report. The first stage is a general statement about snakes, followed by a series of paragraphs, each giving information on one aspect or type of snakes, and ending with a summarizing comment about the role of snakes in an ecosystem. These stages accomplish the purpose of reports, which is to present information in an organized way. Reports are written in the timeless present, and a great deal of the information is packed in complex noun groups. Thus, in choosing a genre for writing, students need to be instructed on the stages or text organization and language features so that their choices allow them to accomplish the purpose of the particular genre. The features of genres in the English-speaking culture have been illustrated by a number of SFL researchers, including Butt et al. (2000), Derewianka (1990), Derewianka and Jones (2012), Humphrey et al. (2012), Knapp and Watkins (2005), Martin & Rose (2008), and Schleppegrell (2004). The genres of specific disciplines have been further analyzed, including history (Coffin, 2006; Schleppegrell & Achugar, 2003), social studies (Bunch, 2006), science (De Oliveira & Dodds, 2010; Veel, 2000), and mathematics (De Oliveira and Cheng, 2011; Marks & Mousley, 1990; Schleppegrell, 2007).

Slinky Scaly Slithery Snakes by Dorothy Hinshaw Patent

You'd think it would be hard to survive in the wild without legs. But look at snakes! More than 2,500 kinds slither and creep throughout the world. Snakes live just about everywhere except on some islands and near the North and South Poles. They can climb the tallest trees or burrow deep into the earth. Some snakes never leave the water. Others remain forever on land.

Snakes have only one shape, but they come in many different sizes. Two-inch-long thread snakes are as skinny as a strand of spaghetti. But a thirty-two-foot reticulated python is big enough to eat a pig or even a small person.

The book continues for 31 pages, introducing on each some aspects of snakes and information about different types of snakes. It concludes with the importance of snakes in nature.

FIGURE 1.1 Sample Text

Patent, D.H. (2000) Slinky, Scaly, Slithery Snakes. New York, N.Y.: Walker & Co, p. 1

In addition to the context of culture, texts exist within the context of situations where language choices vary with respect to three variables: field, tenor, and mode. These variables constitute the *register* and correspond with the three metafunctions of language (Eggins, 2004; Halliday & Matthiessen, 2004; Thompson, 2004). Language reflects the *field* or content of the text (experiential function) through clauses formed by processes, participants, and circumstances. When clauses combine in clause complexes, the logical function serves to express relationships, often signaled by conjunctions. The *tenor* of a text reflects the relationship between language users. In writing, language choices depend on the author's awareness of audience and the intended writer's voice or identity. Language resources used to create a cohesive text constitute the *mode*. Language choices will differ depending on whether the text is oral or written (further detail on the aspect of register will be included in chapter 3). Multimodal texts also include the images that complement the meaning expressed by language. To illustrate the relationship of language and register see the report in Figure 1.1. In this example, the field or topic is snakes. The types, features, habitats, diet, predators, and reproduction of snakes are expressed through clauses and clause complexes. With respect to tenor, the author is an adult writing to upper elementary school children. This is reflected by the use of verb groups, noun groups, and adverbials that offer enough technical information, but which are still comprehensible by that age group. Although the whole book is written in statements and the third person voice gives it an authoritative voice typical of the report genre, the author uses an exclamation, second person voice, and modals in the first paragraph, reflecting an entertaining voice to attract the attention of elementary age children.

The text achieves its cohesion through paragraphs that flow through well-connected themes and new information. For example, the new information on size in the first clause of the second paragraph becomes the theme of the two clauses that follow expanding the concept of size. The reference ties are clear, and the lexicon connects the concept of snakes throughout the piece. Occasionally, because the report is for children, the author uses such terms as *spaghetti*. Although this term is not strongly associated with snakes, it helps create a vivid image. As in most reports, there are no text connectives connecting paragraphs because each paragraph stands on its own with a self-standing subtopic.

The structure of the text is also impacted by the *medium*. Students can produce the pieces they write in the different genres in the form of (but not limited to) essays, picture books, letters, poems, brochures, posters, PowerPoints, and blogs. Each calls for specific organizational structures and language, making it easier or more difficult for students to produce. The traditional English language arts (ELA) literature refers to these structures as genres. Making the distinction between genre and medium needs to be made clear for students because the various genres can be produced in any of the various mediums. For example, *A Ballad of Ducks* and *The Mosquito's Song* are both poems, but the first is a fictional narrative while the latter is an argument.

Teaching and Learning Cycle

The choices that students make while writing are related to the resources available to them. Teachers build these resources through instruction. The teaching and learning cycle (TLC) is an approach to writing instruction that supports student writing through four stages: negotiation of field or developing content knowledge, deconstruction of text, joint construction of text, and independent construction of text (Rothery, 1996). To address issues of reading comprehension, David Rose and his colleagues developed the Reading to Learn project that includes additional steps to the teaching cycle (Rose & Martin, 2012).

During the negotiation of field, students develop the content knowledge of the particular discipline and topic they will be writing about and the language needed to express that knowledge. This particular aspect of the TLC actually takes place in anticipation of writing and during the other stages, as well (Rose & Martin, 2012). Teachers guide the students through deconstruction, or close analysis of mentor texts, that illustrates the stages and the language features of the focused genre. The focus of the deconstruction is linked to the particular objective or unit as determined by the teacher. For example, a kindergarten teacher used the book *Chrysanthemum* to illustrate the stages of fictional narratives by pointing out the orientation, complication, resolution, and ending of the story, and encouraging students to recall the name of the stages as she retold the story using finger puppets (Brisk & Zisselsberger, 2011).

Teachers collaborate with the students in their class to jointly construct the text on the basis of what they have learned through the deconstruction of mentor texts. Teachers and students are familiar with approaching the text as readers, to "read for the sake of gaining new information, novel experiences, and interesting viewpoints" (McKeough, 2013, p. 87). When deconstructing a text, teachers and students should read the text as writers, to "turn the text inside-out to see how it is made, how it is held together, and what makes it work" (p. 87).

With all of the knowledge and experience acquired through deconstruction and joint construction of a text, students can then create their own independent writing. Rothery (1996) represents the TLC as a circle because "there are different points of entry for students according to their development in learning and literacy" (pp. 101–102). She also argues that the TLC is not a linear process, but may go back to a previous stage before moving forward to the next. One teacher working with L2 (second language) learners found it important to make the TLC an iterative process. She repeated the deconstruction, joint construction, and independent construction stages throughout the process of writing biographies (Pavlak, 2013). This greatly facilitated the writing process for the students because they were able to focus on one stage at a time.

An important aspect of the TLC is the development of metalanguage to talk about the genre and language features of students writing. This metalanguage labels with greater precision and function the resources the students need to use to carry out their writing. The more precise the metalanguage, the more helpful it is for students. Thus, using SFL terms like *orientation, sequence of events,* and *conclusion* or *evaluation* to talk about the stages of a personal recount are more descriptive of the content in each stage than the commonly used *beginning, middle,* and *end* terminology. Every genre has a beginning, but they can be very different in nature. Thus, an argument has a thesis statement or claim, a report includes a general statement, an explanation states the phenomenon, and recounts and narratives have an orientation.

Many teachers tell students to "add details." However, the word *details* can mean different things, including reasons ("OK, but we are not going to come up with more ideas, we want to think of supporting details"), events ("Again, we could leave some of those details of the story for later"), and adjectives ("Include details! This makes your reading interesting!") (Daniello, Turgut, & Brisk, in press, pp. 14–15). Only by the context can the meaning of the term *detail* be inferred. Therefore, it is better to replace *detail* with more precise terminology. When Pat, a 4th-grade teacher, asked his students, "If a *reason* is depression, what would some *evidence* be in that paragraph?" there is no question that he was talking about the stages of an argument.

Harris (2011) found that her 4th-grade students were able to make better comments on each other's writings when they were availed of metalanguage to talk about their writing. For example, she reports that, "During a peer conference later in the week, Tom agreed that Adam had 'good action verbs'" (p. 109). Similarly, Williams (1999) found that metalanguage is a useful tool for students to understand the grammar of the text. Gebhard et al. (2014, p. 123) also concluded that

> ELLs benefited from learning how to use SFL metalanguage to read and write disciplinary texts. For example . . . they learned to identify expected genre moves and register features, classify different types of processes and participants, notice how and why authors shift tenses, catalogue different types of conjunctions, and track theme/rhyme patterns in assigned readings and in their own texts to note how coherence is achieved in extended written discourse.

Connection With Process Writing

Process Writing has dominated the teaching of writing in many education settings. Process Writing is iterative, helping a writer create and improve a piece. Children are encouraged to modify their writing numerous times (Graves, 1983). Students work in a classroom set up as a workshop, where they write under the guidance of an expert teacher (Fletcher & Portalupi, 2001). Thus, this pedagogy is often referred to as Writers' Workshop. When using an SFL-informed approach to teaching writing, Process Writing does not have to be displaced because it addresses different aspects of writing. They can complement each other. Process

Writing focuses on the process of creating a piece of writing, which entails planning, drafting, revising, editing, and publishing. SFL provides the content of what to teach during each of these activities. In addition, TLC gives specific suggestions for what teachers need to do to prepare students to write. In Process Writing, the support of the teacher increases after students write through teacher conferences. Children from some cultures are confused with this approach because their expectations at school are to write correctly from the start (Dien, 2004).

The problem with Process Writing is that it does not give students much guidance on what to plan or draft, and there is no clear basis for revision or editing. Research done in Australia on students' writing guided by the process approach where students chose what to write and teachers acted as facilitators illustrated that

> most students had to make use of text types they were familiar with from spoken language outside the school—including short observations and comments on past experience, and recounts of unproblematic sequences of events. This limited experience of writing did very little to prepare students for learning across the curriculum in primary school, for writing in the specialized subject areas of secondary schools, or for dealing with the various community genres they might encounter as the most fluent English speaker of their family.
>
> (Martin, 2009, p. 11)

The approach proposed in this book introduces a variety of genres and guides teachers through a process that draws from the TLC and Process Writing, as well as from modifications developed in cooperation with teachers participating in writing projects. Using this approach, students are apprenticed to the given genre through exploration of mentor texts and writing collaboratively with the teacher and other students. The elements of Process Writing—planning, drafting, revising, and editing—are present, but they have been intertwined with the TLC to make students feel informed and confident in their ability to write. Apprenticing students to writing makes the process easier—for both students and teachers—than if students had been asked to write after a short mini-lesson. Students produce pieces in a variety of genres and media that have been crafted with attention to the context of a situation or register. Teachers allow newcomers to write their individual pieces in their own language if they so desire. When connected with various disciplines, writing extends students' knowledge of the discipline.

"A workshop is a place where people *do* things, usually under the guidance of a master craftsperson" (Elbow & Belanoff, 1989, p. 4). Many of the key aspects of Writers' Workshop are essential in any writing classroom, including having an authentic purpose for writing, organizing students to work on projects, and having students choose topics and own their work (Fletcher & Portalupi, 2001).

In the approach proposed in this book, however, there are some modifications. For example, the topic choices are made within the discipline content in which the writing is embedded, and the purpose is connected to the particular genre. As explained in the TLC approach, the role of the teacher is to apprentice the students to writing through deconstruction and joint construction of text as opposed to students writing with only minimal teaching through mini-lessons and conferencing. Similar to Writers' Workshop, the students learn by doing, but only after having experienced the particular type of writing through analysis of mentor texts and writing with the whole class facilitated by the teacher. Conferencing and sharing are carried out with goals related to the structure of texts and features of language defined by the genre, topic, audience and voice, and need for creating a cohesive text. For example, students in Cheryl O'Connor's 4th-grade class shared their report posters among themselves. She instructed them to provide feedback about the elements and language features of a report rather than simply commenting that they liked the piece (Brisk, Hodgson-Drysdale, & O'Connor, 2011).

Connections With Common Core State Standards

The CCSS (National Governors Association Center for Best Practices & Council of Chief State School Officers, 2010; www.corestandards.org/) consider three broad text types: narratives, informational/explanatory, and arguments. Each of these include standards and sample texts in Appendix B. Using the SFL lens to analyze these text types, it becomes evident that each includes a variety of genres (See Figure 1.2). The CCSS narratives cover personal recounts, fictional narratives, and perhaps autobiographies. The all-encompassing informational/explanatory category includes procedures, reports, explanations, biographies, and historical recounts. The arguments category covers exposition, discussion, and some response to literature genres. There is no indication of where procedural recounts and empathetic autobiographies would fit; perhaps in the all-encompassing informational/explanatory category that seems to embrace what traditionally was known as non-fiction.

The problem with the CCSS broad text types (in circles) is that the genres within, as defined by SFL (rectangles), have different purposes, structures, and language. For example, the purpose of a report is to organize information, its text structure includes a general statement and subtopics, and the verbs are in the present tense and express relations or actions. A biography's purpose is to recount the life of a significant historical figure, the text structure includes an orientation, a sequence of events, and a conclusion stating the significance of the person's life, and the verb types include action, saying, feeling, and thinking, helping to develop the central figure. These are all very different features from reports. Most of the standards under informational/explanatory text types better fit the report genre. There are no standards within this category that support learning procedures, explanations, or the historical genres. Similar lack of specificity is encountered in

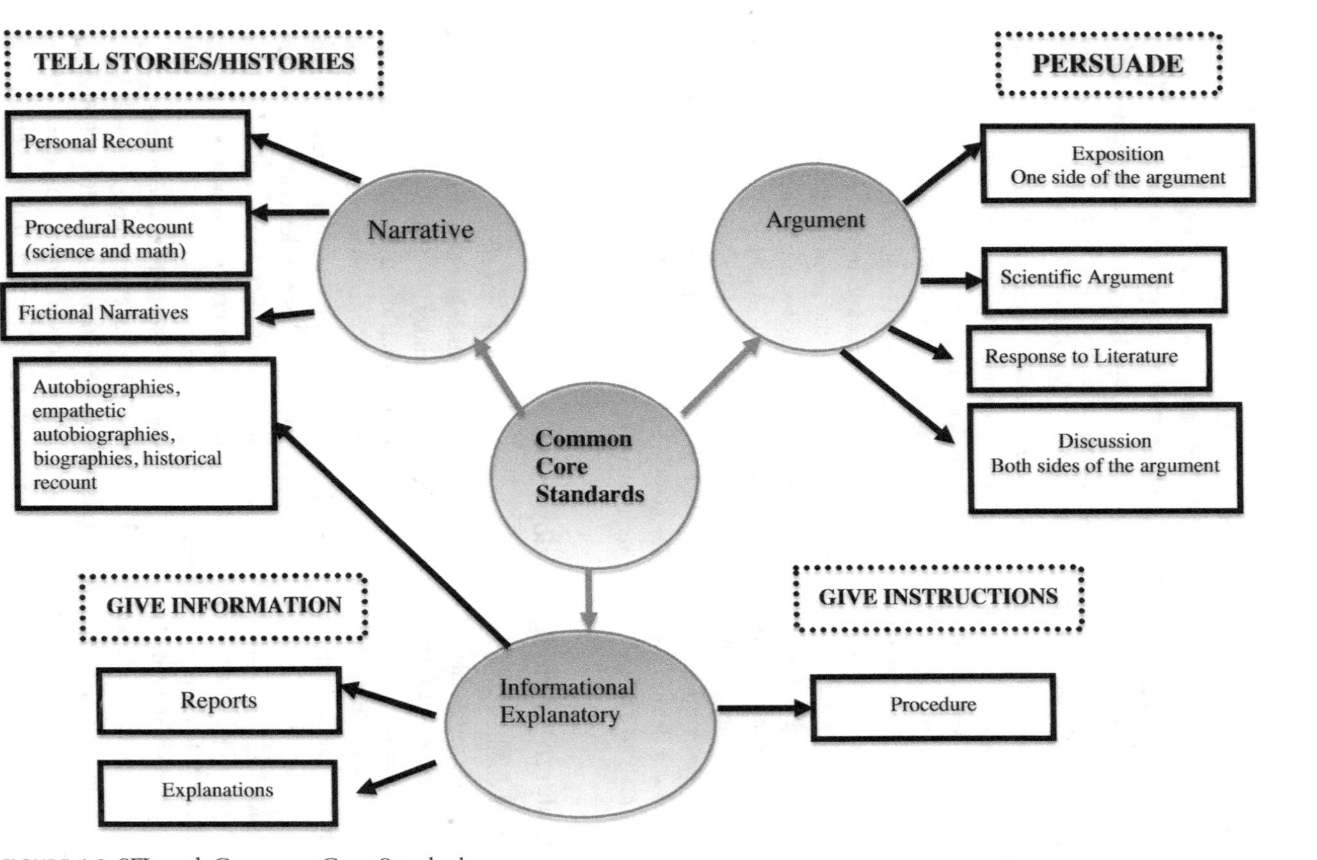

FIGURE 1.2 SFL and Common Core Standards

the other two text types, leaving teachers to make their own guesses and decisions. Thus, using SFL can give specific guidance to teachers implementing the CCSS and enhance learning of writing for students. The genre chapters in Part II of this text further situate the CCSS within the SFL genres.

The CCSS writing standards include text types only. Language is a separate category with generic standards with respect to vocabulary, grammar, and conventions. SFL, on the other hand, shows that specific language features help accomplish the purpose of a genre. For example, a CCSS vocabulary standard for Grade 1 states, "Distinguish shades of meaning among verbs differing in manner (e.g. *look, peek, glance, stare, glare, scowl*) and adjectives differing in intensity (e.g. *large, gigantic*) by defining or choosing them or by acting out the meanings" (CCSS.ELA-Literacy.L.1.5d). SFL considers the choice of these types of words a function of voice. By choosing a particular word, writers show their point of view and try to influence their audience, a critical feature of argument writing (Humphrey et al., 2012). SFL provides information to implement language standards by tying vocabulary and grammar with the genres and register. Therefore, the SFL-informed approach presented in this book provides teachers with much needed direction, clarity, and specificity to implement the CCSS, now demanded in a number of U.S. states (Daniello, 2013). Moreover, even if the CCSS are someday eliminated, teachers can still use the approach in this book because it defines the kind of academic writing expected by culture and provides the tools to change writing to meet these expectations.

Children's Writing Development

Most children develop written language from their experience with the spoken language, but oral and written language play different roles in our society and have features that distinguish these modes. As Halliday (1989) points out, "writing and speaking are not just alternative ways of doing the same things; rather, they are ways of doing different things" (p. xv). In oral discourse, speaker and listener share a specific time and place. However, in writing, the author and reader do not. Therefore, "the writer must be precise in his/her lexical, syntactic and structural choices in order to facilitate the reader's interpretation of text" (Fang, 1997, p. 345). Moreover, in oral communication, intonation and non-verbal forms of expression support linguistic meaning-making.

Learning to write involves acquiring different discourse and lexicogrammatical structures from oral language. Thus, learning to write is comparable to learning a second language, where L2 learners use the resources of their first language. Similarly, children use their oral language resources when writing (Kress, 1994). The initial demands of writing are such that children are usually behind from their oral language development (Christie, 2012; Loban, 1976). Halliday (1993) claims that children are behind by up to three years in their ability to make meaning through writing. Further, as Heath (1983) illustrated in her research, ways of communicating differ among communities of different cultural and social backgrounds. Some of the oral language dialects are closer to the written version than others, making learning to write a different experience given children's background (Kress, 1994).

When learning to write in English, children have to learn the writing system of English, including letter formation, punctuation, capitalization, directionality, and spacing. In addition, they need to develop the ability to create cohesive texts in a variety of genres with effective meaning-making vocabulary and grammar. In school, children encounter a variety of genres. There is a natural tension between the benefit of teachers and students controlling the genres and being controlled by them. Learning the specific demands of each genre can inhibit students' creativity. On the other hand, as a 4th grader expressed it, students feel free and confident to write once having appropriated the language of argumentation (Sánchez Ares, 2012). Thus, control of the genres empowers children to be able to accomplish specific purposes through writing (Kress, 1994).

Elementary school children bring with them rich language resources and an intuitive sense of the functions of language. However, they need to further develop the language of content area disciplines and the ability to express relationships between concepts expressed in writing. It takes a number of years of schooling to fully master writing. According to Christie (2012), children go through four phases of language and literacy development, two of which take place during the elementary years. The first phase starts with the first years of schooling, when children express their ideas through drawings often accompanied with pseudo writing. Letters or groups of letters emerge, but do not always follow the accepted directionality and alignment. The written text usually starts by describing the drawing and later by telling the story illustrated in the drawing about a personal experience. As children grow, texts become longer and more complex. Language increasingly carries meaning, slowly replacing drawings as the vehicle for the message. Parallel to the development of the message is the development of the writing system. Children experiment with words writing approximations of the correct spelling with a few exceptions where words have been memorized and spelled correctly. The writing grows more conventional with further development, mainly related to the ability to pack language into clear, but meaning-rich clauses and sentences. Children move from writing about concrete ideas to include more abstraction (Christie 2012; Kress, 1996). Studies comparing the spoken and written language of elementary age children show changes between 3rd and 6th grades. These changes indicate that these years are important for supporting written language development (Kroll & Lempers, 1981; Lull, 1929). Christie (2012) suggests that children's language in their late childhood and early adolescent stage (ages 9–13) begins "to change, facilitated by a gradual expansion of language resources, so that children can make meanings in new ways" (p. 28). These changes pave the way for the understanding of the grammar of written language. As children make the transition from oral to written discourse, they achieve a growing control of the thematic patterns of their writing and show greater control of internal reference to build cohesion in their texts. Students learn to compress more information into different types of prepositional phrases and to use nominalizations and other strategies to expand noun groups and create denser texts (Hunt, 1965).

In terms of genres, students' ability to write in particular genres has been found to develop over time. As they mature, they become more skillful with specific aspects of the genre and language. Explanations and arguments are the most challenging and are best addressed in upper elementary grades. Procedures and personal recounts can be introduced in the very early grades.

Genre and medium preferences impact students' writing. When children write in their preferred genre or medium, their writing is much better than when they write in those that they dislike. Some children like personal recount, while others prefer fantasies and adventure stories. Often, but not always, these preferences run along gender lines (Franklin & Thompson, 1994; McPhail, 2009). Differences across gender were apparent in the quality of persuasive writing samples of Hispanic 4th-grade students. Female writers' essays "show a greater degree of elaboration and a clearer attempt to express the writer's point of view than those written by male Hispanic students, regardless of proficiency level" (Bermúdez & Prater, 1994, p. 53).

Some of the more pervasive challenges for children are to maintain a third person voice, typical of academic writing (Brisk, 2012). Children seem to feel the need to closely connect with their audience, leading them to use the first and second person. For example, 5th graders finished their animal reports by addressing their audience with a call to action. A 5th grader wrote, *Help!!! Also please try to save these animals. Also protect these animals for* [from] *the hunters. Please put hunting for tigers illegal.*

As in oral language, children's writing is not always concise. Ideas are expressed in separate simple sentences written independently or joined by the conjunction *and*. For example, a 5th-grade student started her biography of a classmate (real name was changed),

> *There is a girl name Millie Perez. Millie is 10 years old and born on 1998 and she was born in hondorous* [Honduras]. *Millie speaks 3 languages. She speaks spanish, english And a little or porkachees* [Portuguese].

These 6 clauses could become one sentence with the use of apposition and embedding: "Millie Perez, a 10-year old girl born in 1998 in Honduras, speaks Spanish, English, and a little Portuguese." The ability to pack writing and form clause complexes is a major challenge for elementary age children (Brisk & DeRosa, forthcoming). However, mastering packing language and forming clause complexes are necessary because they are typical features of written language (Kress, 1996).

As children grow, they express more complex ideas that are encoded in sentences of greater complexity, expressing specific logico-semantic relationships. Sometimes, children are successful: *An animal does not have these things* | | *since animals do not make their own food* (Grade 4). However, others use strings of clauses organized in a temporal order joined mainly with *and* and failing to clearly indicate the relationship between words. For example, a student wrote, *It is the end of the year and I am happy,* meaning "I am happy *because* it is the end of the year" (Brisk & DeRosa, forthcoming).

The demands of writing are related to children's cognitive development, as well. Although chronological order is easier, 5th graders had difficulty distinguishing between major events in a person's life and the detailed information about a particular event when writing biographical recounts. For example, when writing a biographical recount about his parents immigrating to the United States, one student wrote of three main events for the entire recount: who had left, when, and why. These three items simply described his parents' departure, the first major event. Other major events needed to follow to develop the whole biographical recount of their immigration experience.

Similar problems with categorization were apparent when analyzing students' topic sentences in reports. In order to write these sentences, students need to classify the information and name the topic of a particular paragraph. For example, in her report on leopards, a student wrote a paragraph about where leopards are found. Instead of introducing the topic, she started directly writing about where leopards are found, saying,

> *Some live in Africa Like these dark colored leopards live in the warm amazon dark rain forest. They even live in Asia. Did you know that few live in the world because people hut* [hunt] *for there* [their] *skin. Also because ther rainforest is getting Felled.*
>
> (Grade 5, JE, 11/10/09)

Writing Development of Bilingual Learners

Some of the developmental features in children's writing may be because some children are being raised in more than one language or that English is their second language. Bilingual students who are developing writing in their second language go through similar development as native speakers (Fitzgerald, 2006). They also have challenges related to their knowledge of the second language, and cross-linguistic and cross-cultural influences (Brisk, 2011).

Many bilingual students develop biliteracy abilities when they attend schools that promote them (Gort, 2006; Homza, 1995; Lindholm-Leary, 2001) or because they immigrated when they were already literate in their native language. Strong writing ability in the native language supports writing development in the second language (Barratt-Pugh & Rohl, 2001; Carlisle & Beeman, 2000). A correlation between native language writing ability and performance in English writing exists even when the languages have a different script (Cummins, 1991). Second language writers successfully tap their native language resources to solve the problem of composing in the second language. However, when features of the native language are different, the results are not fully successful. For example, Spanish-language features, such as placing adjectives after the noun or omitting personal pronouns, often appear in the English writing of Spanish speakers (Brisk, 2012; Gort, 2006; Simpson, 2004). Khmer speakers have difficulty with English past tense, plurals, use of articles, and prepositions because their language does not indicate past tense or plural with a morpheme added to a verb or noun and does not use articles or prepositions (Barratt-Pugh & Rohl, 2001). In this case, L2 writers need to learn the specific features of the second language.

Grammatical morphemes are one of the greatest challenges for L2 learners and can persist even when students have become very proficient in English (Genesee, Paradis, & Crago, 2004; Menyuk & Brisk, 2005). Genesee et al. (2004) define grammatical morphemes as "little words and inflectional affixes that are the 'glue' that sticks the content words together in the sentence" (p. 122). Errors such as dropping the "s" in plural nouns *(2 cup of sugar)* or regularizing irregular verbs *(He bringed the cake)* are common and persistent.

L2 writers are further impacted by culture. In the English-speaking culture, the writer is responsible for making the text clear and comprehensible for the reader. However, there are cultures where the burden is on the reader to interpret the text, freeing the writer from having to be explicit (Hinds, 1987).

Some genres evidence different characteristics across cultures (Connor, 2002; Hinkel, 2002; Matalene, 1985). For example, most children come to school familiar with narrative genres acquired in the context of the home where oral storytelling or book reading may be part of their daily practice. However, narratives vary in structure across cultures (McCabe & Bliss, 2003; Pérez, 2004). When children are asked to write personal recounts in school, they will use their own cultural patterns of telling stories. Sometimes, children may feel conflicted because it is not appropriate to share personal matters in school in some cultures (Dien, 2004).

It is important not to stereotype cultural differences because the writing of L2 students is not only influenced by culture, but also by personal experiences and instruction (Matsuda, 1997). Further, some bilingual students are raised in a bilingual environment where they become familiar with both cultural patterns. In contrast, those who immigrate as preschoolers experience writing directly in the second language and are not always familiar with the written form of their heritage language (Lisle & Mano, 1997).

In summary, the development of writing is a difficult and complex task. This section has provided an overview of the challenges confronted by elementary age students of different backgrounds (For a thorough study of children's writing development, see Christie, 2012). Throughout the genre chapters in Part II, features of elementary students' writing illustrate the various discourse and lexicogrammatical aspects of each genre.

Conclusion

The approach to teaching writing presented in this book is supported by theory that has emerged from the systematic study of how the English-speaking culture constructs written texts for different purposes within a variety of disciplines. SFL theory and its application to education provide teachers with specific resources that can inform their lessons. In addition, the TLC approach to instruction supports the notion that writing needs to be taught. As students mature and teachers apprentice them to the discourse and language resources of English, students will become more adept at expressing meaning through writing in academic settings.

2

TEACHING AND ASSESSING WRITING

This chapter presents suggestions for schools to plan their writing curriculum and for teachers to prepare writing units. The content of this chapter emerges from experience working with urban schools for over eight years, particularly with a pre-K through grade 5 public elementary urban school and St. Rose School, a pre-K through grade 8 Catholic school in Chelsea. Chelsea is a town comprised predominantly of immigrants just outside of Boston. These schools have over 60% of students who come from homes where a language other than English is spoken. In the public school, for each grade level there is a Sheltered English Immersion (SEI) class for Spanish-speaking immigrants who are emergent bilinguals. These students are taught by a trained teacher—often bilingual—until they are considered ready to work in a standard curriculum class. Both schools felt there was a need to enhance the teaching of writing and have strong leaders who support this effort.

Previous to working with these schools, the little writing children did was mostly confined to personal recounts (referred to by the schools as personal narratives) or response to literature pieces. Occasionally, they also wrote procedures and reports. At the time we began our work, there was no school-wide plan for writing. Individual teachers made decisions on what to teach, largely conducting writing instruction following the Writers' Workshop format of students writing independently after a mini-lesson, followed by sharing. While students wrote, teachers conferred with individual students. Teachers often commented on how tedious it was to read over and over recounts describing how children had visited a water park or played the latest video game. They were also concerned about how to decide what to teach. Teachers working with emergent learners of English complained that students could not really write after a short mini-lesson. Although children were required to write in all content areas, writing instruction was limited to Writers' Workshop time.

Intensive summer sessions, monthly professional development, and weekly in-class support transformed writing instruction school-wide. Initially, teachers focused on teaching the purpose and stages of the various genres. As teachers gained confidence and knowledge, they included more aspects of language into their writing instruction. In the first year, teachers taught only a couple of genres. Currently, they teach three genres in the lower grades and between four or five genres in grades 3–8.

Over time, teachers learning to teach writing using the approach described in this book were interviewed. These are some of the things they had to say:

- "Well, I think it has [affected my writing instruction] for the fact that I know more about the genres of writing and I have more materials to teach the children in an explicit way. We wouldn't have had those materials before, certain books that we have that Dr. Brisk has provided and the knowledge behind each genre of how to teach it and talking about it in grade-level meetings with Dr. Brisk. About what worked, what's successful, what we could change. So I think it's still a work in progress, but we've made gains in that area." (Kindergarten teacher)
- "I've loved it! I've learned a lot. I've learned a lot about me, like in my expectations of students and my expectations and my ideas of what I thought writing was. They've changed, and I think I've told you that, I've always felt that if they weren't writing something down themselves, then they weren't actually writing. I've learned that's not true because I was really limiting their gift. I mean some kids don't have those skills to actually put down on paper what they have in their head. But if they can dictate and someone can scribe, what they come up with is amazing." (1st-grade teacher)
- "It helps break down all the different categories of writing, it helped me understand all the different genres, I didn't really think it could be broken down into all those categories . . . I wanted them to understand the purpose of the writing because without the purpose they are just doing it to do it. So all the subgenres, breaking it down, helped organize it to me. I have never taught writing before." (3rd-grade teacher)
- When the SEI 3rd-grade teacher was asked to comment on the monthly meetings, she said, "I think just by having time to talk to other teachers at the same level to see what has worked for them, to give you the time to talk about the writing—to give you the TIME to do it. Even though sometimes you just get to start the conversation you can continue it later. Just by being around the other teachers that would help me the most. And, also I think when Dr. Brisk brings a specific piece of writing from the kids and she talks about it. That is helpful. How an expert can show us what to pay attention to, so that is what I have learned."

- "It [SFL-informed pedagogy] has brought us back into again breaking it down piece by piece and using a lot of graphic organizers, a lot of mentor texts, building on their background knowledge." (4th-grade teacher)
- "Our work helps to shape how writing is talked about and taught . . . I definitely thought more about language structure through SFL." (SEI 4th- and 5th-grade teacher)
- "It was helpful in the training to learn about the different genres. Before I didn't really think much about the differences. The theme and new information work has been very helpful especially for revision. The graphic organizers were great and gave me a place to start to adapt to my own approaches." (English teacher, middle school)

After the first-year experience, teachers planned their school writing curriculum together, taking into consideration the content demands of each grade level and the suitability of specific genres for the content areas. For example, since the kindergarten science curriculum included the life cycle of animals, cyclical explanations were introduced using oral language and diagrams. As 5th graders studied explorers, they learned how to write biographies of their chosen historical figure.

The remainder of the chapter offers suggestions to teachers on how to plan genre units and how to carry out instruction and assessments to apprentice students to academic writing. Specific information suitable for individual genres will be included in Part II.

Genre Units in the Context of Content-Area Teaching

The preparation of individual units should be based on a whole-school plan where the school staff has agreed on which genres will be taught within which content areas and grade levels. The genre units presented in this book have elements that are common to all units, including:

- Content, writing, and language standards
- Resources
- Classroom organization
- Student products: medium, multimodality, and authenticity
- Content knowledge
- Academic language.

Content, Writing, and Language Standards

Informed by the content and literacy standards, teachers can match the standards with the content of each genre unit. However, writing and language standards tend to be generic. Thus, although a standard may say, "Students write good beginnings," in this book we expect students to write good orientations when working on personal recounts, good general statements when writing reports, and good thesis statements or claims when writing arguments. Given that so many states have adopted the CCSS, individual genre units in this book address how a specific unit fits within the demands of the CCSS.

Resources

In each genre chapter, the specifics of each genre are developed around a mentor text, provided in full. Other mentor texts are suggested at the end of the chapters. Teachers are encouraged to use texts that are part of their regular curriculum. Texts that are appropriate as reading materials for young students can be used as mentor texts with older students, because students are likely to produce writing that is at a lower level than they are able to read. It is better to present the features of the genre with short texts that are not difficult to comprehend. For example, the mentor text for fictional narratives (See chapter 9) is a short fable with a simple plot. However, it includes all the stages of a fictional narrative: the two characters reflect both external and internal features, and the story includes all of the essential aspects of language to be covered in the unit. In addition, teachers will need resources to develop the content knowledge where the genre unit has been embedded. These can include books, Internet resources, videos, maps, games, and others.

Classroom Organization

There is no formula for grouping students. In every unit, students at all grade levels produce texts as a whole class as part of the process of learning to write in a genre. This can be considered the final product for pre-K and kindergarten students and also for beginning English language learners. In the other grades and with intermediate English language learners, students can then produce group texts. Finally, with more confident writers, students can write independently with support from their group or partner. Difficulty in accessing content material or specific genres may necessitate starting with group projects in upper grades. For example, one teacher decided to have her 4th-grade students write group posters for their report unit because the students did not yet have experience writing in this genre. As a school implements genre writing throughout the grades, students in the upper grades will have more expertise and will be able to do more independent work.

Student Products

When planning what students will produce in a unit, factors such as medium, multimodality, and authenticity need to be considered. Real-life products can be models for the various choices students need to make when considering these three variables.

There are a variety of media that can be used to produce writing, including individual or class books, magazines, poems, PowerPoints, brochures, posters, letters, lab reports, dioramas, and diagrams. Each presents different challenges with respect to organization. Some examples include:

- Class books with multiple genres
- Class book with family recipes (procedure unit)
- Posters showing the face of a person, a time line, and the significance of that person's life (biography unit)
- PowerPoints (report unit)
- Brochures inviting someone to visit a country of origin (argument unit)
- Letters to the editor or to the principal (argument unit)
- Labeled diagram of the life cycle of an animal (explanation unit).

Schools usually teach poetry separately. Poems come in all genres but they also have specific textual features that require much instruction. Lab reports common in science classes include a variety of genres: procedure, procedural recount, and explanation or argument.

These different media include not only text, but also images such as diagrams, photographs, charts, and drawings. These images complement the text and allow students to express themselves even if they have not yet mastered the written language.

Josefina (Fifi) Pérez, a 3rd-grade teacher, was concerned that her students, who were relatively new to English, would have difficulty writing biographies. She encouraged them to create books with images downloaded from the Internet. Students added a short caption under the image. Hence, they had to write only a short sentence for each event. Michelle, another 3rd-grade teacher, was concerned that her students, although proficient in English, would also have difficulty with biographies. She had them create a 2-foot long time line to which they attached a drawing of the upper body of their person and a small circle with the significance of the person. This approach eased the construction of paragraphs to describe the events.

Images can be either narrative or conceptual. Narrative images present "unfolding actions and events, processes of change, transitory spatial arrangements" (Kress & van Leeuwen, 1996, p. 79). These are more typical of narrative and historical genres, where drawings, sketches, paintings, or photographs represent the unfolding story. Conceptual images represent "participants in terms of their more generalized and more or less stable and timeless essence, in terms of class, or structure, or meaning" (Kress & van Leeuwen, 1996, p. 79). These are more typical of procedure, procedural recount, reports, and explanations. They convey concepts in the form of diagrams and other abstract designs. Students need to be taught these distinctions. For example, a 4th grader illustrated her report on snakes with narrative images, such as the parent snakes kissing each other. Images in reports tend to be factual, including photographs of the real animal or diagrams. Mary Pike, a pre-school teacher, told her students that when drawing a diagram on the life cycle of a chicken, they could not color their chicks pink. She stressed that they were not producing a story, but rather a cycle explanation of what really happens.

In addition, it is important to consider how authentic students' products will be. Having students produce written artifacts that approximate what they see in real life increases the motivation and care with which they write and, therefore, the quality of their products (Edelsky & Smith, 1984). For example, a teacher had her students create posters on places to visit as part of her argument unit. The teacher asked a local travel agent to exhibit them in their store windows. This authentic task contributed to students' understanding of the language and content choices they needed to make (Stead, 2002).

Content Knowledge

To be able to write, students need to know the content. Because learning and researching the content for writing is time-consuming, it is more efficient to connect writing with content the students have to cover in their various disciplines. Students must acquire the habit of using or seeking knowledge in preparation for writing. They need to be explicitly taught to be researchers (Perry & Drummond, 2002).

> "Cheryl, a fourth-grade teacher . . . introduced the report genre to her class by telling the students that report writing involved becoming an expert on a topic in order to write about it. She repeatedly stressed the need for students to educate themselves before writing about a topic and informing their audience" (Brisk et al., 2011, p. 4).

The exploration of the content moves from what is familiar to the students to new knowledge in the various disciplines they learn through schooling. To make this transition possible, students need to learn how to carry out research and the language connected to this new knowledge. In specific genre units, the students also need to acquire the knowledge that will allow them to comprehend the texts that they will later deconstruct to learn how authors write in that particular genre (Rothery, 1996). Content development needs to continue throughout the genre unit. As students build knowledge of the genre, they continue to build and reinforce their knowledge of the topic of writing.

Students who come from different cultures already have a knowledge base, but for particular concepts their knowledge may be different, which will influence their writing. For example, a 4th-grade teacher had given her students an old prompt from the state test that asked students to tell a story based on what happened when they had a snow day. One of the students from Central America started her piece with, *Yay! It's snowing and it's Christmas day that means there is no school.* She had no concept of a snow day, when schools are closed because of excessive snowfall. She needed the justification of a holiday and Christmas is a holiday which, in her new country, occurs in the winter.

The writing standards of the CCSS include a category called "Research to Build and Present Knowledge" where some generic competencies are outlined for each grade level. In the approach presented in this book, building knowledge is an essential aspect of the writing process. Writing starts with what each student knows to facilitate engagement. At the same time, building new knowledge is an essential aspect of preparing students for writing. For example, for a procedure unit, students can create a book of home recipes or games from their culture and then move on to procedures related to science experiments, involving instruction of new content.

Learning How to Do Research

To build content knowledge, students need to learn how to do research. In preschool and kindergarten, students begin to get a feel for the process of research, but it is done in a concise way, in a shorter period of time, and with material that they are familiar with through life experiences, field trips, books, or videos.

> Mary and her pre-K class decided to write a report on baby chickens because Mary had a colleague who raised chickens and could contribute knowledge to the class. After reading about chicks, the students gathered around the easel where Mary had written "chickens" and brainstormed possible subtopics. The children chose food, habitat, and parents. Mary started a web. Then they focused on each of the three subtopics and developed them further, expanding each arm of the web. Together they developed a sentence or two with respect to each subtopic, writing them on a separate sheet per subtopic. Mary then typed the final versions of the sentences on separate sheets, reproduced them and made individual booklets for the children to illustrate.

With older learners, exposed more formally to research, teachers need to:

- Strengthen students' reading comprehension
- Teach students to use a variety of sources and take notes
- Teach students to transform notes to full text.

Strengthen Students' Reading Comprehension Specific reading strategies can be used to help students gather research from written sources. Some examples of reading strategies include Reader-Generated Questions, where students are asked to think of questions that will be answered by a text after they are told what the text is about. Students then try to guess answers and finally read the text (Brisk & Harrington, 2007). The Reading to Learn program (Rose & Martin, 2012) suggests that teachers first prepare students for reading by providing background knowledge and overviewing the whole text. Followed by detailed reading of one paragraph, students do joint or individual rewriting of the paragraph using the technical language.

Teach Students to Use a Variety of Sources and Take Notes Depending on topic, grade level, English language proficiency, and accessibility, students can use observations, interviews with experts and community members, videos, books, and the Internet to find information (See Stead, 2002, for suggestions on how to secure resources). Students can learn different research skills in connection with different writing projects. For example, in a 2nd-grade classroom, students learned how to interview people to write about the country of their ancestors and how to extract information from books relevant to their report on animals.

Students can obtain information by observing during experiments, field trips, or in other settings. To take full advantage of these observations, it is best to brainstorm what type of information they should be looking for beforehand. After a list of topics or questions is produced, each student should receive a copy (Stead, 2002).

For example, at the beginning of the argument unit, Pat Scialoia, a 4th-grade teacher, asked his students to watch television commercials to determine the intended audience of those commercials given the information presented in them.

One teacher found that interviews with community members were a good alternative to research in books for students new to English. Lipman (n.d.) recommends teaching students to interview through games because solely creating questions is not always enough to help students conduct a successful interview.

The graphic organizers included with the end material for each genre can be used to collect information from various sources and to help students take notes. These graphic organizers match the stages or text structure of the genre.

Teachers can explore a topic together with the students to demonstrate how to extract information and note the important information in the graphic organizer. This can be done over time as the particular topic is explored.

Steps to using genre graphic organizers as research tools:

- Prepare a large graphic organizer for the genre that students will be writing on to project or write on chart paper (See examples in Part II chapters);
- Explain the topic that you will be studying and link to the type of genre that students will be writing;
- Use a variety of resources to fill in the graphic organizer with information in collaboration with the students. Write the information or have students write it on sticky notes and attach them to the graphic organizer;
- Depending on the grade level, have students contribute to the class topic with their own research. Have them practice different strategies using their own copy of the graphic organizer to collect the information;
- Have students add what they find individually to the class graphic organizer;
- Then groups or individual students can choose their own topic and research and take notes following the same process.

Doing group research helps students to share the sources found so that each student has less information to find alone. A 2nd-grade teacher had her bilingual students do research in groups. This group activity was not only helpful with coping with the quantity of information gathered when researching, but also with consulting different sources, which led to animated discussions about the accuracy of information.

Resources may be written in the native language of students. The challenges of doing research in another language are that students may not be literate in that language and it may be difficult to find the vocabulary to express themselves in English once they have the information needed. If students are working with a bilingual teacher, then this language and vocabulary need can be supported in the classroom.

Once students have gathered information, they need to organize and summarize it to make it useful for their writing. Teaching summarization includes the ability to categorize information, which in turn requires students to abstract and name the category that appropriately matches the information. For example, if students research events in the life of a person, such as going to elementary and secondary school and university, then they are talking about *education*. This skill is also useful for creating topic sentences when writing reports. Moreover, summarization requires making decisions to determine which information or details are important and which are superfluous or repetitious (Recht, 1984).

Teach Students to Transform Notes to Full Text Often, students have difficulty transforming notes into well-developed, meaningful clauses and coherent text. Once the information is collected in the class graphic organizer, students need to practice how to turn notes into sentences and paragraphs with the class piece, followed by turning notes into text for their individual pieces. In lower grades, the class piece may be the final product.

Strategies to demonstrate writing from notes:

- Take each note from the graphic organizer, read it aloud, and with the help of the students create a sentence and write it on a sentence strip. Encourage the use of technical terms and be careful that the content is accurately expressed;
- In collaboration with students, organize the sentence strips to create a paragraph;
- Paragraphs of genres such as reports, explanations, and arguments usually include a topic sentence alerting the reader what the paragraph is about. Discuss with the class what the paragraph is about (the name of the category should be in the graphic organizer);
- Ask students if the first sentence of the paragraph they currently have indicates what the paragraph is about. If it does not, then work together to create an appropriate topic sentence.

Jennifer Wyatt, an SEI 2nd-grade teacher, read the mentor text aloud, asking students to suggest which information they should add to their notes. As they pointed at a piece of information, she wrote it succinctly on chart paper in the form of notes. Then, she worked with the students to transform the notes into full sentences. She then wrote the sentences in sentence strips and discussed the order with the students. Using these strips, they put together the text. Finally, they revised the text to suggest possible ways to combine sentences. Students followed the same process for the person they had chosen to research individually. The students' small sentence strips were ordered and then glued in their writing notebook. After students had the whole text completed, the teacher and student teacher conferred with the students to discuss potential places to better combine or connect the text. For example, one student wrote, "JFK graduated from Harvard. JFK enlisted in the navy." The teacher suggested combining them as, "After JFK graduated from Harvard, he enlisted in the navy."

Teach Students to Appropriate Academic Language

A key component to knowing a discipline is to know the language used to express the content of that discipline. Thus, language and content are inextricable from each other. Often, students are told to write in their own words rather than to copy from books. However, if children do not learn the language of books, they will never acquire academic language. Therefore, the task is to support students in learning the language used in books. Children need to learn the language of written texts and to know what it means to be able to express themselves in academic discourse.

While studying content and taking notes, teachers should build the students' academic vocabulary by creating thematic world walls and exposing students to the language through reading, videos, and videos with subtitles. A powerful way to teach this language is to help students convert their everyday expressions—either oral or written—to technical language (Brown & Ryoo, 2008; Gibbons, 2002).

Teachers in the project worked hard at developing technical vocabulary both orally and in writing.

Oral Use. When a student said, *it's not in the magnet's bubble,* Ed, the science teacher asked, *What's the scientific word for the magnet's bubble?* And the students responded with the technical term, *magnetic field.*

Written Use. Holly, the science teacher, noticed that students had used a lot of everyday language in their pieces on rock formation, even after having used the technical language throughout instruction of content. She put up a chart with two columns, one with the students' language and one with the technical expressions (See Table 2.1).

She compared them and discussed their meaning with the class. Then, she asked students to review their pieces to see if they could change their language.

TABLE 2.1

Everyday Phrasing	*Scientific Phrasing*
Rocks are made by	Rocks are formed by
Melted rock	Molten rock or magma
Igneous rocks forming outside	Extrusive igneous rocks
Igneous rocks forming inside	Intrusive igneous rocks
Pieces of rocks	Sediment
Animal skeletons	Fossils

When developing academic discourse, students need to learn more than vocabulary. They also need to learn how to express ideas through simple and complex clauses. For example, Daniel attempted to connect two clauses, but struggled to have them express what he wanted. He wrote,

> *"When snakes slither they make the letter S so they can swim."* The source book included the following sentences: "Snakes' bodies make S shapes as they glide along. This kind of movement also helps snakes swim" (Patent, 2000 p. 6). Therefore, the intended connection from the text is not one of cause (glide/slither) and effect (swim), as Daniel put it, but rather that gliding and swimming are both helped by the S-type movement.
>
> (Brisk et al., p. 8)

Assessment and Instruction Continuum

To cover the material in the genre units and support students needs, two instructional cycles with three assessment points are proposed in this book (See Figure 2.1). An uncoached piece of writing provides the initial information about the students' familiarity with purpose and stages (text structure) of the genre. The analysis of a mid-unit draft provides information on the aspects of language that students still find challenging. The final evaluation shows the impact of instruction on students' writing. In between, there are instructional steps based on a modified version of the TLC resulting from work in urban schools.

In addition to the strategies described within the two cycles, teachers need to make decisions on the use of metalanguage when explaining concepts to students and the use of the bilingual students' native languages as a tool to support learning.

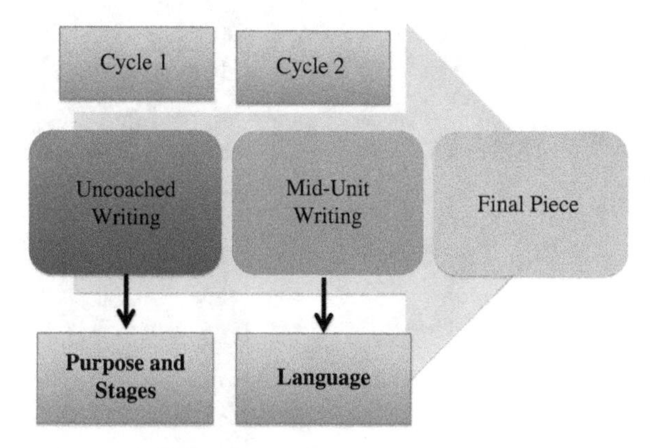

FIGURE 2.1 Assessment and Instruction

Cycle 1

The goal of the first cycle is to develop an understanding of the purpose and knowledge of the stages, that is, how the text is structured in a particular genre. Because decisions for writing are always guided by the audience, the intended audience is determined early in the unit. The first cycle (See Figure 2.2) begins with the analysis of students' uncoached writing with respect to the purpose and stages of the genre. Instruction on purpose is done mostly through deconstruction of texts written in that genre. Instruction on stages is done through deconstruction of a mentor text, joint construction of a class graphic organizer with lessons on stages, and joint construction of students' graphic organizers. Once the students have completed their individual graphic organizers the teacher should confer with them to insure that the plans make sense. The class graphic organizer guides the jointly constructed class product, while the group or individual graphic organizers help students create their own writing products. These can become final products or drafts that inform the second cycle.

Producing Uncoached Writing

The unit starts by having the students write an uncoached piece to gauge students' knowledge of the features of the genre, which guides the planning of instruction (Stead, 2002). In each genre chapter under "Uncoached Writing," there are suggestions for potential prompts to use. It is important to carefully construct the

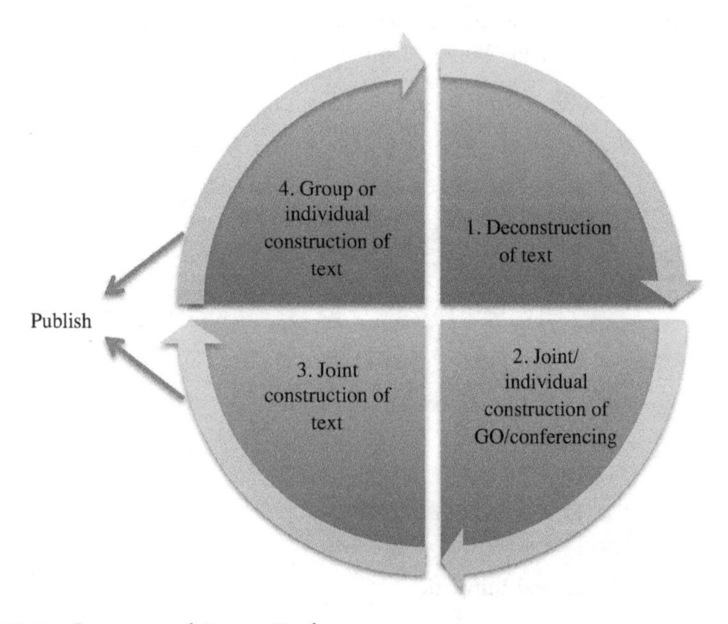

FIGURE 2.2 Purpose and Stages Cycle

prompts because, if written unclearly, they may lead students to write in a different genre. For example, for a report unit students received the prompt "Write about your favorite animal." A number of students wrote an argument piece with information supporting why that animal was their favorite instead of a report on the animal. In kindergarten or early 1st grade, uncoached writing can be done with the whole class. The teacher writes what students suggest to create a class piece.

The 1st-grade teacher in St. Rose did a whole-class uncoached piece. She told the students that they were going to create instructions for new students, describing the steps they need to take when they first come to class each morning. As the students made suggestions, she wrote them on the board exactly as they dictated,

> *Take out our stuff from the back pack.*
> *We take off our bookbags.*
> *We stop at the door.*

The text continued for a few more sentences.

There are genres, especially in the upper grades, where it becomes harder to do an uncoached piece because of the need for content knowledge. Therefore, the teacher will need to draw on previously taught content or something very familiar to students. For example, if the students are going to study the water cycle and write a cycle explanation, the teacher can remind students what they studied about the life cycle of butterflies and ask them to use that prior knowledge to inform their cycle explanation writing. A 4th-grade teacher preparing to support students to write biographical recounts about their parents' or grandparents' immigrant experiences asked the students to interview their subjects and then write. This became the uncoached piece.

Analyzing Students' Writing

Each genre unit includes an Analysis of Student Work form for purpose and stages at the end of the chapter. Given the grade level, teachers determine if for each item the student (1) needs substantial support, (2) needs instruction, (3) needs revision, or (4) meets standard. The criteria for this point system is as follows:

1. *Needs substantial support:* The student writer needs extensive help developing that aspect of the genre.
2. *Needs instruction:* There are gaps in the writer's understanding of the specific aspect. The writer has insufficient control. S/he needs instruction and practice.

3. *Needs revision:* The paper needs revision on one or two instances of the feature. A conference would be sufficient to help the writer meet the standard.
4. *Meets standard:* The paper reflects what the student should be able to accomplish and write independently given the instruction provided for this grade level (National Center on Education and the Economy, 2004).

In addition to each item, there is a specific comment space. Following is a sample uncoached causal explanation by a 4th-grade student, followed by the teacher's analysis of purpose using the analysis form provided at the end of each genre chapter. Analysis of verb tense is included with purpose because it is one of the easiest ways to check purpose.

> ***Why?***
>
> *I think that the dampbread decayed faster because the water couldn't take the water and the bread coudn't fight it. It also needed air to stay fresh. Since it was sealed for 8–9 days, It was hard for the bread to not decay. It decayed because the bread said "I cant take it!" Thats why it decayed.* (See Table 2.2.)

Throughout the genre units, the evaluation forms are used with a student sample to illustrate the features of students' writing addressed in the chapter.

Using the Analysis of Student Work form for purpose and stages, teachers determine what the students already know and what they have not yet mastered. Based on this assessment, teachers identify the lessons that best address students' needs. There may be aspects of the genre that are challenging to only some students. The teacher may do group lessons to address those aspects. There may be issues that are typical of students for whom English is a second language (See chapter 3). The teacher may do group lessons to address those issues for that particular group of students, as well.

TABLE 2.2

	1	*2*	*3*	*4*	*Uncoached Writing Comments*
Purpose					
To explain why something happens. Each event in the sequence causes the next.	✓				Reflects elements of procedural recount: documenting observations and of a narrative such as dialogue and personifying inanimate objects.
Verb Conjugation					
(present)	✓				All in the past, typical of recount and narrative genres.

In order to use these forms, teachers need to know about the purpose and stages of the genre, as well as the essential language features. As opposed to rubrics, where the expected performance is given, analysis of student work requires teachers to look at the writing and note what genre features are reflected.

Once all of the class needs are defined, the teacher plans the unit, deciding when to teach each lesson and for how long. Appendix A has a sample unit planner. Usually, teachers like to develop their own unit in response to their particular students.

Although there is not an explicit focus on language in this first phase of the unit, language issues may be resolved through students' understanding of the purpose and the stages. In the aforementioned example, once the student understood the purpose of explanations, she naturally switched to the present tense. Some students may be already familiar with the purpose and stages of the genre from earlier grades so teachers can work on language early in the unit. Cheryl, who moved with her 4th-grade students to 5th grade, started the argument unit by directly teaching language. This instructional decision was made in response to the request by her students, who had learned the purpose and stages of the genre with her in 4th grade.

Teaching Purpose

Understanding the purpose is essential for students to achieve the goal of the genre, organize the text appropriately, and use language effectively. Specific information about the purpose of each genre is included within the genre chapters.

The best way to teach purpose is to expose students to a variety of texts in the genre. Initially, it is best to choose a text that clearly reflects that genre. Once the students have a clear understanding of a variety of genres, they can be exposed to texts that are a combination of genres or macrogenres (Humphrey et al., 2012; Martin & Rose, 2008). For example, a number of the science texts included in the explanation unit also have biographical recounts of prominent scientists.

Verb conjugation is one aspect of language that is worth exploring with purpose because the two are connected. For example, recounts and historical genres are written in past tense because they chronicle events that happened in the past. Reports and explanations show how things are, thus they are written in the timeless present. Occasionally, these patterns change. For example, recounts for young children may be written in the present and explanations about animal adaptations use past tense because they took place in the distant past.

Choosing an Audience

Children's awareness of audience is usually reflected in their use of asides directly to the reader (Edelsky, 1986) or use of the second person addressing the audience directly. Students need to be further aware that audience impacts their choice of topic, amount of information given, and choice of language. Therefore, it is essential that writing be done with the audience in mind and that as students plan and write they are reminded of how the audience affects their choices. Classroom settings are not ideal for exploring diverse audiences because the natural audiences are always the teacher, the other students, or both. Having groups working on different topics and then sharing is one way to make classmates a more authentic audience. Other audiences are possible, including the principal, school administration, students in younger grades, pen pals, local media, family members, and others. Students should be involved in choosing their audience.

Students in Liz's 4th-grade class decided to write their reports for their former student teacher that was going to come visit the semester following his full-time practice. They wanted to show off how much they had learned about a topic that he had started to work with them before finishing his practice. (Brisk, Horan, & MacDonald, 2008).

It is important to have students write to different audiences, either within a unit or across units. Younger audiences require attention to the clarity of the writing, while writing to adults encourages students to use academic language. For example, Holly, a science teacher, had 4th graders create posters about planets to demonstrate to the principal how much they had learned. They also wrote booklets for 1st graders, predominantly using images and short sentences.

The various genre units include specific ways to attend to both audience and voice. When starting the unit, it is enough to decide on the audience and to refer to it when making specific decisions as students plan, revise, and write.

Teachers can have separate activities to teach about audience. In this book, lessons on the audience and voice (tenor) are included in chapter 8 (Arguments) because audience is essential for persuasion. However, it can be practiced in other content and genres, as the following example shows.

A 4th-grade teacher did two activities to help students understand how to use different language given their audience. For the first task, they jointly constructed letters about being in 4th grade to three audiences: a 3rd grader, their mothers, and the President of the United States. After the letters were written, students discussed the difference in language. The second task was to write a scary story for the teacher. After the students had written their stories, she asked them to rewrite the same story for the kindergarten children. Before changing the language of the stories, students discussed in groups what they would change and why.

Deconstruction of Text

The purpose of deconstructing a text is to show how authors write with attention to a particular aspect of the genre. Teachers have found that after doing a general overview of the stages, it is best to work on one stage at a time (Pavlak, 2013). Thus, teachers run the whole cycle of deconstruction, joint construction, and individual construction one stage at a time. The result is much more writing at each stage.

When deconstructing text, it is best to project the text so that all students can see and the teacher can point out the features. For example, to teach the elements of an orientation in fictional narrative, a teacher might have students ask who, where, when, and what and foreground the problem using the book *Very Last First Time.* To deconstruct the text, the teacher would project the first section and, interacting with students, identify the specific words that give the information. In the following example, the words are in bold to illustrate key words to the reader, but the teacher would project the original text without any markings for the students. Together, they could mark the text and identify the genre feature.

> **Eva Padlyat** [who] lived **in a village on Ungava Bay in northern Canada** [where]. She was Inuit, and ever since she could remember she had **walked** with her mother **on the bottom of the sea** [what]. It was something the people of her village did **in winter** [when] when they wanted mussels to eat.
>
> Today, something very special was going to happen. Today, **for the very first time in her life, Eva would walk on the bottom of the sea alone** [foregrounding the problem].

In this deconstruction activity, students notice not only the concept, but also the specific language. For example, the author uses the character's full name. Students, on the other hand, tend to use categories such as "the girl" or "my cousin." The teacher, through deconstruction and questions, can help the students notice this feature and encourage them to use it in their own writing.

It is often helpful to compare authors who do things a little bit differently to show students that there are choices within expected structures. For example, Maria, a 4th-grade teacher, when teaching students about orientations to biographies, showed two different examples and commented,

> Now you can see the difference between the first author and the second author . . . The second author started not with when she was born, but decided to start with something fantastic about her . . . So you ask yourself, do I want to begin my book with . . . and either way is OK.
>
> (Classroom observation 3/12/13)

Joint/Group and Individual Construction of the Graphic Organizer

Although the TLC recommends that joint and individual construction of text follow deconstruction of mentor texts, teachers have found that first working on the graphic organizers (GOs) helps students learn how to connect the stages. Thus, teachers first work with students on the class project GO, showing the students how the different stages connect. Then, students work on their own sections of the GO.

Conferencing With Completed GO

Before students start writing their individual pieces, teachers have found it very useful to confer with students to look over their GOs, check if the connections make sense, and help students clarify what they propose to write. This results in writing with fewer inconsistencies. Students are more willing to modify their GOs than their drafts. For example, when conferring with 4th-grade students about their fictional narrative GOs, a teacher noticed that there were a couple of GOs where the events did not connect to the problem the students had proposed. After negotiating the changes with the students, they were ready to write a narrative. In another classroom, a 1st-grade teacher asked follow-up questions regarding the very basic events that a student had written about in her GO, prompting the student to add more facts. The student's personal recount was quite informative in the end.

Joint Construction of Text

Next, the students and teacher jointly write a text. This can be done immediately after creating the class GO or after students have created their own GO. The teacher guides students as they write and invites suggestions. The teacher negotiates with the students when suggestions need modification to render a good example of the genre. With students in early grades, emergent English language learners, and students working on difficult genres, this can become the final product of the unit. Joint construction is different from modeling, however, where the teacher writes and the students watch. In joint construction, the students are actively involved in creating the text. It is also different from Language Experience Approach, where the teacher writes exactly what the student says without any negotiation.

For example, Kathy Wallace, a 2nd-grade teacher, jointly constructed with her class the procedure for making coffee filter ghosts. She had carried out the activity first.

Kathy: [*Writes "Title" on the smartboard*] So I'd like you to think of a title for this.

Student: Ghost.

Kathy: Do you think we should make it a little more descriptive than just ghosts?
Student: Scary ghosts.
Kathy: I'm thinking of the materials we used. What kind of paper?
Student: Coffee filter.
Kathy: [*Writes "Coffee filter ghosts"*] What comes next, in the science experiment and the recipe?
Student: Instructions.
Kathy: No, what comes next?
Student: The materials.
Kathy: [*Writes "Materials"*] So let's think. What's the first material? The first thing we used. I should see 21 hands.
Student: Pencil. [*Kathy writes "Pencil"*]

She continued to elicit the materials, writing down the students' suggestions. She did the same with the steps. As the students responded, she wrote the step, changing the language to read like a procedure:

Student: First we crumpled one coffee filter. [*Kathy writes "1. Crumple one coffee filter"*]

Sometimes she asked them to expand their responses to make the directions more specific:

Kathy: Then what did I do?
Student: We took the pipe cleaner and twisted it around.
Kathy: OK. [*Writes "Twist the pipe cleaner around"*] Around what?
Student: The pencil. [*Kathy writes "The pencil"*]

Group or Individual Construction

Although the TLC suggests going from joint to individual construction, producing writing in a group is very helpful and a good intermediary step for young students, students working for the first time on a difficult genre, or students who are emergent English language learners before they write on their own. The group product becomes the publishable piece. Letting the students write in a group is particularly useful when students have to do research to contribute to the writing because they then share the task of consulting resources. Reading academic texts can be difficult; thus, sharing and discussing what students find in the different resources supports comprehension and excites the students.

Cycle 2

The second cycle (See Figure 2.3) begins with the mid-unit analysis of student work followed by instruction about language. Language instruction focuses on the choices writers make given the topic, audience and voice, and the need to

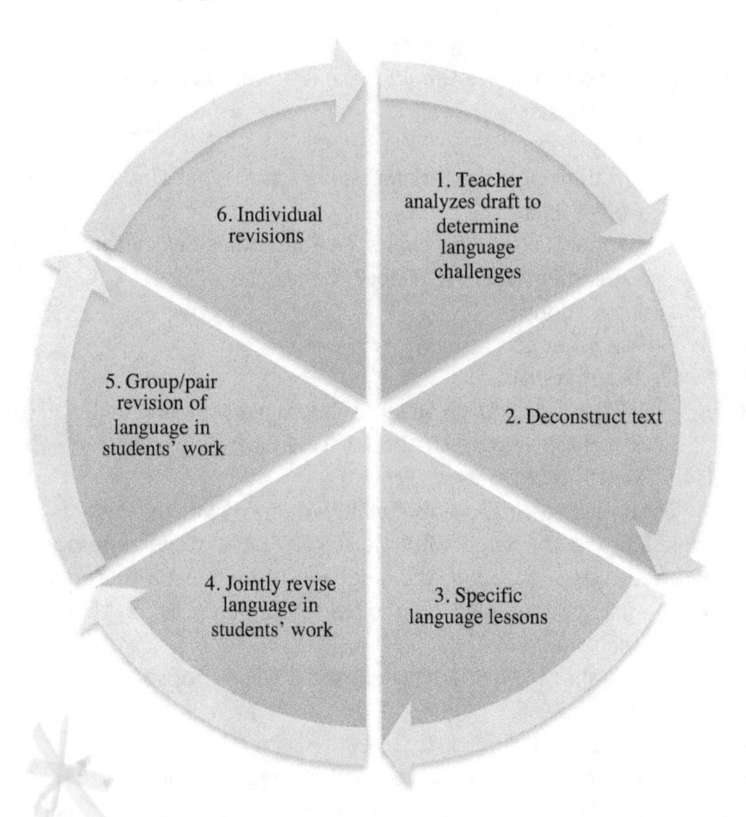

FIGURE 2.3 Language Cycle

create a cohesive text. In order to make choices, students need to develop their language resources. To build these resources, instruction follows cycle 2: deconstruction of text, specific language lessons, joint revision of student work, and group/pair and individual revision of student work. This is an iterative process in which each aspect of language goes through the same cycle. First, the deconstruction of a mentor text is completed, focusing on the specific aspect of language that corresponds with the genre, as determined by the teacher. Each genre chapter illustrates these aspects within the mentor text. Then, the teacher chooses a couple of student writing samples to analyze the chosen aspect of language with the whole class. It is a good idea to choose one writing sample that has captured the focal features of language and another that had challenges. The whole class then jointly revises these samples of student work. When the teacher feels that students are ready, they revise the remainder of the drafts in groups, pairs, or individually. This cycle is repeated for each aspect of language that will be the focus of instruction. The resulting product can constitute the students' final work.

Analysis of Student Work

Teachers choose at least a paragraph from each individual student's work to analyze using the Analysis of Student Work forms. When analyzing student work, teachers check language use to determine where students faced challenges. Based on this analysis, teachers can then plan the language lessons they will cover. Each genre chapter includes examples of language analysis of student writing for the various aspects of language.

Joint and Individual Revision of Student Work

The best way to support students in improving their language is to work with them directly on their writing. In the following example, the teacher felt that the students needed to work on the language of their orientations. On the smartboard, she projected the orientation that Felix had written:

Get me out of here!! I'm thousands of feet above ground. Help me! I shouted.

After reading his orientation, Felix told the class what happened in the plane when he was on his way to visit his grandparents. The teacher and other students gave him suggestions to make his writing more clear and connected to the genre:

Felix:	I was freaking out and started crying.
Chloe [teacher]:	My concern about "freaking out" is that sometimes parents or grandparents might not get that. You might use language, different types of language with [different] people.
Student:	I have a suggestion for Felix. Since he was asking for help, I would use, "I *pleaded*."
Chloe:	[*To another student*] Tell us what you said again?
Student:	I was freaking out and I was crying.
Chloe:	So do we want to use that and switch the words around?
Student:	Yes.
Chloe:	So, we are thousands of feet above ground. Are we in a hot air balloon? We might need to give them [the audience] more information about the *what.*
Student:	No [not in a hot air balloon] . . .
Felix:	I'm in the plane.
Chloe:	I think we need to mention that he's in a plane. What do you think?
Students:	Yes [*droning*].
Student:	[*Offers*] Put "on a plane" after "Help me."
Another Student:	I was thinking to myself, "Will anyone find me?" (Pavlak, 2013, pp. 136–137)

The comments went on. With all of this new information, Felix modified the piece to read:

> *Get me out of here!! I'm thousands of feet above ground. Help me!!" I shouted. Somehow the bathroom door got locked. It was Christmas and I was on a plane to Canada. I was thinking to myself, "Will anyone find me?"*

Finally, students look at their own work in groups or pairs and propose revisions. Teachers can take advantage of this group work time to confer with individual students. The cycle then starts again with another aspect of language.

Use of Metalanguage

During instruction, it is important that teachers use the technical terms when talking about purpose, stages, and aspects of language. Giving students a language to talk about language is an important aspect of this type of instruction. No matter what age, children can learn these words. With names for what they are trying to learn, it is easier to talk with other students and among themselves:

> This metalanguage enabled the teachers to be more explicit with their instruction. For example, during the first year of intervention, teachers in their writing instruction with students frequently mentioned the importance of *"details."* Teachers used the word, *"details,"* when referring to various aspects of language (adjectives, adverbials) and genre structure (additional events). After learning SFL theory, the teachers were provided the metalanguage and knowledge about language and genre that enabled them to more accurately teach writing.
>
> (Daniello, Turgut, & Brisk, in press, p. 11)

Use of Bilingual Students' Native Language

Often, teachers let students write in their native language while mastering a second language. Even when encouraged to write in their first language, students often switch to writing mostly in English within a year (Graves, Valles, & Rueda, 2000). Allowing students to use their native language when planning writing and interacting was found to be more helpful in improving students' attitudes toward school (Fitzgerald, 2006) and comprehension of concepts (Garrett, Griffiths, James, & Scholfield, 1994; Huss, 1995), rather than directly in improving English writing. Even when the teacher does not know students' native languages, allowing students to use their stronger language facilitates engagement in the classroom activities. For example, a 3rd grader who recently arrived from Guatemala wrote her predictions and observations in science class in Spanish and then, with the teacher coaching, looked at the word walls in the classroom and translated the phrases to English:

Yo creo que el agua ba asubir
I think the water will expand
El proximo dia el agua subio
The next day the water up it expand.

Thus, it is a recommended practice that when students do not know words in English, the teacher should encourage them to write (or say) it in their native language and have them teach it to the whole class. The teacher, in collaboration with other students or by any means available, should figure out the meaning of the words and teach the bilingual learners the English equivalent. Both words should be included in the class word wall.

Final Evaluation

Taking whatever writing piece is considered the final product, teachers analyze the student work, addressing all of the areas that have been taught. These results can be compared with the earlier analyses to gauge students' development. This final evaluation should travel with the students to the next grade to help the next teacher assess what students have already produced in each genre.

In the following section, there is an example of a language analysis of two important language features of personal recounts that 4th-grade students were learning in preparation for the state-wide composition exam. The teacher had identified a student as one of her low-performing students at the beginning of the unit. The initial analysis of the uncoached piece showed that the student needed to learn to write using a variety of verbs to express meaning more specifically and using a variety of adjectivals to better describe the participants not only for information, but also to add entertainment to her voice. The final product shows that the student had acquired both of these features.

SAMPLE ANALYSIS OF TWO LANGUAGE ITEMS IN A PERSONAL RECOUNT

Uncoached Piece

Me and my sister gave our dad a mug for Christmas. With a picture of all three of us on it. (my mom took it). It said #1 dad in gren ths look on his face was Priceless it felt so good to give and get he was happy. Giving the gift meant a lot to me because he was happy. It made me happy to.

Final Piece

Two years ago on December 25th 2010 my third-oldest sister, Natasha, gifted me and my 8-year-old sister, Hailee and I a female Chihuahua. We named her Dolce after My sister's favorite presume [perfume]- Dolce and Gabanna.

As the front door opened, Natasha stepped through out white-colored door.'

"Merry Christmas", greeted Natasha while gripping onto something inside her jacket

"Merry Christmas!", my family cheered.

Natasha kneeled on the smooth wooden floor and opened her black wooled coat and hid behind her legs.

I used to be jealous of Natasha's own Chihuahua, but I didn't expect one of my own.

Dolce was terrified- her tail was in between her legs and she was shaking with fear Like a leaf. She was small and white with a spot on her ear and a random spot on her back.

I bend down near Dolce and petted her back. Hailee kissed her on her head. Dolce started to whimper. "Its okay," I said as I continued petting her. Dolce started to warm up to us, pretty soon we were running all around the house playing tug-a-war with Dolce.

Dolce ran around the house all day long- she had long nails that made Scratching sound on the smooth floor. She was skinny with tiny arms and legs, and her paws were rougher then sand paper. That Christmas night as I climbed into my bed I thought of how lucky I was to have my very own Chihuahua.

Key: 1. Needs substantial support; 2. Needs instruction; 3. Needs revision; 4. Meets standard; NA: Not applicable (See Table 2.3).

TABLE 2.3

	1	2	3	4	*Uncoached Writing Comments*	1	2	3	4	*Final Writing Comments*
Verb Groups										
Avoid repetition of the same generic verbs. Variety of types that express what participants are doing, saying, thinking, feeling, sensing, and relational connections. Appropriate tense (past tense)		✓			10 verbs Some repetition: gave, to give, giving; was (3 times) Some variety: doing, saying, feeling, relational Uses past tense				✓	27 verbs All different (except "was" repeated once) accurately indicating the meaning. No use of generic verbs. Doing, saying, thinking, relational. Variety in doing and saying verbs.

	1 2 3 4	*Uncoached Writing Comments*	1 2 3 4	*Final Writing Comments*
Adjectivals				
determiners possessives pre-nominal post-nominal apposition	✓	Limited use: determiners, possessive, two adjectives, two prepositional phrases	✓	Lots of pre- and post-nominal adjectivals richly describing participants. Uses apposition. One odd use: "white-colored door" instead of "white door."

Conclusion

Until teachers gain confidence in trying the genre-based approach to teaching writing, they tend to focus on purpose and stages. While working on purpose and stages, there is some attention to language, but it is not systematically connected to register. Experience in Australian classrooms demonstrates the importance of moving from focus on text types to the language demands of subjects in schools (Rose & Martin, 2012). Therefore, it is important that instruction starts focusing on language by 3rd grade, too. To make it less cumbersome, only the language aspects that are essential for the specific genre are considered in each unit. Specifics about language will be described in more detail in chapter 3, including the challenges for English language learners. Once teachers are comfortable with the content of language lessons, they can start introducing them earlier in the writing process; for example, after students have their piece planned in their graphic organizer and before students start to write their texts.

The assessment and instruction strategies proposed in this chapter are basic guidelines; teachers can make adaptations given their experience and specific students. The one principle that is important to always remember is not to assign writing that students have not been taught how to do. It is important that the features of the genres presented in the genre chapters be considered as basic or typical but not fixed. As students learn the cultural expectations of how genres function in the English-speaking school context and mature as writers, they can introduce their own innovations as long as they do it for a reason with an eye on audience and on accomplishing the purpose of the genre.

3

LANGUAGE RESOURCES THAT SUPPORT WRITING

Chapter Map	
Topic Development (Field) Clause Process (Verb Groups) Verb Types Verb Forms Participants (Noun Groups) Circumstances (Adverbials) Clause Complexes The Structure of the Verb Dependency Logico-semantic Relationships Audience and Voice (Tenor) Text Cohesion (Mode) Development of Language Resources	Cheryl O'Connor continued, or looped, with her fourth grade students to fifth grade. When she announced to them that the first writing unit of the year was arguments, one of the students immediately requested to learn more about the language of persuasion. Students claimed that knowing the language was going to enhance their writing. As Cheryl recollects, "We sat on the rug to co-construct a K/W/L chart about argument writing to find out how much the students knew about arguments. Although we are looping, we have absorbed several children from other schools and an SEI classroom, so I wanted to take an inventory of what they remembered and what the others had been taught. When we got to the 'W' (want to learn) section, Janella added that she wanted to learn how to use the right language to make her argument more convincing or stronger to her reader. A mariachi band started playing in my head because I wanted to introduce modality to them and Janella had come up with it herself!" The students in her school, after five years of implementing SFL informed writing pedagogy, have learned about the power of language to write effectively.

SFL understands language as a "set of resources for making meaning, rather than rules for ordering structures" (Rose & Martin, 2012, p. 21). To create texts, writers avail themselves of these language resources. In this chapter, the resources of English are explained and illustrated. They are by no means exhaustive; there are whole books that attempt this. (Derewianka, 2011 and Humphrey et al., 2012 are contextualized in practice. Eggins, 2004, Halliday & Matthiessen, 2004, and Thompson,

2004 are contextualized in the theory.) The purpose here is to provide sufficient background to understand the particular features of language addressed in the various genre chapters. As these features are explained, connections are made with those specific aspects that are challenging to L2 learners. Again, the issues related to L2 learners are not exhaustive, but show examples frequently encountered in their writing samples. The goal is to illustrate that children writing in their second language have additional challenges. It does not mean that they lack the concepts. Thus, when a student writes, "*Snow leopard are . . .* ," it does not reflect that he does not understand the concept of a noun being plural, but just that he failed to mark it.

Approaches to teaching language focus mostly on vocabulary. Vocabulary can be viewed from a number of perspectives. Vocabulary is needed to develop the topic (field). For example, to write a procedure in relation to a craft, students will need such verbs as *cut, glue, flatten,* and *fold.* Vocabulary is needed in the context of audience and voice (tenor) to express judgment *(a silly man, an intelligent man)* and to express degrees of intensity *(moist, damp, wet, soaked,* and *drenched).* It is further needed to help cohesion, including using synonyms as a tool to connect text without repetition *(Americans, militias,* and *colonials).*

For L2 learners, vocabulary is difficult because of the sheer number of words needed to catch up with native speakers. By first grade, native speakers can produce and understand between 8,000 to 13,000 words (Templin, 1957). One strategy of L2 learners is to use a word for more than one function. For example, students using nouns as adjectives, such as: *It was very fun* [funny], *He is so greed* [greedy]. In addition, specific features of words add to the difficulties, such as acoustic similarity *(Sunday, someday),* length, homophones *(their, they're* and *there),* words with multiple meanings, and others (Menyuk & Brisk, 2005). For example, one L2 learner wrote in his report about snakes, *There* [their] *powerful muscles.* The 4th-grade prompt for a state test asked students to write a story based on the fact that they had found a *trunk* in their backyard. To teachers' dismay, a number of L2 learners were at a loss because they were more familiar with *trunk* in relation to a tree, a car, or an elephant than with a traveling case.

This chapter will describe how language contributes to the variables of the register or context of situation, that is, the language needed to express ideas, the language choices informed by audience and voice, and the language needed to create cohesive texts. Although these dimensions are closely related, this chapter introduces them separately.

Topic Development (Field)

In SFL theory, meaning is not carried by isolated vocabulary, but within grammatical structures. The clause is the first level of grammatical structure where "meanings of different kinds are mapped into an integrated grammatical structure" (Halliday & Mattheissen, 2004, p. 10). Beyond the clause, clause complexes, that is, a combination of clauses also express integrated meanings.

Clause

The grammatical categories that form a clause are verb groups, noun groups, and adverbials. For example, the clause, "With her sharp teeth and speed, she soon caught a small fish," (from *The Moray Eel and the Little Shrimp*) includes two adverbials, two noun groups, and a verb.

With her sharp teeth and speed	*she*	*soon*	*caught*	*a small fish*
Adverbial of manner (preposition + noun group)	Noun group: pronoun	Adverb of time	Verb	Noun group

Clauses contain one verb/verb group to express what is happening (process). They indicate who/what is taking part (participants) and the circumstances surrounding. Not all clauses contain all three of these meanings, but verbs/verb groups are essential. These grammatical categories are meaning-making resources and should be presented to students for the role they play in making meaning, that is, their function and not just as a feature of language form. Thus, the word *sharp* in the phrase, "with her sharp teeth," is not just an adjective, but its function is to describe the *teeth*. It also reveals the features of the character as frightening.

Clauses can be formed with a conjugated verb (finite) or non-conjugated verb (non-finite) (Derewianka, 1998) (See Table 3.1). Non-finite clauses (underlined) contain a verb (bold) that is not conjugated.

TABLE 3.1 Finite and Non-finite Verbs

Type of Structure		*Example*
Finite verb		The Sonoran *is* the only desert in North America that does not *have* cold winters. (from *Saguaro Moon*)
Non-finite verb	**To**- clauses	Scientists *have recorded* more different types of animals and plants in the Sonoran than in any of the other North American deserts, *making* it a truly exciting place ***to explore***. (from *Saguaro Moon*)
	-**ing** clauses	Scientists *have recorded* more different types of animals and plants in the Sonoran than in any of the other North American deserts, ***making*** *it a truly exciting place to explore*. . . . the fangs swing out and pierce the prey, ***injecting*** *deadly poison*. (from *Slinky Scaly Slithery Snakes*)
	-**ed** clauses	***Compared*** *to the Negro League players*, white players *were* very well *paid*. (from *Teammates*) *When* **threatened**, it lifts and flattens its neck, and hisses. (from *Slinky Scaly Slithery Snakes*)

Non-finite clauses help compact the writing. In the first example in Table 3.1, there are two non-finite clauses forming a sentence with three verbs, but only one is conjugated. If the verbs were conjugated, more sentences would be needed, making the writing less clear and concise.

These non-finite clauses have a variety of functions, such as indicating a circumstance of time ("When threatened, it lifts and . . .,") or acting as the subject of a sentence. For example, a 4th grader wrote, *Making the pamphlets* was fun.

Processes (Verb Groups)

Processes are represented grammatically by verb groups. Verb groups can be just one word *(drizzled)* or a group of words *(could crush)*. There are also phrasal verbs formed by a verb and a preposition *(sniff out, hunt down)*. As the preposition changes, so does the meaning. For example, *pass on, pass out, pass away, put off,* and *put out* all have different meanings. These are very difficult for second language learners who may not be sure which preposition to use to express what they want. For students with Romance language backgrounds, the equivalent meaning, often a Latin-based word, would be easier. For example, extinguish (put out) the fire. The word *extinguish* is similar to *extinguir* (Spanish and Portuguese).

Another great challenge for L2 learners is to use a variety of verbs to express meanings more precisely. Because the amount of vocabulary is one of the greatest burdens for a bilingual learner, L2 students tend to be efficient and use the words they know as often as possible. Thus, written work in the second language is characterized by repetition of vocabulary and use of generic verbs. For example, a 3rd grader wrote, *put the bread in the toaster* rather than *toast the bread*. Teachers complained that their students' personal narratives overused the verb *went*. More specific terms, including *drove, run,* and *walked,* were absent.

L2 writers have difficulty distinguishing the difference in meaning between each of two very common pairs of verbs: *be* and *have* and *make* and *do*. For example, a 3rd grader wrote in her autobiography, *I have 8 years* [I am 8 years old] and a 5th grader wrote, *they use teeth to do* [make] *neckless.*

Verb types. There are several types of verbs that express different experiences: action, saying, sensing (including thinking, perceiving, and feeling), relational, and existential (Derewianka, 2011). Action verbs indicate what the participants do. Saying verbs express what somebody says. They can be found in direct speech *("This itch is very big!" groaned the poor moray eel.)* or indirect speech *(Maria's mother told her to knead the masa)*. Sensing verbs describe what a human thinks, sees, hears, smells, tastes, senses, feels, and wants. Relational verbs show the relation between two things. Existential verbs indicate a state.

Different genres tend to favor particular types of verbs.

- Procedures and procedural recounts usually include action verbs: *print out, cut out, color, decorate, glue, plant, filled*

- Reports and explanations mostly include relational verbs: *is, become, represent, appear, turn into, symbolize, have, include, possess, own, lack* (Derewianka, 2011, p. 24); action verbs: *sort, heat, remove, beat, cover*; and existential verbs: There *are* four major deserts in North America.
- Personal and imaginative recounts, all of the historical genres, and fictional narrative genres usually have the greatest variety, including:
  - Action: *waited, caught, waved, traveled, met*
  - Saying: *groaned, asked, told, whispered, said*
  - Sensing (thinking, perceiving, and feeling): *couldn't bear, would like, knew, be forgotten*
  - Relational: he *is* hungry, never *had* another itch.
- Arguments also use a variety of types of verbs. The thesis statement, reasons/evidence, and concluding statement often include relational verbs *(Dogs are better than cats, dogs are strong, dogs are friendly)*. The evidence includes action verbs *(greet, barked, protect)*, sensing verbs *(are considered)*, and saying verbs *(reported, argued)*.

Verb forms. Tense, imperative mood, and passive voice are useful concepts for elementary students to learn. Verb tense includes the present, past, future, and variations of present and past. Tenses and imperative mood closely relate to genres and are the easiest way to notice if students' writing does not reflect the purpose.

Present tense not only means the present, but also can signify a permanent state. It appears in reports, explanations, and the thesis statement and reasons in arguments ("There *are* four major deserts in North America."). It also appears in direct speech in recounts and narratives ("'He'*s* hungry,' the moray thought."). For L2 learners, it is important to know that with the exception of the verb *to be,* the present tense changes only in the third person singular by adding an "s." Whether students come from a language that conjugates verbs like Russian or one that does not change like Chinese, they often leave out the "s" in the third person singular. For example, a 3rd-grade student wrote, *The shark grow on ocean.* A 2nd-grade student writing a report added an "s," but as in a possessive *(My animal eat's little creatures).*

Past tense indicates that something happened in the past. It is found in all forms of recounts and fictional narratives ("Nearby, a little red-and-white banded shrimp *foraged* the food" in *The Moray Eel and the Little Shrimp*). L2 learners do not have trouble understanding the concept of past but they often have difficulty forming the past tense. Sometimes, they omit the *–ed* ending when forming a regular past verb (*I open my eyes,* referring to yesterday). They also need to learn the spelling rules for when the *–ed* ending is added (See www.oxforddictionaries.com/us/words/verb-tenses-adding-ed-and-ing). Irregular verbs pose a challenge because students simply need to learn each form *(I brang a jug)*. Sometimes, L2 writers add the *–ed* ending to an irregular verb *(And we haded so much fun).*

Future tense indicates an action in the future. The auxiliary "will" is used to form the future *(They will never leave us)*. A very common way to form the future is by using "be going to" *(I am going to study law.)*. Other ways to form the future include using the present with an adverbial of time or "about" *("We are about to start")*, and present progressive *("I am seeing James on Thursday.")* (Derewianka, 2011, p. 31). L2 learners familiar with oral English are more likely to have heard "be going to" or the contraction *(We'll take you there)*. They will need to learn that the auxiliary "will" tends to be used more in written language. The future tense is used in direct speech in recounts and narratives, arguments (mostly in evidence), and in the predictions of lab reports.

There are other tenses, such as continuous tenses, that indicate an action happening over time or simultaneously with other actions. They can be in the present, past, or future tenses: *She is coming down the road. She was coming down the road when the accident happened. She will be coming down that road.* L2 learners tend to learn the continuous form very early and apply it to many situations, often dropping the auxiliary *(We playing hide and seek.)*. Perfect tenses indicate actions that occurred in the past in relation to the present *(I have called her three times)* or in relation to the past ("María's mother *had placed* her diamond ring on the kitchen counter" from *Too Many Tamales*). L2 learners may have difficulty with the irregular verbs (*If you haven't went to Santo Domingo . . .*).

L2 learners need to be taught how to form the interrogative by adding the auxiliary "to do" before the subject and the negative by adding "to do" and "not" before the verb. Most languages do not use an auxiliary.

Imperative mood denotes a command and is typical of procedures ("*Color* and *decorate* the clothes using crayons or markers" from *Paper Scarecrow*). This is the simplest form of a verb for L2 learners because it is the name of the verb.

Passive voice is used when the focus is on the participant receiving the action rather than the participant doing the action. Thus, the explanation for how paper is recycled (See chapter 7) includes a number of clauses in the passive voice ("The paper *is sorted out* in the recycling center."). Paper is what the writing piece is about and who is doing the sorting is irrelevant. Sometimes, the doer is named afterwards following the preposition "by" ("Federal judges *are appointed* by the president" from *Limiting Power: Checks and Balances*).

Contractions are common in oral language and when writing dialogue. Young writers often carry these to their written academic language, where it is not considered appropriate. Sometimes, L2 learners write the contraction without the apostrophe *(Im* for *I'm)*. Other times, they create a different structure or meaning by inserting the apostrophe incorrectly *(It's family* for *Its family)*.

Participants (Noun Groups)

Participants are represented by noun groups or pronouns. These participants can be the doers or receivers of an action. For example, in "María moved her nose" (*Too Many Tamales*), María is the doer and her nose is the receiver of the action. Noun groups can include nouns or pronouns.

Subject pronouns are *I, you, he, she, it, we,* and *they.* L2 learners often confuse *she* and *he.* They use one when they mean to use the other. Because some languages do not have the neutral "it" (everything has a gender), L2 writers replace "it" with another pronoun. For example, a Spanish-speaking student wrote, *"She is beautiful"* when talking about a table. In Spanish, *table* is feminine. Spanish speakers omit the subject pronoun because in their language it is not required. The verb declension marks the subject (*If we have to go to school is better . . .*).

Nouns can be proper (María) or common (mother). Proper nouns are often difficult for L2 learners because the words are unfamiliar in English form. This can cause particular difficulty when reading and writing historical texts. In turn, L2 learners' own names (an example of proper nouns) may be difficult for their teachers, resulting in incorrect pronunciation of the names. In the worst cases, teachers resort to changing their names so that they can pronounce them better. Two good children's books that address the topic of name changing are *My Name Is María Isabel* by Alma Flor Ada and *Any Small Goodness* by Tony Johnston.

Nouns can be used alone or can be described by a number of different adjectivals placed before or after. These word groupings form noun groups, which can be quite complex. For example, the noun *types* in the following example is described by pre- and post-nominal adjectivals:

"more different	types	of animals and plants in the Sonoran"
Adverb + adjective	Noun (head)	Prepositional phrase

Pre-nominal adjectivals, or those that precede the noun, include determiners and adjectives (See Table 3.2).

TABLE 3.2 Pre-nominal Adjectivals

Determiners			*Adjectives*					*Noun*
Article	*Pointing word*	*Possessive*	*Quantity*	*Opinion*	*Factual*	*Comparing*	*Classifying*	
								Snow
the								windows
		her						nose
							diamond	ring
							kitchen	counter
	that							ring
			second					batch
		her		full				stomach
a					silvery			light
The						best		tamales

Source: Adapted from Derewianka, 1998

Some L2 learners have first languages where the adjectives usually follow the noun and they may tend to apply that structure to English noun groups. L2 students also need to learn the formation and use of comparison adjectives: *better, best; more expensive, most expensive.* Students need to learn when to use and not to use "more." It is not uncommon for L2 learners to write *more better* or to state *the oldest brother* when there are only two brothers.

A peculiar English structure is the possessive modifying a noun *(Mom's ring),* a pre-nominal construction representing a prepositional phrase *(the ring of my Mom).* Indeed, some languages use a prepositional phrase and students tend to transfer that to English *(a baby penguin drink milk from its mother,* rather than *his mother's milk).* Another difficulty of the possessive is using the apostrophe after the "s" in the case of plural nouns. Thus, a 3rd grader wrote, *Whales enemies are people,* without the apostrophe. Once they learn the possessive form, however, students may over use it (*is gonna be yours falut* [fault]).

Post-nominal adjectivals, or those following the noun, can take the form of appositions *(The student, called Norman),* prepositional phrases *(a spoonful of sugar),* non-finite clauses *(the other cousins tagging along),* and relative clauses ("the beautiful ring *that was now sitting inside Danny's belly*"). These clauses that are part of the noun group are called embedded clauses. Children begin to use embedded clauses in the upper elementary grades (*Their paws have really sharp claws that allow them to climb trees and open all sorts of containers for food.*—5th grader), which has been found to be a sign of maturity (Christie, 2012).

Some academic genres use generalized participants to represent a category. For example, students may write about *volcanoes* as opposed to *the Vesuvius.* Generalized participants are indicated by using the plural form of the noun. L2 learners need to learn plural forms, both regular and irregular. For example, a 3rd grader wrote, *First get two slice of bread.* Another wrote *mouses* for *mice.* They need to learn to add not only the "s" to the singular form, but also "es" in some cases *(classes),* as well as the irregular plural forms (e.g., *feet, lives*), and a number of other variations. (For a complete list of rules on plural formation see www.myenglishpages.com/site_php_files/grammar-lesson-plurals.php#.Ukv2heDipvY.)

Circumstances (Adverbials)

Circumstances are typically expressed with adverbials and subordinate clauses. Adverbials generally say more about the processes (verbs). The meanings expressed by adverbials include how, where, when, or why something happened *(drifted through the streets).* Sometimes, adverbials add more meaning to an adjective *(that is very good)* or to another adverb *(pretty soon everyone else was laughing).* The following text from *Too Many Tamales* illustrates various types of adverbials (in bold):

> Snow drifted **through the streets** and **now that it was dusk,** Christmas trees glittered **in the windows.** María moved her nose **off the glass** and

came **back to the counter.** She was acting grown-up **now,** helping her mother make tamales. Their hands were sticky with *masa.*

"That's **very** good," her mother said.

María **happily** kneaded the *masa.* She felt grown-up, wearing her mother's apron. Her mom had even let her wear lipstick and perfume. If only I could wear Mom's ring, she thought to herself.

María's mother had placed her diamond ring **on the kitchen counter.** María loved that ring. She loved how it sparkled, **like their Christmas tree lights.**

When her mother left the kitchen to answer the telephone, María couldn't help herself. She wiped her hands **on the apron** and looked back **at the door.**

Among the most common circumstances expressed by adverbials are time, place, manner, reason, accompaniment, and cause (See Table 3.3). (For more complete lists, see Butt et al., 2000, p. 65; Derewianka, 2011, pp. 67–68)

Adverbials can take the form of a word *(very, soon),* derivations *(carefully, loudly, gently),* prepositional phrases *(through the streets),* and noun phrases *(Fill it a quarter of the way).* Prepositional phrases often include complex noun groups within them *(on the bottom of the jar),* thus containing a lot of information.

Finite and non-finite subordinate clauses can also express circumstances:

"Place the other cup on top upside down *so that the top of the two cups are touching.*" (finite or conjugated verb/reason)

"Close the two cups together *using duct tape* (non-finite, manner) *to seal them.*" (non-finite/reason).

These types of constructions will be addressed in depth in the next section on clause complexes.

Both adverbials and adjectivals can take the form of a prepositional phrase. The use of prepositions is very difficult for L2 learners. Sometimes, they choose

TABLE 3.3 Adverbials

Type	*Question*	*Example*
Time	When? How long? How often?	now that it was dusk; now
Extent	How much?	Fill it a quarter of the way.
Place	Where	through the streets; off the glass
Manner	How? Like what?	happily; very; like their Christmas tree lights
Reason	What for?	to answer the telephone
Accompaniment	With whom, what?	with the other cousins
Cause	Why?	because of the weather

the incorrect one *(Put the cheese in the bread.)*. Other times they may omit the preposition (*My family is happy living America and hope to someday visit Vietnam*—5th grader). This can be a persistent challenge that is never quite overcome.

Clause Complexes

Simple clauses with one verb are very common in the writing of young children. However, when children reach 4th grade, they often want to express more complex ideas that call for sentences with more than one clause. These are called clause complexes. These sentences can be analyzed in three ways: (1) by the structure of the verb, introduced earlier in the chapter; (2) by the nature of the dependency; and (3) by the logico-semantic relations they convey.

The Structure of the Verb

As shown earlier, clauses can have a conjugated (finite) verb or a non-conjugated (non-finite) verb. These clauses can function as post-nominal adjectivals or subordinate clauses. Children use the non-finite form with "to" quite often (*First, we gathered information about the ecosystem we wanted to write about.*—4th grader). However, they are just as likely to have two clauses with conjugated verbs instead of the non-finite verb. For example, a 4th-grade student wrote, *The water pulled us the whole way, and water splashed everywhere,* instead of "The water pulled us the whole way, *splashing everywhere*" (Brisk & DeRosa, forthcoming).

Dependency

There are two types of dependency: coordination (parataxis) and subordination (hypotaxis). In coordination, the dependency is one of equality. In subordination, one of the clauses is dominant and the other is dependent. Sentences with coordinated clauses are called compound. Those with subordinated clauses are called complex and compound/complex when they combine.

Type	*Example*
Compound	"It covers 100,000 square miles, | and expanded to its present size only about 8-10,000 years ago." (from *Saguaro Moon*)
Complex	"If he did nothing, || Danes would die." (from *The Yellow Star: The Legend of King Christian X of Denmark*)
Compound/Complex	"Electricity flows through the electromagnets | and pulls the striker || so that it hits the bell." (from *Magnetism and Electricity*)

Children tend to overuse coordinated clauses, even when a subordinate, showing the meaning more clearly, would be more appropriate. For example, a 4th-grade student wrote, *We got a floaty and sat on it* instead of "After we got a floaty, we sat on it" (Brisk & DeRosa, forthcoming). Having a clause using *after* shows that the relation between the clauses is one of time, which adds information.

Logico-semantic Relationships

In clause complexes, clauses "are linked to one another by means of some kind of logico-semantic relation" (Halliday & Matthiessen, 2004, p. 363). The interdependence among clauses is usually signaled by conjunctions (Eggins, 2004; Thompson, 2004). There is a wide range of possible logico-semantic relations between clauses (See Table 3.4). The two basic types of relationships are projection and expansion (Halliday & Matthiessen, 2004). In projection, one clause indicates what someone said (locution) or thought (idea). The other clauses express what was actually said or thought, either quoted or paraphrased (Eggins, 2004). There are three ways of expanding a clause: elaboration, extension, and enhancement. In expanding a clause complex, the secondary clause expands what is expressed in the primary clause. There are many different possibilities to build on the meaning, often signaled by a conjunction or other connective. Table 3.4 shows a simplified version of the relationships. Wherever possible, these relationships have been illustrated with examples of student work or mentor texts. When those were not available, the relationships were illustrated with examples from the literature (For full development of logico-semantic relations see Brisk & DeRosa, forthcoming).

TABLE 3.4 Clause Complexes

Type of Relationship	*Conjunctions or Other Connectives*	*Example*
Saying	None	Mr. Rickey *told* him, "I want a man with the courage not to fight back." (from *Teammates*)
	that	*They even told me that it was a two-hour RIDE!!* (5th grader)
Thinking	None	*I thought no one would like me.* (5th grader)
Temporal (when?)	Then, next, afterwards, just then, at the same time, before that, soon, after a while, meanwhile, all the time, until then, now, as	"A snake has no limbs to get in the way || *when* it's chasing after tunneling ground squirrels and burrowing mice" (from *Slinky Scaly Slithery Snakes*)
		"Snakes' bodies make S shapes || *as* they glide along" (from *Slinky Scaly Slithery Snakes*)
		When predators come || the snake waves around in a circle || then vomits. (4th grader)
		After it does its "business" || it plays dead || until the predator leaves. (4th grader)

Type of Relationship	*Conjunctions or Other Connectives*	*Example*
Causal (reason, purpose)	Because, as, since, so, then, consequently, therefore	*An animal does not have these things* || *since animals do not make their own food.* (4th grader)
		New Jersey nickname is the Garden state because it has so much garden and trees. (4th grader)
Conditional	If (positive)	*If snake venom gets in your bloodstream you'll die, but if you swallow venom it cures bad health.* (4th grader)
	Unless, without (negative)	
Manner (how?)	By, thus, in that way, so, similarly	"*By* decomposing dead leaves and branches, insects and micro-organisms help to enrich the soil" (Derewianka & Jones, 2012, p. 227).
Spatial (where?)	Where, wherever, everywhere	"Donovan was hunting her *wherever* she might go" (Eggins, 2004, p. 283).
Comparative	Likewise, similarly, in a different way	"Her sister Louise told her the news carefully. *Similarly*, Richards was cautious . . ." (Eggins, 2004, p. 48).
Concessive	But, yet, still, despite this, however, even so, nevertheless	"Many kinds of snakes can swim, *but* sea snakes are swimming champions" (from *Slinky Scaly Slithery Snakes*).
Extending by adding something new	And (additive)	"When threatened, || it lifts *and* flattens its neck, || *and* hisses" (from *Slinky Scaly Slithery Snakes*).
		If their prey is bigger || *they often hunt in groups* || *and they work together to kill the prey.* (5th-grade SEI group poster)
	Nor (negative)	They were neither pretty *nor* inexpensive
	But, while (adversative)	*An animal cell has all of these things,* || *but a plant cell has a cell wall and chloroplast.* (4th grader)
	Or, instead of, besides, instead of, without, rather than (variation)	"*Rather than* moving around from place to place, animals stay in the same place" (Derewianka & Jones, p. 227).
Elaborating without introducing something new	In other words, for example, for instance, in particular, actually, what I mean, in fact, indeed	*For example when elephants are travelling in a known path . . .* (5th grader)

Thus, when combining clauses, writers need to decide the meaning to be expressed, the connective that will signal the type of expansion, and the order in which they will place the clauses. Using clause complexes allows writers to express more complex ideas and specific relationships useful in academic writing.

Audience and Voice (Tenor)

Tenor "is concerned with the interpersonal in language, with the subjective presence of writers/speakers in texts as they adopt stances toward both the material they present and those with whom they communicate" (Martin & White, 2005, p. 1). Writers constantly make language choices depending on the intended audience and the voice or identity they want to reveal through their writing.

Children have an idea that their audience can differ, but they do not always adjust their language to show it. Kroll's (1984) research showed that children can adapt to different audiences, but this occurs to different degrees.

Audience awareness is reflected by clarifying cultural topics and by choice of topic, specific information, syntactic complexity, and specific language. In the modern world, children write for people of different cultures within their country and using social media, across the continents. Their audience may not be familiar with their experiences and content of their writing. Therefore, students may need to be more explicit about what they write.

Writers aim at making their writing comprehensible and appealing to their audience by choosing topics that will be of interest and by using language that will be understood. For example, in these two opening paragraphs on reports about snakes, the language is very different.

Text 1

You'd think it would be hard to survive in the wild without legs. But look at snakes! More than 2,500 kinds slither and creep throughout the world. Snakes live just about everywhere except on some islands and near the North and South Poles. They can climb the tallest trees or burrow deep into the earth. Some snakes never leave the water. Others remain forever on land.

(from *Slinky Scaly Slithery Snakes,* p. 3, 4th-grade book)

Text 2

Snakes are elongated, legless, carnivorous reptiles of the suborder **Serpentes** that *can* be distinguished from legless lizards by their lack of eyelids and external ears. Like all squamates, snakes are ectothermic, amniote vertebrates covered in overlapping scales. Many species of snakes have skulls with many more joints than their lizard ancestors, enabling them to swallow prey much larger than their heads with their highly mobile jaws. To accommodate their narrow bodies, snakes' paired organs (such as kidneys) appear one in front of the other instead of side by side, and most have only one functional lung. Some species retain a pelvic girdle with a pair of vestigial claws on either side of the cloaca.

(Wikipedia, *Snake*)

Text 1 has less information packed in it, while Text 2 uses technical terms to pack more information and to be more precise. For example, Text 1 repeats the word *snakes,* while Text 2 uses the more technical terms *reptiles* and *serpentes.* Further, Text 1 describes the snakes *without legs,* while Text 2 uses *legless.*

The interpersonal relation also reveals the author's voice through a number of grammatical resources, including type of sentence, person, modality, use of evaluative vocabulary and grading (Droga & Humphrey, 2003). In addition, spelling can be framed for children within voice. Starting approximately with the 20th century, accurate spelling has been viewed as important and poor spelling has been associated with a lack of education. Thus, being careful with spelling in specific situational contexts is advantageous for the writer.

Types of Sentences

There are four types of sentences:

1. Statements or declarative sentences (Dogs are too noisy.)
2. Questions (Can I keep him?)
3. Exclamations (I can keep him!)
4. Commands (Take him back.)

Statements are more assertive. Questions, exclamations, and commands inherently show a relationship between writer and audience. Questions are the least assertive way to address an audience, while commands are the most assertive. Exclamations reveal the feelings of the writer or of a character when there is dialogue. Similar to Text 2, Text 1 is written in statements, except for the second sentence where the author uses an exclamation to rally children's enthusiasm about the topic.

Grammatical Persons

There are three grammatical persons: first (I, we), second (you), and third (she, he, it, they). The first and second persons overtly express the presence of the writer and the audience. The third person places the focus on the topic at hand, hiding the writer and gearing the piece toward a generalized audience. Although the rest of Text 1 is in the third person, the first sentence includes second person, addressing the audience directly. Text 2 is completely in third person, the typical approach of authoritative text that puts importance on the subject rather than on the reader and writer.

Modality

Writers take a position about a phenomenon and express it with *modal verbs, adverbials, adjectivals, nouns,* and *clauses* or *phrases* (See Table 3.5) (Derewianka, 1998; Humphrey et al., 2012). Text 1 has many examples of modality showing the

TABLE 3.5 Modality

	High	*Medium*	*Low*
Verbs	Must, need, has to	Will, would, supposed to	Can, may, might
Adverbials	Certainly, definitely	Probably, usually, likely	Possibly, perhaps, maybe
Adjectivals	Certain, definite	Probable, usual	Possible
Nouns	Certainty, necessity	Probability	Possibility
Clauses and Phrases	I believe that Everyone knows that	I think that In my opinion,	I guess that

Source: Humphrey et al., 2012, p. 97

position of the author or as a way to highlight and draw attention to facts. The modality is medium to low demonstrated by using *would, you'd think,* and *can*. Some modal adverbials in this text highlight facts *(never leave the water)*. This is rather high modality. A report for adults would rarely be as assertive.

Cheryl carried out a lesson on modality following the request indicated in the initial chapter vignette. She wrote,

"The day after the K/W/L lesson, I sat the students down to talk about modality (and referred to Janella's request on the K/W/L). I started by writing down three sentences:

I really wish you would try spinach.
You should give spinach a try.
You MUST try this spinach.

I asked them which sentence would get them to think about trying spinach, which didn't really get them to even think about spinach, and which would just kind of "tick them off." Through a discussion, they agreed that the last sentence was too pushy. People don't like to be forced or yelled at.

I then showed them a chart with what we called "The Goldilocks and the Three Bears Model" in argument writing: Weak, Strong/Pushy, and Just Right.

The students worked in pairs to come up with language that would fit into all three categories, given an argument situation. For example: The argument is hot water in schools. Students came up with language for a weak argument (We would like), strong/pushy (We demand), and just right (We really feel it's necessary). The level of excitement was wonderful!" (E-mail communication, 9/30/13).

Evaluative Vocabulary

Writers use evaluative vocabulary to (a) express feelings "to build up empathy and suspense (Affect)" (Humphrey et al., 2012, p. 101). This is typical of stories;

TABLE 3.6 Evaluative Vocabulary

	Positive	*Negative*
Affect	Happy, trusting, engaged	Sadly, fearful, bored
Judgment	Lucky, powerful, brave, good	Unfortunate, weak, cowardly, bad
Appreciation	Lovely, well-written, meaningful	Boring, simplistic, insignificant

Source: Droga & Humphrey, 2003

(b) make moral judgments of behaviors (Judgment); and (c) assess quality (Appreciation) (See Table 3.6). In Text 1, the author starts with the statement *"hard to survive in the wild"* to draw empathy for snakes. This is more typical of stories than of a report, more evidence that the text is directed to young students.

This type of vocabulary shows either the positive or negative feelings of the writer. It can also show how writers judge or appreciate the topic at hand. These meanings can also be positive or negative. It is important to show not only the literal meaning of vocabulary, but also how it can show the author's perspective. For example, an L2 student asked for the meaning of the word *nasty*. The teacher gave the definition, but needed to add that by using it, the student would also show the writer's point of view with respect to the particular character she was describing.

Grading

Writers use grading to increase or diminish the intensity of meanings (Droga & Humphrey, 2003). In Text 1, the author increases the excitement about snakes by writing that snakes "climb the *tallest* trees" and "burrow *deep* into the earth." These evaluative words can be made to stand out more by increasing or diminishing the level of intensity through the choice of synonyms. For example, "ideal" has a greater level of intensity than "good." "Dire" is more intense than "bad." An author may signal a lower level of intensity to make the argument more persuasive. This is visible in the following poem (from the book *Dirty Laundry Pile: Poems in Different Voices*), where a mosquito wants to convince the audience to let him bite. The mosquito is trying to convince the audience that biting is not such a big deal by using low grading in words, such as *little, simple,* and *tiny.*

The Mosquito's Song

I sing. You slap
I mean no harm
There is no cause
for your alarm.
A **little** drop
Is all I ask.
It really is
a **simple** task.

So please hold still
at this
juncture,
while I
make
a **tiny**
PUNCTURE!

When presented with the notion of grading, children automatically want to increase the intensity. Thus, it is good to expose students to a text such as this poem to demonstrate that lower intensity can also be effective in certain circumstances.

Text Cohesion (Mode)

To produce cohesive texts, writers use a number of grammatical resources that support organization of the text to make it comprehensible for the reader. These resources include how to structure the text so that the whole text connects to the text theme or macrotheme, how the paragraphs connect to the topic sentences that establish what the paragraph is about or hypertheme, and how the theme/new information within each clause connects fluidly across clauses in a text (Coffin, 2006; Halliday & Matthiessen, 2004). In the following argument, the macrotheme of the text is that dogs are good pets. Then, each paragraph describes a quality that makes a dog a good pet. The last sentence connects back to the overarching topic of the piece.

Rhetorical Feature	*Text*
Topic of the text (Macrotheme)	**Dogs are** often called man's best friend and make **good pets**.
Subtopic (Hypertheme)	One quality of a dog is its **faith in its owner and its loyalty**. They always greet us when we come home and they will never leave us even in a bad situation. For example, there was a sick man and the dog barked and barked until the rescue team arrived.
Subtopic (Hypertheme)	Furthermore, dogs are animals that will **protect us**. Houses with dogs are considered safer than even those with burglar alarms. Not only will they stop thieves, but they will also guard against fire. For example, there was a fire and a dog managed to pull its owner out.
Subtopic (Hypertheme)	And finally, dogs **can be trained to help people**. Dogs can do a number of things that people cannot. For example, they can sniff out drugs, find bodies, illicit DVDs, and hunt down prisoners. They're also used to help the elderly and disabled.
Closing theme	To sum up, **dogs are good companions**.

Source for the text: www.jamesabela.co.uk/exams/dogsvscats.pdf

In turn, the paragraphs can be broken down into the theme (what the author is talking about) and the new information (what the writer is saying about the theme or topic). In this paragraph, the focus is dogs and, as a result, most of the themes are the word *dog* or *they.*

Theme	*New Information*
One quality of a dog	is its faith in its owner and its loyalty.
They always	greet us when we come home
and they	will never leave us even in a bad situation.
For example, there	was a sick man
and the dog	barked and barked until the rescue team arrived.

In this text, there are two types of themes (Droga & Humphrey, 2003): experiential (what you are talking about: *quality, dog*) and textual (words that help connect the text: *for example*). There are also interpersonal themes that help connect the writer and reader *(I think that dogs make the best pets).* Children commonly use the interpersonal theme, which weakens arguments. The experiential themes are always present. To help students organize their writing, teachers can analyze or have students analyze a whole text with Worksheet 1: Macro and Hyperthemes and paragraphs with Worksheet 2: Theme/New Information (Worksheets are provided at the end of the chapter.).

Text connectives, reference ties, ellipsis, and lexical ties are additional grammatical features that help the text come together. *Text connectives* link chunks of the text. For example, in the aforementioned text, the last paragraphs start with *And finally,* and *To sum up,* connecting the paragraphs with those previous and alerting the reader to the end of the text. Common connectives clarify *(in other words, for instance, as a matter of fact),* show cause or result *(therefore, consequently, because of this),* indicate time *(then, next, in the end, previously),* sequence ideas *(first, finally, in conclusion),* add information *(furthermore, too, also),* and express condition or concession *(however, besides, still).* (See Derewianka, 2011 for a more exhaustive list). L2 learners have difficulty using these elements appropriately and often overuse them (Hinkel, 2002).

Reference ties mainly involve the use of pronouns and determiners. Pronouns refer to participants that have already been mentioned in the text and help keep the text connected and track the participants. For example, the sample text on dogs read, "One quality of a dog is its faith in its owner and its loyalty. *They* always greet us . . ." *They* refers to *dogs.* When well used, pronouns help track the participants without repeating the noun.

Further evidence of reference is the use of "the" in front of a noun that has already been introduced. Otherwise "a" should be used. L2 writers often have difficulty with the determiners. They either under use them (*Those 7 cats are lion, Tiger, Leopard . . .*) or inappropriately use them. For example, a 3rd grader used *the* in front of *rice* when she had not yet mentioned *rice (we started to cook the rice).*

To avoid repetition, some words can be deleted *(ellipsis)*. This is seen in the sentence, *I read the book and she did too.* In the second clause of the compound sentence, the verb is not repeated.

An important way to make the text connect is through *lexical ties* or associated vocabulary, such as synonyms, antonyms, repetition, collocation or words that usually occur together *(dog, bark, sniff)*. (See extensive analysis of the features of mode in Derewianka, 2011 and Humphrey et al., 2012).

Development of Language Resources

As children mature in their writing, they avail themselves of more and more of these language resources to express what they mean, given the context. Knowing the language and how to use it is an essential component of learning to write. Children need to master the language, not only to be able to write what they mean, but also to have choices and to be intentional in how they express themselves.

Multilingual writers have access to language resources in more than one language and, according to Walters (2005), they make choices at all levels of the production process in the context of the given situation. These choices are dependent on the register variables and on their language proficiency. Content can be connected with a particular language. When writing about cultural aspects of one language, bilinguals prefer to write in that language (Bou-Zeinddine, 1994; Gort, 2006).

Tenor influences language choices among bilinguals. Children who wrote mostly in Spanish, for example, showed awareness of audience when switching to English when writing notes to their English-speaking classmates (Laman & Van Sluys, 2008). Bilingual writers writing in English, not their heritage language, often code-switch to show their cultural identity. For example, Sandra Cisneros (2002) often switches to Spanish in her book *Caramelo.* When bilinguals want to impress their audience, they monitor their language use to make it as close to that of native speakers as possible. They use strategies including rallying the help of native speakers to edit their language. When writing to friends or family, they tend to be less preoccupied with language deviations, especially those that are very common.

Some common issues of L2 writers, with respect to creating a cohesive text (mode), are the overuse of text connectives (Hinkel, 2002) and weak lexical ties caused by limited vocabulary. Acquisition of vocabulary is significantly slower for L2 learners when compared with peers reading in their first language (August, Carlo, Dressler, & Snow, 2005). This difficulty is evident even at the pre-school level, with gaps in bilingual–monolingual vocabulary development persisting until the 5th grade (Paez, Tabors, & López, 2007).

The choices bilingual students make when writing in their L2 are partly related to the resources they have acquired in the language, that is, their level of proficiency. Their ability to express and connect ideas (expressive and logical functions) is dependent on their lexicogrammatical resources available to express those ideas. For example, when a student wrote about *the place where they keep animals,* she had the idea, but not the word *zoo,* to express it. Another student wrote, *It is the end of the year and I am happy* instead of *I am happy because it is the end of year.* She combined the ideas, but was missing the more precise way to express the logical connection with *because* and reversed the temporal order of the ideas (Brisk & DeRosa, forthcoming).

When creating a written text, students make a number of choices from different language systems or levels in order to make meaning. They choose how to organize the text to accomplish the purpose, they choose the vocabulary and how to group the words in clauses and sentences, and they choose which letters and other symbols to use. Students use their language or languages resources when making these choices. The role of teachers is to recognize the resources that students bring with them and to build additional ones, especially those needed to function in academic contexts. These choices are not made in a vacuum, but within the context of the culture where the students are being schooled and the different situations students encounter in the school, such as writing in math class, writing for a test, and writing for a variety of audiences.

Worksheet 1: Macro and Hypertheme

Rhetorical Feature	*Write From Text Here*
Topic of the report (Macrotheme) Is the topic about the whole report expressed in the first paragraph?	
Determine the **subtopic** of each paragraph. Is the subtopic of this paragraph introduced in the beginning sentence? Do all the sentences in that paragraph relate to that topic?	
Subtopic (Hypertheme)	
Subtopic (Hypertheme)	
Subtopic (Hypertheme)	
Subtopic (Hypertheme)	
Subtopic (Hypertheme)	

Worksheet 2: Theme/New Information

Write **themes and new information** in one paragraph. Are they connected? Does the information flow? Does the theme signal what the author is talking about in that paragraph?

Theme	*New Information*

PART II
Genres

This section of the book includes chapters on the different genres to be explored in elementary schools. Each chapter follows a comparable format. The chapter starts with a vignette illustrating instruction in the particular genre followed by a general introduction to the genre, the content areas to which the writing can be connected, and the grade levels where it can be taught. The remainder of the chapter includes information on how to develop a writing unit in the genre. The development of the unit is divided into four parts: general preparation, purpose and stages of the genre, key language features, and resources to support instruction and assessment.

General Preparation

Chapter 2 provides important background and information for the general preparation applicable to all genres. In addition, genre chapters illustrate specific information with respect to topics, the Common Core State Standards, resources, and building content and language, and they give suggestions for an initial prompt to assess how well students can write in the genre.

Purpose and Stages and Language Specific to the Genre

For each genre, purpose and stages are presented first, followed by features of language. For teacher candidates and teachers new to this way of teaching writing, dealing with purpose and stages is easier than addressing language. In addition, as students work on purpose and stages, improvement in language follows. Veteran teachers introduce issues of language in combination with the stages. Only key aspects of language that most impact the particular genre are addressed in each chapter. Teachers can focus on others as they see fit. Chapter 3 explains language resources in more depth, providing support for the linguistic knowledge needed to implement language instruction within the genre units.

In these sections, each aspect addressed includes the theory, features of students' work, and suggested lessons. The theory is explained and illustrated through a mentor text. Students' abilities and challenges are exemplified through an example of an uncoached piece or cold prompt produced before instruction for the purpose and stages and another piece produced after instruction for the language aspects. These have been analyzed using the Analysis of Student Work forms included at the end of each chapter. Other challenges are illustrated from patterns observed in other children's writing collected in the two schools as well as those described by the literature. Each section rounds up with suggestions for lessons. These are briefly described because of space limitations and would need further expansion when planning implementation. They are written in a different font to indicate change of voice. In the interest of avoiding repetition, various aspects of language were included under just one genre but could be applied to others. For example, Lesson 17 in the Reports chapter (chapter 6) about expanding noun groups could be applied with other genres where there is need to teach to expand the noun groups.

The lessons will not include spelling or mechanics, not because they should not be taught but because there is already a lot of emphasis on those aspects in instruction.

For those genres that are too difficult to have students write in the early grades, there is a section with suggestions of oral activities, games, role-plays, and others that will help prepare students for when they have to write in those genres. These can also be used with students who are in the early stages of learning English.

Resources

At the chapter's end there are a number of useful resources for teachers, including forms to analyze students' writing with respect to purpose, stages, and language; graphic organizers; additional books and Internet resources that can serve as mentor texts; and other worksheets specific to particular genres.

Deviations From the Norm

In some genres there are some differences. The Recounts and Historical Genres chapter (chapter 5) covers seven types of recounts: personal, imaginative, procedural, autobiography, empathetic autobiography, biography, and historical recount. Throughout the chapter, the similarities and differences are stated to show how one can build on the other. Although the Explanations chapter (chapter 7) introduces five types of explanations, the genre is illustrated through two of them to be able to go in depth without extending the chapter too much. The

Fictional Narratives chapter (chapter 9) has a different organization, starting with purpose and character development where language plays a key role and ending with learning about the stages or plot of a narrative.

Order of Implementation

The genre chapters do not need to be studied in the order presented. Implementation in schools does not have to follow the order either. However, experience working with pre- and in-service teachers and students suggests that the order in which they are presented corresponds with difficulty.

4
PROCEDURES

<table>
<tr>
<td>

Chapter Map

Grade Levels and Content Areas
Procedures Unit
General Preparation
Part I: Purpose and Stages of the Genre
Purpose of Procedures
Decisions on Audience
Stages of Procedures
A Word About Endings
Part II: Language
Verb Groups
Specificity Through the Use of Adjectivals and Adverbials
Clause Complexes
Text Connectives
Reference Ties
Resources
Analysis of Student Work Forms
Graphic Organizer
Additional Resources That Illustrate the Genre

</td>
<td>

The 1st-grade students are seated in desks, which have been rearranged to make two long tables. Each table seats 10 students, with 5 sitting per side. Jeanine Morris is jointly constructing a procedure for a science experiment that they conducted in the morning. Ms. Morris informs her students that they will give the procedure to their 4th-grade buddies the next time they get together. The 4th graders will then use the procedure to repeat the experiment. Ms. Morris has typed the title of the procedure, "How to Make a Toy Car Move," using a computer connected to the smartboard. As students make suggestions, she types.

Ms. Morris (M): What do we need next?
Student (S): The materials.
M: Can you give me the materials? Even just one.
S: I can't remember them.
M: You can't remember?
S: [*Thinks*] Pencils.
M: Was there anything special about the pencil?
S: It was flat.
M: How many?
S: Two.
M: Why's it important to know that there's two?
S: So it could hold the rubber band.
M: What kinds of pencil did you say we used?
S: Flat.
M: What's another word for flat?
S: Not sharpened.
M: [*Types "2 unsharpened pencils (flat)"*] What else?
S: A hot wheels car.

The activity continues as Ms. Morris negotiates the remainder of the materials and the steps with the class, including discussions on the preciseness of describing the materials, the need to number and order the steps, and whether to use *you* with the imperative.

</td>
</tr>
</table>

The purpose of procedures is to give directions to accomplish a goal. This genre is found in many aspects of people's lives, such as in recipes, instructions for arts and crafts, directions to assemble products, and instructions to play games. In school, students encounter procedures when doing lab experiments.

Procedures are different from protocols and procedural recounts. Procedures contain directions to do or to make something sequentially, while protocols list instructions "that are designed to stay in place simultaneously" (Butt et al., 2000, p. 236). A protocol is "a list of rules which restrict what you can do instead of explaining how to do it" (Martin & Rose, 2008, p. 4), for example, example rules for classroom behavior or bus safety. The language features of protocols are similar to procedures; thus, the suggestions for procedures can be applied to protocols. Procedures should not be confused with procedural recounts, where the writer tells what happened when following a procedure. For example, a procedure describes how to make a paper plane, while a procedural recount tells what happened in the process of making a paper plane.

Procedure is a good starting genre because the texts can be short and the stages are clear. In the case of procedures for children, each step is usually numbered. The verbs are not conjugated, but rather the name of the verb is used, making it easier for L2 learners (e.g., *Cut the paper in half*). One challenging aspect of procedures is the need to be precise. Students need to learn not to write *Put rice,* but *Add 2 cups of brown rice to boiling water,* indicating amount, category, and place. Thus, procedures help to develop the language of clauses by the use of adjectives and adverbials.

Procedure is also a foundational element in the chain of scientific genres. Children need the opportunity to write procedures before they can begin to write scientific reports, explanations, and finally, arguments (Veel, 2000). The language features of each genre become increasingly complex and "work to produce a kind of knowledge path along which ideal pedagogical subjects will move into fully fledged scientific discourse" (p. 190). Although procedural writing might be accessible for children, it is not a genre that they typically engage in when given a choice in their writing (Fang, 1997). If children are to become proficient in this type of writing, teachers need to more deliberately engage them in this work.

Grade Levels and Content Areas

Procedure is a fun genre because it involves making things, including crafts, recipes, and science experiments. It is a good genre for the early grades (pre-K–2) and for beginners to the English language. In the later elementary grades (3–5), procedures can be used with science and math. Some high-stakes science tests require students to set up a procedure for an experiment to prove something. For example, students were asked to design an experiment to test the power of a fertilizer on the growth of tomato plants. They were required to write precise instructions to carry out the experiment.

There are a number of lesson suggestions in the procedure unit that follows this introduction. Following are suggestions on how procedures can be adapted to the different grade levels.

- *Pre-K and Kindergarten:* Procedures written as a whole class following an arts and crafts project (how to make a paper plane) or a cooking activity (how to make applesauce). Students contribute their ideas and even some of the writing as they learn letters and words. Some teachers take pictures as they carry out the procedure and use them as a guide to write the instructions.
- *Grade 1:* Teachers and students jointly construct procedures that have been demonstrated. Students put together procedures with prepared sentence strips. Students add images to procedures.
- *Grade 2:* Students learn in similar ways as in first grade and then write their own procedures.
- *Grade 3–5:* Students write their own procedures, following deconstruction of mentor texts and joint construction with the teacher. Procedures rely increasingly more on language than mainly the images to describe the steps.
- *Grade 5 Science:* Students write procedures to set up simple scientific experiments.

Depending on experience with writing procedures and English language proficiency, teachers may use some of the strategies for lower grades with the upper grade students.

Procedures can be written in connection with various content areas, mostly as part of larger lessons. For example, in science, procedures are the starting point for various experiments. The students carry out the experiment following the procedure. Then they make observations, write procedural recounts of what happened, and end up with some form of explanation or argument. In science classes, all of these writing activities constitute the macrogenre that is traditionally called a lab report (Hyland, 2007). In mathematics, having students verbalize or write procedures for mathematical drawings, problems, or algorithms "helps clarify the nature of mathematical processes for the students and the logical orders in which these might be carried out" (Marks & Mousley, 1990, p. 128). In ELA, procedures can be self-contained lessons. With lower grades, it is best to use crafts because they can be easily carried out in class. Recipes are also appropriate, but they can be more cumbersome to demonstrate in class because they may involve cooking.

If the school has a science teacher, the classroom teacher should work in coordination with the science teacher. For example, a 3rd-grade science teacher taught procedure writing when constructing a crayfish habitat with the students, setting up the graphic organizer with the materials and the steps. This teacher taught technical scientific terms and explained the scientific reasons for each step as they jointly filled out the graphic organizer. Then the classroom teacher worked with the students to actually create final products, writing out the steps, checking their language, and adding illustrations.

Procedures Unit

This procedure unit can be carried out in 3–4 weeks. It is a fun unit to implement because it can be connected with engaging, hands-on activities that help develop vocabulary in a wide variety of topics. It is a good unit to implement at the beginning of the year because it usually does not require a lot of background knowledge. On the contrary, procedures are often used to build background knowledge. For example, in the Explanation unit (chapter 7) where the mentor text describes making recycled paper, teachers can use a procedure to have students actually make their own recycled paper to better understand the process. Many science texts include procedures for experiments that help students understand the scientific principles of the lessons. For example, the book *Animal Senses: How Animals See, Hear, Taste, Smell, and Feel* includes procedures for experiments in connection to each of the senses. Similarly, social studies texts include procedures. For example, the book *The American Flag,* about the creation of the flag, includes a procedure to construct a flag at the end.

General Preparation

In preparation to start the unit and on the basis of the school-wide decisions of which genre to teach at which grade level and in connection to which content area, teachers should:

- Determine the content, writing, and language standards
- Choose resources
- Decide how students will be grouped
- Decide on writing products: medium, multimodality, and authenticity
- Build content knowledge
- Teach students to appropriate academic language
- Plan lessons based on analysis of students' uncoached writing.

There are extensive details about each one of these points in chapter 2. Following are considerations specific to this genre with respect to the CCSS, resources, suggestions for authentic tasks, appropriating academic language, and prompts for uncoached writing.

The CCSS do not include standards that specifically support procedure writing. A statement in Appendix A of the CCSS indicates that they are part of what the CCSS calls informational/explanatory writing: "Informational/explanatory writing includes a wide array of genres, including academic genres such as literary analyses, scientific and historical reports, summaries, and précis writing as well as forms of workplace and functional writing such as *instructions . . .*" (p. 23) [emphasis added]. However, the standards themselves do not support any of the texts or language features of procedures.

There are abundant resources for procedures in books and on the Internet. Some books solely consist of procedures, whereas others include procedures in addition to writing from other genres. Everyday life provides many examples of procedures, such as recipes on canned or boxed products, instructions that accompany products, and instructions to play games. The mentor text used in the unit was drawn from www.enchantedlearning.com/crafts, a webpage that includes numerous crafts. Additional resources can be found in the material at the end of the chapter.

There are books that appear to be procedures by their title (e.g., *How Are Sneakers Made?* by Henry Horenstein). However, this text is an explanation of the process of making sneakers and does not include instructions for somebody to read to make a sneaker.

When students write their own procedure, it is important to make the task authentic. Examples may include:

- Instructions for crafts to give to parents or caretakers for use with younger siblings
- Family recipes to create a class book to share with the community or to enter in a school magazine
- Science experiments to teach future classes or younger students how to carry out experiments, or to show in a science fair
- Math games to share with another class
- Games that come from students own cultural background.

Sometimes teachers use practical examples, including how to brush your teeth, how to wash your hands, and how to dress to play outside in the winter. These are very helpful for very young children and are good to use as examples early in the lessons because students are familiar with the actions. However, once these are learned, procedures do not need to be consulted again. On the other hand, crafts, recipes, math games, and science experiments usually require the use of procedures every time they are carried out.

"Ms. B informed her 5th grade students that recipes would be the next type of procedural text that students would work on. She began the exploration of recipes by asking students to ask their parents about recipes that they enjoyed:

Ms. B: Ask mom how to make your favorite recipe, arroz y habichuelas, empanadas.

Student: Chicken

Omar: Mac and Cheese

Ms. B: Yes, exactly! Ask about the things you like to eat at home, your favorite. We will create a class book of recipes and everyone will get a book of recipes.

There was chatter in the room about favorite recipes and foods as students began packing up to go home. Students were given the same graphic organizer that they used previously in the 'How-To' piece so that they could begin organizing the information for the recipe piece. They were to complete the organizer and bring it in the following day" (Zisselsberger, 2011, p. 152).

The language of procedures has to be precise and specific in order to produce clear and accurate instructions. Because there is often no teaching of content knowledge in procedure writing, the academic language is built simultaneously with teaching how to write procedures. Therefore, to plan the first part of the unit, teachers should:

- Have students write an uncoached piece using a prompt such as *Write instructions on how to make a ham and cheese sandwich.* Care should be taken that the product is something familiar to students given their cultural backgrounds;
- Analyze the pieces using the Analysis of Student Work: Purpose and Stages form in end-of-chapter resources to determine what students can already do and what their challenges may be.
- Enter ideas for lessons mainly related to purpose and stages in the Unit Plan (See Appendix A).

Part I: Purpose and Stages of the Genre

Purpose of Procedures

The purpose of procedures is "to tell how to do something" (Butt et al., 2000, p. 233). Procedures are written in the imperative. The person following the instructions is not named (e.g., *Color and decorate . . .*). Only rarely are "you" or "one" used and, if this does occur, it is mostly found in oral language.

Features of Students' Writing

An SEI 3rd-grade teacher wrote on the board the title *How to Make a Peanut Butter and Jelly Sandwich* and prompted the students to write. Federico, one of the students, copied the title and wrote a piece that includes elements typically found in stories. Without the title, given by the teacher, the reader of this student's writing would not immediately guess that it was intended to be a procedure:

How to make a Peanut butter and Jelly Sandwich.

The first stepe is you go to the store and you buy bred and peanut butter and you buy Jelly and then the prsone of the store, will say good buy see you next time then you go back to yore amportmint and you get the bred and the peanut butter and jelly and you put it together and you make peanut butter and jelly sandwich.

This student also used "you" in front of the imperative form of the verb throughout his piece.

	1	*2*	*3*	*4*	*Uncoached Writing Comments*
Purpose To give directions to accomplish a goal.	✓				Includes story elements (underlined) and the process of getting the ingredients, which in procedures is never done. The ingredients are simply listed.
Verb Conjugation (imperative)		✓			Always use the "you imperative" instead of the straight imperative. Other verb tenses.

In a 2nd-grade SEI class, students never succeeded in getting away from storytelling. They produced booklets where the first page included the materials and each of the following pages had a couple of steps with an image above the step. The images included a girl or boy, depending who the author was carrying out the activity. These images, with an identified participant carrying out the procedure, in addition to the text connective *then* and the use of the second person, is in the style of a story. In contrast, books for children with recipes show images of ingredients and of hands carrying out the step. These features give an impersonal nature to the person carrying out the task, which are more accurately characteristic of procedure writing.

The prevalence of narrative storytelling may be attributable to the types of texts that children are accustomed to reading. In the elementary grades, children are overexposed to texts from recount and narrative genres. Procedures are about generalized participants, in contrast to stories, which are about specific characters or people (Fang, 1997). This underscores the need to provide children with examples and mentor texts that are clear examples of procedures and not told as narratives.

Avoiding personal pronouns to keep the detached voice of instructions is a challenge for students. Like Federico, most children use the second person when writing procedures, rather than not mentioning who executes the procedure. Other changes in voice also occurred. One 3rd grader changed from second, to first and finally to third person (underlined), *you pour flour, next we pour 1/2 cup salt, Next Ms R put the Playdoug in microway.* One 4th grader wrote the whole procedure using the first person: *First I get two slices of bread. Next I get the ham. Then I get the cheese . . .* One of her classmates in this SEI class switched from the imperative to the first person, making her writing more like a story: *Toast two slice of bread. Then I sprout* [spread] *butter on the two bread. Then I put the ham and cheese.*

LESSON 1. Exposing Students to Procedures

Goal: To discover the purpose of procedure writing and learn the imperative form through exposure to different procedures, including those in the students' everyday experiences.

Materials: Procedures in books, Internet examples, games, and household goods, such as boxes or labels from cans for cooking instructions and directions on assembling furniture. Cards to write words. Projector.

Activities

- Depending on the grade level, read the examples of procedures aloud, or have students in groups read them, or do both. Discuss the purpose of giving instructions for somebody to follow in sequence in order to get something done.
- Project a procedure.
- Help students find the imperative verbs.
- Clarify the meaning if needed and point out that the verb is usually by itself and not preceded by "you."
- Give groups of students one procedure each. Have them find the imperative verbs and write them on cards to start creating a word wall that will support their writing later in the unit. With younger students, do this activity as a whole class.

Additional Suggestions: There are a number of games that also help young children practice the imperative, such as Simon Says (Make a crown for students to put on and give an order, which the students then follow. This can be varied by blindfolding a student and having the other students give him or her directions to get to another student or area of the classroom without bumping into anything.).

Fifi, a 3rd-grade SEI teacher, had introduced the purpose of procedures at the start of the unit, but she continued to remind the students for a few following days:

Teacher: What genre are we writing now?
Student: Procedure.
Teacher: What does it mean?
Student: How to do something.
Teacher: It gives you directions, right?
Student: How to make a sandwich
Student: How to choose a pet, how to play Monopoly . . .

Decisions on Audience

Because procedures are short, students will likely produce a number throughout the course of the unit. In preparation to write each piece, regardless if it is by the whole class or an individual product, first discuss the potential audience with students.

Stages of Procedures

The stages of a procedure include the title, goals or aims (sometimes included in the title), materials or requirements (often, but not always needed), method presented in sequential steps, and an optional evaluation (Butt et al., 2000). The title is chosen considering the context of situation and medium. For example, if the product is a recipe by itself, it may be entitled *How to Make Spring Rolls.* But if it were to be included in a cookbook, *Spring Rolls* would be enough. The materials may include utensils, instruments, ingredients, equipment, or others as relevant and appropriate. Some instructions do not require materials (e.g., what to do when first coming to the classroom in the morning or how to operate a machine). The steps follow sequentially, each starting on a separate line and sometimes numbered. Procedures written for children include illustrations of the materials or steps, or both. The images accompanying the steps are essential for students to understand the procedure. They allow for the use of less complicated language in the instructions. Sometimes a procedure ends with a suggestion for how the success of the procedure can be evaluated or with another final comment.

Stages	*Example of a Published Procedure*
Title	*Paper Scarecrow* www.enchantedlearning.com/crafts/thanksgiving/scarecrow (Drawings accompany instructions on the website; links in the instructions lead to additional resources)
Goal or Aim	Make a paper scarecrow for Thanksgiving. This scarecrow makes a wonderful Thanksgiving decoration.
Materials or Requirements	Printer Construction paper Pencil Glue Scissors Markers or crayons Optional: Googly eyes Optional: Real straw or raffia
Method presented in a series of sequential steps	• Print out the scarecrow template or draw your own. • Print out the scarecrow clothes or draw your own. • Cut out the scarecrow, shirt, overalls, shoes, and hat. • Color and decorate the clothes using crayons or markers. • Glue the clothes on the scarecrow. Optional: glue on some straw (real straw, raffia, or thin strips of light brown paper) at the edges of the clothing. • Add eyes, nose, and mouth.
Evaluation or final comment (often omitted)	This scarecrow makes a fun Thanksgiving decoration.

Procedures are not written in traditional paragraphs. Instead, each stage is set up differently. If not part of the title, the goal or aim is included right after the title. If the procedure has materials or ingredients, they are listed under the title or goal. The steps follow, each starting on a new line. Often, procedures include images so that the instructions accompany these images either to the side or underneath.

"To assist her 5th grade students with remembering the steps taken to complete the skeleton piece, Ms. B decided to incorporate a lesson on using diagrams and illustrations with procedures. She relied on mentor texts to illustrate how diagrams were helpful in most how-to manuals. She provided students with their own copies of diagrams of how simple machines work. She asked students to look at their skeleton pieces and go back and draw out, step-by-step, how they glued the pasta onto the black construction paper. She gave students paper with blank boxes for them to sequentially draw out the steps they took to create the pasta skeletons. Students were instructed to complete the diagrams before going back to finish the skeleton drafts" (Zisselsberger, 2011, p. 172).

Features of Students' Writing

Following is the analysis of the stages from the uncoached student piece presented earlier.

	1	*2*	*3*	*4*	*Uncoached Writing Comments*
Title (if required by the medium)					N/A because it was given by the teacher.
Goal or Aim					N/A it was included in the title.
Materials or Requirements	✓				Instead of listing them, told how to get them. No quantities or specific features of ingredients.
Method presented in a series of sequential steps	✓				Presented as a narrative rather than a list of steps. Steps are vague.
Evaluation or Final Comment	✓				Repeated the goal, "and you make peanut butter and jelly sandwich."
Layout of stages	✓				Written as a narrative rather than each stage separately with materials listed, etc.

The main problem that students have with the stages is providing a vague list of materials. For example, in a science experiment, the students listed soap, water, and oil, but with no specific quantities. With respect to the steps, there are two challenges: (1) steps can be vague or missing, and (2) the first steps tend to be related to getting the materials *(Get the ornaments in a Christmas tree store, take the milk from the refrigerator)*. Procedures do list the materials, but the steps are related to doing something with them and not simply obtaining them. In addition, students tend to write procedures as a narrative rather than laying out each stage in its appropriate format.

Lessons to Practice the Stages of the Genre

The following lessons help the students become familiar with the stages. As stages are taught, it is also helpful to teach the format in which they are to be written. Initially, it is best to present good examples of the genre and deconstruct them with the students to see how authors accomplish the goals of the genre. Graphic organizers can help show visually what the various stages of the text are. It is always important to point out both the standard features of the genre and how authors vary within the standard structure. Because procedures are generally short, all of the activities involve working on the three stages simultaneously.

LESSON 2. Deconstruction of Texts

Goal: To learn how a procedure is organized in stages. The pattern and format of stages facilitates reading of a procedure to accomplish the goal of the particular procedure.

Materials: Resources used earlier for teaching purpose. Examples brought by students from things they find at home. Graphic organizer (See end-of-chapter materials) on chart paper or smartboard.

Activities

- Have students in groups look at a sample of procedures and notice stages and how they are laid out.
- Discuss and write stages on chart paper. Alternatively, introduce students to multiple examples of procedures by reading them.
- Point out the stages in each example and insert the various stages in the graphic organizer. Show how they are laid out.

LESSON 3. Carry Out Procedures

Goal: To reinforce the purpose and stages by actually implementing procedures.

Materials: Procedure written on chart paper. Materials or ingredients needed to carry out the procedure.

Activities

- Carry out the procedure with the students.
- Take pictures or have students draw each step.
- In collaboration with students, paste pictures or drawings down the side of chart paper in the correct order and write down each step.

Depending on the age and language ability of students, you may repeat this lesson with different activities, including science experiments.

LESSON 4. Organizing the Stages and Learning How to Sequence Steps

Goal: To learn the order of the stages and the order of elements within the stages, in order to make the procedure comprehensible for the reader.

Materials: Large sentence strips with the goal (could be in the form of a title), materials, and steps written on them for a specific procedure. Chart paper. Materials or ingredients to carry out the procedure.

For an alternative or follow-up activity: Envelopes for each group with small sentence strips with the goal (could be in the form of a title). Materials or ingredients and steps written on them. A sheet of blank paper for each group.

Activities

- Remind students of the three stages: goal, materials, and steps.
- Tell students that you will read each sentence strip and they have to tell you to which stage it belongs. Sort the strips in three piles.
- Take the goal, reread it, and ask the students where it goes. Place it on the sheet of chart paper.
- Take the strips in the material pile and discuss them in the order the students choose. Place the strips on the chart paper.
- Read each strip in the steps pile and have the students decide the order. Place them on the chart paper.
- Using the materials you brought, have students follow the procedure as written to check its accuracy. Encourage revisions if needed.

Alternative or follow-up activity:

- Give each group an envelope with sentence strips and a sheet of paper.
- Have students work in groups to order the sentence strips following the same process as before.
- When students have agreed on an order, have them glue the strips on their worksheets.
- Have them share with the whole class.

In Kathy's 2nd-grade classroom, students regularly work at literacy centers during the ELA block. Small groups circulate through centers such as listening station, smartboard, and guided reading, spending 20 minutes at each center. During the procedure unit, after procedures had been introduced and the students had jointly constructed a few writing pieces, Kathy set up a sequencing center. She wrote out a procedure that was familiar to the class on strips of paper, putting the title, each material, and each step on separate strips. During her ELA blocks, small groups of students worked together, spreading out the strips on the table in front of them and reorganizing them to put the stages and steps in order. As the unit went on, Kathy added two procedures for students to sequence. Over the course of a month, students had multiple opportunities to reconstruct the procedures, becoming increasingly familiar with the stages of a procedure.

LESSON 5. Joint Construction of Procedures (Pre K–5)

Goal: To write procedures together to gain confidence before writing individual pieces.

Materials: Materials needed to carry out a procedure. Camera or sheets of paper to draw on. Large chart paper.

Activities

For kindergarten or 1st grade:

- Carry out the procedure with the students.
- Take pictures of every step. (If you do not have a camera, have students draw each step on separate sheets of paper.)
- Work to produce a class procedure together:
  - o Brainstorm with the class what the title should be.
  - o Brainstorm the materials or ingredients needed and list them. Encourage the use of quantities.
  - o Have students put the pictures or drawings on chart paper, ordering them in sequence. Have them dictate the instruction for each picture, letting students come up to the chart paper to write the letters or words that they know.

For 2nd grade and up:

- Discuss the *content*, the *medium*, and the *audience* with the class.
- Carry out a procedure, teaching the vocabulary connected with the materials and the actions. Write any new vocabulary on word cards and create a word wall.

- Jointly construct the stages with the students. As this occurs, point out the layout:
  - Decide on the title. Include a goal if not contained in the title.
  - Ask students to tell you the materials that were used and list them. Encourage the use of adjectives describing materials precisely.
  - Ask students to suggest every step. Keep reminding them that these are directions to be used by the audience reading the procedure so that they can repeat the steps.
- Repeat with other procedures, if necessary.

LESSON 6. Group Construction of Text (Grades 2–5)

Goal: To start releasing teacher responsibility by having students produce procedures while working in groups.

Materials: Images of the materials and steps for a procedure (for example, Linda used directions to assemble IKEA furniture with her SEI students). Have either one copy of the same procedure per group or use different procedures for each group.

Activities

- Ask students (in groups) to label the materials and write the step next to the image.
- If students have the same procedure, have the groups compare and discuss any discrepancies.
- If each group has a different procedure, have the groups share and discuss whether the others can understand the directions.

LESSON 7. Individual Construction of Procedures (Grades 2–5)

Goal: To demonstrate that students have learned to write procedures by producing their own.

Materials: Copies of the graphic organizer for each student.

Activities

- Have students research things from their own experience to share with others. When there are students from multiple backgrounds and cultures, students can consult with their families for information on family recipes, games, or other activities that require a procedure. Alternatively, they can think of procedures found in school, including math games that they have played in class and science experiments that they have done in science.

- Have students fill out the graphic organizer with the materials and steps (or in consultation with a family member).
- Bring the graphic organizer to class and share them in groups to determine if all of the stages are complete.
- Have students write their procedures using the information in the revised graphic organizer.

JEANNINE'S 1ST-GRADE CLASS AT ST. ROSE WRITES A PROCEDURE

Jeannine had practiced a number of procedures with her class. Her culminating activity for this procedure unit, implemented at the onset of the year, involved students preparing the instructions for how to make play dough to give to their buddy 4th-grade class (at her school, all grades have a buddy grade). She had distributed strips with the title, each material, and each step needed to all of the students. The strips with the steps had numbers on the back of the instructions to help students with the order. As she brainstormed what needed to go first and the following order with the students, the student with the appropriate strip came up and glued it to the chart paper. At the end, they added numbers to each step.

A Word About Endings

Procedures usually end with the final instruction. Occasionally, the last sentence may be of a different type. For example, recipes end with instructions on how to serve: "Serve cold, garnished with mint leaves," or "Serve right away" (Johnson Dodge, 2008). They may also simply end with how many the recipe serves, such as "Serves 4." Games often finish with a statement describing how players win or lose the game. Crafts may include comments instructing what to do with the craft such as, "hold the maraca around the middle and shake" (www.ehow.com/how_4855654_make-cheap-maracas.html) or in reference to the end product, such as, "You now have a beautiful Kokeshi doll," or "You now have a great butterfly decoration" (www.enchantedlearning.com/crafts). In books for children, an encouraging note may be found at the end of a procedure in very rare occasions. For example, in a book of craft activities, only one craft ended with an exclamation, "Prepare to sail off!" (Boursin, 2007, p. 45).

However, almost all of the students in a 3rd-grade class changed their voice at the end of the procedure to address the audience with an encouraging exclamation. For example, Yarissa finished her recipe with *Tada! The ensalada mixta is done! Enjoy!*

LESSON 8. End of a Procedure

Goal: To explore how different types of procedures end to include the most appropriate ending in students' own writing.

Materials: Examples of different types of procedures for different audiences, such as cookbooks, craft books, instructions in boxes, cans, other products found in a household, math games, and science experiments. Chart paper. Markers.

Activities

- Sort out the procedures by type (crafts, recipes, science experiments, games). Give each group of students one type of procedure, a sheet of chart paper, and markers.
- Have students look at the end of the procedure and write down the last sentence on the chart paper. Then have students discuss the type of procedure, the type of sentence, the similarities and differences among the various examples, who was the author and the audience, and why the author did or did not use a final exclamation to encourage the audience.
- Have groups share and display the sheets with the different ending sentences around the class.
- Have students look at the last sentence in their own procedure and decide whether the voice is appropriate. Make sure that students do not feel that all of the sentences should have the same voice.

Part II: Language

Topic development, audience, and voice are closely connected in procedures. Instructions show awareness of the audience if they are clear and precise in order so that the audience can carry out the procedure successfully. In writing a procedure, authors show awareness of their audience by the amount of information they provide through language, as opposed to images and the specific choice of language. The mentor text *Making a Paper Scarecrow* at the beginning of the chapter is for young children. The author uses very simple clauses such as "Glue the clothes on the scarecrow" accompanied with images that show exactly where each piece of clothing fits the body of the scarecrow, thus avoiding complicated language to explain where each piece of clothing fits. Given that a procedure is a set of directions, sentences are written as commands without directly engaging the audience. Images are also used to disengage the audience by illustrating what to do, but not including the person doing it.

To plan the remainder of the unit with emphasis on refining the language of procedures, teachers should analyze samples of students' writing using the Analysis of Student Work: Language form in the end-of-chapter materials. The lessons in this section can be carried out after students have drafted initial pieces on the basis of what they have learned about the genre stages. In connection to the lessons, students can revise the draft or drafts that they want to publish or they can keep the lessons in mind when producing new drafts.

Francisco, another 3rd grader in the SEI class, wrote the following procedure after the initial lessons of the unit. Analysis of the following piece using the Language form illustrates the various aspects of language that are helpful to cover in the unit.

How to make a ham and cheese sandwich

First you get the braed and put
the bread in the toster for a kopl
minets in tell it pops. 2 When the
bread pop up you get it and
you get the cheese and put the cheese
in the bread. 3 When you put
the cheese in the bread you put
the Ham in the bread. 4 after
you did your bread you get a
drike and eat it.

The following aspects of language will be covered in the remainder of the chapter:

- Verb groups: variety and reinforcing the use of the imperative, if needed
- Specificity through the use of adjectivals and adverbials
- Clause complexes
- Text connectives
- Reference ties.

Clause complexes and reference are topics more appropriate for the upper grades.

Verb Groups

In procedures, the verbs used in the instructions are usually action verbs written in the imperative *(Color and decorate the clothes using crayons or makers)*. It is important to develop a variety of actions to help students be precise when describing the action.

	1	*2*	*3*	*4*	*Mid-unit Writing Comments*
Verb Types Uses precise action verbs to indicate what needs to be done.		✓			Uses frequently generic verbs like "get" and "put" ("put the bread in the toaster" rather than "toast the bread").

As Francisco does, children tend to use generic verbs such as "put" and "get." For example, he wrote, *First you must get all the things,* rather than *assemble all of the materials;* or *put the pastelitos in the frying pan,* rather than *fry the pastelitos.* A 4th grader wrote in her uncoached recipe for making a ham and cheese sandwich: *Put a ham on top of the mayonesa. Put some onions on top of the ham. Put some pickels on top of the onions.* She could have simply written, *Layer the ham, onions, pickles, yellow cheese, and tomatoes on top of the bread,* using the more descriptive verb "to layer."

LESSON 9. Deconstruction of Text

Goal: To use the language of procedure as a resource and a model for the verbs in order to enrich the vocabulary.

Materials: Procedures comparable to what students will be writing in their own procedures, such as crafts, recipes, math games, and so on. Cardboard strips to make word cards. Projector.

Activities

- Project a procedure.
- Ask individual students to come up to the screen and find the imperative verbs. As each student finds an imperative, give him or her a card and have the student write it on it.
- Clarify the meaning, if needed, and point out that verbs are usually not preceded by *you*.
- Create word walls with "Crafts verbs," "Recipe verbs," or other relevant type of procedure used in class that students can refer to when writing their own procedures later on.
- Do a whole-class activity with one or more procedures and then, if students are old enough (2nd grade and up), distribute the rest of the texts and have students do the same activity in groups.
- As a follow-up activity, put the cards in a hat.
- Have students take turns taking a card out of the hat and forming a clause with the verb.

This lesson can be repeated with different topics in preparation for writing other types of procedures. For example, you may start with crafts and then do science experiments.

Jack, a 2nd-grade teacher, had noticed that in the first set of procedures his students had written, most of the commands were the verbs "put" and "get." To help students revise their writing using more precise action verbs, he divided a piece of chart paper into four squares. On top of the first square he wrote, "Cooking," and asked students for suggestions of commands that would appear in a procedure related to cooking. Students suggested such words as *pour, fry, squeeze, flip,* and *heat.* In the next square, he wrote, "Arts & Crafts," and asked for suggestions for that type of procedure. Students called such words as *fold, cut, tape, glue,* and *draw.* Then, he asked for other procedures that they had written. One student said, "How to make a snowman." He asked how many people had written that one and, seeing a few hands go up, he wrote "Snowman" over the third square and asked for suggestions. He did the same thing with the last square.

Then, he asked for volunteers to read aloud their procedures. As a student read her piece on how to decorate a Christmas tree, which included several of the commands starting with "Put," Jack chose one sentence ("Put the jingle bells on the Christmas tree") and asked the class to give the author suggestions for words other than "put." One student said, "hang." After a few more students read their pieces and received excellent suggestions, Jack asked the children to go back to their seats, read their procedures, and change a few of the "put" and "get" verbs to a more precise action. Students could refer to the examples in the chart paper. Most of the students made appropriate changes.

Specificity Through the Use of Adjectivals and Adverbials

Adjectivals and adverbials give precision to instructions and are essential in procedures (See chapter 3 for more information on adjectivals and adverbials). Adjectivals (adjectives, prepositional phrases, or embedded clauses with finite or non-finite verbs) describe the participants with precision, for example, *thin* **strips** *of light brown paper.* Adverbial prepositional phrases or adverbs indicate circumstances, particularly of place and manner, that support the instructions, for example, *Color and decorate the clothes using crayons or markers* (manner); *Glue the clothes on the scarecrow* (place).

Francisco used no adjectives to help make the ingredients more specific. Some adverbials were repeated several times.

	1	*2*	*3*	*4*	*Mid-unit Writing Comments*
Noun Groups Various types of adjectives are used to give specificity.		✓			No description of ingredients.
Adverbials Adverbs, especially of place and manner, are used to make the instructions specific.			✓		Uses adverbials of time and place. There is unnecessary repetition.

Like Francisco, children tend to name the participants without including much information about them. For example, a 3rd grader listed the materials for her recipe on *How to Make Hot Coco* as *"ingredient: pot, chocolate bar, canela, milk, sugar, stove, spoon, cups"* without specifying any quantities or classifiers for the ingredients.

Children do not always use these adverbials of time, place, manner, and degree to help make the instructions more precise. When they do, they mostly use prepositional phrases rather than adverbs, such as *slowly* or *carefully.* For example, the 4th graders in an SEI class were directed to write their uncoached piece on how to make a ham and cheese sandwich. One of the students wrote, *Get the bread. Get the cheese. Get the ham,* while another more specifically indicated, *Put the ham on the bread,* using a prepositional phrase of place (underlined).

LESSON 10. Deconstructing Text for Adjectivals and Adverbials

Goal: To help students understand the function of adjectivals and adverbials in making instructions/directions precise.

Materials: A couple of procedures projected or written on chart paper with adjectivals and adverbials blocked by a piece of paper. Materials needed to demonstrate the steps of the procedures. Projector. For the Ice Cube experiment, have two identical bowls [same size] and ice cubes.

Activities

- Show or read one of the procedures with the adjectivals and adverbials covered.
- Have a few students come to the front of the class. Give them the materials and have them try to carry out the procedure. For example, *paper* versus *one sheet of construction paper* or *fold* versus *fold in the middle.*
- Uncover the adjectivals and adverbials and have the students try again.
- Discuss the differences.

Repeat the process with the procedure from a science experiment because being precise is absolutely essential in this context. For example, do the following Ice Cube Experiment (adverbials are underlined and adjectivals are bold). When you show the piece without adjectives or adverbials, also be sure to cover the title and goal.

Stress the importance of the language that describes measurements and quantities. When writing procedures, students often forget to include the quantities.

Ice Cube Experiment

Goal: To measure melting time relative to the size of the ice.

Materials: 2 **identical** bowls; 2 **ice** cubes.

1. Put the bowls *on the counter.*
2. Take **two ice** cubes *out of the freezer* and place one *in each bowl.*
3. Break one of the **ice** cubes *into smaller pieces that are no larger than 1/4 the size of the whole ice cube.*
4. Time how long it takes for all of the ice to melt.

LESSON 11. Using Adjectivals and Adverbials to Be Precise

Goal: To apply the knowledge of adjectivals and adverbials to giving precise directions.

Materials: Materials to make something simple (e.g., a paper hat or paper airplane). With younger students, it is better to choose something you have already done as a class.

Activities

- Tell students that you have brought the materials to make a paper hat (or other simple object) and ask them to give you the directions so that you can make it.
- Follow the directions exactly as they tell you. For example, if they tell you to "fold the paper," do it any odd way.
- Discuss why you folded it that way and what the students need to tell you so that you fold it the way they want.

LESSON 12. Using a Barrier Activity to Show the Importance of Being Precise

Goal: To apply the knowledge of adjectivals and adverbials to giving precise directions and to understand the implications of not being precise.

Materials: Several copies of a simple drawing, cardboard screens, paper, and pencils. The drawing needs to be something that the students are familiar with so that they have the vocabulary to describe it.

Activities

- Sit students in pairs across from each other with a screen in between them.
- Give one student a drawing and another student a blank paper. Don't let the student with the blank paper see the drawing.
- The student with the drawing tells the other student what to do to create a similar drawing. Then, they compare their drawings.
- Discuss potential language that would have helped to make the drawing more accurate.

LESSON 13. Add Adjectives and Adverbials With the Help of Questions

Goal: To revise students' work to give more specificity.
Materials: Samples of students' procedures to project or write on chart paper. Blank sheets of chart paper to add questions. Projector.

Activities

- Using one of the students' procedures, demonstrate how to ask questions to make the students' procedures more precise. You may create an anchor chart with questions to help students when they are writing procedures on their own.
  - Ask questions to describe materials more precisely. For example, "sugar" questions: How much sugar? "2 tablespoons." What kind of sugar? "Brown sugar."
  - Ask questions about verbs that would help students add adverbials and be more precise. For example, for the instruction, "cut each potato," ask the following questions: Cut how? "In half lengthwise." For the instruction, "spread the potatoes," ask the following questions: Spread where? "Onto the prepared pan." For the instruction, "pour the boiling water," ask the following questions: Where? How? "Carefully, pour the boiling water in the sink."
- As you ask questions, negotiate the suggestions given by the students and add the agreed upon revision.
- Repeat with another piece.
- Have students work in groups or pairs to do this activity with their other procedures.

Ms. B., a 5th-grade teacher, gave students a few suggestions for writing procedures and directed them to fill out a graphic organizer with the information. Before writing their drafts, she wrote a procedure to make a kite on the whiteboard and led the whole class in a text analysis of the adjectival and adverbial phrases followed by a discussion of the function of this language in making the instructions more precise. When writing their procedures from their graphic organizers, the students added the elements of language from the lesson, demonstrating the impact and influence. For example, one student had "put rocks in" in her graphic organizer. In her draft, she wrote, "put in your *small* rocks *in the tank*" [emphasis added] adding an adjective and adverbial phrase. Another student wrote, "cut the banana into eight pieces," in his draft, while his graphic organizer just showed "cut the bananas" (Zisselsberger, 2011 p. 141). To further help students revise their pieces, Ms. B had partners acting out the procedures, as well as filling out a worksheet with comments, to help improve the accuracy of the instructions.

Clause Complexes

Procedures for older students or adults sometimes include clause complexes with either finite or non-finite (non-conjugated verb) clauses. However, procedures for elementary age children tend to be predominantly written with simple clauses or occasional dependent clauses with non-finite verbs (underlined): *Using the black paint*, paint a jack *o'lantern face on your jar. Cut the cheesecloth into squares large enough to drape over your bottle.*

A science teacher required students to include not only the steps for a procedure, but also the scientific reason for that step, thus demanding a complex sentence. For example, when writing the procedure to create a crayfish habitat in a 3rd-grade class, a student wrote, *Step 3 cut pieces of black paper and glue it on the tank. You need black paper because crayfishes lives under a rock and under a rock is dark.*

Francisco's piece on making a ham and cheese sandwich includes a series of simple clauses that could be combined into one: *First you get the braed and put the bread in the toster for a kopl minets in tell it pops* could be written as *Toast the bread for a couple of minutes.* Further, *When the bread pop up you get it and you get the cheese and put the cheese in the bread,* could become *When the bread pops up, put the cheese on it.*

	1	*2*	*3*	*4*	*Mid-unit Writing Comments*
Clause Complex With Finite and Non-finite Verbs Help specify instructions, pack information (in procedures for upper elementary).		✓			Simple and coordinated sentences could be packed or combined.

This type of writing is frequently found in students' work. Another common problem is having a string of directions joined by *and* or *then* that could be simply written as separate clauses, each starting on a new line, to make the directions more clear. For example, a 3rd-grade student used *then* 8 times within 70 words, connecting every step of the procedure. Zisselsberger (2011) shows a similar pattern with 5th graders: "2. If the fish bowl is dirty you can clean by using a long tube filer *and* press the top hole with your finger *and then* let your finger go *and* it should suck all the nasty stuff in there" [emphasis added] (p. 142).

LESSON 14. Edit Sentences

Goal: To teach students how to pack or separate a string of clauses in order to make the instructions more clear.

Materials: Students' work samples that need editing with sentences that could be packed (underlined in green) or separated (underlined in blue). Choose either sentences that need to be packed or those that need to be separate every time you carry out the activity so as not to overwhelm the students. Blank paper.

Activities

- After checking with the authors, put the complex sentences that could use packing up on a smartboard or the board. Do two or three examples with the whole class.
- Ask for suggestions from students, identifying and underlining the verbs to determine the number of clauses.
- Ask for suggestions from students, underlining conjunctions, especially "and."
- Demonstrate how a sentence could be packed. For example:
  - *Put the pastelitos in the fring Pan and wait 10 minutes and the cheese melts.* could become *Fry pastelitos for 10 minutes until the cheese melts.*
  - *First wrap thumb with bandage. If you don't your hand is going to hurt.* could be written as *To avoid hurting your thumb, wrap it with a bandage.*
  - "Take the ice cream scooper and start scooping the chocolate ice cream into the ice cream cup" (Zisselsberger, 2011, p. 168). This clause complex could be packed either by simply stating, *Scoop the chocolate ice cream into the ice cream cup* or by including a subordinate clause with a non-finite verb, *Using the scooper, scoop the chocolate ice cream into to the ice cream cup.*
  - Get the pan, put water in it, and put it on the stove. Put the potatoes in the pan to boil until tender. This string of sentences could be packed and the ubiquitous put and get verbs eliminated by writing something like, Boil the potatoes in a pan filled with water.
- Give students the rest of their work with one or two sentences underlined that they need to work on. Have students work in groups, look at their writing, and focus on the sentences underlined in green.
- Have students suggest how they could pack a sentence that you have marked.
- Have students write their agreed-upon alternative on a separate sheet.
- Work with groups to review their proposed revisions or have them share with the whole class.
- Agree upon a final revision and have the authors make changes to their procedures.

Repeat the activity with strings of sentences that could be separated first with the whole class and then worked on in groups. This time, students will focus on the sentences underlined in blue. For example, a 3rd grader wrote, . . . *then put it in the microwave for 1 minute then take it out of the microwave then touch it just a piece then stired it then put it in the microwave for 4½ minuetes then take it out of the microwave then take it out and stire it then get some play do* [dough]. Each of the "then"s could be eliminated, creating new sentences with a command written on a separate line, for example, *Put it in the microwave for a minute. Take it out and stir it . . .* Some of the sentences could be combined by joining the two actions with "and."

Text Connectives

Procedures do not use text connectives, except sometimes, especially in procedures for children, numbers precede each step. Often, teachers encourage children to use connectives such as *first, next,* and *last*. However, these connectives are never used in published texts. Therefore, students should not be taught to write them. It is important to check published texts because they often illustrate what the culture expects.

Francisco learned his lesson about the use of numbers, except for the first instruction that begins with "first." However, he wrote the piece without breaks and with numbers embedded in the text rather than using each number to start a new sentence.

	1	*2*	*3*	*4*	*Mid-unit Writing Comments*
Text Connectives Use of numbers or no text connectives. (Connectives such as "then," "next," and "finally" are more appropriate for procedural recounts.)			✓		Uses numbers, but does not start each instruction on a new line.

LESSON 15. Text Connectives

Goal: To have students use appropriate connectives, if any.

Materials: Sample mentor text previously used that has different formats, including numbers, bullets, and a list of instructions with each listed on a new line.

Activities

- Give groups of students a set of mentor texts that use different formats, for example, numbers, bullets, or starting on a new line.
- Ask students to identify how authors indicate that there is a new step.
- Show a student sample that requires editing and correct it with the whole class.
- In their groups, have students edit their work, especially editing out words like *the first, step, you,* and others unless they are essential.

Reference Ties

For reference ties in procedures, it is essential to check that if students mention a material or ingredient in the instructions, this material or ingredient must appear in the list at the beginning of the text. Otherwise, the person following the instructions will not know the kind or quantity. When materials are named in the steps, they don't require the quantity any longer unless portions are used in different steps.

Francisco failed to write the list of ingredients, so clauses like *get the bread* and *put the cheese* have no reference.

	1	*2*	*3*	*4*	*Mid-unit Writing Comments*
Reference Materials included in steps have been introduced in materials list.		✓			Materials were not initially listed, yet they were named in the instructions with "the": "First you get the bread."

One student wrote in the opposite way. Not only did he have all of the measures with the materials, but he repeated the measures during the steps, an unnecessary redundancy: *first put in the plastic continer 1 cup of flour 1/2 cup of salt 4 spoons of oil.*

LESSON 16: Reference

Goal: To help students see the connection between the materials in the list and those named in the steps.

Materials: Sample student work, a couple that are appropriately done and a couple that need revision.

Activities

- Show a sample student work. Circle the materials in the steps and look for them in the materials list. Are they present in the list? Did they repeat the quantity in the instructions? Is it necessary to state the quantity?
- Repeat with the other pieces of sample student work.
- Have students work in groups to edit their own work.

Resources

- Analysis of student work: Purpose and stages
- Analysis of student work: Language
- Graphic organizer
- Additional resources that illustrate the genre

Procedure—Analysis of Student Work: Purpose and Stages

Content Area: **Medium:** **Intended Audience:**

Key: 1. Needs substantial support; 2. Needs instruction; 3. Needs revision; 4. Meets standard; NA: Not applicable

	1	*2*	*3*	*4*	*Uncoached Writing Comments*	*1*	*2*	*3*	*4*	*Final Writing Comments*
Purpose To give directions to accomplish a goal.										
Use of Imperative Person carrying the action is not named. Rarely is referred to by the use of "you" or "one."										
Title (if required by the medium)										
Goal or Aim										
Materials or Requirements										
Method presented in a series of sequential steps										
Evaluation or Final Comment (optional)										
Layout of stages Materials in a list. Each step starts flush against the left margin.										

Criteria

1. Needs substantial support: The student writer needs extensive help developing that aspect of the genre.
2. There are gaps in the writer's understanding of the specific aspect. The writer has insufficient control. S/he needs instruction and practice.
3. The paper needs revision on one or two instances of the feature. A conference would be sufficient to help the writer meet the standard.
4. The paper reflects what the student should be able to accomplish and write independently given the instruction provided for this grade level. (National Center on Education and the Economy, 2004).

Procedure—Analysis of Student Work: Language

Type: **Content Area:** **Medium:** **Intended Audience:**

Key: 1. Needs substantial support; 2. Needs instruction; 3. Needs revision; 4. Meets standard; NA: Not applicable

	1	*2*	*3*	*4*	*Mid-unit Writing Comments*	*1*	*2*	*3*	*4*	*Final Writing Comments*
Verb Types Uses precise action verbs to indicate what needs to be done.										
Noun Groups Various types of adjectives are used to give specificity.										
Adverbials Adverbs, especially of place and manner, are used to make the instructions specific.										
Clause Complex With Finite and Non-finite Verbs Help specify instructions, pack information (in procedures for upper elementary).										
Text Connectives Use of numbers or no text connectives. (Connectives such as "then," "next," and "finally" are more appropriate for procedural recounts.)										
Reference Materials included in steps have been introduced in materials list.										

Criteria

1. Needs substantial support: The student writer needs extensive help developing that aspect of the genre.
2. There are gaps in the writer's understanding of the specific aspect. The writer has insufficient control. S/he needs instruction and practice.
3. The paper needs revision on one or two instances of the feature. A conference would be sufficient to help the writer meet the standard.
4. The paper reflects what the student should be able to accomplish and write independently given the instruction provided for this grade level. (National Center on Education and the Economy, 2004).

Procedure Graphic Organizer

Goal:

Materials:

__________________ __________________

__________________ __________________

__________________ __________________

__________________ __________________

Steps:

1. ____________________________________
2. ____________________________________
3. ____________________________________
4. ____________________________________
5. ____________________________________
6. ____________________________________

Evaluation or Final Comment (Optional)

FIGURE 4.1 Procedure Graphic Organizer

Additional Resources That Illustrate the Genre

For All Elementary Levels

Bolton, F., & Snowball, D. (1986). *Growing radishes and carrots.* New York, NY: Scholastic.

Boursin, D. (2007). *Folding for fun: Origami for ages 4 and up.* Buffalo, NY: Firefly Books.

Burke, J. (1999). *Look what you can make with paper bags: Over 90 pictured crafts and dozens of other ideas.* Honesdale, PA: Boyds Mill Press.

Coy, J. (2003). *Two old potatoes and me.* New York, NY: Alfred A. Knopf.
Gould, R. (1998). *Making cool crafts & awesome art: A kids' treasure trove of fabulous fun.* Charlotte, VT: Williamson Publishing.
Griffin Llanas, S. (2012). *Easy lunches from around the world.* Heshan City, Guangong, China: Leo Paper Group.
Hickman, P. (1998). *Animal senses: How animals see, hear, taste, smell, and feel.* Buffalo, NY: Kid Can Press.
Irvine, J. (1996). *How to make holiday pop-ups.* Toronto, ONT, Canada: Kids Can Press
Parker, S. (2005). *The science of water: Projects and experiments with water science and power.* Chicago, IL: Heinemann Library.
Wiseman, A. (1973). *Making things: The hand book of creative discovery.* Boston, MA: Little, Brown.
Yanuck, D. L. (2003). *American symbols: The American flag.* Mankato, MN: Capstone Press.

For Grades 3–5

Braman, A. (2000). *Kids around the world cook! The best foods and recipes from many lands.* New York, NY: John Wiley & Sons.
Fletcher, R. (2002). "How to make a snow angel" in *Poetry matters: Writing a poem from inside out* (pp. 122–123). New York, NY: HarperTrophy.
Johnson Dodge, A. (2008). *Around the world cookbook.* New York, NY: DK Publishing.
King, D. C., & Moore, B. (1998). *Colonial days: Discover the past with fun projects, games, activities, and recipes.* New York, NY: John Wiley & Sons.
Long, L. (2001). *Measurement mania: Games and activities that make math easy and fun.* New York, NY: John Wiley & Sons.
Mebane, R. C., & Rybolt, T. R. (1995). *Water & other liquids.* New York, NY: Twenty-First Century Books.
Rainis, K. G. (2003). *Microscope science projects and experiments: Magnifying the hidden world.* Berkeley Heights, NJ: Enslow. (This book has a number of procedures for experiments, each followed with suggestions for a science fair.)
Rau, D. (2004). *Jump rope.* Mankato, MN: Compass Point Books.
Rau, D. (2005). *Card games.* Mankato, MN: Compass Point Books.
Robbins, K. (1992). *Make me a peanut butter sandwich and a glass of milk.* New York, NY: Scholastic.
Wiseman, A. (1973). *Making things: The handbook of creative discovery.* Boston, MA: Little, Brown.

Internet Resources

Marshall, H. *How to make no-cook play dough easily.* Retrieved from www.ehow.com/how_5271462_make-nocook-play-dough-easily.html
www.youtube.com/watch?v=I0a0p8ygfQM (Video on how to make a paper plane)

5

RECOUNTS AND HISTORICAL GENRES

<table>
<tr>
<td>

Chapter Map

Grade Levels and Content Areas
Stories and Histories Unit
General Preparation
Part I: Purpose and Stages of the Genre
Purpose of Recounts
Decisions on Audience
Stages of Recounts
Orientation of Recounts
Sequence or Record of Events in Recounts
Conclusion
Creating a Coherent Text and Paragraph Formation
Part II: Language
Verbs
Noun Groups
Adverbials
Development of Audience and Voice (Tenor)
Development of Clause Complexes
Text Connectives
Reference Ties

</td>
<td>

The 5th-grade teachers started a unit on empathetic autobiographies connected with different periods in history. Linda Drueding's students wrote about historical characters in the Revolutionary War. Beverly chose the Holocaust. She collected a number of books on the topic and had the students search the Internet for information on the Holocaust. She read aloud *Star of Fear, Star of Hope*, a book where the author takes the identity of a young French girl who tells how she escaped the Holocaust persecution, but her best friend disappeared. Pat Scialoia's class had a field trip to Plymouth Plantation, where there was staff who impersonated colonials and Wampanoag (a Native American tribe) during the early settlement. The students interviewed the interpreters, noticing their language, dress, and customs. One of the children addressed an elder in passing by removing his hat and saying, "Hello, my good man," already behaving in character. As soon as they returned, they started working on their empathetic autobiographies, choosing one of the characters and one of the customs to feature. They worked intensely on content-specific language, evident in their writing:

My faced [face] burned as I stirred the rabbit stew. I made sure the squash was soft & the garlic was mixing. All the deer skin on my back kept me warm. The smoke from all the wetu fires burned my eyes.

</td>
</tr>
</table>

Resources Analysis of Student Work Forms Graphic Organizers Additional Resources That Illustrate the Genre	The writing goes on for a couple of pages accompanied with photographs. Students shared their drafts and made suggestions for improvements. Their enthusiasm and knowledge of the content was evident. To reinforce another person's perspective, Holly, the science teacher, who works in coordination with the classroom teachers, had the children write imaginative recounts, telling the life story of a water drop to learn about the water cycle.

This chapter will cover a family of genres with a number of similarities and differences. The following genres will be covered (the genre initials in bold will be used throughout the chapter to help spot information about each one):

Stories	*Histories*
PersR Personal Recount	**A** Autobiography
ProR Procedural Recount	**B** Biography
IR Imaginative Recount	**EA** Empathetic Autobiography
	HR Historical Recount

Each of these genres has a different purpose but they share a number of features. As they are taught over the elementary grades, instruction can build on the previously taught genre. For example, when writing autobiographies, students learn to choose important events in their lives, which can be applied later when writing biographies. When learning to write biographies, students need to learn to write in third person, which will be useful for historical recounts.

Although *fictional narratives* are a type of story, they are covered in a different chapter. The skill of developing character is very involved and lengthy, requiring a different set of cognitive and linguistic demands than those of the genres included in this chapter.

PersR A *personal recount* is a story genre used to tell what happened based on a personal experience, to document a sequence of events, and to evaluate their significance in some way. This genre is often called a personal narrative. Genre theory distinguishes between recounts that include a sequence of events and narratives that include a problem, crisis, and resolution. Personal recounts allow the narrator to share their experiences with others, providing a tool to create community. Children from other cultures will likely follow the norms of narratives in their cultures when writing personal recounts.

ProR The purpose of a *procedural recount,* also called factual writing, is to tell what the writer observed. For example, reporting on an incident that the writer witnessed, such as a dispute during a break, would fit in this category. In science, procedural recounts are used to record what has been done in an experiment in order to use it as evidence for the final argument. In math, procedural recounts are commonly demanded of students to explain how they went about solving a problem. Procedural recount is different from procedure. Procedure includes the instructions for how to do something, whereas procedural recount tells what happens based on observation.

The purpose of the historical genres included in this chapter is to record history (Coffin, 2006). These include autobiography, biography, empathetic autobiography, and historical recount. Each has its own purpose.

IR The purpose of an *imaginative recount* is similar to the personal recount, but the writer takes the identity of an object. For example, one would write from the point of view of the teacher's desk in the classroom or of a shoe. This genre can be helpful to prepare students to write empathetic autobiographies. This genre is common as a school activity because it supports children in learning to take another person's point of view, an essential skill needed to comprehend text (Scollon & Scollon, 1981).

A An *autobiography* retells "the events of the author's life in order to both inform and entertain" (Coffin, 2006, p. 49). A memoir is a form of autobiography that focuses on some aspect of a person's life. When written by students, autobiographies and memoirs are a way for members of the classroom community to get to know each other. **B** A *biography* tells "the life story of a significant historical figure" (p. 53). They are tools used to add depth to students' knowledge of history. **EA** In an *empathetic autobiography,* the author assumes the identity of a historical figure, defined or general, for example, Paul Revere or a colonial soldier. The purpose of this writing is to inform and entertain (Christie & Derewianka, 2008). This genre is a powerful tool to engage students in learning the sociocultural context of a time in history. **HR** The purpose of a *historical recount* is "to chronicle past events regarded as historically significant, and designed to inform rather than entertain"(Coffin, 2006, p. 56).

Each of these genres is increasingly more difficult (terms underlined signal the new aspect introduced in the genre). *Autobiographies,* like personal recounts, are in the first person. Unlike personal recounts, the events are *episodic* rather than serial. Episodic means that only certain events are chosen to be included. In personal recount, the events are serial because every detail of what happened in a short amount of time is recounted. *Empathetic autobiographies* are written in the first person and are episodic, but the story is not about the writer. *The writer takes the personality of somebody else.* For example, a student might be instructed to write as if he or she were Christopher Columbus crossing the Atlantic. *Biographies* are episodic, but written in the *third person.* The focus is on one person. *Historical recounts* are episodic and written in the third person, but the focus is not just on one person as in biographies, but a whole event in history, for example, the French Revolution.

TABLE 5.1 Recount Instruction Across Grades

Grade Level	*Content Area*			
	ELA		Social Studies	Science/Math
Pre-K	Personal Recount			
K				
1				Procedural Recount
2				
3	Imaginative Recount	Autobiography	Biography	
4		Personal Recount*	Empathetic Autobiography	
5			Historical Recount	

* Some state tests demand personal recount for their long composition in 4th grade. If that is the case, it should be reviewed in this grade.

Grade Levels and Content Areas

Schools should plan to teach these genres across all of the grades, building from one level to the next. In pre-school, kindergarten, and 1st grades, children can start with personal recounts. One of the historical genres can be added at each grade level (See Table 5.1 for a potential distribution of the genres covered in this chapter). Each one of the genres is appropriate for different content areas. Personal and imaginative recount and autobiographies are appropriate for ELA, procedural recount is appropriate for science and math, and the remainder of the historical genres is appropriate for social studies.

Stories and Histories Unit

The purpose of combining these seven genres under a recount chapter is to avoid repetition—given that these genres share so many features—and to show how one genre builds on the previous one. When preparing a unit, teachers would do it for one of the seven genres described, extracting ideas from each of the elements that pertain to the unit they are preparing. For example, when preparing a unit on autobiography, teachers should isolate features particular to autobiographies within the sections on purpose, stages, and language.

To help build on students' skills acquired through each of these genres, it is important for teachers in a school to plan their writing calendar together and understand what is required at each grade to support the more difficult tasks encountered as the students move up in grades and compose writing in advanced genres. Table 5.1 suggests how these genres can be distributed across the grade levels.

PersR/ProR/IR *Personal recount* is a good starting genre with younger students because they can use their personal experiences as the content for the writing. There is no need to research topics. One of the problems with personal recounts is that students often skip events, making the progression of the story confusing to the reader. A *procedural recount* helps students understand that they need to clearly describe what happened to create a complete observation. When students skip events in their observation, the teacher can easily point to the omission. An *imaginative recount* should be done as a quick write, rather than as a whole unit, to have students practice taking another person's point of view. This practice is useful for empathetic autobiographies and literacy, in general.

A/EA *Autobiography* is a good genre to incorporate by third grade and should be done at the beginning of the year to get to know the students. It can be difficult for students to think in terms of a time line and having to choose and develop just significant aspects of what happened and not everything that happened as in a personal recount. *Empathetic autobiography* is a genre only found in school contexts. Its purpose is to immerse students in a period of history to understand it better, while having fun imagining life during that period. The features of text structure and language are comparable to autobiographies. However, this genre can be difficult because it requires students to take another person's point of view. Further, students' historical and socio-cultural knowledge of the time period must be accurate to make their writing authentic. Therefore, it should be implemented in the upper elementary grades.

B/HR A *biography* introduces the skill of writing in the third person. The detached perspective that the third person brings, a more typical voice of academic writing, is very difficult for children (Brisk, 2012). A *historical recount* is similar in structure and language to biographies. They are also written in the third person. However, writing about a period in history, rather than one person, is more difficult to construct and sort out what is important to cover. For example, the Civil War is a more abstract participant than Abraham Lincoln.

General Preparation

In preparation to start the unit and on the basis of the school-wide decisions of which genre to teach at which grade level and in connection to which content area, teachers should:

- Determine the content, writing, and language standards
- Choose resources
- Decide how students will be grouped
- Decide on writing products: medium, multimodality, and authenticity
- Build content knowledge
- Plan lessons based on analysis of students' uncoached writing.

There are extensive suggestions about each one of these points in chapter 2. Following are considerations specific to this genre with respect to content areas, CCSS, resources, medium, and prompts for uncoached writing.

As suggested earlier, these genres best fit specific content areas.

PersR/IR/A For *personal* and *imaginative recounts,* students do not have to do research because they are both based on personal experiences. It helps to introduce personal recounts and guide the students through the structure of the text and language by basing writing on a shared experience. Teachers can better help students incorporate all of the events if students know what happened. For example, a kindergarten teacher walked her class to the nearby fire station, took pictures along the way (including pictures of individual children), and helped them construct their first personal recount based on this experience and supported by the photos. Although *autobiographies* are based on the students' lives, they still require some basic research interviewing family members who can tell the students about their birth and earlier years of their lives.

ProR *Procedural recounts* are best embedded in science and math lessons. In science lessons, the procedural recounts are based on observations that students make when carrying out an experiment or when they observe the habits of a class animal. In math, students solve a problem and then write their procedural recount on the basis of how they went about solving it.

B/EA/HR For *biographies, empathetic autobiographies, and historical recounts,* students must carry out research. The unit should be embedded in a social studies unit. For example, a 3rd-grade class wrote biographies during Black History month. Students conducted research and wrote biographies on various African American historical figures. A 5th-grade class wrote empathetic autobiographies in the context of their unit on explorers, choosing historical figures from the 16th century to current times. Another 5th-grade class wrote a historical recount about the crossing of the Bering Strait while studying about the Ice Age.

In the CCSS, these genres are included either in narratives (personal recounts), informational/explanatory (biographies, empathetic autobiographies, and historical recounts), or not at all (imaginative and procedural recounts). Because the CCSS genres are so broad, there is very little specific information about the different features of each of the seven genres included in this chapter. Moreover, the historical genres seem to be included in informational/explanatory because they fit the old "non-fiction" classification. Personal recounts and procedural recounts are also not fictional, but they are not grouped with the informational/explanatory but rather the narrative text types. The standards, themselves, mostly support the characteristics of what, in this book, is called *reports.* For example, when contrasting reports and biographies by what is specified in CCSS (See Table 5.2), it is obvious that the standards match the purpose and stages of reports, but they do not remotely approximate those of a biography.

There is no clear evidence in the Standards proper that informational/explanatory includes biographies and historical recounts, only examples included under informational/explanatory in Appendix B of the CCSS reveal that the authors also had these genres in mind. The sample texts for the narrative text types are mostly fictional narratives and some personal recounts.

TABLE 5.2 CCSS Standards as Applied to the Genres Within Informational/Explanatory

CCSS ELA-Literacy.W.5.2 a, W.5.2e	*Report vs. Biography, as Defined in This Book*
• Write informative/explanatory texts to examine a topic and convey ideas and information clearly. • Introduce a topic clearly, provide a general observation and focus, and group related information logically; include formatting (e.g., headings), illustrations, and multimedia when useful to aiding comprehension. • Provide a concluding statement or section related to the information or explanation presented.	**Purpose** • Report: "A factual text used to organize and store information." • *Biography: "Tell the life story of a significant historical figure."* **Stages** • Report: General statement, information organized by subtopics, conclusion. • *Biography: Orientation, record of events, significance of the life of the person.*

TABLE 5.3 Mentor Texts

Genre	*Mentor Texts*
Personal Recount	*Alexander and the Terrible, Horrible, No Good, Very Bad Day* *Come On, Rain!*
Procedural Recount	*One Bean*
Imaginative Recount	*Dirty Laundry Pile: Poems in Different Voices*
Autobiography	*My First American Friend*
Biography	*Mae C. Jemison 1956–* (Chapter 6 in *African-American Astronauts*)
Empathetic Autobiography	*Tapenum's Day: A Wampanoag Indian Boy in Pilgrim Times*
Historical Recount	*A Murder That Rocked the Nation* (a chapter in *The Civil Rights Movement*)

Mentor texts listed in Table 5.3 are used to illustrate instruction of this genre. For other suggestions, check "Additional Resources" in the end-of-chapter materials.

PersR *Personal Recount:* The mentor texts suggested for personal recounts are written as personal recounts, but do not necessarily recount experiences that happened to the author. The two books listed have complementary features that support this genre. *Alexander and the Terrible, Horrible, No Good, Very Bad Day* would appeal to boys, is written in the past (expected of narrative genres), and has language accessible to young students. *Come On, Rain!* illustrates the use of descriptive language. It would appeal to girls because all of the characters in the story are female. It is an excellent example of taking a short event that occurred in a day in the life of a child and turning it into an interesting story, as opposed to children's "bed-to-bed" personal recounts describing their day.

ProR *Procedural Recount: One Bean* is a procedural recount about growing a bean plant from its seeds. In a couple of occasions, it has language that does not belong in a science procedural recount, but rather in a personal recount. The author, considering that her audience would be young children, tried to add some "fun" language when she inserted phrases like, "just like in the story of Jack and the beanstalk—something wonderful happened!" and concluded with "I picked a few pods and ate the beans that grew inside them. And they were very, very good!" If a teacher chooses to use this book as mentor text, then these language choices should be discussed with students so that they do not add personal recount elements to their procedural recounts unless they have a valid reason.

IR *Imaginative Recount:* The suggested mentor text for imaginative recounts is a book of poems entitled *Dirty Laundry Pile: Poems in Different Voices*, each written from the perspective of a pile of laundry, a broom, and others.

A *Autobiography: My First American Friend* is a good mentor text to use with young writers because it was written by a 3rd grader who moved to Boston from China. The language is very accessible and the examined life span of the author is short, as it will be for the students.

B *Biography: Mae C. Jemison 1956–,* chapter 6 of the book *African-American Astronauts* is a short biography that is both accessible and current. There are also many biographies written by David Adler that can be used as mentor texts. The stages in his books are straightforward, making it easy for children to learn the text structure of the genre. *A Picture Book of Helen Keller* tends to be a particular favorite text for many children. Biographies should be selected in connection with the social studies topics being studied.

EA *Empathetic Autobiography: Tapenum's Day: A Wampanoag Indian Boy in Pilgrim Times* is one of several books that Kate Waters has written in this genre. This type of literature is uncommon because writing in this genre is used mostly for social studies activities to help students immerse themselves in a historical topic.

HR *Historical Recount: A Murder That Rocked the Nation* is a chapter in the book *The Civil Rights Movement,* a topic usually covered in the upper elementary grades. Teachers should use additional texts related to the social studies unit that anchors the historical recount unit and serves as an additional source.

Strategies to find research content are presented in the section on Learning How to Do Research (chapter 2). It is important to note that the approach to developing content knowledge for various types of recounts varies.

PersR *Personal Recount:* Students need to search their memories for events, not only of what they have done, but also of what was happening in their surroundings in those moments. They need to choose a memory worth writing about because it was exciting, funny, or it reveals something about themselves. Although children do not need to do research for personal recounts, it is worth teaching students how to explore what and why they want to write. They should be conscious of choosing a topic that will entertain their audience.

ProR *Procedural Recount:* In the case of science experiments, students take notes while they carry out the experiment and use them to write. In the case of math problems, students need to refer to the problem and their memories to recount how they solved it.

A *Autobiography:* As a whole class, teachers and students can construct a graphic organizer in the form of a time line that students can take home and fill out with their parents or guardians. Photographs can be used to help document memories.

B/EA/HR *Biography, Empathetic Autobiography,* and *Historical Recount:* For these types of writing, students need to do research using primary and secondary sources in books, magazines, newspapers, or through the Internet.

Depending on the genre and age, different mediums of writing can be used. Personal recounts can take the form of picture books, letters, diaries, or journals. Procedural recounts often combine visuals illustrating the steps in the science experiments or math problems. They can also be a form to record eyewitness accounts of incidents. The historical genres can simply be time lines, posters, PowerPoints, or books with visuals or photographs accompanied by captions.

Sample Prompts for Uncoached Student Writing:

PersR *Personal Recount:* Because this genre is recommended for kindergarten and 1st grade, there is no need to do an uncoached piece. When using the genre in preparation for 4th grade high-stakes tests, teachers can ask the students to write about something that happened to them in the past week.

ProR *Procedural Recount:* There are several writing topics that can be connected with daily activities: (a) Feeding the classroom pet, asking students to observe what happens, and then writing it up, and (b) Asking students to choose a student, observing that student during break, and then writing it up. Students can take notes if they want.

IR *Imaginative Recount:* Most of these writing samples will be done as uncoached quick writes because it is not the type of genre found in the literature. It just serves the purpose of having students practice taking something else's perspective and is fun.

A *Autobiography:* Students write about their previous year in the school.

B *Biography:* Students write about a family member's life story on the basis of an interview.

EA *Empathetic Autobiography:* Students write about an event that took place in a book from the perspective of a character.

HR *Historical Recount:* Students write about some event that happened in the past few weeks on the basis of a newspaper article.

Teachers analyze students' writing using the Analysis of Student Work: Purpose and Stages form found in the end-of-chapter resources to determine what the students can already do and what their challenges are. Teachers can use the Unit Plan (Appendix A) to plot the necessary lessons.

Part I: Purpose and Stages of the Genre

Purpose of Recounts

All the genres covered in this chapter have as their purpose to recount the past, either from a personal experience or from history. Except for within dialogue, the verbs are in the past tense. Young students and L2 learners will need coaching on how to form both the regular and irregular form of verbs. In autobiographies and empathetic autobiographies, the author switches to the present tense at the end of writing or conclusion to refer to current times. Some authors do write in the present tense when books are for young children. If using such books, teachers should discuss issues of audience and the reasons why the author decided to use the present tense.

Jeanine Morris, a 1st-grade teacher who used the book *Come On, Rain!*, written in the present tense, wrote, "Most, if not all, of the personal narratives we read were written in the present tense, yet, the children automatically told their stories in past tense. I decided to not even call attention to tense when explicitly teaching unless there was a need, as I didn't want to add any confusion since we hadn't learned tense yet. The children never used any language other than past tense. I did however continually reiterate that a personal recount is an event that had already happened" (E-mail communication, 4/19/13).

As mentioned earlier, these genres have different purposes: **PersR** *Personal recounts* document a sequence of events in an entertaining way and evaluate their significance. **ProR** The purpose of *procedural recounts* is to "describe in sequence the steps taken to achieve a particular goal or outcome after the activity or procedure has been completed" (Derewianka & Jones, 2012, p. 142). **IR** The purpose of *imaginative recounts* is similar to personal recount, but the writer takes the identity of an object. **A** *Autobiographies* retell "the events of an author's life in order to both inform and entertain" (Coffin, 2006, p. 49). *Empathetic autobiographies* also inform and entertain, but from the point of view of a historical figure, defined or general, for example, Paul Revere or a colonial soldier. **B** *Biographies* tell "the life story of a significant historical figure" (p. 53). **HR** The purpose of *historical recounts* is "to chronicle past events regarded as historically significant, and designed to inform rather than entertain" (p. 56).

Features of Students' Writing

Of the two purposes of a personal recount (telling what happened and entertaining), the first seems to develop more naturally in students' writing. The latter is much harder to accomplish. A teacher commented that boys sometimes interpret "entertaining" to mean being crude. This can be a good time to have the students think about their audience and whether it is appropriate to be crude.

Initially, kindergarten and 1st-grade students tend to draw a picture and simply describe it. For example, the first uncoached piece by a 1st grader early in the year had a picture of children eating doughnuts that were hanging from strings and the writing underneath said, *We wr Eating the donuts.* The rest of her classmates had similar products. However, an author may choose to describe a picture as part of a personal recount. For example, in the book *Family Pictures,* each page includes a memory from the author's childhood in Mexico, accompanied with a picture and its description. By 2nd grade, as the following example shows, students understand that they need to describe what happened on the basis of their experiences, but they often feel the need to begin their writing by describing when they wake up and conclude with the end of the day, that is, "bed-to-bed" stories.

My First Day of School

Hello! My name is [student's name]. This morning My Dad said, Wake up Cinderalla! Sometimes My Dad calls me Smelly Marshmellow. Then I brushed my teeth, and changed my clothes.

Then Me and Helen also Kelvin. And all 3 of us combed our hair. And I had to comb Helen's hair first. Then my hair. Then we got in the car at 5:00 AM and we got to school at 6:30 Am Then we went in our classrooms. and I saw Mrs. W and [student's name].

People: Mrs. [teacher's name], My Dad, and [student's name]

	1	*2*	*3*	*4*	*Uncoached Writing Comments*
Purpose Varies depending on the specific type.		✓			Tells what happened, not entertaining.
Verb Tense (past, except in direct speech)			✓		Uses the present to introduce herself, unnecessary in a personal recount.

The second purpose, to entertain, is absent in the uncoached piece. There is no sense of excitement or anticipation in the writing and no description of anything in particular that happened that first day of school. The student did add images to her writing, such as a heart over the "i" in her name and images of a marshmallow face, her clothes, and of her and her siblings labeled with their names.

With instruction and natural development, students' writing will eventually focus on one aspect of their experience and become more entertaining. For example, in this section, a 4th grader recounted his experience of going snowboarding. In this piece, the student makes the account exciting and focused through actions and descriptions:

> I got my gear and went to the chairlift. I waited less 5 seconds, it was coming towards me and the chairlift scooped me up. When I pulled the bar down, I was so scared. But when I looked out, it was so beautiful. The towering trees covered in a sheet of white snow, the animals in the

trees and the other snowboarders below. I was seconds away from the mountain so I pushed the car up and got ready to jump on top of the mountain. The chairlift was on top of the mountain, I closed my eyes and jumped, when I opened my eyes, I was on the surface of the mountain. I took 3 deep breaths and I went down the mountain.

Sometimes, the prompts given to students to encourage writing derail the purpose. For example, a class was directed to write a personal recount of their favorite thing to do. One of the students wrote what read like a list of everything he likes to do, rather than choosing one thing and telling what happened one time.

By the time students start writing historical genres, they have a sense that the purpose is to recount events in their lives, the life of a historical figure, or a historical event. For example, Timothy, a 5th grader, understood the purpose of biographies when he was asked to write about his parents' immigration experience:

My mom and dad left Vietnam they came to America they didn't speak english so it was very hard to get job and get food. Once they got money they bought two boat tickets and traveled to Hong Kong by boat. My sister was born in Hong Kong. Then three years later my brother was born. Then they came back to America then another brother was born. They got help from my sister by communicating. Then I was born and that's the story of how my parents got there from Vietnam.

The End.

	1	2	3	4	*Uncoached Writing Comments*
Purpose Varies depending on the specific type. (Biography: Tell "the life story of a significant historical figure.")				✓	It is about a person's life, yet the assignment was to tell only about the immigration experience. This piece goes beyond.
Verb Conjugation (past, except in direct speech)				✓	All verbs in the past.

Young children and L2 learners sometimes write in the present tense, not necessarily because they are unaware that it should be past tense, but because they do not know how to form the past. For example, a 1st grader wrote the following in his graphic organizer for a personal recount: *We went back home in the car and eat chickin nugets.* He changed the verb to "ate" in the final version after conferring with the teacher. Another common problem is the use of the past continuous, *I was going to New York City,* instead of the simple past, *I went to NYC.* There are two possible explanations. The first is that when children draw first before writing, they often write as if describing the picture. The other is that the continuous is the preferred initial tense of L2 learners. They commonly apply it to the present, past, and future.

Lessons to Teach Purpose

Depending on the specific genre, the lesson content will vary.

LESSON 1. Purpose of the Genre

Goal: To discover the purpose of personal recount (or other type of recount) through exposure to different texts in the genre.

Materials: Specific recounts in books. Internet examples of recounts. Good examples of recounts written by students in previous years.

Activities

- Read to the students or let students read the examples.
- Discuss the purpose (See description of purpose for each genre earlier in the chapter). This can be done during reading time.

LESSON 2. Purpose Is to Be Entertaining (Personal Recount, Autobiography, Empathetic Autobiography)

Goal: To learn what makes a text entertaining for a given audience.

Materials: Texts in the genre. Chart paper. Markers. Samples of student writing that could be edited to make the writing more entertaining (for example, the uncoached piece "My First Day of School" shown earlier).

Activities

- Read the mentor text and other sample texts in the genre to students.
- After reading each text, ask students the following: Did you like it [the text]? Was it fun? What made it fun?
- Jot down the ideas that described what made the text fun on chart paper. Use the list to help remind students when they are writing or revising their stories to add some of those entertaining features. For example, in *Come On, Rain!,* descriptions of the character's activities use language that makes them sound enjoyable to readers:

> "It streams through our hair and down our backs. It freckles our feet, glazes our toes. We turn in circles, glistening in our rain skin. Our mouths wide, we gulp down rain."

- Show the students the uncoached piece of writing that is not entertaining.
- Ask students what they could add to make the writing describing that event more fun. For example, students could suggest things that may happen on the first day of school that can make for an entertaining story.

LESSON 3. Teach Use of Past Tense (For L2 Learners in Particular)

Goal: To learn how to form the past tense, both regular and irregular. This is important for L2 learners who are not familiar with English grammar.

Materials: Projector. A paragraph of the recount, such as an excerpt from the biography of Mae C. Jemison:

> As a child, Jemison once **told** a teacher that she **wanted** to be a scientist. The teacher **told** her to become a nurse instead. Jemison **did not listen** to her teacher. She **did** science projects in school. She also **studied** dance and art.
>
> (p. 39)

Activities

- Project the paragraph.
- Make two columns labeled "*–ed* past" and "Irregular past." Write the verbs from the paragraph under the corresponding column. Ask the students to name the irregular verbs. For the regular verbs, have students explain how to form the past tense with the *–ed* ending.

  In the case of the example provided, there are two additional things to teach: (1) When negative, the past tense is marked by the auxiliary and not the verb, thus *did* marks the past, but not *listen;* (2) There are spelling rules for *–ed* verbs. When the verb ends in *–y,* then the "y" turns to "i" as in *study—studied.* When the verb ends in a consonant, the consonant sometimes doubles, as in *tripped* and *dropped,* but for others it does not, as in *wanted* (for additional spelling rules, see chapter 3).
- With permission from one of the students, project his or her writing.
- Ask the class to point out the verbs in the students' writing, identifying those verbs that are part of direct speech (dialogue) and adding quotation marks when the dialogue does not include them.
- Focus on the verbs outside of the dialogue. Ask the students if they are in the past. If the verbs are not in the past, ask students how they would change the verbs to be in the past.
- Continue to add to the list of irregular past tenses (e.g., *bought, took, thought*).
- Working in their groups or with a buddy, have students edit verb tenses in the pieces that they wrote.

Decisions on Audience

The different genres lend themselves to different audiences. For example, a pre-K teacher had the students illustrate and label a personal recount written as a book with all the activities that they did during the day to take home and show their parents. The 5th-grade class produced a book about their visit to Plymouth Plantation that included their empathetic autobiographies, as well as photographs from the experience. They used software to publish the book and showed it to visitors to the school. The audience for autobiographies can be the other students in the class as a way to build community. The principal can be the audience for historical genres as a way for students to show off how much they have learned.

Stages of Recounts

The stages of the various recounts and historical genres are similar. However, the beginnings and endings tend to differ. The major difference in the body of the text between stories and histories is that the events in stories are serial (a series of events in a row), while the events in histories are episodic (selected events over time). Table 5.4 shows the various stages of stories and where the similarities and differences occur.

Personal and imaginative recounts are quite similar, with the exception that the main participant in imaginative recounts can be an object (thing). Procedural recounts are different, starting with the aim of the experiment, math problem, or event. While feelings are expressed in the conclusion of personal and imaginative recounts, a procedural recount concludes with what was accomplished or learned. Ed, a 3rd-grade teacher, found that writing the sequence of events in a procedural recount helped students to understand the need to include all of the events that make the sequence clear. In a personal recount, it is more difficult to avoid gaps because the events are less tangible when the students write them.

The historical genres share a similar way to write the body of the text, where selected events (chosen to be worthwhile) are included in the order in which they occurred (See Table 5.5). However, there are more differences in the orientation and conclusion.

TABLE 5.4 Stages of the Text: Stories

Stage/Genre	*Personal*	*Imaginative*	*Procedural*
Title	Reflects topic and genre		
Orientation	Who, where, when, what happened	Who or what, where, when, what happened	Aim
Sequence of events: serial	In order in which they occurred. A reorientation is optional. It rounds off the sequence of events.		In order in which they occurred.
Conclusion	Draws some implications from experience. Gives personal evaluation of the significance of the events and the author's feelings about the events.		May include what has been learned or accomplished.

TABLE 5.5 Stages of the Text: Histories

Stage/Genre	*Autobiography*	*Empathetic Autobiography*	*Biography*	*Historical Recount*
Title	Reflects the topic and the genre			
Orientation	Who, where, when		Who, where, when, background if needed	Background: summary of the previous historical events
Record of events: episodic	Episodes in order in which they occurred			
Conclusion	What is happening in the present or a reorientation: "rounding off with a comment or an expression of attitude" (Coffin, 2006, p. 50).		Significance of the life of the person	Significance of the event

Lessons to Learn About Stages of Recounts

These lessons present the stages in a general way. Later, each stage (orientation, sequence or records of events, and conclusion) is presented in more depth, including challenges that students encounter. Teachers are encouraged to review all of the lessons related to the stages and decide what will be appropriate for their own grade level. In early grades, especially if done at the start of the year, it is best to cover the stages in general. With late elementary students, or if the genre is revisited with younger students later in the year, it is better to do each stage in more depth as presented later in this chapter.

Depending on the grade level and the particular students in a given class, deconstruction and joint construction of text can be repeated several times before giving students the opportunity to write their own individual recounts. For pre-K and kindergarten, the joint construction writing can become the final product. Students can create a big book and illustrate it.

Oral recounts can continue throughout the unit, directing the questions to the focus of the lesson. For example, when the focus of a lesson is to teach students to name their participants, if a student says, "I went with my cousin . . . ," the teacher should ask for the name of the cousin. Observations of oral recounts provide data for future lessons. For example, if an L2 learner says, "She bringed me a toy," the teacher should note to include the irregular past of this verb when teaching the past tense.

When working with 4th graders to prepare them for high-stakes tests, it is important to focus on the orientation. An entertaining and well-written orientation impresses the evaluator from the start. When going over their students' personal recounts, a group of 4th-grade teachers noticed that many were interesting and well written. However, many of them began with "One day . . . ,"—a rather uninteresting start.

LESSON 4. Deconstruction of Text to Learn About Stages

Goal: To notice in a broad way the stages of the genre in published texts.
Materials: Mentor texts. Graphic organizer on large chart paper.

Activities

- Re-read some of the books, including the mentor text.
- Discuss the stages in a general way. For example, ask students to notice what kind of information the author includes at the beginning, in the body of the text, and at the end. Point out the stages in the graphic organizer as you discuss them.

LESSON 5. Practice Through Oral Retelling (Personal Recount, Pre-K–Grade 1)

Goal: To practice telling a personal recount orally in order to enhance the components of the recount.
Materials: A class list with the days of the week to keep track of which student has shared when.

Activities

- Sit in a circle. Tell students that a few will be sharing something that happened to them.
- Tell your own (the teacher's) personal recount the first time to model.
- Choose one or two students each day to tell something that happened to them.
- Probe when more information is needed. For example, when students start telling their recount, have them make it clear when it happened, where it happened, who (other than the narrator) was there. If students skip events, making the recount unclear, probe them and encourage other students to do the same. This practice can be done throughout the year even before this unit is implemented.

LESSON 6. Joint Construction of a Personal Recount (Pre-K–Grade 1)

Goal: To apprentice students to write recounts by doing them together. This activity can be done several times. For young learners, especially when done early in the year, these can be their final products.
Materials: Chart paper or projector.

Activities

- There are two ways to do the joint construction:

  1. Choose one of the recounts that a student told orally that sounded interesting, remind the class about it, and have the whole class participate in

writing the recount on chart paper or project it so that all can see. The (student) author should provide the necessary information.

2. Do an activity together, such as a field trip or a walk around the block. Then, have the whole class construct the recount together. The only problem with this activity is that it will be told in the first person plural using "we" instead of "I," differing from the students' individual pieces.

- Students can copy the joint product in their own notebook and illustrate it. In the case of a field trip, they can take their writing (and drawing, if illustrated) home to share with their families.

Jeanine Morris carried out the following sequence of lessons with her 1st-grade class:

1. Teacher read aloud and then deconstructed several texts using the graphic organizer.
2. Students did oral retelling of personal recounts with the theme of weather, which was the theme of the mentor text. The teacher gave the first recount, and then students told their own personal recounts.
3. Teacher discussed with the students the purpose of a personal recount, comparing and contrasting with procedure, the genre they had written previously.
4. Teacher and students jointly constructed a graphic organizer using a class story.
5. Teacher and students jointly constructed various stages of the personal recount using the information in the graphic organizer. Steps 4 and 5 were repeated with several class stories.
6. Students wrote individual personal recounts.
7. Teacher modified graphic organizer to facilitate listing of events.
8. Class played the writing orientation game.
9. Students worked in groups to create their graphic organizers and wrote a group story. Working with one group, the teacher and students jointly constructed the graphic organizer. She then let them work on the writing on their own while she worked with other groups.
10. Students began independent construction of their personal recounts.
11. Students inserted the information for the orientation and the list of events in their graphic organizer.
12. Teacher taught students how to extend each event by writing probing questions next to the events that needed more information.

13. Teacher conferred with the students and added the information they mentioned in response to her questions in the boxes for each event.
14. Students used the information in the graphic organizer to write their individual personal recounts.

Orientation of Recounts

The orientation in personal and imaginative recounts are quite similar, and include answers to the questions of *who, where, when,* and *what happened.* In procedural recounts, the orientation usually includes the *aim,* although the aim may be missing in some recounts for and by children (See Table 5.6). When the procedural recount is part of a lab report, it goes directly to the events because the aim is inferred from the preceding steps.

Some of the features are shown indirectly or through images. For example, in *Come On, Rain!,* the author indicates that it is summer by talking about "endless heat" and "parched plants." She also shows the *where* through images and by providing the detail that the mother was working in their garden.

Orientations of personal recounts can be written in different styles. These styles can include traditional narrative *(Yesterday morning, I drove to New Hampshire with my Uncle Nestor and his family.);* action *(I got up early in the morning and rushed to get dressed and have breakfast. Shortly after, my Uncle Nestor came by to pick me up to go to New Hampshire.);* and dialogue *("Hurry up and get dressed," my mother ordered, "your Uncle Nestor is coming in 5 minutes to take you to New Hampshire with his family.").*

The orientation of autobiographies and empathetic autobiographies are rather simple, placing the person in time and place (See Table 5.7). Biographies often include some historical background needed to situate the significance of the person. For example, In *America's Champion Swimmer: Gertrude Ederle,* the author explains the status of women in the early 20th century to help readers understand what an accomplishment it was for Gertrude to succeed in sports. Historical recounts start by placing the focal event in the context of the historical times

TABLE 5.6 Matrix Illustrating Orientations in Recount Mentor Texts

Aspect/Text	*Alexander*	*Come On, Rain!*	*One Bean*
When	morning	summer	
Who	I (Alexander)	I (Tessie), her mother	
Where	His bedroom and bathroom	Their home	
What	Having a terrible day	Wishing for rain	
Aim	NA	NA	Missing

TABLE 5.7 Matrix Illustrating Orientations in Historical Mentor Texts

Aspect/Text	*Autobiography* My First American Friend	*Biography* Mae C. Jemison 1956-	*Empathetic Autobiography* Tapenum's Day	*Historical Recount* A Murder That Rocked the Nation
When	6 years	October 17, 1956	During colonial times	In 1955
Who	I, grandparents, parents	Mae C. Jemison, her family	I (Tapenum), strangers	Emmett Till, family
Where	China	Decatur, Alabama; Chicago, Illinois	His land	Mississippi
What	Moving to America	Wanted to be a scientist		Murder of Emmett Till
Historical background	Birth to 6 years			Civil Rights movement, important events

when it occurred. Thus, the murder of Emmett Till is situated in the context of the Civil Rights movement.

Because the autobiography *My First American Friend* focuses on the time the author spends in the United States, the first six years of the author's life are all packed within the orientation.

Features of Students' Writing

The 2nd grader who wrote "My First Day of School" (shown at the beginning of the unit) had mixed success in writing an orientation in her first uncoached personal recount.

	1	*2*	*3*	*4*	*Uncoached Writing Comments*
Orientation Personal/Imaginative: who, where, when, what Procedural: Aim Histories: who, where, when (may need background)		✓			Starts by addressing the reader directly. Includes the main participant and her father and "when." "Where" is assumed. Doesn't tell the "what," except in the title. Uses dialogue.

She starts by addressing the reader, a feature often found in children's writing, but rarely found in published recounts. This habit was pervasive among 4th graders' writing analyzed at the beginning of the personal recount unit in preparation for the state test.

Before coaching, orientations may be missing from student writing altogether or be limited, missing some elements, as in the case of the 2nd grader's piece and the biography of the 5th grader writing about his parents' emigrating from Vietnam (shown earlier).

	1	*2*	*3*	*4*	*Uncoached Writing Comments*
Orientation Personal/Imaginative: who, where, when, what Procedural: Aim Histories: who, where, when (may need background)		✓			No "when" and no background explaining the motivation to come.

Another 5th grader started his biographical recount about his parents moving from Vietnam by directly describing the events, skipping the orientation completely. Several of the kindergarten students early in the year drew elaborate pictures and dictated a sentence that mostly included the *what* of the orientation *(I went to target* or *I went swimming.)*. Next, *where* usually appears *(I go to sports to swimming at the doorchestr hoese.)*. A 3rd grader, rather new to English, also included the *when* (*In the furst Day of somr* [summer] *I whit* [went] *two* [to] *waturcochree* [Water Country].).

After coaching, the elements begin to emerge in student writing, but there are still some challenges. First graders included the information, but in multiple short sentences *(I went in my car with my Dad and sister. we drove to the aquarium.)*. This could have been simply said, *I drove to the aquarium with my Dad and sister.*

Even when all of the information was present, the style in personal recounts did not change until students reached the upper grades when actions and dialogue were introduced. However, when students are first introduced to these features, they have a tendency to overuse them. For example, a 4th grader wrote, *It was march 25th the best day of this whole year Relax day !!! I screamed till the top of my lungs every one came down the stairs like a bullet* . . . . Only is it in later grades and toward the end of the unit that students use indirect ways of indicating elements of the orientation. For example, a 5th grader showed that her recount started on a road in the winter through her descriptions: *In the back seat in my mom's black Honda . . . I saw towering pine trees covered in a sheet of white snow.*

Lessons to Teach the Orientation

There are two aspects to consider when writing an orientation: the information needed and the style. Identifying the information to be included in the orientation can be done with students of all ages. Orientations in personal recounts can have a variety of styles. Styles are best examined and taught with grades 3 and up.

LESSON 7. Deconstruction of Text—Orientation Information (Grades 1 and Up)

Goal: To learn the information that goes in the orientation to help students write informative orientations.

Materials: Several mentor texts in the same recount genre, for example, personal recounts, autobiographies, or historical recounts. Orientation graphic organizer on chart paper. Copies of the graphic organizer, one per group. The graphic organizer slightly varies depending on which recount genre you are teaching (See Tables 5.6 and 5.7).

Activities

- Read the orientation in the mentor text. The length of the orientation will vary. Sometimes, the orientation will be the first paragraph, but more often will be the first couple of paragraphs.
- Discuss which information will go in which column of the graphic organizer. Point out that authors sometimes give the information indirectly through images or descriptions. You may fill out the graphic organizer or just have there to point at the elements.
- Repeat the activity with a couple of other books.
- Give each group one or more texts and a copy of the graphic organizer. Have them write down the information from the book in their graphic organizer. Walk around the room checking their work and noting anything that will further instruction.

LESSON 8. Deconstruction of Text—Style of Personal Recount Orientation (Grade 3 and Up)

Goal: To learn to write orientations in different styles to make them more interesting and varied.

Materials: Mentor texts familiar to the students with different orientation styles (traditional, action, and dialogue).

Activities

- Distribute the mentor texts among groups in your class.
- Have students describe the style used in the mentor texts.
- Ask groups to read selections aloud and say which style the author used. For example, in *Come On, Rain!,* the orientation is written as a dialogue. In *Owl Moon,* the style is more traditional: "It was late one winter, night, long past my bedtime, when Pa and I went owling." In *Alexander,* the information of the orientation is included in a series of actions.

LESSON 9. Jointly Constructed Orientations (All Recount Genres, Grades K–5)

Goal: To practice defining information and translating it to a written orientation with the students.

Materials: Orientation graphic organizer on chart paper, corresponding with the specific genre.

Activities

- Establish the content of the class recount:

  a. **PersR** *Personal Recount:* Ask a student to recount something interesting that happened to him or her. (By now, students should be familiar with telling recounts orally and be ready to do so.) Take brief notes (yourself, as teacher) on the events to use later.
  b. **ProR** *Procedural Recount:* Solve a math problem or do an experiment together as a class. You can also ask a student to tell how he or she went about solving the problem to get the class involved. You may choose a student who could use help with his or her writing.
  c. **A** *Autobiography:* Choose one student who could use help with his or her writing and do his or her autobiography as the class project. Ask him or her to offer the information and get the class involved by asking questions and making additional suggestions.
  d. **B** *Biography:* Choose one person related to the theme of your biography unit to do as a class project.
  e. **EA** *Empathetic Autobiography:* Choose one person related to the historical topic that the students will draw from to write their own independent empathetic autobiography.
  f. **HR** *Historical Recount:* Choose one aspect of the historical period you are studying. For example, if the mentor text came from a book on the Civil Rights movement, then choose one event from this movement to make the class recount.

- Create a large Orientation graphic organizer.
- Using the content from the focus genre, solicit ideas from the students and write the information on the Orientation graphic organizer.
- Take information from each column of the graphic organizer and ask the class for suggestions on how to write it. Propose revisions if needed.
- For personal recount, use the style graphic organizer to get suggestions from the class on how to write three different orientations. Ask the class if they want to change anything in the orientation to indicate some of the information indirectly (this does not have to be done every time). Ask the class to vote for the orientation that they like best and use it as the beginning of the class recount.

LESSON 10. Group or Independently Constructed Orientations (Grades K–2)

Goal: To start releasing responsibility and encourage the students to create orientations more independently.

Materials: Copies of the orientation graphic organizer corresponding to the genre.

Activities

- Group or pair the students.
- Give each group of students a copy of the orientation graphic organizer.
- Ask each group to discuss the recount that they will write about.
- Ask the groups to say, draw, or write the information in the graphic organizer (depending on age and ability to write).
- Depending on students' ability and preference, have students draw before or after they write, illustrate the events, or dictate the recount. In the case of procedural recounts, the visuals tend to be diagrams, rather than narrative illustrations.
- Have students dictate or write their group or individual orientations, depending on their ability to write.
- For personal recount, ask students to finish their recount and then start with a new story to practice aspects beyond orientation.
- For other genres: This orientation will be the beginning of the group project in that genre. In genres other than personal recount, students have to do research, so there is less chance to write multiple projects. For example, when working on biographies, there will be one person chosen for the class project and each student will choose one person to write about.

LESSON 11. Group or Independently Constructed Orientations (Grades 3–5)

Goal: To start releasing responsibility and encourage the students to create orientations more independently.

Materials: Copies of the orientation graphic organizer corresponding to the genre.

Activities

- Give each group or individual student a copy of the orientation graphic organizer.
- Ask students to discuss the recount that they will write about in their groups or with a partner.
- For personal recount, have students write three different types of orientations in their style graphic organizer. Then, have students choose one orientation

and write it as the beginning of their personal recount. Ask students to finish writing their recount and then start with a new story to practice the other aspects of the genre beyond orientation.
- For other genres: This orientation will be the beginning of the group/individual projects in that genre.

Sequence or Record of Events in Recounts

Personal, imaginative, and procedural recounts include a sequence of events in the body of the text that follows the order in which they occurred. For example, the first few events in the personal and procedural recount mentor texts are the following:

Come On, Rain!	*One Bean*
• Asks to wear a bathing suit	• Has a dry bean
• Observes what is happening in the neighborhood around her house	• Moistens it
• Sees the rain clouds	• Plants the bean
• Runs out to look for her friend Jackie-Joyce	• Waters the bean
• Runs back home and makes some iced tea for her mother	• Bean sprouts

In personal recounts, writers make these events interesting by developing each of them with details. In the case of the *Alexander* mentor text, the full meaning is rendered through language and the images.

The following two examples from mentor texts describe how an event was further developed:

Come On, Rain!	*Alexander*
Event: Runs out to look for her friend Jackie-Joyce	*Event*: Went to his Dad's office
• Crosses a path	• Played with the copy machine (image of paper flying off the copy machine)
• Goes by Miz Glick's window	• Careful, except with elbow (image of ink and other objects spilled over the desk)
• Peers inside and sees a phonograph playing	• Used the phone to call Australia (image of the phone off the hook)
• Smells the tar and garbage	
• Gets to Jackie-Joyce's house	
• Jackie-Joyce comes out wearing shorts	
• Asks her to put on her bathing suit and come over to her house	
• Runs back home	

Personal recounts sometimes include a reorientation before the conclusion rounds up the events. For example, in *Come On, Rain!* before the conclusion it says: "As the clouds move off, I trace the drips on Mamma's face. Everywhere, everyone, everything is misty limbs, springing back to life." *Alexander* does not include a reorientation, but instead a final unfortunate event before the concluding evaluation.

The historical genres include a record of events in the body of the text. These are episodes in the order in which they occurred. For example, the first few major events in *Mae C. Jemison* and *A Murder That Rocked the Nation* (squiggly line indicates that more events follow) are as follows:

Mae C. Jemison	*A Murder That Rocked the Nation*
Childhood exchange with a teacher	Allegedly flirted with a White woman at a store
Attended Stanford for college	Emmett was kidnapped and killed
Went to medical school	Emmett's funeral
Served in the Peace Corps	Two men tried and freed
Was accepted for astronaut training	Two men sold their story

These events are also made interesting by developing them with more detail. For example:

Mae C. Jemison	*A Murder That Rocked the Nation*
Event: Served in the Peace Corps (PC)	*Event*: Funeral
• Goes after medical school	• Public funeral with open casket
• Members of the PC help people	• 50,000 people attended and saw the beaten body
• Was in PC for more than 2 years	• Pictures appeared in the newspapers
• Worked in West Africa	• The nation was enraged
• Taught people about health care	
• Wrote rules for health care and safety	
• Left in 1985	

Features of Students' Writing

In the early writing, the entire recount is one simple event *(My uncle brought in a pigeon.)*. The richness of this kindergartener's recount is in the elaborate drawings that included several family members watching the pigeon in amazement. With maturity, the number of described events increases, as we saw earlier in the 2nd grader's recount on the first day of school. However, minimal information about each event is included and additional details would be more helpful.

	1	*2*	*3*	*4*	*Uncoached Writing Comments*
Sequence of Events (personal, imaginative, procedural)		✓			Includes 4 events that span over time, giving little information about them, except #2.

Similarly, Timothy simply listed the events in his parents' aforementioned biography without giving much information about each event.

	1	2	3	4	*Uncoached Writing Comments*
Record of Events (historical genres)		✓			It is unclear whether they came to America and then they went to Hong Kong or vice versa. Events not developed at all.

Only some of the better writers in 4th grade, with much coaching, were able to elaborate on individual events, as we saw in the snowboarding recount.

Often, young writers include a reorientation at the end of their recount describing going to sleep at the end of the day. Rather than rounding up a particular well-developed story, they round up the day.

Lessons to Teach Sequence and Record of Events

Students need to learn how to not only write a sequence of events, but also to make each event interesting by including several related actions and descriptions. When deconstructing text, it is best to outline the major events and then deconstruct one of them in detail. Further practice of deconstructing individual major events can be done with other recounts that students read.

The lessons used to teach students how to better describe each event can be postponed, particularly with younger writers, until they have had experience deconstructing, jointly constructing, and individually constructing the general events of a text.

LESSON 12. Deconstruction of Text—Sequence of Events (Grades K–5)

Goal: To have students identify major events to learn how this aspect of recounts is written and realize that recounts are not bed-to-bed stories.

Materials: Chart paper or projector. Mentor text.

Activities

- Project a time line or put up onto chart paper.
- Re-read the mentor text in chunks and ask students to name the major events (See earlier examples).
- Write what the students suggest, negotiating changes when necessary. If working on personal recounts, point out that the stories do not start with waking up and end with going to sleep.

LESSON 13. Deconstruction of Text—Development of Events (Grades 1–5)

Goal: To teach students to develop each event to make their writing more interesting.

Materials: Chart paper or projector. Mentor text.

Activities

- Take one of the major events and write it on top of the chart paper (See earlier example).
- Re-read the passage from the major event chosen and ask students to identify the detailed information that the author gave.
- Write these notes in collaboration with the class on the chart paper. Leave the chart paper up as an example.
- For grades 2–5, give groups of students a mentor text from the genre of the unit and a worksheet with space to write the major event from the text at the top. Have students look at the text, choose one major event, write it on top of the worksheet, and then write the sub-events below.

LESSON 14. Jointly Constructed Sequence of Events

Goal: To apprentice the students to writing a sequence of events in order to learn to avoid gaps and be informative.

Materials: A large time line (See options in sequence of events graphic organizer at the end of the chapter). Chart paper.

Activities

- Choosing the topic: For personal recount, start with a fresh story, either from an individual student who could use extra help or from an experience that you (the teacher) and the students had together. For the other genres, continue with the topic you started.
- Using the time line, ask the class what they would put as major events and write them down.
- Check for gaps with the class. With historical genres, discuss what students will write at the end of the piece (with respect to significance) and check if they have included the major events that will support this significance. Add any missing events or details.
- Choose one event and write it on top of the chart paper. Have the class suggest information that could be included under that subtopic. Work with the class to come up with suggestions and write them on the chart paper.
- Repeat with one or two more of the items in the time line.
- Use all of the material produced to create a class product. For pre-K and kindergarten, this piece becomes the final product.

LESSON 15. Individual or Group Construction of the Sequence of Events (Grade 1)

Goal: To apply what students have learned about writing a sequence of events to their own recounts.

Materials: Graphic organizers for young learners with the orientation information already completed. Packet with 4 or 5 sheets of paper per student with space for drawing and writing (or their notebook, in which they can write and draw).

Activities

- Give students the graphic organizer and have individual students or groups fill in the events.
- As students create their graphic organizers, confer with them, asking questions to enhance the information for each individual event. Write down what they say in their graphic organizer.
- Give students new paper.
- Have them write the orientation of their recount on one piece of paper.
- Ask them to write each event from their graphic organizer onto individual pages and then add illustrations.

> Elena, a 3rd-grade teacher working with English language learners, asked the students to bring photographs from home from different periods of their lives. They used these to create a time line for their autobiographies. Then, they pasted each photograph on a separate piece of paper and wrote about that episode in their lives. Elena allowed students to write in their native language if they wanted.

LESSON 16. Individual or Group Construction of the Sequence of Events (Grades 2–5)

Goal: To apply what students have learned about writing a sequence of events to their own recounts.

Materials: Copies of the grade 2–5 graphic organizer that has the orientation information. Packet with 4 or 5 sheets of paper per student (or their notebook, in which they can write and draw).

Activities

- Give students the graphic organizer.
- Have individual students or groups fill in the main events in the time line of the graphic organizer.
- Have students further develop each event in the lines underneath (See Figure 5.1):

FIGURE 5.1

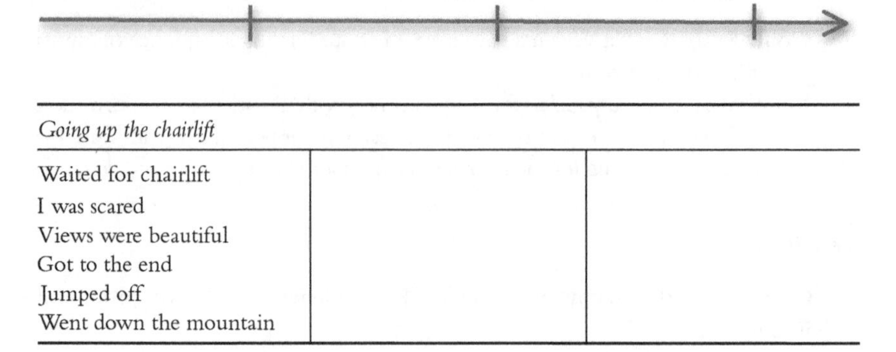

Going up the chairlift		
Waited for chairlift I was scared Views were beautiful Got to the end Jumped off Went down the mountain		

- As students work on their graphic organizers, confer with students to make sure the text is coherent.
- Give students several sheets of paper.
- Have students write the orientation of their recount on one page.
- Ask students to write about each event using the time line and the additional information on a separate page so that they do not feel restricted and can add more information if they want. For example, the information in a student's aforementioned graphic organizer resulted in the following paragraph:

> I got my gear and went to the chairlift. I waited less 5 seconds, it was coming towards me and the chairlift scooped me up. When I pulled the bar down, I was so scared. But when I looked out, it was so beautiful. The towering trees covered in a sheet of white snow, the animals in the trees and the other snowboarders below. I was seconds away from the mountain so I pushed the bar up and got ready to jump on top of the mountain. The chairlift was on top of the mountain, I closed my eyes and jumped, when I opened my eyes, I was on the surface of the mountain. I took 3 deep breaths and I went down the mountain.

- Have students keep this draft to make any additional modifications resulting from additional language lessons.
- Once all modifications are done, students can type a final draft using a computer or write it on clean paper.
- Then, have students take clean paper and write the whole recount, starting with the orientation, followed by detailed major events based on their notes, and a conclusion. They can also wait to write the conclusion until they learn how to do it.

Conclusion

Conclusions in personal recounts may end with a feeling, an evaluation of the events, a thought, or one last event.

Feeling: "'We sure did get a soaking, Mamma,' I say, and we head home purely soothed, fresh as dew, turning toward the first sweet rays of the sun" *(Come On, Rain!)*. Notice that the feeling is expressed indirectly through the actions and descriptions.

Evaluation: "It has been a terrible, horrible, no good, very bad day. My mom says some days are like that. Even in Australia" *(Alexander and the Terrible, Horrible, No Good, Very Bad Day)*.

One last event that gives closure: "When he was finished, he raised his head and turned away slowly and walked off into the night" *(Salt Hands)*.

Final event and thought of the narrator: "I picture them back here, dancing in the streets of La Perla, and I lie there, watching the moon shine on the Christmas star till I fall asleep" *(Going Home)*.

In the other genres, there is not much individual difference among conclusion styles. The conclusions tend to follow the patterns shown in Table 5.8.

TABLE 5.8 Conclusions in Procedural Recounts and Historical Genres

Genre	*Type*	*Example From Mentor Text*
Procedural Recount	Optional. May include what has been learned or accomplished.	"I picked one [a bean pod]. I split it open and looked inside . . . I saw some smooth and shiny beans shaped just like the one bean that had started it all!" *(One Bean)*
Autobiography	What is happening in the present or a reorientation: "rounding off with a comment or an expression of attitude" (Coffin, 2006, p. 50).	"This year, I am in the third grade, and my English is perfect! I have many friends now, and I'm very happy. But I'll always remember Ali, my first American friend." *(My First American Friend)*
Empathetic Autobiography		"I am tired from hunting and fishing and thinking so much today. The warmth of the fire puts me to sleep. *Wunniook*. Be well." *(Tapenum's Day)*
Biography	Significance or impact of the life	"She became a teacher at Dartmouth College. She encourages African-American students and other minority students to study math and science. Jemison encourages students to do all they can with their imagination, creativity, and curiosity." *(Mae C. Jemison)*
Historical Recount	Significance or impact of the event	"The murder of Emmett Till enraged both blacks and whites, causing many people to join the civil rights movement." (*A Murder That Rocked the Nation*)

Features of Students' Writing

Conclusions do not come easy for children. In their first attempt at writing, they are often either omitted or *the end* is used to close all types of recounts. Even after coaching, 1st graders concluded their writing with *it was fun*.

Timothy had a rather dry conclusion for a life story that was probably quite dramatic (*that's the story of how my parents got there from Vietnam. The End.*).

	1	*2*	*3*	*4*	*Uncoached Writing Comments*
Conclusion Varies depending on type. (Biography: Significance or impact of the life)		✓			Very factual; not evaluative of the significance or impact of the move on the family. Uses "the end."

Older students can improve their conclusions through coaching and conferencing. For example, a 3rd grader concluded his biography on Diego Rivera as follows: *Diego Rivera's murals inspired the North America artist to paint in the walls. Diego created a style of art that was entirely Mexican* . . . He goes on for three more sentences elaborating on the importance of these murals. Yet another student in 5th grade ended the final version of his biographical recount describing his parents' journey to America rather flatly writing, *My family is happy living America and hope to someday visit Vietnam*.

Lessons to Teach Conclusions

Conclusions are structured differently and may have different styles for different types of recounts (See Table 5.8).

LESSON 17. Deconstruction of Text to Learn About Conclusion (Personal Recounts)

Goal: To learn the features of different types of conclusions.
Materials: Sets of mentor texts with different types of endings. Examples of each type of ending written on separate sheets of chart paper.

Activities

- Find mentor texts with different endings. Group them by type.
- On chart paper, show one example of each of the different types of conclusions using the mentor texts and other books familiar to the students.
- Read the endings on chart paper aloud and discuss what type of conclusion they are. Leave the chart paper up so that students can refer to it when writing their own endings.
- Read other endings and discuss which kind they are.

LESSON 18. Deconstruction of Text to Learn About Conclusion (Procedural Recount, Autobiography, Empathetic Autobiography, Biography, and Historical Recount)

Goal: To learn the features of the endings in the genre in which students are writing.

Materials: Mentor texts. Examples of endings. Chart paper or projector. Handout with examples of conclusions.

Activities

- Project the endings (or post on chart paper) and distribute a handout including them to help students refer to them when they are trying to compose their own conclusions.
- Discuss the type of conclusion common to this genre with the class.
- Give each group of students one text and have them read and discuss the conclusions.

LESSON 19. Joint and Individual Construction of the Conclusion

Goal: To learn to write the conclusion on the basis of what students have learned in lesson 18.

Materials: Chart paper. Student notebooks.

Activities

- Given what students have learned about conclusions, ask the students to provide a good conclusion for the recount they worked on as a whole class.
- Negotiate the conclusion with the class as you write.
- In a group or with a partner, have students write the conclusion for their own work.
  - If working on personal recounts, have students look at the conclusion of one of their previous personal recounts and decide whether it has the appropriate features or if it could use revision.
  - If working on the other genres, have students compose an appropriate conclusion with the features previously discussed.

    Titles. Titles in recounts either name the topic *(One Bean, My First American Friend, Mae C. Jemison, Tapenum's Day)* or are more elaborate and include descriptions *(Alexander and the Terrible, Horrible, No Good, Very Bad Day, A Murder That Rocked the Nation)* or action verbs *(Come On, Rain!).*

LESSON 20. Titles

Goal: To learn how to write a title that is informative and interesting.

Materials: Mentor texts with different types of titles.

Activities

- Read titles of several texts from the genre.
- Discuss the words that the author uses to communicate the topic and, in the case of personal recounts, stir interest.
- Have the class decide on a title for their jointly constructed piece.
- Have two or three students share their recounts.
- Have the author (student) discuss possible titles with the class.
- Have students work in pairs or groups on titles for their group or individual pieces.

Creating a Coherent Text and Paragraph Formation

After and even during lessons on stages, it is important to check that the different stages relate well to each other and create a coherent text that makes sense. Instruction on stages is also a good place to teach paragraph formation. In recounts, paragraphs relate to the sequence of events. In children's picture books, there are no real paragraphs, just a few sentences per page with many illustrations.

Features of Students' Writing

The first uncoached pieces often do not have the stages well developed and are difficult to clearly understand. Teachers are so used to interpreting students' writing that they often fail to see what does not make sense. Usually, the first uncoached pieces have no paragraphs, mostly because the writing tends to be a collection of undeveloped events. With coaching, most of the students in upper elementary classes are able to develop the events with coherence.

The 2nd grader introduced earlier in the chapter entitled her piece *My First Day of School,* yet she recounts little of what actually happened in school. Instead, the focus is on getting up and getting to school. Because events are not developed, the whole piece is structured as one paragraph.

	1	*2*	*3*	*4*	*Uncoached Writing Comments*
Coherent Text (The stages relate well to each other and make sense)	✓				Although the title is *My First Day of School*, there is little information on what happened that day in school.
Paragraph Formation (For Histories: Each paragraph includes information on one aspect of the recount)	✓				Because each event is barely developed, the whole recount is one paragraph.

As students learn to develop the stages, they also learn to create longer text separated in paragraphs. However, students often need more help to write coherent text. Collaboration and sharing helps students to realize when their writing does not make sense, that is, when it is lacking coherence and clarity.

LESSON 21. Sharing and Reviewing the Structure of Recounts (Grades 3–5)

Goal: To learn to create a piece of writing in which all of the stages come together and relate well to each other.
Materials: Selected samples of student work. Projector.

Activities

This activity can be done with any grade to the depth that they have gone into learning about the stages.

- Project one of the pieces, especially one that is complete, and have the author (student) read it aloud.
- Go over the three stages of recounts and discuss with the class if the student example has all of the elements that they have learned about and whether these elements go well together. For example, in *My First Day of Class,* it should become evident that the student did not write much about what actually happened in school.
- Encourage students to suggest what was done well and why, and also to suggest improvements. Then, they can re-read and share their own pieces and decide if they want to make any changes.

LESSON 22. Creating Paragraphs (Grades 3–5)

Goal: To teach students how to separate the content of their recount by using paragraphs that focus on the orientation, individual events, or the conclusion.
Materials: Mentor texts. Students' samples. Projector.

Activities

When doing this lesson, you can address the fact that a paragraph is usually indented in manuscripts. In printed books, paragraphs may be indicated by extra space. In picture books, they may be indicated by a different (or new) page. The important thing to remember is that content makes a paragraph and not indentation.

- Project a mentor text.
- Identify the paragraphs. Discuss their content and how the information is distributed in the paragraphs.
- Project a student recount and the student's graphic organizer of the stages.
- Check to see if the paragraphs correspond with the graphic organizer.
- Discuss any needs for revision.
- Repeat with other student work.

- Ask students to look at their planning graphic organizers to see if each sentence or paragraph corresponds with the steps they had planned for their recount.
- Have students make modifications, if needed.

Part II: Language

Students' writing can be improved by working on the elements of the clause: verbs, noun groups, and adverbials. In the upper grades, it is also important to support students in their formation of the clause complex, including the ability to use dialogue. The specific language choices will depend on audience and voice. Development of paragraphs, the use of text connectives, and attention to reference ties further helps improve recount writing (See chapter 3 for general descriptions of these various aspects of grammar).

Grades 4 and 5 should attend to all of these aspects of language in order to support students in writing texts that make sense to a reader. At this age, students want to express more complex ideas and they need the language to do so. In lower grades, teachers may select certain language elements, building language skills as students progress through the grades.

Veronica's book about her father's immigration experience illustrates the various aspects of language that require attention. Each paragraph was written on a page and accompanied with illustrations.

Dad's Journey

My dad left El Salvdor in 1992 He felt very sad to leave El Salvdor, but he needed to find work to help his parents. On October 5th 1992 he traveled to America. He arrived in Boston. He coold not believe his eyes. Boston was huge! He was so thrilled to be here, but sad too.

Then my dad found a house and a job at the car wash. When the first check came in he got $100.00. He was so happy he mailed his parents $50.00 and he kept $50.00 but he was still was homesick

A few years later he met my mom and my four-year old sister Amber. Theay got married. One year later something amazing happend. The date was March 29th 2002. I was born When my eyes first opend, My Dad screamed in excitement. My mom, dad My six year old sister Amber, and My self were all one big happy family!

The End

2013

I know it was very hard for dad to Leave his parents but at least now he is living a better life.

Verbs

Verbs are very important in recounts. They express actions, feelings, thoughts, and what the participants say, know, and sense. Students need to build their vocabulary (specifically, of verbs) to better communicate these meanings. In addition, they need to be able to write with a variety of vocabulary. Often, students repeat the same verb. For example, one teacher commented that *went* was prevalent in his students' personal recounts. He encouraged them to think of other possible verbs, such as *dashed, drove, walked,* or *took the bus.*

Students may need to use the passive voice in procedural recounts when using the third person (e.g., *the plants were watered twice a day*). Passive voice is useful in science when the focus is on the experiment rather than on the person doing the experiment. The switch in person is particularly difficult for children who are more likely to write, *I watered the plants twice a day.*

Features of Students' Writing

Veronica's writing shows that students can master the use of verbs after instruction. She could still improve, through instruction, in using verbs to reflect her dad's emotions. For example, she could write, *he hurried to mail his parents $50.00* to denote excitement about his earnings.

	1	*2*	*3*	*4*	*Mid-unit Writing Comments*
Verb Groups Avoid repetition of the same generic verbs. Variety of types that express what participants are doing, saying, thinking, feeling, sensing, and relational connections. Appropriate tense (past tense).			✓		Verbs are varied, expressing a variety of actions. They are in the past and at the very end appropriately change to the present to describe present times. Verbs do not reflect the emotions she describes in the characters.

Besides the use of past tense discussed earlier in the chapter, other challenges in verb use include using a variety of verb types to develop characters, make the story more exciting, and avoid repetition.

1. *Use of a variety of verb types to develop character and make the story more exciting:* For example, this uncoached empathetic autobiography by a 4th grader is factual, but flat: *We sometimes sleep in places that are not comfortable like rich beds but we are used to it and some of us get sick and die before entering Plymouth.* However, after coaching and experiencing Plymouth Plantation, a 5th grader painted a richer picture with her writing: *My faced burned as I stirred the rabbit stew . . . In the garden I worked even harder. With two hands firmly on my rake, I flipped over the*

moist dirt . . . Next I heard a familiar voice. It was my husband, who just came back from canoeing with the other Wampanoag men.

2. *Avoid repetition:* A 3rd grader's uncoached first personal recount included 23 verbs. Of them, *was/were* was repeated 10 times, *went* 4 times, and *saw* 3 times. The 5th grader who wrote the empathetic autobiography about Plymouth Plantation also had 23 verbs in her draft. However, after the teacher emphasized the need for being precise, only one verb was repeated. She had verbs related to cooking *(stir, cook,* and *eat),* gardening *(flip* and *work),* other daily activities *(hurry, rest, pass,* and *finish),* interpersonal relations *(call, hear,* and *greet),* and feelings *(feel, sniff,* and *thank).*

Lessons to Improve the Use of Verbs

When working with young writers, it is best to address the following verb use issues: being specific to the topic, avoiding repetition, and using the proper tense. These can be addressed as you (the teacher) work with students in the earlier joint construction lessons or during conferencing. These moments provide an opportunity to see what students are trying to write, instead of simply addressing verb issues as separate lessons.

Jeanine, a 1st-grade teacher, worked to enhance verb use when conferring with the students about their graphic organizers, in which they had planned their personal recounts. Students revised any problems with tenses and, through her questions, helped students increase and vary the actions and feelings they had planned to include. As students made suggestions orally, she wrote them down in their graphic organizers. For example, a student had written in one of the event boxes, *Then we went inside the aquarium.* After answering questions and discussing the material from the graphic organizer, the new sentence read, *We went inside. I saw a piranha. It was big. I felt a shark. It felt soft. It was cool. I wasn't afraid. My sister was a little afraid. A shark almost bit her!* As the student transferred this information to his final piece, he added more things that he saw.

By doing the revisions in the graphic organizer, the teacher helped the student before he produced the full recount, during which it would have been more difficult for the student to be willing to make changes.

LESSON 23. Deconstruct the Text for Verbs (All Genres, Grades 3–5)

Goal: To get ideas of how authors use verbs and learn vocabulary related to different topics typically found in recounts.

Materials: Paragraph(s) of a mentor text. Chart paper or projector. Copies of additional paragraphs.

Activities

- Isolate the verbs in the paragraph using chart paper or a projector.
- Discuss with the students how the verbs all relate to the topic of the recount and how they are varied. Describe verbs as words that tell us what the participants are doing, (e.g., saying, feeling, thinking, sensing, relating). Procedural recounts are the only recount genre that includes mostly action verbs. The other genres include all verb types:

PersR *Personal Recount:* At the beginning of *Alexander,* the mentor text, we find the following verbs related to going to bed, getting up, and bad things happening *(went to sleep, got out, tripped, dropped, was running, could tell, was going to be).*

ProR *Procedural Recount:* Related to plant development and growth *(plant, filled, laid, covered, watered, poked up).*

A *Autobiography:* The mentor text starts with travel *(get up, traveled, met, took, was flying, flew, were waiting).* Because a 3rd grader wrote the mentor text, it also includes several relational verbs, such as *was* and *had.*

B *Biography:* Initial paragraph after the orientation deals with education *(attended, studied, participated, graduated).*

EA *Empathetic Autobiography:* The verbs relate to various activities that the boy carried out, such as hunting *(walking, follow, look, listen, watch, turn, shoot, need to concentrate).*

HR *Historical Recount:* The mentor text describes the murder of a Black boy in the South *(arrested, found, beat, killed).*

- Repeat with one or two more paragraphs, depending on whether you feel students need more practice.
- Working in groups or pairs, distribute the copies of additional paragraphs and have students repeat the activity. They should notice that sometimes the verbs are more clearly connected with the topic than others.

LESSON 24. Deconstruct Their Writing for Verbs (All Genres, Grades 3–5)

Goal: To revise student writing on the basis of what they have learned in Lesson 23.

Materials: Sample(s) of student writing. Chart paper or projector.

Activities

- Project one of the draft recounts written by a student. You may choose writing from a student who may not be able to do this revision on her or his own.
- Together with the class, identify the topic of a paragraph. If recount is short, identify the topic of the whole piece.

- Working with the whole class, find the verbs and
  a. discuss if they reflect the topic
  b. note if the same verb is repeated too often
  c. brainstorm other verbs that are connected with the topic
  d. brainstorm the feelings of the characters. Ask if the actions reflect those feelings.
  e. suggest revisions.

For example, the uncoached piece presented earlier has several types of verbs (following, in bold). Although the piece is entitled, *My First Day of School,* the verbs describe getting up in the morning and going to school. There are no actions, feelings, or talk related to things that happened that day in the school, except for the very last sentence when the student sees her teacher.

> *Hello! My name* ***is*** *[student's name]. This morning My Dad* ***said,*** *Wake up Cinderalla! Sometimes My Dad* ***calls*** *me Smelly Marshmellow. Then I* ***brushed*** *my teeth, and* ***changed*** *my clothes.*
>
> *Then Me and Helen also Kelvin. And all 3 of us* ***combed*** *our hair. And I* ***had to comb*** *Helen's hair first. Then my hair. Then we* ***got*** *in the car at 5:00 AM and we* ***got*** *to school at 6:30 AM Then we* ***went*** *in our classrooms. and I* ***saw*** *Mrs. W and [student's name].*

The actions do not reflect any emotions about the first day of school. The student could have written, *We jumped out of the car and rushed to meet our friends outside the classroom,* with the verbs reflecting excitement.

- Repeat with one or two more pieces, depending on whether you feel the students need more practice.
- Have students work in groups or with a partner to do the same activity with a paragraph or two of their own writing.

LESSON 25. Improve the Variety in Verbs

This lesson can be done instead of the previous one (Lesson 24) with lower grades.

Goal: To learn how to use verbs that better describe the actions and events than generic verbs.

Materials: Sample of student writing. Chart paper or projector.

Activities

- Choose a student who can use help with vocabulary. Tell the class the topic of their piece that they will work on together. For example, in the aforementioned uncoached piece, there are two topics: getting up in the morning and driving to school.

- Have the whole class suggest verbs that are related to the topic. Write them on another piece of chart paper with columns.
- Project the student's piece and compare the verbs in the piece with those suggested by the students. Show how he or she could make revisions to eliminate repetition of generic verbs. For example, the verbs in relation to getting up are quite varied and give a clear picture of what was happening. But the clauses, *Then we got in the car at 5:00 AM* and *we got to the school at 6:30 AM,* have the generic verb *got* twice. The student could have used, *we drove to school for one and half hours,* or *It took one and half hours to drive to school,* to describe the action more accurately.
- Repeat the activity with one or two more pieces.
- Have students work in groups or with a partner to do the same activity for their own writing.

Noun Groups

Well-developed noun groups help to precisely describe what the author is talking about, making the reading of their pieces more enjoyable for their audience. Even the simplest personal recount can show the author's knowledge of the subject through the nouns and adjectivals used (See chapter 3 for more information). For example, in *Come On, Rain!* there is substantial vocabulary related to summer weather, such as nouns *(thunder, lightning, heat, heat waves, clouds, sweat, breeze, wind),* adjectives *(broiling, gray, bunched, bulging, purple, crackling-dry, stuffy, hot, sizzling),* and similes *(sizzling like a hot potato, streaks like night lightning).*

In historical genres, adjectives, appositions, and embedded clauses help pack information by extending the noun group rather than by using multiple clauses. For example, the first sentence in the historical recount mentor text, *The Murder That Rocked the Nation,* has numerous adjectives and prepositional phrases: *One of the most tragic* ***events*** *was the* ***murder*** *of a 14-year-old* ***boy*** *named Emmett Till.* All of these give more information about the *event,* the *murder,* and the *boy.* Each phrase also has a complex conglomerate of nouns and adjectivals within. The last one includes an embedded clause, *named Emmett Till,* giving more information about *boy.*

Features of Students' Writing

In her example, Veronica used few adjectivals in her biography and some were repeated.

	1	*2*	*3*	*4*	*Mid-unit Writing Comments*
Noun Groups **(a) Describes nouns with adjectivals** *(pretty, blue, named Ali, beautiful, one of the most tragic, that rocked the nation)*		✓			Limited use, mostly related to feelings. Not much description of other things in the biographical recount.

Students tend to use generic nouns, numerals, a series of short sentences (mostly with the verb *to be*), and few adjectivals, instead of complex noun groups.

1. *Use of generic nouns:* For example, a 3rd grader used the word *thing* throughout his biography of Ben Franklin rather than naming the objects or their category: *Ben invented so many things and had many jobs, and invented things like the stove, and discovered many things, and invented many things . . .*
2. *Limited use of adjectivals:* To a great extent, the limited use of adjectives is caused by the lack of descriptions surrounding events. For example, a 5th grader's first uncoached piece of his biographical recount read as a series of facts with no descriptions or emotions:
   My mom and dad left Vietnam they came to America they didn't speak English, so it was very hard to get job and get food. Once they got money they bought two boat tickets and traveled to Hong Kong by boat.

It goes on to enumerate that each of his siblings was born, how the family returned to America, and then ends with the author's own birth. Including descriptions of places, hardships, feelings, and motivations in the writing would have given more opportunities to use adjectives to make the recount more interesting and engaging for the audience.

3. *Multiple short sentences:* Students use multiple short sentences instead of adjectives. For example, a 1st grader wrote, *I saw a piranha. It was big . . .*, rather than simply adding the adjective to the noun group, *I saw a big piranha.* The first draft of a 5th grader's biography of her classmate read, *There is a girl name Laura Garcia. Laura is a 10 year old and born on 1998 and she was born in hondorous [Honduras]. Laura speaks 3 languages. She speaks Spanish, English And a little or porkachees [Portuguese]* (Original name of the classmate was changed.). These sentences could be better packed to form one sentence with an apposition (underlined) and a non-finite embedded clause (bold), *Laura Garcia, a 10-year old girl* ***born in Honduras****, speaks Spanish, English, and Portuguese.*

Lessons to Improve the Use of Noun Groups

To improve their noun groups, students need to be precise in the nouns they use and add adjectivals to further describe the nouns. For example, when writing empathetic autobiographies after a visit to Plymouth Plantation, one of Pat's 5th-grade students wrote, *I stirred the soup.* Through questions, Pat guided that student to write *I stirred the rabbit stew* instead.

LESSON 26. Adjectivals in Mentor Texts (Grades 3–5)

Goal: To impress upon students the power of adjectivals when portraying a picture of what they are writing about.

Materials: One or two paragraphs of a mentor text with adjectivals. Chart paper or projector.

Activities

- Show one or two paragraphs from the mentor text, covering the adjectivals.

  For example, if you are teaching autobiographies, project this example paragraph with adjectivals covered (crossed in text):

  I was sitting at ~~my~~ desk during playtime when ~~a~~ girl ~~named Ali~~ came over to play with me. Ali had ~~blue~~ eyes, ~~a pretty~~ smile, and ~~beautiful blonde~~ hair. I had never seen such ~~pretty~~ hair before. Even though I could only speak ~~a little~~ bit ~~of English~~, Ali and I had ~~lots of~~ fun together. She let me touch ~~her pretty~~ hair (*My First American Friend,* p. 13).

- Ask the students to describe Ali.
- Uncover the adjectives, read the selection again, and ask the students to describe Ali again.
- Discuss with the students the difference that adjectivals make.

LESSON 27. Adding Adjectivals to Students' Work (Grades 3–5)

Goal: To revise students' own work using what they have learned about the function of adjectivals.

Materials: Sample paragraphs of student work. Chart paper or projector.

Activities

- With a student's permission, project an event from her or his recount. If needed, first ask questions to further build and describe the event. Then, ask questions that could enhance the description of the event with the addition of adjectivals. Post questions that can help students, such as:
  - What?
  - Which ones?/Whose?
  - How many?
  - What like? (qualities: facts)
  - What like? (qualities: opinion)
  - What kind?
- Repeat with a few other student examples.
- Have students work in pairs or groups with an event from their current project. Have students add adjectivals that describe more precisely what they are talking about in their writing. Encourage students to use the list of questions for guidance.
- Confer with students who need extra help in carrying out this activity.

This activity is best to do with one chunk of a student's writing, instead of the whole piece, which could be an overwhelming task. Sometimes, children overdo the use of adjectives, especially in the upper elementary grades. Having students read their pieces aloud helps them to recognize when there are too many adjectives, allowing them to work towards achieving a balance.

LESSON 28. Packing Language Through Complex Noun Groups (Grades 4–5)

Goal: To have students learn to pack their short sentences into complex noun groups to make their writing look more like written language, instead of oral language written down.

Materials: Samples of students' writing that require this kind of revision. Students' drafts with one or two clauses underlined that could potentially be packed.

Activities

- Take a group of short sentences from a student's writing and demonstrate how they can be packed by putting the information in a noun group rather than in separate sentences.

Students' Writing: Separate Clauses	*Packed in a Noun Group*
I digged it out it was a trunk.	I dug out a trunk.
And for snack I ate plum and a sandwich. The plum was so sweet	For snack I ate a sandwich and a very sweet plum.
I went at summer to water park. I went with My Famly	This summer my family and I went to . . .
I won a pupet. I wont a lithered and a monkey	I won a puppet, a lizard, and a monkey.

- Repeat the activity with another example.
- Give students their drafts with the groups of clauses underlined and have them work in pairs or groups to try to rephrase the sentences. Work with individual groups as students do this activity.

Adverbials

There are a number of potential adverbials to use in writing, but the most important ones in recounts are those that indicate time and place. As recounts unfold, time passes and the action may occur in different places. The *Come On, Rain!* mentor text has a number of adverbials of place *(down the block, over rooftops, inside, in the dim, stuffy cave of her room, against her screen, in the kitchen)* and of time *(while Mamma weeds, as the clouds move off)*. Adverbs of manner also help express how things happen *(quietly, purely, hard, tromping through puddles)*.

An important function of adverbials of time in recounts, especially the historical texts, is appearing at the beginning of paragraphs to move the action forward, such as these from *Tapenum's Day: Before the sun is up, As I start to run, When he asks me to stay*.

Features of Students' Writing

Veronica's aforementioned book about her father's immigration experience had a variety of adverbials of time and place that gave information about her biography. On one occasion, she used an adverbial phrase of time *(A few years later)* to start a new paragraph.

	1	*2*	*3*	*4*	*Mid-unit Writing Comments*
Adverbials Place: *down the block, in the kitchen; time: while Mamma weeds, as the clouds move off*; Manner: *quietly, purely, tromping through puddles*				✓	Mostly used adverbial phrases and clauses of place and time, in addition to adverbs such as "still" and "very."

Most students use adverbial phrases and clauses of time and place. It is rarer to find students using adverbs with *–ly* endings, such as *carefully* and *sadly*.

Lessons to Improve the Use of Adverbials

All students should be taught to use adverbials. With the youngest students, teachers should let them use the adverbials that they know and encourage them to use those of time and place first, especially in the form of prepositional phrases. As students advance in grades, adverbials describing different types of circumstances can be added. Although adverbials can say more about adjectives and other adverbials, the most common use is to say more about a verb.

LESSON 29. Adverbials (Grades 3–5)

Goal: To teach students to use adverbials to describe the circumstances surrounding the meaning expressed by verbs.

Materials: Questions *(when, where, how, with whom,* and *why)* written on chart paper or the board (See additional questions in chapter 3). Drafts of students' work with one or two verbs that could use additional information with circumstances underlined.

Activities

- Put a simple clause on the board and ask the questions (e.g., *when, where*) for the verb. Let the students propose answers. For example: *He came.*

  When? He came yesterday.
  Where? Yesterday he came home.
  How? Yesterday he came home angry.
  With whom? Yesterday he came home angry with his friend.
  Why? He came because he wanted to see you.

- Repeat with clauses from the students' work and have them propose revisions or additions.
- Have students work in groups or pairs to do the same in their drafts that have been prepared.

LESSON 30. Hunt for Adverbials Phrases of Time (Grades 2–5)

Goal: To explore how authors use adverbial phrases of time to move the recount forward.

Materials: Mentor text that use these adverbial phrases (for example, *Tapenum's Day*). Additional texts that have examples of these phrases or clauses. Projector.

Activities

- Read the mentor text aloud and ask students to signal when they hear an adverbial of time at the beginning of the paragraph. If you have L2 learners, project the text so that they can hear and see the text.
- List the adverbials of time on the board or chart paper.
- Give students other books and, working in pairs or groups, have them look for additional examples.
- Have students add examples to the class list.
- Go through the list and ask students to suggest variations. For example, for *Before the sun is up,* they could suggest *Before eight o'clock, Before the sun rose,* or *Before my father arrived.*
- Working in groups, ask students to examine their writing and see where they could add an adverbial of time to improve the meaning of their recount (You may want to demonstrate with one or two students' samples first.).

Development of Audience and Voice (Tenor)

Specific choice of verbs, noun groups, and adjectivals reflect tenor. The level of technicality of the words and the complexity of the noun groups demonstrate awareness of the audience. In the biography mentor text, *Mae C. Jemison,* when the author recounts that she wanted to be a scientist, but the teacher told her to be a nurse instead, the author writes, "Jemison did not listen to her teacher." However, in Wikipedia, written for adults, the same information reads, "Jemison would not let anyone dissuade her from pursuing a career in science." The latter biography includes more complex sentences and advanced vocabulary. At the same time, complex language and use of technical words reflect an authoritative voice.

In personal recounts and autobiographies, the use of evaluative vocabulary and grading (See chapter 3 for explanation of these concepts) allow the author to express the feelings of the characters. For example, in *Alexander,* the repeated use of the words *terrible, horrible, no good, very bad* throughout the entire book shows the negative feelings of the character. In contrast, *Come On, Rain!* uses the words *purely soothed, fresh,* and *sweet* to reflect happiness and peacefulness at the end of the recount. In historical genres, the author can show his or her point of view through the choice of words. For example, in the mentor text, *A Murder That Rocked the Nation,* the use of such words as *tragic, horror,* and *enraged* in relation to Emmett's murder shows that the author disapproves of those actions.

Features of Students' Writing

Veronica does not seem to be aware that her audience does not know her father. She provides little information about his immigration experience. Interestingly, the strongest expression of point of view, reflected in the word *amazing,* is related to herself rather than her father, the focus of the recount.

	1	*2*	*3*	*4*	*Mid-unit Writing Comments*
Audience o Choice of amount of information		✓			Limited information. Mainly because instead of concentrating on just the immigration years and describing those years with more information, she goes on all the way until the present times, with limited descriptions for each episode.
Voice o Use of evaluative vocabulary o Grading		✓			Some evaluative vocabulary reflecting the main character's attitude: "thrilled," "happy," and the author's point of view, "amazing." Only one example of grading: "screamed."

Children do not naturally think much about audience. However, when they are made to think about audience, upper elementary students have an intuitive sense that the language needs to be different depending on their audience. The ability to show point of view and the feelings of their characters differ among children. For example, in contrast with Veronica's description of her father's feelings, a Vietnamese 5th grader's writing is very flat. He started his revised biographical recount with,

> *My mom and dad left Vietnam because they wanted to visit America where their parents lived. When my mom and dad arrived in Massachusetts they decided to stay in America.*

Once students understand the notion of grading or turning up or down the intensity, students often tend to exaggerate. They prefer to turn the intensity up rather than down.

Lessons to Improve Audience and Voice

It is important to make all children aware of their audience from the very beginning of their writing. When conferring with students, refer to the audience as you're making suggestions. For example, it is helpful to say, "You haven't told your audience when the event took place." This strategy is sufficient for younger children. For the upper grades, the modifications should be more purposefully made, considering the audience.

LESSON 31. Identify Audience on the Basis of the Language of Texts (Grades 3–5)

Goal: To identify how authors use different language for different audiences in order for students to learn how to make appropriate language decisions for their own writing.
Materials: Text with same topic, but written for different audiences. Projector.

Activities

- Project two or more chunks of texts on the same subject written for different audiences.
- Have students guess the audience for each text.
- Have students identify elements in the text that signaled the audience.

LESSON 32. Write for Different Audiences (Grades 3–5)

Goal: To have students practice writing for different audiences.
Materials: Paper or students' notebooks. Projector.

Activities

- Choose or have students choose two or three audiences.
- Have students write a short piece for one of the audiences.
- Have students choose one of the other two audiences and rewrite the piece for another audience (Different students can choose different audiences.).
- Choose one example of each audience, project those pieces, and ask students what made them different. Make sure that students focus on aspects of language that have been previously discussed.

LESSON 33. Appropriate Amount of Information Given the Audience (Grades 3–5)

Goal: To identify information missing given the audience in order to revise the writing.
Materials: Sample student work. Projector.

Activities

- Project student work. Focus on one or two paragraphs.
- Have the class ask questions of the author to explain or describe more of her or his writing to make the meaning clearer. For example, in Veronica's first paragraph, she could say more about El Salvador, about how her father traveled to Boston, or whether he came by himself.
- Have the author propose modifications and have the student revise right away. If students wait to revise later, they tend to forget the suggestions.
- Repeat the activity with another piece.
- Working in pairs or groups, have the rest of the students look at their own pieces and revise using the same strategy.

LESSON 34. Use of Evaluative Vocabulary and Grading (Grades 3–5)

Goal: To understand how authors express point of view through words and how they turn up or down the intensity through the specific choice of words.

Materials: Examples of phrases from mentor texts. A picture that has action and expressions in people's faces with a list of adjectives and verbs to choose from to best describe the emotions and actions in the picture (for example, a picture of a group of kids jumping with the following choices for an adjective: *pleased, glad, happy, jolly,* and *delighted,* and for a verb: *giggled, chuckled, laughed, howled, roared*). Student work.

Activities

- Take the phrases from the mentor text, *Come On, Rain!*, such as "in the broiling alleyway," and make some modification to the evaluative vocabulary or change the grading. For example, "in the alleyway," could become "in the cool alleyway" and the class could describe or draw this new scene. Discuss the differences between the original and modified phrases.
- Show the picture and lists of adjectives and verbs and ask the students to choose the word that best describes the emotions and actions. If students differ in their opinion, ask them to explain their answers. You may discuss that it is not always necessary to use vocabulary to exaggerate.
- Show a sample of student work. Have students propose modifications that will help to reflect emotions and attitudes in the participants' feelings and actions.
- Have students work in groups or pairs to make revisions in their own work.
- Have students read the revised versions aloud. Once students learn about evaluative vocabulary and grading, they tend to exaggerate. Discuss the need for students to check their modifications by reading their new writing aloud to ensure that it sounds appropriate.

LESSON 35. Revise to Show Point of View (Grades 3–5)

Goal: To learn how to express point of view through the use of selected vocabulary.

Materials: Paragraph from a mentor text, especially a biography or historical recount. For example, "One of the *most tragic* events was the murder of a 14-year-old boy named Emmett Till. The *horrifying* event . . .". Sample of student work in the same genre. Projector.

Activities

- Project and read the paragraph from the mentor text, *A Murder That Rocked the Nation.*
- Ask the following questions: How do you think the author feels about what happened to Emmett? What language in the text gave you this feeling? (You may point out that the author does not say "I think . . .," a common tendency among children, but uses adjectives, such as *horrifying* and *tragic* to describe the event that shows his point of view.)
- Show a sample of student work:

My mom and dad left Vietnam because they wanted to visit America where their parents lived. When my mom and dad arrived in Massachusetts they decided to stay in America.

- Ask the author how he feels about his parents moving. Given his response, ask the author and the class what they can add to show the point of view. For example, if the author is glad, then he could add *fortunately* to the clause, *they decide to stay in America.* If he is not glad, he can add *unfortunately.*
- Repeat the activity with another piece of student writing.
- Have students work in groups to look at their own writing, asking similar questions and adding expressions of point of view.

Development of Clause Complexes

Once in 4th grade, students often start expressing more complex thoughts in their writing. This requires sentences with more than one clause expressing a variety of relationships (See chapter 3). One type of relationship found in recounts is *projections.* In projections, one clause indicates what someone said (locution) or thought (idea). The other clauses express what was actually said or thought, either quoted or paraphrased (Eggins, 2004). When paraphrased, the two clauses are often joined by *that* (See Table 5.9).

Non-finite clauses of all three types are abundant in recounts (See chapter 3 for discussion of non-finite clauses). For example: (1) *–ing:* "'Come on, rain!' I say, *squinting into the endless heat*" *(Come On, Rain!)*; (2) *–ed:* "a 14-year-old boy *named Emmett Till*"; and (3) *to + verb:* "It needed a bigger place *to live and grow*" *(One Bean).*

TABLE 5.9 Types of Projections

Type of Relationship	*Conjunctions or Other Connectives*	*Example*
Quoting	None	Mr. Rickey told him, "I want a man with the courage not to fight back." (*Teammates*)
Reporting	"That" or none	I decided it takes all kinds of Pilgrims to make a Thanksgiving. (*Molly's Pilgrim*)

Features of Students' Writing

Students write more complex sentences when trying to express relationships. Sometimes they have difficulty expressing these relationships and using the appropriate conjunction. Other times, the use of non-finite clauses or adjectivals can help to pack their sentences more (Brisk & DeRosa, forthcoming). Although use of direct speech is a form of clause complex, students have no difficulty constructing it. However, they have difficulty with determining when to use dialogue and how to use punctuation. Students either do not use dialogue at all or overuse it. When they use dialogue, they often omit all of the punctuation, making it difficult for the reader to sort out the dialogue.

Veronica used mostly coordinated sentences and non-finite clauses *(to + verb)* to express complex ideas. She used many simple sentences, some of which help to give a dramatic effect to her story, but others could be packed. As found in many of the students' writing, there was no dialogue.

	1	*2*	*3*	*4*	*Mid-unit Writing Comments*
Use of Clause Complexes Appropriate use, including appropriate relationships. Packing of simple clauses to make clause complexes.			✓		Uses many *to + verb* non-finite clauses to pack ideas. Other complex clauses are mostly additive with "and" and adversative with "but." Some clauses could be packed.
Use of Dialogue (Quoting) Some dialogue.	✓				NA, no dialogue.

Challenges found in students' clauses complexes include:

1. *Difficulty expressing relationships:* A 3rd grader wrote, "He hate the smell of waxs and hate making candles." What he meant was, "He hated making candles because he hated the smell of wax."
2. *Packing sentences:* In Veronica's piece, the sentences, "My dad left El Salvdor in 1992 . . . . On October 5th 1992 he traveled to America. He arrived in Boston," could have been packed into one: "On October 5th 1992 my dad left

El Salvador for Boston, U.S.A." A 4th-grade student wrote, "I slid down and laughed the whole way." It could be packed as, "I slid down, laughing the whole way."

3. *Use of direct speech:* Veronica's piece is one of many that the 5th graders wrote about their family's experience immigrating to the United States. None included dialogue. The one occasion when students used a lot of dialogue was in the Catholic school in a religion class where they had to write parables, a type of narrative found in the Bible. This genre is characterized by dialogue moving the action forward (Brisk & DeRosa, forthcoming).
4. *Non-finite clauses:* Most students use the *"to + verb"* type of non-finite clause, for example, *he needed to find work to help his parents.* Students rarely use the *–ing* form and seldom use the *–ed* form. The use of these forms would help students to pack language and add more information to their writing.

Lessons to Improve Clause Complexes

These lessons are most appropriate for students in 4th and 5th grades. Specific lessons should be chosen depending on students needs. Some lessons can be done with other genre units.

LESSON 36. Formation of Clause Complexes

Goal: To identify clause complexes in mentor texts and break them apart to see how an author puts ideas together. To apply what students have learned to their own writing.

Materials: Chunks of mentor texts with clause complexes. Samples of students' work with simple clauses that could be combined. Students' notebooks with one or two groups of sentences underlined that could be combined. Projector.

Activities

- Project an example from the mentor texts: "Her family moved to Chicago, Illinois, when she was three years old." *(Mae C. Jemison)* and separate the ideas into simple sentences (for example, *Her family moved to Chicago, Illinois. She was three years old.*).
- Discuss how the author combined the separate ideas and sentences and why.
- Repeat with other examples.
- Show samples of students' work that require changing from simple to clause complexes, for example, the first paragraph of Veronica's biography "Dad's Journey," shown at the beginning of "Part II: Language."
- Working in groups or pairs, have students combine the sentences that you have underlined in their notebooks. Confer with the groups as they are doing this work.

LESSON 37. Expressing Relationships Accurately

Goal: To teach students how to combine sentences with the conjunctions that express the relationship, rather than always resorting to *and*.

Materials: Clause complexes from mentor texts that express relations similar to the ones which students have had trouble expressing themselves. Sample of students' writing that needs revision. Additional students' work with a sentence underlined that requires revision. Projector.

Activities

- Project a clause complex from the mentor text, break it into separate clauses, and discuss the order in which events or steps happened. For example, the clause complex "Soon after I got to America, I started first grade" *(My First American Friend)* has two clauses: (1) Soon after I got to America, and (2) I started first grade. Ask students how the author conveys the time and meaning in the events. Have students point at the words that help give the meaning.
- Show the student example (for example, *We changed into our bathing suits and found a place to sit.*). Have students break it up in clauses.
- Ask students similar questions about time and meaning and have them propose a revision. In this sentence, there is a connection of *time* between these two sentences that could be indicated as follows: *After we changed into our bathing suits, we found a place to sit* rather than simply with *and,* which does not indicate time as *after* does.
- Repeat with another set of examples.
- Working in groups or pairs, have students revise sentences that you have underlined in their notebooks. Confer with the groups as they do this work.

LESSON 38. Finite to Non-finite Clauses

Goal: To show students how to pack writing or add information by using non-finite clauses.

Materials: Paragraphs from mentor texts with non-finite constructions. Samples of students' writing that could be packed by changing clauses with conjugated verbs to non-finite clauses. Samples of students' writing to which non-finite clauses could be added to enrich the description. Projector.

Activities

Project or show on chart paper examples of non-finite clauses from the mentor text. For example, in *Come On, Rain!,* there are many such constructions. In the last sentence of the text, there is one non-finite construction within another:

"'Three weeks and not a drop,' she says, *sagging over her parched plants.*"

". . . gray clouds, *bunched* and *bulging under a purple sky.*"

"Mamma says, *lifting the glass to her lips [to take a sip].*"

- Ask students to convert the clauses into clauses with a conjugated verb (for example, *She lifts the glass to her lips, she takes a sip.*). Write the new clauses down next to the original version.
- Have students compare and discuss how much more compact the writing is.
- Give groups mentor texts opened to a specific page that has these constructions. Ask students to identify them and read them aloud.
- Show an example of student work in which all the sentences include conjugated verbs. For example,

When the first check came in he got $100.00. He was so happy he mailed his parents $50.00 and he kept $50.00.

- Ask the students to change, if possible, one sentence to include a non-finite construction. For example, the first sentence could become, *Sharing his first $100 paycheck with his parents made him feel happy.*
- Repeat with additional student work.
- Working in groups or pairs, have students look at their own writing and see if they can make similar changes. Confer with the groups to help them, as needed.

LESSON 39. Teach to Insert Dialogue

Goal: To teach students how to create dialogue to provide insights into the characters in their recounts and to learn the proper amount of dialogue to include.
Materials: Mentor texts with dialogue. Student text with no dialogue that could be enhanced by including dialogue. Projector.

Activities

- Project a couple of pages of the mentor text that has dialogue and narrative. For example:

"I am sizzling like a hot potato. I ask Mamma, 'May I put on my bathing suit?' 'Absolutely not,' Mamma says, frowning under her straw hat. 'You'll burn all day out in this sun.'" *(Come On, Rain!).*

- Discuss the following questions with students:
  - How much dialogue is there in comparison to the narrative?
  - What does the dialogue show?
  - What does the author use to distinguish the dialogue from the narrative, for example, punctuation?
- Show a student text without dialogue. For example:

I got my gear and went to the chairlift. I waited less 5 seconds, it was coming towards me and the chairlift scooped me up. When I pulled the bar down, I was so scared. But when I looked out, it was so beautiful. The towering trees covered in a sheet of white snow, the animals in the trees and the other snowboarders below.

- Ask the author to pretend that she was going on the chairlift with her brother. Choose a student to act as her brother and have them act out the sentences underlined (These sentences express feelings from the narrator.).
- Jointly construct a dialogue with the class to replace those sentences.
- Repeat the activity.
- Working in groups or pairs, have students look at their writing to see if there is a place where dialogue would enhance the writing. Make sure that students do not feel that they always have to use dialogue. You may want to show other texts that do not use dialogue and discuss the differences between the two and why the authors did or did not decide to use dialogue.

Text Connectives

In recounts, text connectives (See chapter 3) are mostly adverbials of time and sometimes of place, as discussed in the section on adverbials. Sometimes, there is no connective and the paragraph starts with the person who is the focus of the recount or a new participant. For example, in *A Murder That Rocked the Nation,* the beginning phrases mostly introduce the central events and participants: "The civil rights movement," "Emmett Till," "Till's mother," "Two local men," "The murder of Emmett Till," and one adverbial of time, "After the trial." Very rarely do recounts use such words as *then* or *next,* which are so often taught to elementary children.

The overuse of connectives such as *then* is prevalent in student writing. For example, in a 248-word recount, a 5th grader used the word *then* 11 times. There were no instances of adverbial phrases of time. By the time Veronica had revised the writing shown earlier, the teacher had instructed the students to avoid *then* and uses adverbial phrases or clauses instead. The students showed that they had absorbed the lessons and reflected them in their writing.

	1	*2*	*3*	*4*	*Mid-unit Writing Comments*
Text Connectives No overuse of connectives.				✓	Uses "then" once and the adverbial phrase, "A few years later."

LESSON 40. Text Connectives

Goal: To teach students how to use text connectives to move the action forward.
Materials: Mentor texts. Student samples. Projector.

Activities

- Show students the mentor text.
- Highlight the beginning of each paragraph. Discuss how the paragraph begins (it may or may not be a text connective).

- Project student work, especially those that are good examples and include text connectives, as well as those that need support in the use of text connectives.
- Highlight the beginning of the student paragraphs. Discuss and decide together whether it is appropriate or needs modifications.
- Repeat, if necessary.
- Working in groups or pairs, ask students to work on their own pieces and revise, if necessary

Reference Ties

Another essential grammatical feature that helps the reader is the appropriate use of reference ties, or using a pronoun when the person referred to has been named before or, on occasion, immediately after. When using the determiner *the,* the participant has been previously named. For example, the title of a story would say *A murder* because the reader does not yet know about this event. But after it has been explained, the author uses *the murder.*

A typical feature of personal recounts in students' writing is the use of *we* early in their recount before naming who the participants are who make up *we.* For example, a 4th-grade student started his personal recount with, *"Hurry up, we are going on a trip," my dad yelled.* For the rest of the orientation, it would appear that the narrator and the father are going somewhere together. In the next paragraph, the mother is mentioned and two paragraphs later the sister is mentioned. Thus, *we* stood for all four people. However, there is no way to know that *we* refers to four people from the first paragraph.

Younger children have difficulty tracking the appropriate use of pronouns and names of the participants described in their involved recounts. For example, a 3rd grader wrote a recount about being injured during break. As she describes being taken to the nurse, she refers to *he* and *they* helping them, but it is not clear who *they* are and whether the *he* and *they* represent different participants.

Veronica did not show any of these issues described. The teacher had taught these aspects when the students were revising during earlier writing.

	1	*2*	*3*	*4*	*Mid-unit Writing Comments*
Track Participants Through Reference Ties The referents for pronouns are clear and named.				✓	No confusion on who she is talking about.

LESSON 41. Reference Ties

Goal: To teach students that pronouns need a referent to be able to track participants and understand who or what the author is talking about.

Materials: Mentor text that includes pronouns with referents. Student sample work, some of which are good examples of proper reference tie use and some that need referents.

Activities

With younger students, teachers have often focused on the first paragraph of a mentor text to clarify what the ubiquitous *we* represents.

- Take a mentor text and highlight the pronouns. For example:

  "I run back home and slip up the steps past Mamma. **She** is nearly senseless . . ." or

  "Jackie-Joyce chases Rosemary who chases Liz who chases **me.** Wet slicking our arms and legs, **we** splash up the block . . ." *(Come On, Rain!).*

  - Ask the students who the pronouns stand for, writing the proper name above, and asking them how they know (evidence for their answer). Point out that when there is the possibility of ambiguity, authors use a noun instead of a pronoun.
- Show a chunk of student writing. For example, I screamed till the top of my lungs every one came down the stairs like a bullet, eating breakfast like a pig. Then **we** planned what where going to do.
- Do the same activity. Unlike in the mentor text where the author names the participants before using *we,* this student uses *we* and, only later, introduces the participants over the course of several paragraphs. Thus, *we* has no referents when it is first used.
  - If students are having difficulty identifying the referents, then discuss the possible modifications.
  - Repeat, if necessary.
  - Have students do the same activity with their drafts and make necessary modifications.

Resources

- Analysis of student work: Purpose and stages
- Analysis of student work: Language
- Graphic organizers:
  - Personal recount (K–2)
  - Personal recount (3–5)
  - Autobiography, empathetic autobiography, and biography
  - Historical recount
  - Procedural recount
- Additional resources that illustrate the genre

RECOUNT—ANALYSIS OF STUDENT WORK: PURPOSE AND STAGES

Content Area: **Medium:** **Intended Audience:**

Key: 1. Needs substantial support; 2. Needs instruction; 3. Needs revision; 4. Meets standard; NA: Not applicable

	1	*2*	*3*	*4*	*Uncoached Writing Comments*	*1*	*2*	*3*	*4*	*Final Writing Comments*
Purpose Varies depending on the specific type.										
Verb Tense (past, except in direct speech)										
Title (if required by the medium)										
Orientation Personal/Imaginative: who, where, when, what Procedural: Aim Histories: who, where, when (may need background)										
Sequence of Events (personal, imaginative, procedural)										
Record of Events (historical genres)										
Conclusion Varies depending on type.										
Coherent Text (The stages relate well to each other and make sense)										
Paragraph Formation (For Histories: Each paragraph includes information on one aspect of the recount)										

Criteria

1. Needs substantial support: The student writer needs extensive help developing that aspect of the genre.
2. There are gaps in the writer's understanding of the specific aspect. The writer has insufficient control. S/he needs instruction and practice.
3. The paper needs revision on one or two instances of the feature. A conference would be sufficient to help the writer meet the standard.
4. The paper reflects what the student should be able to accomplish and write independently given the instruction provided for this grade level (National Center on Education and the Economy, 2004).

RECOUNT—ANALYSIS OF STUDENT WORK: LANGUAGE

Type: Content Area: Medium: Intended Audience:

Key: 1. Needs substantial support; 2. Needs instruction; 3. Needs revision; 4. Meets standard; NA: Not applicable

	1	*2*	*3*	*4*	*Mid-unit Writing Comments*	*1*	*2*	*3*	*4*	*Final Writing Comments*
Verb Groups Avoid repetition of the same generic verbs. Variety of types that express what participants are doing, saying, thinking, feeling, sensing, and relational connections. Appropriate tense (past tense).										
Noun Groups **(a) Describes nouns with adjectivals** (pretty, blue, named Ali, beautiful, one of the most tragic, that rocked the nation) **(b) Packs noun groups in place of multiple clauses** "I saw a big piranha" rather than "I saw a piranha. It was big."										
Adverbials *Place:* down the block, in the kitchen *Time:* while Mamma weeds, as the clouds move off *Manner:* quietly, purely, tromping through puddles										
Use of Clause Complexes (grades 3–5) Appropriate use, including appropriate relationships. Packing of simple clauses to make clause complexes.										
Use of Dialogue (Quoting) (grades 3–5) Some dialogue.										
Audience Choice of amount of information										

(*Continued*)

	1	2	3	4	*Mid-unit Writing Comments*	1	2	3	4	*Final Writing Comments*
Voice Use of evaluative vocabulary Grading										
Text Connectives No overuse of connectives										
Track Participants Through Reference Ties The referents for pronouns are clear and named.										

1. Needs substantial support: The student writer needs extensive help developing that aspect of the genre.
2. There are gaps in the writer's understanding of the specific aspect. The writer has insufficient control. S/he needs instruction and practice.
3. The paper needs revision on one or two instances of the feature. A conference would be sufficient to help the writer meet the standard.
4. The paper reflects what the student should be able to accomplish and write independently given the instruction provided for this grade level (National Center on Education and the Economy, 2004).

Personal Recount Graphic Organizer (Grades K–2)

WHO	WHEN	WHERE	WHAT

Personal Recount Graphic Organizer (Grades 3–5)

WHO	WHEN	WHERE	WHAT

FIGURE 5.2

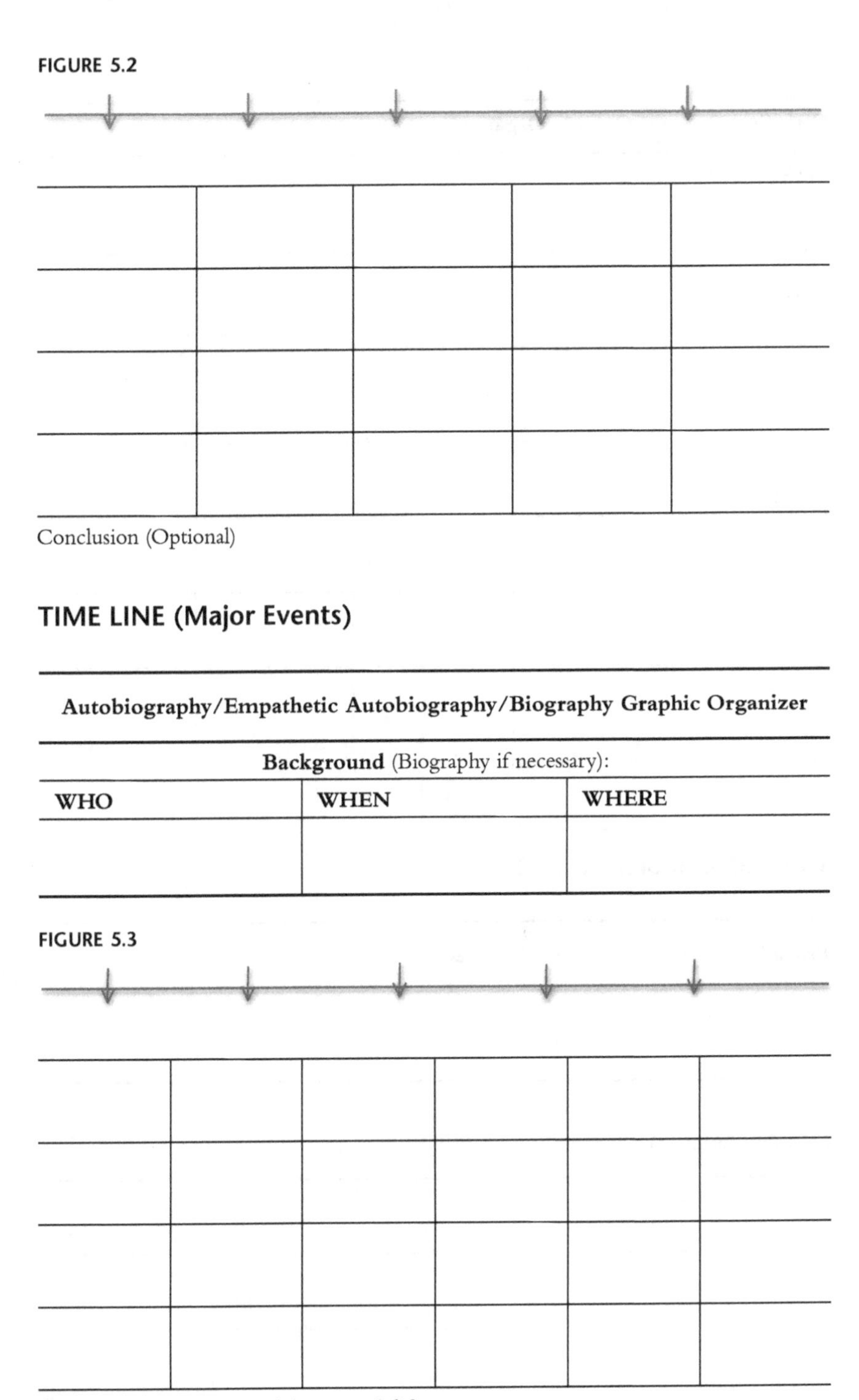

Conclusion (Optional)

TIME LINE (Major Events)

Autobiography/Empathetic Autobiography/Biography Graphic Organizer

Background (Biography if necessary):

WHO	WHEN	WHERE

FIGURE 5.3

Conclusion: Significance of the person's life

TIME LINE (Major Events)

Historical Recount Graphic Organizer

Background

FIGURE 5.4

Conclusion: Significance of the event

TIME LINE (Major Events)

Procedural Recount Graphic Organizer

Aim

Individual Events (Observations)

Additional Resources That Illustrate the Genre

Personal Recount

(Note: Books often are written as a personal recount, but the author may be writing as if he or she were a child at the moment.)

Books for lower grade levels can be used in upper grades if the writing is closer to the children's writing level.

Aragon, J. C. (1989). *Salt hands.* New York, NY: A Puffin Unicorn.

Browne, A. (1998). *Voices in the park.* New York, NY: DK Children.

Bunting, E. (1998). *Going home.* New York, NY: HarperCollins. (This recount is told in the present tense, unlike more traditional recounts. Sometimes, authors use the present tense in books for young children to make it easier to read.)

Cohen, B. (1983). *Molly's pilgrim.* New York, NY: Scholastic.

Crews, D. (1998). *Bigmama's.* New York, NY: Greenwillow Books.

Fitzgerald, E. (2003). *A tisket, a tasket.* New York, NY: Philomel Books.

Hesse, K. (1999). *Come on, rain!* New York, NY: Scholastic.

Howard, E. (1995). *Aunt Flossie's hats (and crab cakes later).* Boston, MA: HMH Books for Young Readers.

Lomas Garza, C. (2005). *Family pictures.* San Francisco, CA: Children's Book Press.

MacLachlan, P., & MacLachlan, E. (2006). *Painting the wind.* New York, NY: HarperCollins.

Martin, B. Jr, & Archambault, J. (1987). *Knots on a counting rope.* New York, NY: Henry Holt.

Parry Heide, F., & Heide Gilliland, J. (1995). *Sami and the time of the troubles.* Boston, MA: HMH Books for Young Readers. (This is an interesting story about a boy living during war times and remembering peace times. War and peace events alternate. The war times are told in the present tense and the peace times in the past tense.)

Perez, A.I. (2002). *My diary form here to there/Mi diario de aquí hasta allá.* San Francisco, CA: Children's Book Press. (Written as a bilingual diary)

Polacco, P. (1994). *Firetalking.* Katonah, NY: Richard C. Owen. (Her autobiography)

Pratt-Serafini, K. J. (2002). *Saguaro moon: A desert journal.* Nevada City, CA: Dawn Publications. (Includes sections that are reports, but also has others that are diaries.)

Ringgold, F. (1996). *Tar beach.* Decorah, IA: Dragonfly Books. (In this book, it is necessary to clarify that the narrator is imagining some of the things described. The book is an interesting personal recount with several instances of imagination as a girl daydreams and wants to make the world a better place for her and her family. The book uses multiple verb tenses and pans the past to the present and future. The grammar changes, which can be difficult for children, causing confusing about what is real and what is a daydream.)

Rohmer, H. (1997). *Just like me: Stories and self-portraits by fourteen artists.* San Francisco, CA: Children's Book Press.

Rylant, C. (1993). *When I was young in the mountains.* New York, NY: Puffin. (Written as what used to happen regularly rather than what happened once)

Stewart, S. (2006). *The journey.* New York, NY: Farrar, Straus, and Giroux. (Diary)

Viorst, J. (1989). *Alexander and the terrible, horrible, no good, very bad day.* New York, NY: Atheneum Books for Young Readers.

Yolen, J. (1987). *Owl moon.* New York, NY: Penguin Putnam.

Procedural Recount

Coy, J. (2003). *Two old potatoes and me.* New York, NY: Alfred A. Knopf. (Procedural recount embedded in a personal recount that ends with a procedure.)

Rockwell, A. (1999). *One bean.* London, England: Walker Books.

Imaginative Recount

Leavitt, P. (2001). *Dirty laundry pile: Poems in different voices.* New York, NY: HarperCollins.

Autobiography

Aldrin, B. (2005). *Reaching for the moon.* New York, NY: HarperCollins.

Cha, D. (1996). *Dia's story cloth: The Hmong people's journey to freedom.* New York, NY: Lee & Low Books.

Jin, S. (1995). *My first American friend.* Boston, MA: Houghton Mifflin.

Parks, R. (1992). *My story.* New York, NY: Dial Books.

Taylor, M. (1990). *Mississippi bridge.* New York, NY: Dial Books. (Written as an autobiography by the person's daughter on the basis of what her father told her.)

Biography

Adler, D.A. (1992). *A picture book of Harriet Tubman.* New York, NY: Holiday House. (Adler has numerous other biographies.)

Capaldi, G. (2008). *A boy named Beckoning: The true story of Dr. Carlos Montezuma, Native American hero.* Minneapolis, MN: Carolrhoda Books.

Deedy, C. (2002). *The yellow star.* London, England: Cat's Whiskers.

Jones, S.P., & Tripp, L.O. (1998). *African-American astronauts.* North Mankato, MN: Capstone Press.

Mochizuki, K. (1995). *Baseball saved us.* New York, NY: Lee & Low Books.

Nivola, C. (2008). *Planting the trees of Kenya: The story of Wangari Maathai.* New York, NY: Farrar, Straus, and Giroux.

Rappaport, D. (2001). *Martin's big words: The life of Dr. Martin Luther King, Jr.* New York, NY: Hyperion Books CH.

Say, A. (1989). *The lost lake.* Boston, MA: HMH Books for Young Readers.

Say, A. (1993). *Grandfather's journey.* Boston, MA: HMH Books for Young Readers.

Surat, M.M. (1983). *Angel child dragon child.* Basingstoke, England: Raintree Publishers.

Winter, J. (2009). *Sonia Sotomayor: La juez que creció en el Bronx/A judge grows in the Bronx.* New York, NY: Atheneum Books.

Empathetic Autobiography

Hoestlandt, J. (1996). *Star of fear, star of hope.* New York, NY: Walker Childrens.
Say, A. (1990). *El chino.* Boston, MA: HMH Books for Young Readers.
Waters, K. (1993). *Samuel Eaton's day: A day in the life of a pilgrim boy.* New York, NY: Scholastic.
Waters, K. (1996). *Tapenum's day: A Wampanoag Indian boy in pilgrim times.* New York, NY: Scholastic.

Historical Recount

Edmonds, S. (1993). *Native peoples of North America.* New York, NY: Cambridge University Press.
Malaspina, A. (2013). *The Boston tea party.* Minneapolis, MN: ABDO.
Ortiz, S. J., & Graves, S. (1988). *The people shall continue* (Rev. ed.). San Francisco, CA: Children's Book Press. (Written as a poem)
Rissman, R. (2013). *The declaration of independence.* Minneapolis, MN: ABDO.
Wood, M., & Williams, B. (2003). *Cultural atlas for young people* (Rev. ed.). New York, NY: Facts on File.

6
REPORTS

Chapter Map

The kindergarten class was preparing to start animal reports when Jeannette Sullivan's class went on a field trip to the Children's Museum. When they returned, Jeannette told the children that they were going to write a brochure with information about the exhibits in the museum. She had to stress that the report was not a personal recount about their visit, but that it was something that they would give to somebody who wanted to visit the museum and wanted information on the different types of exhibits. Using folded papers, the children drew the different exhibits that they remembered visiting and labeled them with Jeannette's assistance. The drawings appropriately illustrated the exhibits. Only occasionally did the drawings appear more story-like with an image of the writer visiting the exhibit. Jeannette pointed this more story-like element out to the children so that they could revise the images for their final version. Given that the children had made such a great effort to conceptualize the writing as a report, Jeannette thought that just labeling the exhibits was enough because as soon as longer text was attempted, the children wanted to write stories.

A report is a factual text used to organize and store information. Reports present information clearly and succinctly (Schleppegrell, 2004). Reports usually provide information about a whole class (e.g., *dogs*). A report can also be about a member of a class (e.g., *My Dog Spot*), and in this case is referred to as a "description"; Martin & Rose, 2008). Martin and Rose further distinguish between descriptive, classifying, and compositional reports. Descriptive reports "classify and describe a phenomenon" (e.g., a report on jaguars) (p. 142). Classifying reports "subclassify members of a general class" (e.g., jaguars, lions, and tigers as members of the class of wild cats) (p. 144). Compositional reports present information on parts of wholes (e.g., a forest and all its parts or the digestive system with its various components). For the purpose of teaching reports to elementary students, this chapter uses the term *report* to include descriptions and all three forms of reports. Elementary students tend to write descriptive reports. The focus of the lessons included here is on reports that provide information to a whole class, rather than to one individual.

Reports can be a good basis for other genres, including fictional narratives, explanations, or arguments. Reports allow students to become knowledgeable about a topic, making it easier to enrich a fictional narrative, form the basis of an explanation, and form the basis for the evidence in arguments.

Reports can be found in magazine articles, brochures, books, textbooks, and in the findings of a research paper. Often, there is confusion between reports, the genre, and teaching about informational texts used in school. An informational text usually includes reports, but it can also include other genres. For example, in the book *Saguaro Moon: A Desert Journal,* each page includes several boxes with short reports and one with a diary entry or personal recount. The first half of the book *Massachusetts: The Bay State* contains historical information in the historical recount genre, while the second half is written as a report describing the land, animals, businesses, capital, and tourist sites.

The word *report* is used in other contexts, but it does not always refer to the report genre. Some teachers have students work on research reports. These can be written in the report genre, as well as others. Students can do research on wild animals and write a report on them. But they can also do research on the Civil War and write a historical recount or a biography on Abraham Lincoln. The term *report* is also associated with what journalists write. Although journalists "report" on something, they tend to write it as a news story and not in the report genre.

Reports tend to be implemented after students have worked on genres that organize information chronologically, such as personal recounts and procedures. Moving from organizing text chronologically to clustering topics in a logical order is a challenge for students (Brisk et al., 2008; Christie & Derewianka, 2008). As the initial vignette in this chapter illustrated, the teacher had to repeatedly stress that students were not writing a recount of their field trip, but a report about the exhibits at the Children's Museum.

Grade Levels and Content Areas

Research on the development of the ability to write reports has revealed that students come to school in kindergarten and 1st grade with some basic knowledge of writing that enables them to create reports by drawing, labeling, and making lists (Newkirk, 1987) and distinguishing between the genres of stories, poems, and science reports (Kamberelis, 1999). Langer (1986) found that students in 3rd, 6th, and 9th grades had basic knowledge of report writing but did not improve much throughout the grades. Thus, students had the requisite knowledge and ability, yet without adequate teaching only marginal improvement was observed. However, appropriate teaching can produce positive results (De La Paz & Graham, 2002).

The choice of medium is one way to adjust the level of difficulty to different grade levels (See Table 6.1). For example, in an elementary school, students in pre-K through 2nd grade and also in 5th grade wrote books using images and different amounts of language. Pre-K children simply added labels to their images. In the early part of the year, kindergarteners filled in blanks in prepared sentences (e.g., ______ live in _____), while they dictated or wrote full sentences later in the year. First graders added one or two sentences to their illustrations, while 2nd graders wrote a short paragraph on each page. In addition, their books included a title page with author and illustrator information, a table of contents, a glossary, a bibliography, and information about the author at the end. Third and 4th graders used different media. Third graders created brochures, while 4th graders designed large posters with images and abundant text. Fifth grade reports included several paragraphs of text, occasionally including one general image.

TABLE 6.1 Report Instruction Across Grades

Grade/Medium	*Pre-K*	*K*	*1*	*2*	*3*	*4*	*5*
Co-constructed posters or books	✓	✓					
Picture books			✓	✓	✓		
Group or individual posters				✓	✓	✓	✓
Brochures		✓	✓	✓	✓	✓	✓
Informational books						✓	✓

Reports Unit

Reports are fun for children because they like to learn about new things. When a 2nd grader relatively new to the United States was introduced to the report genre, he would not stop producing written texts about insects. Schools use this genre for students to display what they have learned. The most frequent type of report found in elementary school science is an animal report. Although animals are a good topic to start students on this genre, it is important not to repeat it throughout the grades. Table 6.2 (p. 11) suggests other appropriate topics. Book reports, a common practice in literacy lessons, is not included in this type of genre, but rather the response to literature genre.

TABLE 6.2 Social Studies and Science Sample Topics and Mentor Texts

Grade	*Social Studies Topics*	*Mentor Texts*	*Science Topics*	*Mentor Texts*
Pre-K, K	Family members	*American celebrations.* New York, NY: Av2 by Weigl. Book series.	The seasons	Hall, M. (2007). *Seasons of the year.* Mankato, MN: Capstone Press. [pp. 10–19 is a report, the remainder of the text is an explanation]
	U.S. holidays and celebrations	Foran, J. (2012). *Independence Day: Remembering the freedom granted by the Declaration of Independence.* New York, NY: Av2 by Weigl.		
1	American symbols	Foran, J. (2012). *Independence Day: Remembering the freedom granted by the Declaration of Independence.* New York, NY: Av2 by Weigl. [pp. 16–17 includes Independence Day symbols]	Animals	Bancroft, H., & Van Gelder, R. (2009). *Animals in winter.* Newton, KS: Paw Prints.
2	Holidays around the world	*Cultural traditions in my world.* (2012). New York, NY: Crabtree Publishing Co. Foran, J. (2012). *Independence Day: Remembering the freedom granted by the Declaration of Independence.* New York, NY: Av2 by Weigl. [p. 11 includes independence holidays around the world]	Insects	Gallagher, D., & Gallagher, B. (2012). *Ladybugs.* New York, NY: Marshall Cavendish Benchmark. [part of a series on insects] http://kids.sandiegozoo.org/animals/insects/

(*Continued*)

TABLE 6.2 (*Continued*)

Grade	*Social Studies Topics*	*Mentor Texts*	*Science Topics*	*Mentor Texts*
3	Why countries have governments	Bedesky, B. (2009). *Your guide to government.* New York, NY: Crabtree Publishing Co.	Earth as a planet in the solar system	Richardson, A. (2005). *Earth.* Mankato, MN: Capstone Press [p. 4 includes a historical recount; pp. 12 and 20 includes explanations]
4	States in the region where students live. If there are children born in other parts of the United States, states where students were born.	*Explore the United States* book series. www.enchantedlearning.com/usa/states www.usa4kids.com/states http://kids.britannica.com	Plants	Taylor, B. (1992). *Green thumbs up! The science of growing plants.* New York, NY: Random House Children's Books.
5	Native American tribes in the United States	Sonneborn, L. (1999). *Amazing Native American history.* New York, NY: The Stonesong Press, Inc. [Much of the text is written in the past because it describes how things were]	Types of rocks and minerals	Hantula, R. (2007). *Rocks and fossils.* Pleasantville, NY: Gareth Stevens. From Gareth Stevens Vital Science Earth Science series. [Contains good examples of explanation]

Teachers have taken different approaches to teach reports depending on the grade level, time of year, and content area to which it is connected. In pre-K, in collaboration with the science teacher, students created small books about turtles, as well as the concepts of hot and cold and reflections when that content was taught. The books included two or three pages with drawings and labels. A kindergarten teacher did mini-reports in connection with various content topics. She gave students sheets with a place to draw and a sentence with blanks to be filled (e.g., *Lions live in _______; alligators live in _______;* or even more blanks: _______ *live in* _______). As students studied about animal habitats, they filled in the blanks, added illustrations, and assembled their habitat books. Similar projects were done with other topics. Later in the year, students can carry out more complete projects. Lillian Pinet, a kindergarten teacher, developed a whole unit in the second half of the school year when children produced a big class book on goldfish and guppies, a topic in the science curriculum. In later years, as she gained confidence in implementing reports with her students, the children produced their own PowerPoints on their chosen animal.

In one school, the 1st- and 2nd-grade teachers planned report writing together related to their favorite content area. The 1st-grade teacher chose animals, and the 2nd-grade teacher, who preferred social studies to science, chose holidays around the world. The 2nd graders, who were primarily first- or second-generation immigrants, chose a holiday celebrated in their country of origin. Their research consisted of interviewing family members about the holiday, as well as looking for additional information in books. Students worked in groups to produce posters, sharing what they had learned.

A 1st-grade teacher started the year asking students to create a book reporting on family members. Each page of the book included the picture of the person and a short description. The topic was very accessible to the students and helped the teacher and students to get to know one another. A 4th-grade teacher decided to do reports in the form of posters as the first unit of the year. Another team of 4th-grade teachers, who implemented report writing in the second half of the school year, had students write short informational books about states, with each student working on a different state. A group of 5th-grade teachers, who wanted to do a short report unit, had students produce group posters. Groups of two or three students shared in the research and writing. Producing posters instead of a book was particularly helpful for bilingual learners who were newcomers to the English language.

A science teacher used the tools of reports to help students read and comprehend their texts. She noticed that her students would look for information in their books in the text, but skip what was included in the images or side boxes, which in many cases contained information not included directly in the text. She gave her students the report graphic organizer with the key subtopics to fill out to prompt them to look at all of the material on a given page.

Reports provide a lot of flexibility with respect to content and media. The key feature that all of these types of projects share is that students write to give information about a topic organized in various subtopics. The text is not a story but, rather, a set of facts describing or classifying information in an organized way.

General Preparation

In preparation to start the unit and on the basis of the school-wide decisions of which genre to teach at which grade level and in connection to which content area, teachers should:

- Determine the content, writing, and language standards
- Choose resources
- Decide how students will be grouped
- Decide on writing products: medium, multimodality, and authenticity
- Build content knowledge
- Teach students to appropriate academic language
- Plan lessons based on analysis of students' uncoached writing.

There are extensive suggestions about each one of these points in chapter 2. Following are considerations specific to this genre with respect to webbing content and writing instruction, CCSS, resources, writing authentic products, academic language, and prompts for uncoached writing.

A report unit should be planned in conjunction with curricular content to be covered in the particular grade. It is important that the various grade teachers plan together or check in with each other in order to connect the report unit with different topics and content areas across the grade levels. Table 6.2 illustrates examples of different science and social studies lessons that could be covered in reports in the various grade levels.

Development of content knowledge and teaching the report unit should be webbed together so that the teaching of content and writing reinforce each other. The starting point is the content. However, aspects of the writing unit can be incorporated early on. Teaching of purpose and general organization of stages, including using the graphic organizer included with the resources at the end of the chapter, can be introduced when teachers introduce the content of the unit (Figures 6.1 and 6.2). In this way, the students can use the graphic organizer to begin collecting information related to the content of their reports. For example, if reports were incorporated in a unit about the states of the United States, students could create a graphic organizer and start collecting information on the particular state they have chosen, while the teacher presents the general content on states. As students begin to learn how to write the different stages in more detail, they go deeper in their research. Sharing their final report with their fellow students will help expand everyone's knowledge on specific states.

A great deal of the information in reports is contained in extended noun groups. As students build knowledge on the topic of the content unit, the teacher should build word walls with nouns groups related to the topic. Students need to understand the meaning of these noun groups so that they can use the vocabulary when talking and writing about the topic. When revising papers for language, it is important to help students change their everyday language to language that is more specific to the topic (See chapter 2 for examples).

Report writing is included within informational/explanatory genres in the ELA standards of the CCSS. The purpose and stages of the genre are addressed in the Writing Standards (CCSS ELA-Literacy.W.K/1/2/3/4/5.2). Although the informational/explanatory genres overlap with a number of genres, the majority of the standards best fit reports. However, there are some exceptions. For example, for all grade levels, a conclusion is recommended. However, published reports do not always include a concluding statement. Within genre theory, a conclusion is optional. In addition, the upper grade standards include, "Use linking words and phrases (e.g., *also, another, and, more, but*) to connect ideas within categories of information" (CCSS. ELA-Literacy.W.3.2c). Published reports rarely have those text connectives, but student reports often do, making for poor writing. For example, the first report of a 5th grader had 17 sentences, 15 of which were connected with *also*.

The CCSS Language Standards for K–5 are generic, so a report unit will cover several. For this reason, the CCSS provides only some language standards that support reports. The Conventions of Standard English section of the CCSS includes some conventions important for reports, such as the use of capital letters (CCSS. ELA-Literacy.L.3.2a). Reports often include proper nouns. Thus, children need to learn the use of capitals other than at the beginning of sentences. Although proper use of various tenses is mentioned, the use of present tense, a mark of reports, is not included. "[U]sing adjectives and adverbs to describe (e.g., *When other kids are happy that makes me happy*) (CCSS. ELA-Literacy.L.2.6.), an important aspect of reports, is included, but the example comes from a personal recount. Teachers, however, know that children need to be taught how to create noun groups with a number of adjectivals to provide information within a report unit in a compact way.

Because the CCSS informational/explanatory section includes procedures, reports, explanations, and historical genres, the suggested texts included in Appendix B include a mixture of these genres. There are a few that can be considered reports (e.g., *Discovering Mars: The Amazing Story of the Red Planet* and *A Tree Is a Plant*).

Table 6.2 illustrates possible topics and mentor texts for reports in social studies and sciences typically taught at the corresponding grade levels.

Prompt for Uncoached Writing: *Write about an animal or a family member.* The prompt should not include the word *favorite* because students will write a persuasive piece to justify why the animal or person is their favorite one. For example, to avoid students' persuasive writing, a 5th-grade teacher asked her students to write a report on their school.

Teachers analyze the writing that emerges from the prompt using the Analysis of Student Work: Purpose and Stages form found in the end-of-chapter resources to determine what the students can already do and what their challenges are. Teachers can use the Unit Plan (Appendix A) to plot the necessary lessons.

Part I: Purpose and Stages of the Genre

Purpose of Reports

A report "is a factual text used to organize and store information . . . Students at school are often expected to write information reports to display what they have learned" (Butt et al., 2000, p. 238). The purpose of scientific reports is "to organize information about things by setting up taxonomies of classes and subclasses; or by dividing a phenomenon into its parts or steps, or through description or listing of its properties" (Scheleppegrell, 2004, p. 115).

A 5th-grade class decided to do biographical reports on explorers. Instead of organizing the life of the person in a time line like a biographical recount, they organized it by subtopics, including personal background, motives, sponsors, route of exploration, details of explorations, and impact. Teachers may find this organization easier to apply to most historical figures, rather than creating a different time line for each subject. However, it is much easier for students to write about a historical figure in the form of a chronological recount (See chapter 5).

Features of Students' Writing

When students have been writing narrative types of genres, such as personal recounts or biographies, they have difficulty switching the purpose of their writing from a story to organizing information in subtopics. Another challenge they encounter is their initial tendency to write using the purpose of the genre that they have just finished learning about.

Students in 5th grade were given the prompt, *Write about the [Name] School,* for the uncoached piece at the beginning of the unit. Alicia wrote:

> *In the [name] school there are healthy snacks like brocoli, pinapple, Cubecumbers, oranges, apples, pears, Asian pears and others. Here we got smart and needs improvement students. There are education, subjects like math, writing, reading, and social studys.*
>
> *There are grades from ko to 5 grade. Ko, k1, k2, 1st grade, 2nd grade, 3rd grade, 4th grade, and 5th grade, then your off to middle school 5th grade is hen you graduate form Elemantry school to middle school.*
>
> *There are hobies like art, computers, science, (P.E.) gym. In art you can do creative things like clay pots and others. In computers you can (find) search up what you need. In science, all students learn scientific nature and learn more of are solar system. In gym (PE.) we get some good exersise like jugging, running, walking, football and others.*

	1	*2*	*3*	*4*	*Uncoached Writing Comments*
Purpose Organize information about a topic.			✓		The whole piece is a report on the school. At the very end, switches the focus to the author and other students.
Verb Conjugation (present)				✓	Present tense

This uncoached report has room for improvement, but Alicia shows that she has a clear idea that the purpose of reports is to give information about something organized in subtopics. This student learned about written reports in 4th grade, so she was able to apply the knowledge into the next year. The prompt indicates that the topic is not about a class of things (e.g., schools), but about a particular member of that class.

For younger students with no experience with reports, writing the uncoached piece was more challenging, as Fred, a 2nd grader, demonstrates in his piece about Thanksgiving:

> *At Thanks Giving peopole eat corn, rice, beens, fish and turkey. cousin hangout with you. they go to the park with you. my favorit part is you get to go to store. you get to buy something then we go relax.*

	1	*2*	*3*	*4*	*Uncoached Writing Comments*
Purpose Organize information about a topic.		✓			Switches to a personal recount after the first sentence.
Verb Conjugation (present)				✓	Present tense

The beginning of Fred's writing showed the purpose by giving information, but it soon turned into a personal recount of the student's own experiences at Thanksgiving.

Even after coaching, some students were unclear of the purpose of reports. For example, one 1st grader wrote a procedure of how to take care of a hamster, instead of a report on hamsters; a 3rd grader started his report on cheetahs with a sentence more appropriate for a story *(It's a dark night in the savvan sound are all around you all a sudon something orange flashes by it a cheetah);* and one 5th grader ended his report with, *that is the end of my story,* using inappropriate metalanguage. These errors may be the consequence of often hearing teachers talking about their writing as stories (Martin & Rose, 2008).

LESSON 1. Purpose

Goal: To teach the purpose of reports and distinguish them from recount genres.
Materials: Mentor texts. Example of a report and a recount. Chart paper or projector.

Activities

- Brainstorm the purpose of reports (to present information in an organized way) as you look at books, brochures, and other texts written in the report genre.
- Show examples of a report and a recount and discuss the differences with respect to purpose, especially if students are confused.

Audience: In collaboration with students, teachers should determine the audience or audiences. This is essential because, as explained later, the stages of a report are greatly influenced by the choice of audience.

Medium: The organization of a report given the medium is different from the organization given the stages of the genre. However, these are often confused. Sometimes, teachers start a report unit talking about the table of contents, subtitles, and glossary, which are features of an informational text and not necessarily that of reports, the genre. Reports can be written in the form of posters, brochures, PowerPoints, or informational books. These different media have different language demands, with posters at one end of the continuum and informational books at the other. The choice of medium depends on the grade level, time of the year, difficulty of the content, and other media that students have already tried. It is important to differentiate between text organization in relation to genre and layout in relation to medium. All media require subtopics, but some, like posters or brochures, do not require an initial general statement. The subtopics in posters and brochures are grouped in different sections of the page and can be in the form of short paragraphs, bullets, and images with labels. In informational books, subtopics are written in paragraphs arranged in sequence. Informational books also include subtitles for each of the subtopics, including a table of contents at the beginning and a reference list and glossary at the end. It is important to point out that informational books typically include a variety of genres. For example, the book *Halloween* includes historical recounts about the origin of the holiday, reports on the various symbols including Jack O' Lanterns, black cats, and bats, and procedures on how to construct the various symbols.

All of the different media types include images. These images can be diagrams, maps, sketches with labels, or photographs. They should represent facts and not tell stories.

LESSON 2. Teach How to Organize the Text Given the Medium

Goal: To teach students how to organize the text in the medium chosen for their reports.

Materials: Samples of reports or other genres in the particular medium.

Activities

- Review a number of examples of reports in different media and have students identify features. For example, Cheryl walked around the school with her students looking at all of the posters and discussing their features in preparation to produce reports as posters.

- With your students, plan how you will organize the report that you will write together.
- Working in groups, have students draw the layout of their own report.

Stages With Attention to Tenor

The stages of a report consist of a general opening statement and factual information grouped by subtopic and written as paragraphs (Butt et al., 2000; Derewianka et al., 1990). Although teachers often encourage students to write a concluding statement, published reports sanctioned by the culture do not require such conclusions (Butt et al., 2000; Martin & Rose, 2008).

Specific content of the various stages is closely related to tenor, that is, audience and voice. Because reports are used to provide factual information about a subject, they generally present the author as an expert on the topic. Therefore, the tenor, or relationship between writer and audience, is "relatively formal and objective," and the text is written in the third person. "The use of first person pronouns (I, we) and the writer's opinions are not generally appropriate in this type of writing" (Derewianka et al., 1990, p. 53). However, reports for children often include language that is more familiar and directed to the reader in the beginning paragraph for the purpose of arising children's curiosity about the topic of the report. These reports may also include an engaging phrase or sentence at the end. The language in these entries deviates from that expected of reports, such as the use of second person, questions, exclamations, and everyday vocabulary. Mentor texts are likely to include this more familiar tenor at the beginning, end, or both. However, if the students are writing a report for adults, they should avoid addressing the reader with informal language, whereas if they are writing for their peers or younger children they could use strategies to convey age-appropriate familiarity.

The following mentor text has been deconstructed into its stages with a general statement, four subtopics, and a final non-finite clause meant to excite children. The first two subtopics are included as one paragraph because the piece is rather short. The piece includes some technical language, but should be comprehensible to children. The voice is mostly authoritative, written exclusively in statements and in the third person. Only in the very last sentence does the informative voice change to include an appeal to children to make them interested in the topic.

Stages	*Mentor Text*
Title	*Meet the Sonoran Desert*
General Statement (Identification and classification of the topic; what and how this is classified in the universe of things)	There are four major deserts in North America: the Chihuahuan, the Great Basin, the Mojave and the Sonoran. Together they cover roughly 500,000 square miles in the southwestern part of the United States and northwest Mexico.

(*Continued*)

Stages	*Mentor Text*
Information organized in bundles (or categories, subtopics) by topic	The Sonoran is the only desert in North America that does not have cold winters. This makes it a tropical desert. It covers 100,000 square miles, and expanded to its present size only about 8-10,000 years ago, which makes it a medium-sized, but very young desert. The Sonoran Desert is also thought of as an arborous desert, which may seem like a contradiction, since 'arborous' means trees. It is not that the Sonoran Desert is covered with forests, but there are tall cacti and many trees—it is more like a sparse woodland. Scientists have recorded more different types of animals and plants in the Sonoran than in any of the other North American deserts,
Summarizing Comment (optional)	making it a truly exciting place to explore.

Source: Pratt-Serafini, K. J. (2002). *Saguaro moon: A desert journal.* Nevada City, CA: Dawn Publications, (p. 3)

An important aspect of the stages in a report is that they are logically connected to the topic of the report. To create a report that is clear to readers, writers indicate the topic of the whole report (or macrotheme) in the initial general statement and the subtopics of each paragraph in the topic sentence (hypertheme). For example, the *Saguaro Moon* mentor text would include the following:

Macrotheme: Major deserts in North America	There are *four major deserts in North America*: the Chihuahuan, the Great Basin, the Mojave and the Sonoran. Together they cover roughly 500,000 square miles in the southwestern part of the United States and northwest Mexico.
Hypertheme: Climate	The Sonoran is the only desert in North America that does not have *cold winters*. This makes it a tropical desert.
Hypertheme: Size	It covers *100,000 square miles*, and expanded to its present size only about 8-10,000 years ago, which makes it a medium-sized, but very young desert.
Hypertheme: Vegetation	The Sonoran Desert is also thought of as an *arborous desert*, which may seem like a contradiction, since "arborous" means trees. It is not that the Sonoran Desert is covered with forests, but there are tall cacti and many trees—it is more like a sparse woodland.
Final summarizing statement	Scientists have recorded more different types of animals and plants in the Sonoran than in any of the other North American deserts, making it a truly exciting place to explore.

Features of Students' Writing

Children have great difficulty with signaling the main topic and subtopic. They directly develop them without naming them. In Alicia's piece describing her school, she failed to introduce her school; instead, she just named it. She succeeded in introducing some subtopics, but for others she just wrote about them. The first paragraph has a combination of topics. The sentence topics were snacks (first), type of student (second), and subject matters (last). Paragraphs with multiple instances of unrelated information are common, especially in the uncoached pieces.

	1	*2*	*3*	*4*	*Uncoached Writing Comments*
Cohesive Text (Macrotheme and hypertheme, based on graphic organizer for the genre)		✓			There is no introduction to the macrotheme. Some paragraphs introduce the subtopic, others are a collection of subtopics without introduction. They all relate to the central theme.

Fred's piece about Thanksgiving is too short for topics and subtopics to be introduced and developed.

A paragraph from a 5th-grade report on jaguars starts, *What Jaguars eat is Deer cause the size of their horns. Also they may sometimes eat elephants . . .* The student goes on to list each prey in a different sentence. However, he did not indicate that he was going to write about the jaguars' diet or type of prey at the beginning of the paragraph.

Even when coached and following a set of questions, 2nd graders often went directly to giving information about a topic, or as in the case of one student, starting a report about pigs with *pigs are omnivore so they eat chicken*. The first clause, *pigs are omnivores,* would have been a good topic sentence for a paragraph on diet, but the second clause limits the topic.

Lessons to Learn About Stages of Reports

In order to write the various stages of the report, students should have researched the information that they will include (See chapter 2 for how to teach students to do research). One useful strategy is to have students collect information in the report graphic organizer included at the end of the chapter. As students fill in their graphic organizers, teachers should confer with them to check for inconsistencies and gaps. Having students construct these graphic organizers in groups also helps with the development of content knowledge.

Initial lessons present the stages in a general way and direct students to create their graphic organizers for their report. Later, each stage is presented in more depth by including a description of the stage and the possible challenges for students. Initially, it is best to present good examples of the genre and deconstruct them with the students to allow them to see how authors accomplish the goals of the genre. Graphic organizers can help to visually show the various stages of the text. It is always important to point out both the standard features of the genre and how authors vary within the standard structure.

After this general introduction, lessons first present how to develop the subtopics then offer suggestions for how to write the opening and closing statements and title. Students often have an easier time with the body of the text than with the beginning or ending. Additionally, in the case of posters or brochures, opening and closing statements are not necessary. With pre-K students, teachers jointly construct the text without going into too many explanations of the stages of a report. Audience and voice will be addressed in connection to each of the stages.

"The science teacher, who taught about live turtles, helped the four-year-olds write a four-page book about turtles. He taught the content at the same time that he modeled each page on chart paper, and the students followed the model as they drew and wrote on their own papers. One of the pages included the picture of a turtle with the body parts labeled. To focus on the food eaten by turtles, he gave them a page with four numbered squares and the question, 'What do Diamondback Terrapin Turtles eat?' The students drew and labeled a type of food in each of the squares. Two more pages included turtles' nests and turtles' habitats with labels such as *baby turtles, beach,* and *moon* to indicate they hatch in the evening" (Brisk et al., 2011, p. 4).

LESSON 3. Deconstruction of Text to Learn About Stages

Goal: To familiarize students with the stages of the genre.

Materials: Reports (preferably short, even from a lower reading level from the grade, and in the topic of the content unit). Large graphic organizer on chart paper. Copies of the small version of the graphic organizer for the students.

Activities

- Read the reports aloud.
- Show a graphic organizer that reflects the stages of reports. As you read the different reports, point to the place in the graphic organizer in which that section of the report belongs.

- Divide students into small groups and distribute reports among them, giving each a graphic organizer.
- Ask students to fill in the graphic organizer with the stages of the report that they have.

Cheryl, a fourth grade teacher "provided mentor texts that were written as reports but at a lower level than the fourth-grade books they usually read, such as *Fantastic Bats* (J. M. Martin, 2006). Cheryl presented a graphic organizer on chart paper with the components of a report including the general statement, subtopics, and an optional concluding statement . . . As she read the book on bats and discussed the components with the students, they filled in the graphic organizer. Cheryl read aloud a number of these books, and for each book the students had a similar graphic organizer to complete, based on the information in the teacher's read-alouds. Some students had difficulty with the graphic organizer because they needed to think not only about the information they would write, but also, to consider the topic to determine the column in which the information would be written. She gave these students a . . . web that provided space for the information to be written without the need to categorize it at the same time. Later, they grouped the information into categories" (Brisk et al., 2011, pp. 4–5).

LESSON 4. Creating a Graphic Organizer for a Report

Goal: To teach students to plan the stages of their report defining the topic and subtopic of the report by using a graphic organizer. This can take a number of classes or sessions, depending on how much support students need with researching the content knowledge, learning how to categorize it, and developing the technical language.

Materials: Chart paper with graphic organizers, both web and boxes (See end-of-chapter resources), and graphic organizers for students. Texts that the class has been using to develop the content area in which the report unit is nested.

Activities

- Discuss the topic of the class report that the students will jointly construct and then have students choose the topic of their own group or individual reports. To facilitate, yet limit, the choice of topics, it is a good idea to provide students with resources to research their topic. For example, students in a 4th-grade class chose their own state for the class report and they had to choose their states from those in the same region. An exception could be made if a student moved from a different region and wants to write about the state where she or he was born.

- Choosing and Researching Subtopics.

There are three ways to go about choosing subtopics for reports: (1) teacher defines the subtopics, (2) students brainstorm subtopics, and (3) teacher and students read through reports on the type of subject and agree on the topics that tend to be covered in that subject. In all styles, try to use the technical language that defines the category.

- o Teachers define the subtopics (pre-K–Grade 3). It can be done in two ways:

1. On chart paper, draw a graphic organizer with four squares labeled with the subtopics. For example, a 1st-grade graphic organizer for an animal report had *body, habitat, food,* and *predators.*
2. On chart paper, write 3 to 5 questions (depending on the grade level) that represent the topics in an order that makes sense. For example, 2nd- and 3rd-grade teachers gave questions such as *What do they look like? Where do they live? What is their diet? Who are their enemies?*

- o Students brainstorm subtopics (Pre-K–Grade 5). To use this approach, students first have to be familiar with the topic.
  - o Ask students what subtopics would be of interest to explore with respect to the topic of their report.
  - o Create a web and note student suggestions.
  - o Group any subtopics that belong together.
  - o Ask for further suggestions for each subtopic and expand the web. With upper elementary students, transfer this information to the report graphic organizer (See end-of-chapter resources).
- o Students use mentor texts to define subtopics (Grades 4–5).
  - o Prepare a large version of the report graphic organizer.
  - o Ask students to scan various readings about the topic on which they will write. For example, if students are going to write a report on states, students can work in pairs or groups to go through books on different states.
  - o As a whole class, discuss the suggested subtopics, write them down in a web, group related information, and number the subtopics in the order in which they will be written. Different books may have a different order, but there usually is information consistently found early in the texts.
  - o Write the subtopics into the report organizer in the order that was agreed on.

- Review the whole-class graphic organizer for logic and organization.
- Confer with students for logic and organization of their own report graphic organizers.

Subtopics

The body of the report includes a series of subtopics that group information and need to be organized in an order that makes sense to readers. For example, the mentor text *Saguaro Moon* starts with a type of desert followed by the size, plants, and animals found in that desert. Reports about animals usually start with the description of the animal followed by other features including habitat, food and prey, and predators. A report about states might include location, main cities, physical description, businesses and sources of work, heroes, and tourist attractions. The order in which the information is presented and consistency of information within each cluster are features of a clear report.

Features of Students' Writing

Alicia had written reports the previous year, so she included a number of subtopics in her uncoached piece about her school. However, the subtopics were not all fully developed and she did not plan the organization.

	1	*2*	*3*	*4*	*Uncoached Writing Comments*
Information organized in bundles or subtopics.		✓			Six topics unevenly developed. No sense why the particular order.
Audience					
Information and language level of difficulty and amount appropriate for the audience.			✓		Appropriate for an audience the age of the student. It is not clear if this was intentional.
Voice					
Body of text in third person.		✓			Body in third person. One switch to second person in the question. It is not clear if it was intended for a young audience.
General statement and conclusion in voice appropriate for audience.					No general statement. The last subtopic in first person, not consistent with the rest in third person.

Alicia's language was appropriate for a young audience. The voice, however, was inconsistent, including a question early on and a switch to the first person in the last subtopic section.

Fred's uncoached piece included just one subtopic before he went on to write a story.

	1	*2*	*3*	*4*	*Uncoached Writing Comments*
Information organized in bundles or subtopics.	✓				Just one paragraph that mixed description with recount.
Audience Information and language level of difficulty and amount appropriate for the audience.		✓			Appropriate for an audience the student's age. With more content knowledge, could address older audiences.
Voice Body of text in third person. General statement and conclusion in voice appropriate for audience.		✓			Starts in third person, but the switch of genre introduced the second person.

At this age, the technicality of the language depends on how much students learn through research, as well as their language maturity. Fred's voice was inconsistent because he switched genre.

Students in Pre-K through 3rd grade organized topics in a logical manner because the teachers coached the students on the order of the subtopics through modeling or questions. It became more challenging when the students chose their own order. One 5th grader started with a paragraph about what jaguars eat, followed by where they live. Only in the third paragraph, just before the conclusion, did he describe the features of a jaguar. A more logical order would have been the exact reverse.

LESSON 5. Voice: Teach to Write in the Third Person

Goal: To teach students to use the third person because the author and the audience stay hidden while the topic of the report stands out.

Materials: Sample of students' reports with or without clauses in the first and second person. Projector. Mentor texts.

Activities

- Report samples written only in the third person. Ask students what the reports are about. Circle the topic.

- Project samples with first and second person within the subtopics. Discuss what these samples are about. Discuss the presence of the author or audience.
- Give mentor texts to students and have them look at the subtopics and see if they find "I" or "you" in them. (Just have students look at the body of the text because, as described later, authors sometimes address the audience directly when writing for children.)
- Have the class suggest revisions.
- Working in groups, have students go over their subtopics and make revisions, if needed.

"One aspect of language that required repeated discussion was the students' tendency to insert themselves into their writing. They often started sentences with *I think, I believe,* or *I learned.* Cheryl pointed out that the report was not about the author but about the topic they were researching. Often she had students read through the mentor texts to see if they could find such clauses" (Brisk et al., 2011, p. 5).

LESSON 6. Writing the Subtopics

Goal: To apprentice students to write the subtopics.
Materials: Class and individual graphic organizers. Chart paper or projector.

Activities

For each of the subtopics, follow the same process.

- Choose the subtopic from the graphic organizer and ask students to describe what it is about.
- Create a topic sentence for the paragraph on the basis of student responses.
- Ask students what information they have written in their graphic organizer about this subtopic. Write sentences that reflect their responses on chart paper or by using the projector. Reinforce the notion of writing in the third person. Negotiate the construction of the sentences with the students so that they are well formed and carry the meaning intended. With 3rd through 5th grades, start modeling clause complexes (See chapter 3 and Part II: Language, found later in this Report chapter). For example, if students propose to write the following on the basis of their notes in the graphic organizer: *Snakes can't hear well* or *Snakes feel vibrations through the ground,* suggest that

these sentences could be combined because they are related in meaning and changed to *Snakes cannot hear well, but they feel vibrations through the ground.* Let the students try first to combine the sentences. If they struggle, provide assistance.

- Re-read and make any revisions.
- Have students work in groups or pairs to work on their group or individual pieces.
- Repeat with the next subtopics. All can be addressed or, after modeling a couple, students can draft the remainder of the subtopics on their own.

General Statement

Reports start with a generalization that gives a broad sense of the topic. For example, the mentor text contrasts the Sonoran desert with the rest of the deserts in North America. The book *Antarctica* starts, "In the cold far south, in Antarctica, live emperor penguins, Weddell seals, and Adélie penguins." This type of statement reflects an authoritative voice and requires abstraction, making it rather difficult for children to construct a precise image.

As mentioned earlier, when authors write for children, they often start reports with a friendlier voice: "*You'd think* it *would* be hard to survive in the wild without legs. *But look at snakes!* More than 2,500 kinds *slither* and *creep* throughout the world" (my emphasis; from *Slinky Scaly Slithery Snakes*). This beginning includes use of the second person, modal verbs, an exclamation, and vocabulary that appeals to children. A report on telescopes included both types of beginnings, the first with a familiar voice and the second more authoritative:

> You can see planets, stars, and other objects in space just by looking up on a clear night. But to really see them—to observe the craters on the moon, the rings around Saturn, and the countless other wonders in our sky—you must use a telescope.
>
> A telescope is an instrument used to produce magnified (enlarged) images of distant objects.
>
> (CCSS.ELA/Appendix B, p. 75)

The voice switches from second to third person. The rest of the report is written entirely in the third person.

Features of Students' Writing

Throughout the grades, the initial general statement is usually absent, as both of the students' uncoached pieces shows.

Alicia	*1*	*2*	*3*	*4*	*Uncoached Writing Comments*
General Statement Identification and classification of the topic	✓				No general statement introducing the school. Goes directly to describing.
Fred	*1*	*2*	*3*	*4*	*Uncoached Writing Comments*
General Statement Identification and classification of the topic	✓				No introduction of Thanksgiving as an American holiday.

With coaching, students tend to include these initial, general statements. For example, Christine (Grade 2) appropriately started her report with *A penguin is a kind of bird.*

Some students start with a question that directly addresses the audience, "*Do you like Jaguars? You should cause their lots inform information I could give you*" (Grade 5). Students are often told that starting with a question "gives reports a voice." As stated before, this is just one possibility, but shows a familiar voice appropriate for a young audience, as opposed to an authoritative voice for an adult audience. Questions usually indicate that the author knows more than the reader. Therefore, it would not be appropriate to start with a question if 3rd-grade students write a report to show the principal how much they know about planets. A question would sound rather pejorative.

Another problem with the initial statement is assuming the readers' background knowledge. The beginning sentence of a report on the solar system, *The sun is hot* (kindergarten), assumes the readers' knowledge on the subject. Similarly, Alicia assumed that the reader was familiar with her school. As students develop knowledge, language, and a sense of audience, their initial statements become more informative.

LESSON 7. Teaching How to Write the Opening General Statement

Goal: To learn how authors write opening statements.

Materials: Reports that have different kinds of opening statements: (a) generalizations as in the mentor text; (b) friendlier beginnings that use second person, exclamations, and questions; and (c) a combination of a friendlier beginning followed by a generalization.

Activities

- Read aloud or give students reports with different types of beginnings and ask them to describe them.

- Write on chart paper examples of the three different types of opening statements from the books researched. Keep these chart papers up for the next lesson.
- Discuss the type of beginning, the appropriate audience that matches, and why.

LESSON 8. Joint Construction of the Opening General Statement

Goal: To apprentice students to write an opening statement for their reports.
Materials: Class work that begins by writing subtopics.

Activities

- Have students think of the intended audience and the type of opening statement that they want for their class report.
- Jointly construct an opening statement with the class.
- Have students think of a different audience and propose a different opening statement.

LESSON 9. Write the Opening Statement of Their Group or Individual Reports

Goal: To have students apply what they learned in the previous lesson to write an opening statement for their own reports.
Materials: Group or individual work that begins by writing subtopics.

Activities

- Have students work in groups or pairs.
- Remind students of the audience that they had decided on for their reports.
- Have students write an opening statement given their audience and on the basis of the models discussed.
- Have students read the opening statement of their report aloud to their group or to each other if working in pairs.
- Have students discuss whether it is an appropriate opening statement given their audience.
- Walk around listening to student discussions.
- Have one or two groups or students share their decision with the class. Choose individuals or groups that you heard giving appropriate responses to model for the other students.
- Have one or two students that you think need revision present. Have the class react and suggest revisions.

Summarizing Comment

Most reports conclude with one last subtopic. For example, the telescope sample text in the CCSS last paragraph reads,

> Some telescopes are launched into space. These telescopes gain clearer views. And they can collect forms of electromagnetic radiation that are absorbed by the Earth's atmosphere and do not reach the ground.
>
> (CCSS.ELA/Appendix B, p. 75)

Some reports for children conclude with an advisory or engaging statement to keep the interest of the children, for example, "It is important to realize that all animals, including snakes, have a place in nature" (from *Slinky Scaly Slithery Snakes*); "The seals and penguins cannot tell yet whether they will share or destroy their beautiful Antarctica . . ." (from *Antarctica*); and the mentor text's conclusion, "making it a truly exciting place to explore" (from *Saguaro Moon*).

Features of students' writing. Neither of the uncoached pieces included a concluding statement, which is fine. However, students' reports tend to have an ending beyond a final subtopic. A kindergarten student expressed an attitude, *Pandas are cool.* Many students are directed by teachers to conclude with a "fun fact" or "something interesting." This is not a requirement of reports and often leads to listing irrelevant information, such as *Humpback whales can dive for up to 30 minutes. The humpback whale has about 330 pairs of dark baleen plates . . .* (Grade 2). Fifth graders often addressed the audience: *So now you know about the most mysterious snow leopard; As you can see tigers are interesting; Rocks are made out of different minerals. I know because I used the minerals test.* Daniel, a 4th grader, wrote as his last entry on his poster, *Never go in the Jungle and grab a vine because it might be a SNAKE!* He added a bubble pointing to this warning, *Plz read the suggest* [Please read the suggestion]. In this sentence, Daniel not only addresses his audience directly, but indicates that this is a child writing to other children by using text message language.

LESSON 10. Deconstruction of Reports Concluding Paragraph

Goal: To have students learn about concluding paragraphs from published text.

Materials: Mentor texts with concluding paragraphs that just include a final subtopic and others include a final reflection on the topic aimed at keeping children interested in the topic. Projector.

Activities

- Read the mentor texts aloud while projecting them for the students to see.
- Discuss with students what the authors do in these final paragraphs and compare the different endings.

- Discuss the intended audience and the grammatical structures, such as person or type of sentence, that signal the intended audience. Were these written for different audiences? Which type would be appropriate for older readers? For younger readers? Why?

LESSON 11. Joint Construction of the Final Paragraph

Goal: To apprentice students to writing a final paragraph given their audience.
Materials: Class report. Chart paper or projector.

Activities

- Have students decide what kind of final paragraph they want to write given the audience.
- Jointly construct a closing statement with the class.
- Read and revise if needed.

LESSON 12. Write the Ending of Their Group or Individual Reports

Goal: To have students apply what they have learned about endings to write a final paragraph given their audience.
Materials: Group or individual reports.

Activities

- Have students work in groups or pairs.
- Have students read their reports aloud.
- Have students discuss whether the current ending is an appropriate ending for their report given the audience or if they want to add a different ending. If students want to change their ending, have them explain why.
- Walk around and listen to student discussions.
- Have one or two groups or students share their decision with the class. Choose individuals or groups who have appropriate endings to model for the other students.
- Have one or two students that you think need revision present. Have the class react and suggest revisions.

Title: The title of reports tends to be simple, indicating what the report will be about (such as *Bats* or *Volcanoes*). In books for children, authors sometimes try to make their titles fun. A favorite book of students is a report about snakes called *Slinky Scaly Slithery Snakes.*

Features of Students' Writing

Neither of the uncoached pieces included a title. When asked to include a title, students tend to write a title that names what they are writing about, such as, *Florida, Pennsylvania, Tigers,* or *Leopards,* as appropriate for the genre.

LESSON 13. Titles

Goal: To learn how to write a title that reflects the topic of the report and the audience.
Materials: Mentor texts with different types of titles.

Activities

- Read the titles of several texts in the genre.
- Discuss the words that the author uses to convey the topic and how authors sometimes use language to make reports appealing to children.
- Have the class decide on a title for their jointly constructed piece.
- Have two or three students share their reports.
- Have the student author, along with the class, discuss possible titles. If the student has a title, have students discuss if and why it is appropriate.
- Have students work in pairs or groups on titles for their group or individual pieces.

Part II: Language

In a report, topic development is very demanding because it requires knowledge of the topic and knowledge of language to adequately express meaning. In order to convey factual information in a precise manner, report writers employ technical vocabulary to form clauses that include verbs, complex noun groups, and adverbials. Often, ideas expressed in individual clauses are connected to form clause complexes or sentences to express different logical relations. Word choice depends not only on topic, but also on audience. Depending on the age and language proficiency of the audience, authors control the difficulty of the technical terms and complexity of clause elements and clause complexes. For example, the first excerpt below comes from a 4th-grade book about snakes. It includes several uncomplicated clauses and sentences.

> You'd think it would be hard to survive in the wild without legs. But look at snakes! More than 2,500 kinds slither and creep throughout the world. Snakes live just about everywhere except on some islands and near the North and South Poles.
>
> (from *Slinky Scaly Slithery Snakes*, p. 3)

The second, geared for adults, comes from Wikipedia, and consists of just one 25-word sentence with complex noun groups and adverbials, as well as a subordinate clause.

> Snakes are elongated, legless, carnivorous reptiles of the suborder Serpentes that can be distinguished from legless lizards by their lack of eyelids and external ears.
>
> (Wikipedia)

In the case of children's writing, their language maturity plays a role in how technical the language can be regardless of audience.

Verbs are not very complex in reports; they are mostly relational and action verbs, usually in the present tense. Relational verbs describe characteristics and varieties. For example, the verbs *be, have,* and *seem* are used to show features of the Sonoran desert in the mentor text. Action verbs describe behavior or activity, as in *cover, make,* and *record*.

Adverbials of place, time, manner, reason, and others express circumstances providing important information about the topic, for example, "8–10,000 years ago," "in North America," and "roughly." Students also use adverbials in their writing, especially of time, place, and reason, for example, *since 1972, into caves,* and *for their warm skin*.

Although reports do not usually use text connectives, children tend to start sentences with new information by using *also*. Using the Reformulation Approach (See Brisk & Harrington, 2007), in which the teacher rewrites the piece without *also,* students realize that use of *also* is not necessary.

This section on language will address those areas that reflected the greatest challenges in students' writing, including participants and the ability to pack information through noun groups and clause complexes. In addition, in order to provide clear information about the topic of the report, writers need to create paragraphs with a well-defined topic sentence and clauses that connect to each other when developing the subtopic.

The following two examples of mid-unit student writing illustrate the language strengths and challenges students have even after some coaching. Both classes were working on animal reports. The 5th grade class was focusing specifically on wild cats. Timothy writes,

> *Leopards are real interesting animals because leopards climb trees to sleep and protect their food from other animals. Did you know that one kind of leopards is snow leopards? These leopards live in the mountains and grassland of centorial Asia Snow leopards have been listed as endangered since 1972. Female snow leopards give birth to two to four cubs at a time.*

Some live in Africa like these dark colored leopards live in the warm Amazon dark rain forest. They are only a few left in the world because people hunt for their warm skin. Also because there forest is gettin felled little by little. Leopards eat goat, hores, deer and bunny's. They climb trees to protect their food by climbing trees, and also they sometimes camouflage to eat/protect. Also that when they sometimes take them into caves. Also Some not all go where they live and hunt them/eat them there.

Leopards are very but very cool and interesting animals!! More than people think they were. The Leopards are cool and interesting. Cause where there from. Like where they live, eat. Even how they protect their food from other people and anmails.

Second graders could choose any animal to write about. Ruben, a student in the SEI class, wrote approximately 10 reports. What follows is one paragraph of his book on octopuses:

Labeled drawing of an octopus (rubbery arms, eyes, blower, suckers, mouth)

Octopus have 8 rubery arems. When an octopus is mad it trun barck [turns dark] red. Octopus have 240 suckers. Their body is round and soft. They also have big round eyes.

Participants

The participants that are the focus of the report are usually generalized, that is, they represent a class of things, such as *deserts.* To indicate this kind of participant, the noun is in the plural. There are reports, also called descriptions, that are about one participant, such as *the Sonoran desert.* Having to write about a category or generalized participants rather than an individual is a new experience for children who are used to writing recounts about specific participants. Although meaning to express a generalized participant, students often alternated between appropriately using the plural form and the singular form. For example, a 5th grader wrote his first draft about tigers with the title in plural, while references to tigers in the first paragraph were singular and all references in remaining paragraphs were plural. However, omitting the "s" at the end of a plural noun is a common error for L2 learners. Rather than the error being an issue of gender, it is a problem of second language grammatical accuracy (Brisk, 2012). When coached by teachers, students can keep the generalized participants consistent as illustrated in Timothy's writing analysis:

	1	*2*	*3*	*4*	*Uncoached Writing Comments*
Participants Are clear, if generalized, they are consistently used.			✓		There is no clear switch from talking about snow leopards and back to leopards in general.

Ruben also understood how to use generalized participants, as demonstrated in his other reports, but the problem in this writing sample was that he did not know the plural of *octopus.*

	1	*2*	*3*	*4*	*Uncoached Writing Comments*
Participants Are clear, if generalized, they are consistently used.			✓		Consistently used but does not know the plural of octopus, "octopuses."

LESSON 14. Generalized Participants vs. Specific Participants

Goal: To teach students the difference between writing about a category and an individual.

Materials: T-chart. Chart paper or projector. Students' draft reports.List of review questions on chart paper: *Have they written about a generalized or a specific participant? If generalized, is the noun in the plural form* (unless it is a collective noun like *water*)*? Is the information appropriate for that type of participant?*

Activities

- Draw a T-chart with a whole category on one side, for example, *volcanoes,* and an individual participant, for example, *Vesuvius,* on the other.
- Discuss when you would write one type versus the other.
- For young children, individual participants are easier to write about.
- Point out that the generalized participant is written in the plural form.
- Brainstorm the kind of information that you would include in one type or the other. For the generalized participant, the information will be in categories, for example, *components of a volcano.* For individuals, the information will be specific, for example, *height.*
- Project one student sample. Point at each of the questions on the list and solicit comments from the class.
- Working in groups or pairs, have students review what they have written, assisted by the list of questions.

Noun Groups

Noun groups carry a great deal of the information in reports. Therefore, the vocabulary used needs to be semantically connected with the topic of the report. The structure of the noun group can be complex to pack this information. The nouns and adjectives used by the writer reflect the topic of the report (lexical ties). For example, the mentor texts include such nouns as *desert, miles, Sonoran, Great Basin, trees, forests, cacti, woodland, animal,* and *plants.* They also include adjectives including *four major, northwest, tropical arborous,* and *exciting.* Interestingly, the adjective *exciting* is the only generic adjective, and it is used at the end when the author changes her voice to address children directly.

Noun groups are abundant in reports and tend to be complex. Even simple sentences (sentences with only one clause) can be complex due to extended noun groups. For example, this simple sentence in the mentor text has two multi-word noun groups (underlined): "Together they cover roughly 500,000 square **miles** in the southwestern **part** of the United States and northwest Mexico."

A noun group includes a head noun and adjectivals before or after the noun, or both (See Table 6.3). These adjectivals define and describe the noun. Determiners and adjectives precede the noun. Prepositional phrases, apposition, and non-finite and relative clauses follow the noun (See chapter 3 for more information). The adjectives are factual and precise.

Many reports, even for children, include multiple adjectivals crowding lots of information around the nouns. This can be seen in an example from the mentor text (noun in bold, adjectival underlined):

- *Four major* **deserts** *in North America: the Chihuahuan, the Great Basin, the Mojave and the Sonoran.* [adjective + adjective + NOUN + prepositional phrase]
- *more different* **types** *of animals and plants* [adjective + adjective + NOUN + prepositional phrase]
- in the **Sonoran** . . . *making it /a truly exciting* **place** *to explore/* [NOUN + non-finite clause /determiner + adjective + adjective + NOUN + non-finite clause]

TABLE 6.3 Types of Pre-nominal and Post-nominal Adjectivals (underlined).

Type	*Example*
Determiners	*A/This/My* book
Adjectives	*Two difficult history* books
Prepositional phrase	The books *on the table.*
Apposition	The book, *called Moby Dick*
Non-finite embedded clause	The book *purchased by your mother/ lying under the table/to buy*
Relative clause	The book *that your mother gave you*
Adjective group after a relational verb	The shell of a snake's egg is *tough and leathery, not hard like a bird's egg.*

The last example is a very complex structure with a non-finite clause saying something about the Sonoran desert that includes another noun group with a second non-finite clause adding information about "place," which refers to "it," which in turn refers to the Sonoran.

These complex noun groups are also found within adverbials, also making adverbials complicated structures. For example, the adverbial "in *the southwestern part of the United States and northwest Mexico*" includes a complex noun group (underlined) [determiner + adjective + prepositional phrase].

Children in general use very few adjectivals. The pre-K texts have illustrations with labels to inform the reader about the participants. For example, Michael's report on turtles started with the image of a turtle labeled with *HEAd, claw, FEET,* and *sheLL.* Throughout the grades, the description of participants (nouns) is limited. If description is found, it is mostly as adjectives as part of the noun group, as in *sharp teeth* (grade 3), *a snakes tail* (grade 4), or *The most biggest and dangerous* cat (grade 5), or connected by relational verbs, especially *to be* and *to have.* For example, *Venus is the hot planets* (kindergarten), *it's cold* and *freezeing* (grade 2), and *some of them are huge large* (grade 3) demonstrate this element in student writing. The adjective groups after the relational verb are not complex structures like those found in books. They could easily join the noun to make a complex noun group. For example, Ruben's sentence, *Their body is round and soft,* could become the beginning of a sentence (*Their round and soft body . . .*) that tells what octopuses do with their body. Ruben reflects what is typical of young writers. He uses only adjectives, with some connected by a relational verb. There are no prepositional phrases or embedded clauses. However, he uses more adjectives than is commonly found in uncoached writing and his adjectives are specific to the topic of octopuses.

	1	*2*	*3*	*4*	*Mid-unit Writing Comments*
Noun Groups **(a) Lexical Ties:** Nouns and adjectives used are semantically connected to the topic of the report. **(b) Adjectivals** to pack information: - Adjectives - Prepositional phrases - Embedded clauses with finite or non-finite verbs - Adjective group after a relational verb.			✓		Uses a number of nouns and adjectives semantically related to octopuses. Uses mostly prenominal adjectives and adjective groups after a relational verb. No prepositional phrases or embedded clauses.

A 2nd grader, when researching the attributes of penguins, located the relevant information, but had difficulty creating noun groups. She wrote, *A baby penguin drink milk from its mother,* rather than *Baby penguins drink their mother's milk* and *The belly color is yellow at the top* instead of *The top of the belly is yellow.*

Timothy also uses only adjectives, but was less successful than Ruben with respect to variety and semantic connection to the topic.

	1	*2*	*3*	*4*	*Uncoached Writing Comments*
Noun Groups **(a) Lexical Ties:** Nouns and adjectives used are semantically connected to the topic of the report. **(b) Adjectivals** to pack information: - Adjectives - Prepositional phrases - Embedded clauses with finite or non-finite verbs - Adjective group after a relational verb.		✓			Uses some technical terms related to leopards. "Interesting" and "cool" are generic adjectives not reflective of the topic. Uses some adjectives, some repeated. In addition, several in adjective groups connected by a relational verb. No prepositional phrases or embedded clauses.

Some 5th graders could write relative clauses to further describe the noun: *Their paws have really sharp claws that allow them to climb trees and open all sorts of containers for food.*

Other features of the students' noun groups included:

- *Difficulty with ordinal numbers:* For example, *earth is the three pnt* [planet] (kindergarten).
- *Omission of the determiner:* For example, *a habitats of a penguin is* [the] *tundra* (grade 2).
- *Inappropriate use of* the*:* For example, *the sharks have sharp teeth* (grade 3).
- *Inclusion of the plural "s" marker when it was not needed:* For example, *a habitats of a penguin* (grade 2).
- *Omission of the plural "s" marker when it was needed:* For example, *snake come* (grade 4).
- *Omission of the apostrophe to indicate a possessive:* For example, *snakes pray* [prey] (grade 4).
- *Formation of the possessive as a prepositional phrase rather than by using the possessive:* For example, *a habitats of the penguin* (grade 2).
- *Formation of the comparative structure:* For example, *most biggest* (grade 5).

These challenges could be developmental or second language difficulties because all of these students spoke a language other than English at home.

LESSON 15. Teach Students to Appropriate Academic Language

Goal: To have students become familiar with the language of the topic they are studying in order to use it with understanding.
Materials: Resources that have been used to introduce the topic. Chart paper.

Activities

- Read aloud a short text on the topic of the unit content, such as *Ladybugs.*
- As you re-read the text, ask the students to stop you whenever you read a chunk of text that has vocabulary that expresses specific meaning related to the topic (e.g., "five thousand species," "dark blue lady beetles," and "eat insects that are pests on farms and in gardens, such as aphids").
- Write the expression provided by the students on chart paper. Then discuss, illustrate, or have students draw or diagram the meaning.
- Depending on the grade level and reading ability of your students, read aloud a few more sources or have them read additional sources in groups and add terms to the chart paper. Have them explain the terms that they have added.

LESSON 16. Deconstruction of Text To Learn About Noun Groups

Goal: To teach students to add descriptions about the participants by using different types of adjectivals.
Materials: Paragraph from a mentor text with different types of adjectivals. Paragraph from a mentor text with nouns circled and adjectivals covered. Projector.

Activities

While doing this activity, take advantage to continue developing vocabulary and content knowledge.

- Project a paragraph of a mentor text, circle nouns and pronouns, and underline adjectivals. Discuss how the adjectivals say something about the noun and how they make the noun more specific. For example, you and the students could discuss the following sentence:

  Some harmless king **snakes** and milk **snakes** look enough like poisonous **ones** that predators leave them alone.

- Project a different paragraph with nouns circled and adjectivals covered. Have students draw a picture of the noun.
- Uncover the adjectivals and ask students if they would draw a different picture. For example, how would the following sentence change their picture: ***Snakes** that slither away have striped **bodies**.* The students would first draw *Snakes have bodies*, and then see the whole sentence, including the adjectivals, to draw their new picture.

As students perused texts for structure and content, Cheryl reminded them to think about language; vocabulary is important, and their language needed to be descriptive to educate their audience on the subject. She used the mentor texts and the descriptive language in them as examples. On an overhead projector, she compared parts of the mentor texts with and without the author's descriptive language, and the students were asked which piece was more informative and why. The students all came to the same answer: The descriptive knowledge helped to serve the author's purpose, which is to inform the reader. Cheryl also discussed with them the role of the illustrations to complement the written text and reflect important information (Brisk et al., 2011, p. 5).

LESSON 17. Expanding Noun Groups (Grades 2–5)

Goal: To teach students how to add pre-nominal adjectives to nouns and to expand students' vocabulary.

Materials: Example of how to build up nouns using the following questions. Chart paper or projector.

Questions

What? bones
Which ones? / Whose? Those bones/Her bones
How many? Those three bones
What like? (qualities: facts) Those three white bones
What like? (qualities: opinion) Those three white smelly bones
What kind? Those three white smelly lamb bones

Activities

- Read the aforementioned example.
- Ask a student to find a noun. Write it on the board or chart paper.

- Using a couple of the questions, have the class add one, two, and three things about the noun. Write them next to the noun. If there are L2 learners in your class, you may need to explain the meaning of the adjectives suggested by students or you may need to give the adjective that they may be trying to express.
- Have students repeat the activity in groups.
- Project a student sample with a noun or two underlined.
- Using the questions, have the class and the student author suggest adjectives that will help to describe the noun.
- Working in groups, have students look at their own writing, choose a noun, and add one or two adjectives. This can also be done during conferencing.

LESSON 18. Expanding Noun Groups (Grades 4–5)

Goal: To teach students how to describe participants by adding or transforming a clause into post-nominal adjectivals (See more information in chapter 3).
Materials: Examples of post-nominal adjectivals. Examples generated in the previous lesson from students' writing samples.

Activities

- Read the following examples and discuss the meaning and function of these prepositional phrases or embedded clauses.
  - Prepositional phrase: Those three white smelly lamb bones on the table
  - Embedded clause with non-finite verbs: Those bones lying on the floor/ buried in the backyard
  - Embedded clause with a relative pronoun and a finite verb (relative clause): Those bones that belong to the butcher
  - Chunk of the mentor text with these types of adjectivals underlined:

    "The Sonoran is the only desert in North America that does not have cold winters."

    ". . . a truly exciting place *to explore.*"

- Re-examine the nouns given by the students in the previous lesson. Ask them to further describe the noun by adding something after the noun.
- Show a student sample with a noun or two that could use a post-nominal adjective. Ask the class to propose additions (Point at the examples to remind them of the structures).
- Show a student sample that has a noun's information in more than one clause that can be combined into a noun group. For example, *These leopards live in the mountains and grassland of centorial Asia Snow leopards have been listed as endangered since 1972,* could be written using an embedded clause

with a non-finite verb: *These leopards listed as endangered since 1972 live in the mountains . . .*

- Working in groups, have students add to or revise their writing. This can also be done through conferencing and questions.

Clause Complexes

In the upper elementary grades, students encounter texts that include sentences with multiple clauses connected to denote different meanings. Even texts for younger students include some clause complexes. By the upper elementary grades, students start to express complex ideas that require these types of grammatical structures. Grammar classifies these sentences as compound, complex, or compound/complex (More information in chapter 3). Sometimes, a dependent clause in a compound sentence is compacted by eliminating the conjunction and noun. The conjugated verb is replaced by a non-finite or unconjugated verb. For example, ". . . the fangs swing out and pierce the prey, ***injecting*** *deadly poison*" (from *Slinky Scaly Slithery Snakes*), uses a non-finite clause instead of writing "and then they inject deadly poison" (More information on non-finite clauses in chapter 3).

The other way to analyze clause complexes is by the relation that they express. The two basic types of relationships are projection and expansion (Halliday & Matthiessen, 2004). Projections were addressed in chapter 5 because they are more likely to occur in recounts or narratives. In expansions, one clause expands what is expressed in the other. There are many different possibilities to build on the meaning, often signaled by a conjunction or other connective (See chapter 3 for more information). Table 6.4 illustrates the relationships most commonly found in reports for elementary students (for full range and analysis of logico-semantic relations, see Brisk & DeRosa, forthcoming).

Thus, when combining clauses, writers need to decide the desired meaning to be expressed and the connective that will signal the type of expansion.

Clause complexes are mostly found in 4th- and 5th-grade students' writing, both in compound and complex sentences. Of the non-finite constructions, the most frequent is *to + verb* to indicate cause, for example, *The snakes use there powerful muscles to move around freely* (grade 4). The most common of the finite constructions were temporal, causal, and additive, for example, *When predators come // the snake waves around in a circle // then vomits,* (temporal, grade 4); *An animal does not have these things // since animals do not make their own food,* and *New Jersey nickname is the Garden state because it has so much garden and trees,* (causal mostly of reason rather than purpose, grade 4); and *If their prey is bigger // they often hunt in groups// and they work together to kill the prey,* (additive, grade 5). Other relations expressed in children's reports were conditional (*If*

TABLE 6.4 Logico-semantic Relationships

Type of Relationship	*Conjunctions or Other Connectives*	*Examples From the Children's Texts* Slinky Scaly Slithery Snakes *and* Rocks and Fossils
Temporal (When? How long? How often?)	Then, next, afterwards, as, just then, at the same time, while, until, before that, soon, after a while, meanwhile, all the time, until then, now, every time, whenever	A snake has no limbs to get in the way *when it's chasing after tunneling ground squirrels and burrowing mice.* Snakes' bodies make S shapes *as they glide along. (Slinky Scaly Slithery Snakes)*
Causal (reason, purpose)	Because, as, since, so, then, consequently, therefore	Even the fastest snake has a hard time escaping from an animal with four legs, *so some snakes have ways of tricking their enemies.* (reason) Other snakes use their color *to hide.* (purpose)
Conditional	If, as long as, in case, on condition that (positive), Unless, without (negative)	*If that doesn't work*, the snake violently twists its body about . . .
Manner (How?)	By, through, with Thus, and + in that way, so, and + similarly, as if, as though, as, like	Sidewinders seem to swim over the surface of the desert, *looping their way quickly from place to place.* (non-finite clause that is not connected by a conjunction)
Comparative	Likewise, similarly, in a different way	A method good for measuring ages in millions of years is of no use on an object that is only a few thousand years old. *Likewise, a method that works well for a short time spans is undoubtedly worthless for much longer periods. (Rocks and Fossils)*
Concessive	But, yet, still, despite this, however, even so, nevertheless, although, even though, even if, while, whereas, much as	Snakes can't hear well, *but they easily feel vibrations through the ground.*
Extending by adding something new	And, as well (additive)	When threatened, it lifts *and flattens its neck, and hisses.*
	But, while (adversative)	Many kinds of snakes can swim, *but sea snakes are swimming champions*
	Or, instead of, besides, instead of, without, rather than (variation or replacement)	Some snakes attract their prey *instead of ambushing it.*
Elaborating without introducing something new	In other words	Certain types of materials, such as uranium, are radioactive. *In other words, they give off radiation.*
	For example, for instance, in particular	That picture, however, is incomplete. *For example, creatures with soft bodies, which easily decay, are not very likely to leave fossils behind.*

Sources for content: Brisk & DeRosa (in press); Derewianka (2011); Eggins (2004); Halliday & Matthiessen (2004); Thompson (2004).

snake venom gets in your bloodstream you'll die, grade 4); concessive (*If snake venom gets in your bloodstream you'll die, but if you swallow venom it cures bad health,* grade 4); and adversative (*An animal cell has all of these things, // but a plant cell has a cell wall and chloroplast,* grade 4).

Children sometimes had difficulty expressing the relation that they intended. Daniel (grade 4) wrote on his poster about "Snakes," *When snakes slither they make the letter S so they can swim.* The source book included the following sentence: "Snakes' bodies make S shapes as they glide along. This kind of movement also helps snakes swim" (Patent, 2000, p. 6). Therefore, the connection is not one of cause (glide/slither) and effect (swim), as Daniel puts it, but rather that gliding and swimming are both helped by the S-type movement. He also wrote, *Certain Snakes live in water but never leave their habitat.* "And" would be a more appropriate conjunction since he is adding information. Oscar (grade 5) used multiple complex sentences that were difficult to understand or made ambiguous connections. For example, he wrote, *What Jaguars eat is Deer cause the size of their horns,* leaving the reader to wonder what it is about the size of the deer's horns that allows jaguars to eat.

Given the clause complexes that elementary students attempt to create on their own, writing instruction should be initially limited to those types illustrated in the examples of students' writing. When students encounter the other types while reading texts, teachers should explain the meaning and structure. This instruction should be limited to 4th and 5th graders and should include creating clause complexes as well as revising their writing to pack simple sentences and express the correct relationships.

LESSON 19. Clause Complex Puzzles (Grades 4–5)

Goal: To learn how different conjunctions signal different relations.

Materials: Sentence strips with clause complexes from a report cut up to separate each clause and the conjunction. Envelopes with sentence strips inside similarly cut up and taken from the report texts that you are using for the given subject area. The sentences can all be the same or be different. Chart paper or projector.

Activities

- Project the conjunctions or put them up on the board or chart paper.
  - Working with the whole class, read aloud or have students read aloud the sentence strips. For example:

    The shell of a baby tortoise does not completely harden + until + it turns 5 years old.
    Their life span is about 35 to 40 years, + but + some can get to be 100 years old.
    Turtles spend more time in the water, + so + their feet are better for swimming.

- Pick one sentence strip and ask the students to pick a conjunction and another sentence that, when put together with a conjunction, makes sense.

- Have students read aloud the new sentences to test that they make sense. Have students explain the meaning in the new sentences.
- Repeat with other sentence strips and conjunctions.
- Ask if students can make different combinations of sentences (and related meaning).
- Give each group of students one of the envelopes and have students carry out the same activity with the small sentence strips. Have students share their sentences and explain what each means. (This activity helps students appropriate the language of books. By manipulating sentences from books, children can internalize the structures of written language.)

LESSON 20. Deconstruct Clause Complexes

Goal: To learn how to express ideas through clause complexes from authors.
Materials: Page of a report with examples of clause complexes. Chart paper or projector. Copies of a page or two of a report that has examples of clause complexes. For both examples, choose sections of the text(s) that have essential content needed to understand the topic being studied.

Activities

- Project the chosen text and have students identify the verbs. Ask students if the clauses are simple or if they are combined to express a relation. For example, the sentence "**When** *threatened,* it *lifts* **and** *flattens* its neck, **and** *hisses*" has four verbs (the first one is non-finite) and the clauses are all connected.
- Ask students what connects the verbs and clauses and what the conjunctions tell you about the relation signaled. In the example, the first is temporal (telling when the snake shows these behaviors) and the other two are additive (*lifts* and *flattens* are connected with each other in relation to *neck* and *hisses* is connected to both previous behaviors). You can also show how the commas help to group the meanings.
- Repeat this analysis with other clause combinations. Discuss their meanings and content.
- Give the student groups the copies of the text. Have them do the same activity and go around working with individual groups as they work. Make sure that students pay attention to both form and meaning.

LESSON 21. Revising Clause Complexes

Goal: To teach students to revise their work to include well-formed and meaningful clause complexes that make their writing look like the language of books.

Materials: Selected pieces of student work. Projector. Students' drafts with one or two sentences underlined that could be either combined or that have an unclear relation.

Activities

- Project one of the students' pieces. Have the student author read it aloud. Depending on what the writing needs, ask the author for the meaning in the sentences or how could they be combined.
- Ask the author and the class to suggest revisions, and write the suggestions on the board or smartboard. Then, discuss which suggestion seems to best express the author's meaning.
- Repeat with one or two more examples.
- Have students work in groups and do the same activity with the underlined sentences in their drafts. Have students first propose revisions, then discuss with the group and make a final choice. Students may not end up with the best choice alone, so it is important for you to walk around and help out, as needed.

Cohesive Paragraphs

Two features help develop clarity in paragraphs for reports. One is that paragraphs usually start with a topic sentence introducing the subtopic of the paragraph, and the second is the internal flow of the paragraph. Within paragraphs, clauses relate to each other. Each clause starts with the *Theme* or "the starting point for a text, paragraph, or clause" (Droga & Humphrey, 2003, p. 89). The Theme "alerts us to the topic which is being developed, while the end of the sentence introduces the new information about the topic" (Derewianka, 1998, p. 105). The term *Theme* refers to a grammatical category and not to the "theme" or "deep meaning of a literary work" used in literary analysis (Fang & Schleppegrell, 2008, p. 98).

The Theme usually consists of the initial part of the sentence until the verb of the main clause. After the initial sentence of a paragraph, the Themes of clauses that follow either connect to the new information of the previous sentence or to the original Theme. Authors choose the information included in the Theme position to direct the reader to the focus of the writing. For example, in recount genres, the initial Theme of paragraphs tends to include an adverbial of time to denote passage of time, for example, "Soon after he . . . ," "About four months after he . . .," and "In 1985 his autobiography, *The Narrative of the Life of Frederick Douglass, An American Slave* . . ." (From *A Picture Book of Frederick Douglass*). In reports, the initial Themes relate to the focus of the subtopic of the paragraph. Following Themes provide more detailed information about the initial. For example, in the CCSS text "Telescopes" (CCSS.ELA/Appendix B, p. 75), analysis of the third paragraph shows the strategies used by the writer.

Theme	*New Information*
There	Are many different types of telescopes, both optical and non-optical.
Optical telescopes	Are designed to focus visible light.
Non-optical telescopes	Are designed to detect kinds of electromagnetic radiation that are invisible to the human eye.
These	Include radio waves, infrared radiation, X rays, ultraviolet radiation, and gamma rays.
The word "optical"	Means "making use of light."

The writer presents the concepts of optical and non-optical as new information in the first sentence, elaborates on optical in the second, and non-optical in the third sentence, with optical and non-optical in the Theme position. In the third sentence, the author introduces "kinds of electromagnetic radiation" referred to as "these" in the Theme of the fourth sentence and described in the New Information. The fifth sentence goes back to the theme of optical, which signals that it could have been placed as a second sentence when the concepts of optical and non-optical were introduced.

It is important for the reader to know what the writer is referring to when a topic, idea, or information is introduced more than once. For example, in the aforementioned passage, the Theme of the fourth sentence has a weak reference when the sentence starts with "these" because a Theme can refer to the "kinds of electromagnetic radiation" or the previous Theme, "non-optical telescopes."

In the early grades, children tend to write short reports or picture books with images accompanied by one or two sentences. These sentences can be related to the topic, especially if guided by the teacher, but the information or ideas in the sentences do not necessarily relate to each other. For example, a page from a 2nd-grade report on spiders read, *A spider is a carnivore. Young spiders are often cannibals. Also to catch up prey they jump out of no where.* From 3rd grade up, students start writing longer pieces that include paragraphs for each subtopic. Here, students may have difficulty writing a topic sentence abstracting the topic of the paragraph and keeping the paragraphs to one main topic. Table 6.5 shows the Theme/New Information analysis of the first paragraph in Timothy's leopard report.

TABLE 6.5 Timothy's Theme/New Information Analysis

Theme	*New Information*
Leopards	are real interesting animals because *leopards climb trees to sleep* and *protect their food* from other animals.
Did you	know that one kind of leopards is snow leopards?
These leopards	live in the mountains and grassland of centorial Asia
Snow leopards	have been listed as endangered since 1972.
Female snow leopards	give birth to two to four cubs at a time.

Timothy starts his piece giving specifics about leopards; however, the first paragraph is not limited to one subtopic. In the first sentence, he introduces that leopards climb trees to sleep and to protect their food. However, the following Themes are all related to snow leopards, instead of further developing the new information in the first sentence. Only later does he write about the initial Theme. Although the sentences that follow are all related to snow leopards, they read like a list with leopard in the Theme position and the new information following. None of the new information is further developed. Christie and Derewianka (2008) found similar characteristics in children's writing collected in Australian schools.

LESSON 22. To Create Paragraphs

Goal: To teach students the concepts of Theme/New Information to apply it to their writing so that they can create paragraphs that flow.

Materials: Paragraphs in mentor texts broken up into Theme/New Information (such as the example on p. 206 of this book, no arrows included). Paragraphs from student writing broken up into Theme/New Information. Chart with a list of published texts' themes (first column) and a list of the themes in one of the students' paragraphs (second column). It is better if students have not seen the published text before. Example:

Themes in Published Text	*Themes in Student's Sample*
Massachusetts	Also that they . . .
New Hampshire and Vermont	Also that they . . .
New York	Also that they . . .
Connecticut and Rhode Island	Also that just by licking it prey it
The Atlantic Ocean	

The published text paragraph reads, "Massachusetts shares borders with five states. New Hampshire and Vermont are north. New York is west. Connecticut and Rhode Island are south. The Atlantic Ocean is east" (Murray, 2013, p. 6).

The student paragraph reads,

> *Also that they use their eyes to find their way through the dark. Also that they got a good sense of smell so they could smell their prey from far away. Also that they also use their wiskers to go through the dark. Also that just by licking it prey it could taste it blood.*

Activities

- Show students the chart with the two lists of Themes. Ask them what the published text is about and what the student's text is about. (A 3rd-grade teacher mentioned that when she did this activity, the students realized what they needed to do with their writing instantaneously.)

- Show the Theme/New Information table with the mentor text paragraph. Discuss it. What is the New Information? Is it related to Themes that follow? Is the new information further developed throughout the Theme/New Information of the sentences that follow? When the theme is a pronoun, is it clear what the author is referring to?
- Show a student text analyzed with the Theme/New Information table. Have students discuss it in the same way and propose revisions, if needed.
- Repeat with other students' texts.
- Have students work in groups to examine other paragraphs of their writing in the same way.

Once all the students were satisfied with their final products, they had a publishing party that was open to the school. Cheryl gave her students a set of questions for the authors to ask as they viewed the posters. These questions were all related to process. The students were told that they must provide feedback that was relative to the elements of a report. For example, they could not respond with, "This is very good. I liked it." Their feedback responses had to show their knowledge of the genre as well. For example, one student said, "Your use of the words *predator, habitat, prey* show that you have done your research on the snake." Another said, "Your word choice 'The slithery, sneaky, venomous cobra' captured my attention and showed me that you were thinking of word choice for effect" (Brisk et al., 2011, p. 5).

Resources

- Analysis of student work: Purpose, stages, and tenor
- Analysis of student work: Language
- Graphic organizers:
  - Brainstorming phase
  - Organizing information phase
- Additional resources that illustrate the genre

Report—Analysis of Student Work: Purpose, Stages, and Tenor

Content Area: **Medium:** **Intended Audience:**

Key: 1. Needs substantial support; 2. Needs instruction; 3. Needs revision; 4. Meets standard; NA: Not applicable

	1	*2*	*3*	*4*	*Uncoached Writing Comments*	*1*	*2*	*3*	*4*	*Final Writing Comments*
Purpose Organize information about a topic.										
Verb Conjugation (present)										
Title (if required by the medium)										
General Statement Identification and classification of the topic.										
Information Organized in bundles or subtopics.										
Conclusion (optional)										
Cohesive Text (Macrotheme and hypertheme, based on graphic organizer for the genre)										
Audience Information and language level of difficulty and amount appropriate for the audience.										
Voice Body of text in third person. General statement and conclusion in voice appropriate for audience.										

Criteria

1. Needs substantial support: The student writer needs extensive help developing that aspect of the genre.
2. There are gaps in the writer's understanding of the specific aspect. The writer has insufficient control. S/he needs instruction and practice.
3. The paper needs revision on one or two instances of the feature. A conference would be sufficient to help the writer meet the standard.
4. The paper reflects what the student should be able to accomplish and write independently given the instruction provided for this grade level (National Center on Education and the Economy, 2004).

Report—Analysis of Student Work: Language

Type: **Content Area:** **Medium:** **Intended Audience:**

Key: 1. Needs substantial support; 2. Needs instruction; 3. Needs revision; 4. Meets standard; NA: Not applicable

	1	*2*	*3*	*4*	*Mid-unit Writing Comments*	*1*	*2*	*3*	*4*	*Final Writing Comments*
Participants Are clear. If generalized, they are consistently used.										
Noun Groups Lexical Ties: Nouns and adjectives used are semantically connected to the topic of the report.										
Adjectivals: To pack information - Adjectives - Prepositional phrases - Embedded clauses with finite or non-finite verbs - Adjective group after a relational verb.										
Clause Complexes: To pack information. Meaning, conjunction, order										
Cohesive Paragraphs (Theme/New Information)										

Criteria

1. Needs substantial support: The student writer needs extensive help developing that aspect of the genre.
2. There are gaps in the writer's understanding of the specific aspect. The writer has insufficient control. S/he needs instruction and practice.
3. The paper needs revision on one or two instances of the feature. A conference would be sufficient to help the writer meet the standard.
4. The paper reflects what the student should be able to accomplish and write independently given the instruction provided for this grade level (National Center on Education and the Economy, 2004).

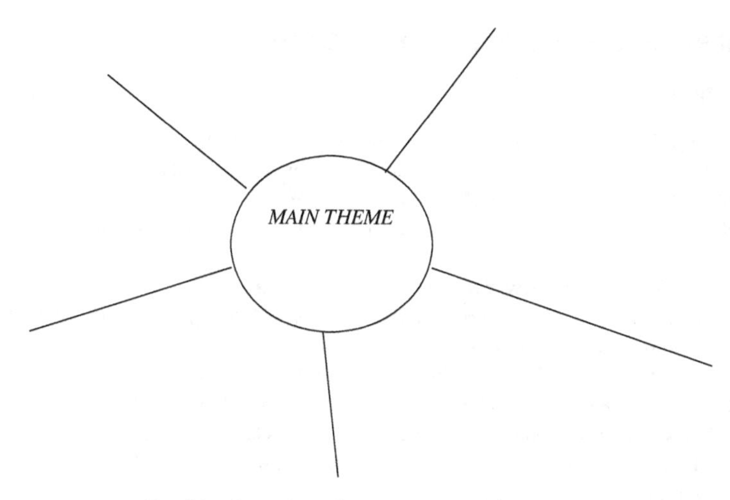

FIGURE 6.1 Graphic Organizer: Brainstorming Phase

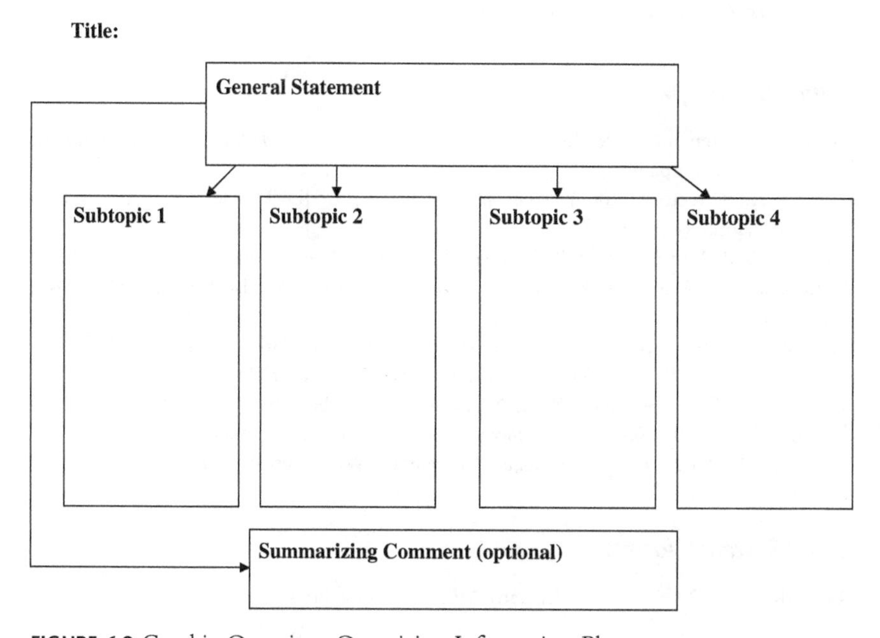

FIGURE 6.2 Graphic Organizer: Organizing Information Phase

Additional Resources That Illustrate the Genre

States/America

Downey, T. (2010). *Massachusetts: The bay state.* New York, NY: Power Kids Press.

Isaacs, S.S. (2001). *Picture the past: Life in a colonial town.* Portsmouth, NH: Heinemann.

Isaacs, S.S. (2001). *Picture the past: Life in America's first cities.* Portsmouth, NH: Heinemann.

Klein, T. (2008). *Rhode Island: Celebrate the states* (2nd ed.). Tarrytown, NY: Marshall Cavendish Benchmark.

Leotta, J. (2008). *Massachusetts.* New York, NY: Children's Press.

LeVert, S., & Orr, T.B. (2008). *Massachusetts: Celebrate the states* (2nd ed.). Tarrytown, NY: Marshall Cavendish Children's Books.

Murray, J. (2013). *Massachusetts.* Minneapolis, MN: ABDO Publishing Company.

Orr, T. (2011). *Florida (America the Beautiful*; 3rd ed.). New York, NY: Scholastic.

Polh, K. (2009). *Looking at the United States.* New York, NY: Gareth Stevens.

Raven, M.T., & Brett, J. (2002). *M is for Mayflower: A Massachusetts alphabet.* Chelsea, MI: Sleeping Bear Press.

Shirley, D., & Hart, J. (2008). *Alabama: Celebrate the states.* Tarrytown, NY: Marshall Cavendish Corporation.

Simpson, J., Thomas, D.H., Pendleton, L.S., & Halliday, H. (1995). *Native Americans.* Alexandria, VA: Time-Life Books. (This is a period piece because it contains reports on a variety of topics related to Native Americans only and not in a chronological way like Christie & Derewianka, 2008).

Animals

Burton, M., French, C., & Jones, T. (1999). *Ocean animals.* Pelham, NY: Benchmark Education Company.

Crawley, A. (Director). (2009). *What makes a fish a fish?* [DVD]. Seattle, WA: DiveInto YourImagination.com.

Jeanesse, G., & Moignot, D. (1997). *Frogs.* New York, NY: Scholastic.

Jenkins, S., & Page, R. (2003). *What do you do with a tail like this?* Boston, MA: Houghton Mifflin.

Kajikawa, K. (1999). *Sweet dreams: How animals sleep.* New York, NY: Henry Holt.

Lesser, C. (1984). *The goodnight circle.* San Diego, CA: Voyager Books.

Martin, J. (1997). *Frogs.* New York, NY: Crown Publishers, Inc.

Patent, D.H. (2000). *Slinky scaly slithery snakes.* New York, NY: Walker & Co.

Schwartz, D. (2001). *La rana de bosque.* Milwaukee, WI: Gareth Stevens.

Solar System/Planets

Richardson, A. (2005). *Saturn.* Makato, MN: Capstone Press.

Miscellaneous Science Topics

Bjorklund, R. (2008). *Circulatory system.* Tarrytown, NY: Marshall Cavendish Corporation. (Chapter 1 is a report)

Blackaby, S. (2003). *Green and growing: A book about plants.* Mankato, MN: Capstone Press.

Hantula, R. (2007). *Rocks and fossils.* Pleasantville, NY: Gareth Stevens.
Hoffman, G. (2008). *Digestive system.* Tarrytown, NY: Marshall Cavendish Corporation. (Chapter 1 is a report)
Kudlinski, K. (2005). *What do roots do?* Minoqua, WI: NorthWord Press Inc.
O'Donoghue, M. (2005). *Rocks and minerals of the world.* Chicago, IL: World Book, Inc. (Includes procedures to carry out experiments)
Stille, D. (1998). *The circulatory system.* New York, NY: Children's Press.
Symes, R.F. (2004). *Rocks and minerals.* New York, NY: DK Publishing, Inc. (From the Eyewitness Books series)

Miscellaneous Social Studies Topics

Crampton, W. (1994). *The world of flags.* Skokie, IL: Rand McNally and Company. (Teacher resource: The last 10 pages have flags from all states and countries)
Goldsworthy, K. (2012). *Halloween.* New York, NY: AV2 books.
Hunter, R. (1998). *Into the sky.* New York, NY: Holiday House. (About skyscrapers)
Komatsu, Y. (2004). *Wonderful houses around the world.* Bolinas, CA: Shelter Publishing, Inc. (Photos and explanations of life and culture in various countries around the world)
Peppas, L. (2012). *Cultural traditions in Japan.* New York, NY: Crabtree. (Series of books about different countries)
Simpson, J., Thomas, D.H., Pendleton, L.S., & Halliday, H. (1995). *Native Americans.* Alexandria, VA: Time-Life Books. (This is a period piece because it contains reports on a variety of topics related to Native Americans only and not in a chronological way like historical recounts).

7

EXPLANATIONS

Chapter Map

- Grade Levels and Content Areas
- Explanations Unit
  - Oral Explanations (Pre-K–5)
  - Written Explanations (Grades 3–5)
    - General Preparation
    - Part I: Purpose and Stages of the Genre
      - Purpose of Explanations
      - Stages of Explanations
      - Sequential Explanation
      - Systems Explanation
    - Part II: Language
      - Verbs
      - Generalized Participants
      - Noun Groups
      - Adverbials
      - Clause Complexes
      - Lessons on Formation of Clause Complexes
      - Audience and Voice
      - Creating a Cohesive Text

Liz, a literacy coach, and Mia, a 4th-grade teacher, followed these steps to teach explanations:

1. *Explanation immersion for several days:* In pairs, the students read multiple texts and discussed their purpose at the end of the lesson. During the next lesson, they read more explanations and explored the stages. The last activity was to define the stages and the language features of the water cycle explanation.
2. *Class rubric:* On the basis of what students had explored with purpose, stages, and language, the students created a class rubric.
3. *Instruction on stages, language, and type of explanation using everyday themes:* This step included a number of lessons. The first lessons worked on identifying themes, oral rehearsing, and writing. Then, lessons addressed the specific stages: statement of the phenomenon, type of explanation, organization of the body of the explanation (either by a series of events with or without causality, events in a cycle, and factors), and finally the conclusion. To teach these stages, Liz and Mia had the class revise a few students' pieces, highlighting the various stages in sample explanations, and then putting together cut-up explanations. They also taught adjectivals, adverbials, and text connectives in connection to different types of explanations. Students prepared one explanation for publication and added a diagram to it.

Resources Analysis of Student Work Forms Graphic Organizers Additional Resources That Illustrate the Genre	4. *Instruction using scientific explanations:* To carry out the instructions for scientific explanations, the teachers followed similar steps as the previous set of lessons, but also included time dedicated to research once students had selected topics from a bank provided by the teacher. While doing research, the students were taught how to take notes in an explanation graphic organizer and write scientific words and their definitions at the bottom of the graphic organizer. While writing their explanations, they turned the definitions into appositions (Harris, 2011).

Explanations share a number of features with reports. The major difference is that reports have chunks of information that stand on their own and the author chooses which ones to include. For example, when writing animal reports, teachers typically encourage students to describe the animal and write about diet, habitat, and predators. There are many other things that one could write about animals, but a report can stand alone with just those few. In explanations, the chunks of information are connected with each other. Ignoring any of them will make the explanation incomplete. For example, in the sequential explanation on how recycled paper is made (included in this chapter), skipping a step will make the explanation inaccurate. Further, in the systems explanation about the branches of government (another example included in this chapter), all three branches and their relationships need to be included. The writer cannot decide to skip one because the explanation would then be truncated.

Explanations seek to explain *how* or *why* things come to be the way they are or to analyze *how* things work. There are a variety of types of explanations (See Table 7.1): sequential, causal, cyclical, systems, factorial, consequential, conditional, and interpretive (Christie & Derewianka, 2008; Coffin, 2006; Derewianka & Jones, 2012; Martin & Rose, 2008; Veel, 2000). Explanations are found mostly in science and history texts, except for interpretative explanations that are found in English and the creative arts (Knapp & Watkins, 2005).

Explanations are a difficult genre. Before starting explanations, it is beneficial if children have had the opportunity to write procedures and reports, as the language features of those genres become increasingly complex. Within the explanation genre, there is also increasing complexity. In the earlier grades, most explanations in school science are based on events that children can observe or visualize, but others are based on cause-and-effect relationships and, eventually, very complex theories (Veel, 2000). Sequential, causal, and cyclical explanations are the types that children typically encounter and acquire in the elementary grades (Christie & Derewianka, 2008; Derewianka & Jones, 2012). Systems and factorial explanations are appropriate for the upper elementary grades. Consequential, conditional, and interpretative explanations can be taught in middle school.

TABLE 7.1 Types of Explanations

Type of Explanation	*Purpose*	*Example*
	Elementary Grades	
Sequential	Explain phenomena in a linear sequence.	How recycled paper is made; how a bill becomes a law
Causal	Explain phenomena in a linear sequence showing how one step causes the next.	How a volcano erupts; solar eclipse
Cyclical	Explains phenomena in a cyclical way, where the last step is also the beginning of the cycle.	The life cycle of a frog; the water cycle
Systems	How a system works. Includes description of the components and how they relate and interact with each other.	How the desert works as an ecosystem; how the branches of government work
Factorial	Factors that contribute to an event or outcome.	Factors that create the conditions for a tornado; factors that led to World War II

This chapter will focus on the five types of explanations appropriate for elementary school. Sequential, causal, and cyclical explanations require the information to be presented in a temporal sequence, making it easier for young learners to understand and practice. The other two types require categorization and relationships, which are more difficult cognitive skills for children.

Sometimes, explanations can be confused with recounts or procedures. For example, when children are asked to "explain" how they solved a math problem, it is actually a recount because they are describing what they did one time when solving a math problem. It would be better to ask them to "tell" how they did it. If they are giving instructions on how to solve the problem, then that is a procedure. When a teacher requested examples of books that included procedures, a librarian included the book *How Are Sneakers Made?,* which is not a book of instructions describing how to make sneakers, but an explanation of how they are made in a factory.

Grade Levels and Content Areas

Writing any kind of explanation is difficult for children. The sentences need to accurately express the scientific or historical meaning. With pre-K to 3rd grades, writing explanations can be limited to just using diagrams with labels, accompanied by an oral explanation. Fourth- and 5th-grade products should include writing as well as diagrams (See Table 7.2).

TABLE 7.2 Types of Explanation by Grade Level

Type of Explanation	*Content Area*	*Oral + Labeled Diagram*			*Written + Labeled Diagram*	
		Pre-K–2	3	4–5	3	4–5
Sequential	Science	✓	✓	✓	✓	✓
	History			✓		✓
Causal	Science		✓	✓		✓
Cyclical	Science	✓	✓	✓	✓	✓
Systems	Science			✓		✓
	History			✓		✓
Factorial	Science			✓		✓
	History			✓		✓

Explanations fit with a number of topics included in the science curriculum as well as some of the social studies curriculum of elementary schools (See Table 7.3). The topics themselves distinguish the level of difficulty. The level of technicality can be adapted to facilitate understanding among children. Science explanations, especially of familiar phenomena, are probably easier for younger children than explanations related to historical topics, which are more abstract and difficult to demonstrate. Within science explanations, explaining *how* is easier than explaining *why*. Table 7.2 suggests explanations to introduce at each grade level and in which mode—oral, written, or both.

It is also a good idea to reinforce the students' ability to write explanations by carrying out lessons in different content areas. For example, in 5th grade, students could start with a unit on making recycled paper during ELA, do an explanation on evolution and animal adaptation by writing a sequential explanation on how reptiles evolved to become birds during science (See *How Birds Fly*, pp. 4–5), and write an explanation of how a bill becomes a law for social studies (See Table 7.3 for sample mentor texts). If the school has a science specialist, he or she could work together with the classroom teacher.

Explanations Unit

There are two approaches to teaching explanations: (1) oral explanations with labeled diagrams and (2) written explanations in which students learn the stages and language of various types of explanations dependent on their grade level. The oral explanations are best implemented as lessons within content units that lend themselves to explanations. Therefore, these explanations can be done as short oral activities with all grade levels whenever those topics are covered throughout the year. For example, students can do the life cycle of an animal

TABLE 7.3 Sample Topics and Mentor Texts

Type of Explanation	*Content Area*	*Example*	*Mentor Text*
Sequential	Science	The process followed to recycle; respiratory system (how air travels through the system)	www.factmonster.com/ipka/A0934633.html (*Includes glass, plastic, aluminum, and paper*) www.ehow.com/how-does_5387071_human-respiratory-system-works.html
	History	How a bill becomes a law	http://kids.clerk.house.gov/grade-school/lesson.html?intID=17
Causal	Science	How a volcano erupts; solar eclipse	www.ask.com/question/how-do-volcanoes-erupt www.hko.gov.hk/gts/event/event-solar-eclps11_e.htm
Cyclical	Science	The life cycle of a frog; water cycle; carbon cycle; electricity circuit	www.tooter4kids.com/Frogs/life_cycle_of_frogs.htm www.sciencekids.co.nz/sciencefacts/weather/thewatercycle.html http://eo.ucar.edu/kids/green/cycles6.htm www.youtube.com/watch?v=VnnpLaKsqGU (Video of an electrical circuit)
Systems	Science	Circulatory system; ecosystems; electric circuit system	The website WatchKnowLearn.org has a number of videos on the circulatory system http://education.nationalgeographic.com/education/encyclopedia/ecosystem/?ar_a=1 (General and specific explanations of ecosystems) http://kids.discovery.com/tell-me/curiosity-corner/science/how-do-electric-circuits-work (Short explanation) www.petervaldivia.com/technology/electricity/moving-charges.php (Electric circuit diagram with explanation)
	History	Checks and balances in the Constitution	"14.7. Limiting Power: Checks and Balances" in *History Alive!: America's Past* (p. 148)
Factorial	Science	Factors that create the conditions for a thunderstorm	www.uwec.edu/jolhm/eh/barnier/tornado.htm (the factors for a thunderstorm are included in the first paragraph within a larger sequential explanation of thunderstorms that may turn to tornadoes)
	History	Factors that led to World War II	www.historyonthenet.com/WW2/causes.htm (*Difficult*) www.johndclare.net/RoadtoWWII7a.htm

in kindergarten, the water cycle in 1st grade, and how something becomes a temporary magnet in 4th grade. A full explanation unit should be planned only from grades 3 to 5.

The remainder of the chapter first offers suggestions for how to teach oral explanations that can be implemented at all grade levels, followed by how to teach students to write explanations through two examples (and two types): a sequential scientific explanation on how recycled paper is made (appropriate for grades 3 and up) and a systems explanation on the branches of government (typically taught in grade 5). Teachers can adapt the suggestions for these two particular explanations to teach the other explanation types. (See Figures 7.1–7.4 for all graphic organizers.)

Oral Explanations (Pre-K–5)

This lesson's suggestions assume that children have not been exposed to explanations previously. Once a school implements the teaching of explanations throughout the grades, teachers will be able to expect more of children as they advance from year to year. This lesson will be illustrated using the life cycle of a frog. Similar lessons can be done throughout the year with other topics and other types of explanations.

LESSON 1. The Life Cycle of a Frog

Goal: To teach students how a cycle explanation works by manipulating and talking about the components.

Materials: YouTube animation: www.youtube.com/watch?v=7NhA9SHunKs. Mat with the Life Cycle of a Frog: www.communication4all.co.uk/Screen%20Shot%20Images/Frog%20Life%20Cycle%20Word%20Mat.png. PowerPoint for Grades 2–3 and up: classroom.jc-schools.net/sci-units/frog-cycle.ppt; Printable Book: www.enchantedlearning.com/subjects/amphibians/books/froglifecycle/. Chart paper with the statement of the phenomenon on top: "A frog goes through four stages from egg to adult." For older students, the statement should be more technical: "The metamorphosis of a frog includes four stages." Labeled cards with images illustrating each event in the cycle: adult frog, eggs, tadpoles (with and without legs), and froglet, as well as arrows or cards that include only the images with space for the students to label or blank cards for students to draw the images and label them. Chart paper.

Activities

- Show the video on the life cycle.
- Alternatives depending on grade level:
  a. Show the labeled cards and discuss with the students.
  b. Show the cards with images and have students label them.

c. Have students create their own cards and labels.
d. Have students create their own cards and write a short sentence for each stage of the cycle.

- Create the cycle on the chart paper with input from the students using the statement of the phenomenon and the cards and the arrows.
- Reproduce the life cycle mat. Cut it as a puzzle with each stage having a separate section. Give the pieces to student groups to put together. The puzzle can either have the labels left blank, requiring students to label them, or students can write sentences, depending on age.
- Ask a few students to show their puzzle and orally explain the life cycle of the frog. Make sure that students express themselves accurately and encourage the use of technical terms, making sure that students understand them.

Written Explanations (Grades 3–5)

General Preparation

In preparation to start the unit and on the basis of the school-wide decisions of which genre to teach at which grade level and in connection to which content area, teachers should:

- Determine the content, writing, and language standards
- Choose resources
- Decide how students are going to be grouped
- Decide on writing products: medium, multimodality, authenticity
- Build content knowledge
- Teach students to appropriate academic language
- Plan lessons based on analysis of students' uncoached writing.

There are extensive suggestions about each of these points in chapter 2. Following are considerations specific to this genre with respect to the CCSS, resources, appropriating academic language, and prompts for uncoached writing.

In the CCSS, explanations are included within informational/explanatory genres in the ELA standards. The purpose and stages of the genre are addressed in the Writing Standards section on Text Types and Purpose. The CCSS informational/explanatory genres include procedures, reports, explanations, and the historical genres. However, the CCSS does not distinguish all of these genres within information/explanatory. Rather, it is only the sample texts in Appendix B that reflect that the CCSS authors had all of these genres in mind. Most of the explanation texts are examples of sequential explanations *(Wind Power, Fire! Fire!; Follow the Water From Brook to Ocean; From Seed to Pumpkin; About Time: A First Look at Time and Clocks)*. The text *Volcanoes* is an example of causal explanation. There are no examples given of the other types of explanations.

The CCSS are rather general and, for the most part, fit best with reports. There is no indication of the differences among the types or text organizations of explanations. There is a generic reference to linking ideas "using words, phrases, and clauses (e.g., *in contrast, especially*)" (CCSS.ELA-Literacy.W.5.2c). As shown later, depending on the type of explanation, specific types of text connectives are needed.

The language standards for K–5 are generic, so an explanation unit will cover a number of them. For this reason, the CCSS provide some ELA standards that support explanations, but do not address all elements of an explanation. In explanations, the use of technical and abstract vocabulary is essential. The CCSS does list a number of standards related to "Vocabulary Acquisition and Use." However, most of them describe how to learn vocabulary, with only one standard for each grade level related to use. Although proper use of various tenses is mentioned, the specific use of present tense, a mark of many explanations, is not included. References to grammar are found in simple standards related to student use. For example, the standard "use adjectives and adverbs, and choose between them depending on what it is to be modified" does not address the complexity of these functions or how students are to use them in writing (CCSS.ELA-Literacy.L2.1e). Further, the importance of learning how to create noun groups with a number of adjectivals to provide information in a compact way or the need for adverbials to include specific and accurate information is not included. The grammatical standards are simply whether students use the features. They do not support functional grammar, or how these elements contribute to the meaning in a particular genre.

The Internet and science and social studies textbooks are good sources of explanations (See Table 7.3).

Simultaneous with learning content, students need to learn the language that they need to understand the mentor texts and to write about a given area of content. For example, to understand the mentor text for the systems explanation introduced later in this chapter, students need to understand such concepts as the *Constitution, check, balance, pass/veto a law, challenge a law in court, unconstitutional,* and *impeachment.* Because this reading assumes that students have already studied the three branches of government, students should be able to understand such concepts as *branches of government, president, Congress, Senate, Legislature, Supreme Court,* and *Judicial.* Even though this may be assumed, this content is likely worth reviewing.

Unlike the science explanations, vocabulary in social studies explanations is more difficult to introduce because it cannot be as easily demonstrated with hands-on activities. Further, social studies vocabulary can be difficult because there are often multiple meanings of words. Students may be familiar with one meaning of a word but not with the one used in social studies or science. For example, the word *branch* will most likely be associated with trees and not with components of a system.

If the school has a science specialist, this teacher should teach not only science content, but also the academic language needed to express the scientific concepts accurately (See chapter 2 for examples).

> **PROMPT FOR UNCOACHED WRITING**
>
> *Write an explanation based on the diagram on the board.* The diagram represents an explanation covered in an earlier lesson that has only been done orally. The explanation should be of the same type as the one the students will write.

Teachers analyze the writing that emerges from the prompt using the Analysis of Student Work: Purpose and Stages form found in the end-of-chapter resources to determine what the students can already do and what their challenges are. Teachers can use the Unit Plan (Appendix A) to plot the necessary lessons.

Part I: Purpose and Stages of the Genre

Purpose of Explanations

Different types of explanations have different purposes (See Table 7.1). The differences between sequential and cyclical explanations are minimal. They both explain the phenomenon in a sequence, but in the cyclical the last event becomes the first event to complete the cycle. Causal explanations add cause to the explanation sequence. The purpose of systems and factorial explanations are quite different from each other and from the other three. A systems explanation shows how a system works and a factorial explanation includes the factors that contribute to an event or outcome.

The verbs in an explanation are usually in the present tense. If an explanation is about something that no longer exists (e.g., dinosaurs), the verbs will be in the past tense (Knapp & Watkins, 2005). For example, in the explanation of the evolution of reptiles to birds, all of the verbs are in the past tense: "Some scaly reptiles **began** climbing trees to escape from enemies" (*How Birds Fly*, p. 4).

Features of Students' Writing

Students understand that they have to explain the ideas in their writing. Their writing usually includes the word "because" to do so. However, without instruction, it is difficult for students to write good explanations. To elicit the uncoached piece, a 4th-grade teacher carried out an experiment with students putting one piece of moist bread and one piece of dry bread in separate plastic bags. They observed how long each piece of bread took to decay. On the basis of this experiment, the teacher asked students to write why the bread decayed. Rachel wrote:

Why?

I think that the dampbread decayed faster because the water couldn't take the water and the bread coudn't fight it. It also needed air to stay fresh. Since it was sealed for 8–9 days, It was hard for the bread to not decay. It decayed because the bread said "I cant take it!" Thats why it decayed.

	1	*2*	*3*	*4*	*Uncoached Writing Comments*
Purpose					
Causal: One step causes the next.	✓				Reflects elements of procedural recounts, such as documenting observations, and of a narrative, such as dialogue and personifying inanimate objects.
Verb Tense					
Present unless the participant does not exist any longer (e.g., dinosaurs). Factorial historical (past tense)	✓				Mostly past tense, consistent with the recount genre.

Instead of explaining why the pieces of bread decayed, Rachel described what happened. Her attempt to give reasons was not accurate. She also personified the bread. Knapp and Watkins (2005) found similar switches of purpose in children's explanation writing.

It is possible that using an experiment in connection to the explanation prompt caused students to write recounts because they naturally want to write about what happened rather that why it is a particular way. Most students in the same class had elements of recounts in their writing.

LESSON 2. Becoming Familiar With the Type of Explanation and the Purpose

Goal: To understand the purpose of a particular type of explanation by being exposed to examples.

Materials: Examples of the type of written explanations that students will write (See Table 7.3 for suggestions).

Activities

- Read aloud and discuss the purpose. Include explanations that students have encountered before in various content area lessons. In the case of scientific explanations that are demonstrated through an experiment, distinguish between the procedure followed in the experiment and the explanation of how or why things happen repeatedly and not just in this one experiment.

- Explore videos. For example, the following videos are good examples of sequential explanations (the easiest for students to learn):
    - "From Tree to Paper | How Paper is Made | The Office Supplies Supermarket": www.youtube.com/watch?v=jGH7kQ30SKo
    - "How It's Made Marbles": www.youtube.com/watch?v=RU_lCrjfMaw
    - "How It's Made—Copy Paper—Jeans—Computers—Plate Glass": www.youtube.com/watch?v=U4HlUVdsoKU
    - "How It's Made, Playing Cards": www.youtube.com/watch?v=rsrrMgotapQ
- Discuss the difference in purpose for genres that the students have encountered, especially recounts and procedures.

FEATURES OF ED BALLARD'S EXPLANATION UNIT ON ELECTRICITY (4TH GRADE)

1. Developed content knowledge by introducing a new concept every week through written resources and experiments. For example, to teach which materials are good conductors and which can serve as insulators, he read aloud the book *Conductors and Insulators* and had his 4th graders create an electric circuit to test different materials for being either conductors or insulators of electricity. Students noted their findings in their notebooks.
2. Taught the structure of an explanation starting with the statement of the phenomenon followed by the explanation sequence, by modeling explanations orally and reading mentor texts.
3. Noted the difference between explanations and procedures, already familiar to students.
4. Jointly constructed explanations with the students.
5. Taught action verbs to be used in the present and generalized participants, pointing out that they do not describe what happened one time, but how it works.
6. Taught technical vocabulary throughout the lesson by creating a word bank with the words and a simple definition and diagram. He also used oral discussion to deepen the understanding of the terms. Both teachers and students created labeled diagrams, while the students used new terms in theirs.
7. Students independently wrote a full explanation with the accompanying diagram at the end of the unit (Hodgson-Drysdale & Ballard, 2011).

Stages of Explanations

The structure of explanations differs depending on the type and the content area (See Table 7.4).

All explanations start with a general statement to introduce the phenomenon by describing or classifying it (Knapp & Watkins, 2005). For example, a general statement could read, "With the aid of pumps, fluids—gases such as air, and liquids such as water and oil—are able to transmit great power and drive machines" (*How Things Work*, p. 38) or "Wind turbines use the power of moving air currents to spin their propellers. These are huge windmill-like blades on top of a tall tower. As they spin, generators inside the turbines make electricity, which is sent via cables underground" (*How Things Work Encyclopedia,* p. 66).

The generalized statement is distant from the immediate experience of students' inquiry activities, so they need to be taught to shift from writing about specific activities to the broader phenomenon using generalized nouns such as *electricity* and *volcanoes.* Sometimes, a broader noun is preceded by an indefinite article (e.g., *a closed circuit, a bulb*).

In historical explanations, in addition to the identifying statement, there is some historical background that provides the context. For example, an explanation about the factors that caused World War II would be preceded by background information on that time in history.

TABLE 7.4 Type of Explanation and Stages

Type of Explanation	*Stages*	
	Science	*History*
Sequential	• Phenomenon identification • Explanation sequence	• Identifying statement • Explanation sequence
Causal	• Phenomenon identification • Explanation sequence indicating causality	
Cyclical	• Phenomenon identification • Cyclical explanation sequence	
System	• Phenomenon identification • System description • System explanation and interaction among components • Generalization	• Identifying statement with historical background • System description • System explanation and interaction among components • Generalization
Factorial	• Outcome • Factors • General statement	• Outcome • Factors • Reinforcement of the factors

Sources: Coffin (2006); Derewianka & Jones (2012)

The body of an explanation differs depending on the explanation type, with each type demanding different skills. Sequential, causal, and cyclical explanations all require events following each other, but causal explanations involve one event causing the next while cyclical explanations have the last event mark the beginning of the cycle. Factorial and systems explanations require students to sort out elements that are not organized in a sequence, but in factors or components. In addition, in factorial explanations, the factors need to be listed in order of importance, while systems explanations require that relationships among components be indicated. Sequential, causal, and cyclical explanations conclude with the last event, while factorial and systems explanations have a concluding statement.

Features of Students' Writing

When students like Rachel switch the purpose, they typically do not include the stages of an explanation. There was no statement of the phenomenon or explanation sequence in Rachel's piece, nor in the writing of other students who wrote something closer to a recount. Both Harris (2011) and Hodgson-Drysdale & Ballard (2011) found that students had difficulty writing the identifying statement of the phenomenon, even after instruction. In one writing sample, "the student begins 'A circuit can make a lightbulb turn on,' which would be a more complete initial statement if it were phrased as 'Electricity flowing through a complete circuit can make a lightbulb turn on,'" (Hodgson-Drysdale & Ballard, p. 40). Even when students attempt an explanation sequence, their writing sometimes reveals limited understanding of the scientific phenomenon or that the sequence has gaps. Thus, instruction needs to constantly focus on content as well as structure.

Lessons to Teach Stages

Instruction of stages will be illustrated through lessons related to two different types of explanations, a sequential explanation for science and a systems explanation for social studies. These were chosen because the first represents the easier type of explanation with a temporal organization. As we saw in earlier genres, chronological organization is always easier for children. Systems explanations do not include clear sequential paths but rather more complex relationships, making them more difficult for children.

Lessons introduce the mentor text and suggest how to teach the stages for each of the two examples. Teachers can use the ideas presented in these lessons to teach the structure of the other types of explanations.

The lessons on language, audience and voice, and creating a cohesive text will be presented together and applied to both mentor texts because the issues are comparable regardless of the type of explanation.

Sequential Explanation: How Paper Is Recycled (Grades 3 and Up)

Before working with the mentor text, students need to be introduced to the related technical vocabulary: *recycled, fibers, pulp/pulping facility, vat, chemical, debris, spit out,* and *screen.* One way to introduce all of this vocabulary can be by creating recycled paper in class (See instructions at http://voices.yahoo.com/recycled-paper-project-fun-kids-adults-3082080.html). In this procedure on how to make recycled paper in class, the process described is similar to how recycled paper is produced at a plant and terms like *pulp, recycle,* and *screen* are introduced. If there are L2 learners in the class, other everyday vocabulary may be also difficult. In this case, after the initial work with the text, work in a group with L2 learners, ask them to point out or underline the words that they do not recognize, and teach those words to them.

Stages	*Mentor Text*
Title	**How Paper Is Recycled**
Phenomenon identification	Recycled paper is made from used paper. Paper is made of tiny fibers. Because these fibers eventually become weak, paper cannot be recycled forever.
Explanation sequence	• The paper is sorted out in the recycling center and transported to a pulping facility. • The paper is soaked and heated in huge vats, becoming pulp. Chemicals in the liquid separate the ink from the paper. • The pulp is screened and cleaned to remove glue, other debris, and the remaining ink. • The pulp is refined and beaten to make it ready to become paper again. • The pulp is fed into a machine that spits out the pulp onto a flat moving screen where it forms sheets. • The sheets are rolled and dried and ready for their new life.

Source: Adapted from www.factmonster.com/ipka/A0934633.html

Because the text is for children, the explanation sequence is facilitated by writing it as a bulleted list.

LESSON 3. Stages of a Sequential Explanation

Goal: To familiarize students with the stages of explanations using published texts.

Materials: Texts with examples of sequential explanations (See Table 7.3 and additional resources at the end of the chapter). Large version of the sequential graphic organizer (See examples at the end of the chapter). When working with 3rd grade, the graphic organizer should include the statement of the phenomenon. For 4th and 5th grade, however, it should not because students will learn how to write the statement of the phenomenon in later lessons.

Activities

- Read aloud the mentor text.
- As you read, point to the graphic organizer to indicate from which stage of the explanation you are reading.
- Repeat with other sequential explanations.

LESSON 4. Writing/Diagramming the Explanation Sequence

Goal: To learn how to put together an explanation sequence by diagramming and writing short captions, helping the students to create explanations without using too much written language.

Materials: Large version of sequential graphic organizer (See end of the chapter). Diagram of a sequential explanation broken up into sections (or you can have students draw each step after rereading the mentor text). Copies of small versions of the graphic organizer. List of a few sequential explanations and resources with the content of such explanations.

Activities

- Take the diagram or drawing of each event in the explanation sequence and discuss the appropriate order.
- Have students paste each event on the class graphic organizer on the left side of each box.
- Ask the class to verbalize what is in the illustration and write captions or labels next to the respective drawing or photograph. Make sure that students express themselves accurately and encourage their use of technical terms, ensuring that students understand each term. For example, *pulp* is something soft like the inside of the fruits they eat.
- Divide the class into groups and have them choose one explanation from the list you prepared. Provide them with a graphic organizer and the resources for them to research the explanation. Have students, as a group, produce a diagram with labels (3rd grade) or captions (4th and 5th grades). Then, have each group explain the diagram orally to the class. Encourage accuracy and use of technical terms.

LESSON 5. Write Full Explanations (Grades 4–5)

Goal: To fully develop written explanations using scientific language that clearly expresses the ideas.

Materials: Class and individual graphic organizers with explanation sequence and notations that were developed in the previous lesson.

Activities

- Show the class graphic organizer with notations and have students propose full sentences. Negotiate each sentence with the students before you write to make sure that the content is accurate and that the language is technical.
- Working in groups, have students take one of the graphic organizers produced in the previous lesson and orally propose full sentences. When the group is happy with the sentence, then students can write it down. Take turns working with individual groups to make sure their explanations are accurate.

LESSON 6. The Statement of the Phenomenon (Grades 4–5)

Goal: To teach students how to write the statement of the phenomenon.
Materials: Graphic organizers with the explanation sequence produced from previous lessons.

Activities

- Using the graphic organizer with the explanation sequence of the mentor text, ask students what phenomenon the sequence explains, for example, "recycled paper is made of used paper." Write this phenomenon at the very top of the graphic organizer.
- Ask groups which explanation they worked on during the previous lesson. Have them orally propose the statement of the phenomenon. Some sample statements could be, "Animals evolve in order to survive. As birds slowly evolved, they became better able to escape danger, find food, and defend themselves" (*How Birds Fly,* p. 4); "Creating laws is the U.S. House of Representatives' most important job. All laws in the United States begin as bills. Before a bill can become a law it must be approved by the U.S. House of Representatives, the U.S. Senate, and the President" (*How a Bill Becomes a Law;* see Table 7.3).
- Discuss if the statement needs revisions.
- Have students write the final version at the top of their graphic organizers in the designated space.

Systems Explanation: Checks and Balances in the Constitution

The text "Limiting Power: Checks and Balances" illustrates a systems explanation. Following is the text broken up in the various stages.

Stages	*Mentor Text*
Title	**Limiting Power: Checks and Balances** In *History Alive!: America's Past*, p. 148.
Historical background	The men who wrote the Constitution wanted a strong and lasting government. One way that they tried to achieve this goal was by designing a system of "checks and balances."
Identifying statement	The Constitution gives each branch of government the power to "check" (stop) certain actions of the other branches. It also balances each branch's powers with the powers of the other branches.
Systems description*	
Systems explanation Interaction between components *(a labeled diagram showing this interaction accompanies the text)*	Checks and balances help to make sure that no one branch becomes too powerful. For example, Congress can pass laws, but the president approves or vetoes them. The president's power is a check on the power of Congress. What if Congress and the president agree on a law that disagrees with the Constitution? If the law is challenged in court, the judicial branch has the power to decide whether it is unconstitutional. The court's power is a check on the power of the other two branches. How are the powers of the different branches balanced? Suppose the president wants one thing and Congress wants another. Congress cannot make laws without the president's signature, and the president needs Congress to pass the laws he wants. Their powers balance each other. And even though the courts can declare laws unconstitutional, federal judges are appointed by the president with the approval of the Senate. Another example of checks and balances is impeachment. Suppose members of the executive or judicial branch try to abuse their power. Congress can impeach them and remove them from office.
Generalization	In these ways, the Constitution tries to make sure that no one branch of the government becomes too powerful.

* This text is missing the systems description because each branch was thoroughly described earlier. Teachers could create with their class three sentences describing each branch of government.

LESSON 7. Stages of a Systems Explanation

Goal: To introduce students to the stages of a systems explanation by reading and deconstructing the mentor text.

Materials: On chart paper, draw the systems explanation graphic organizer (See graphic organizer Figure 7.3 at the end of the chapter). Mentor texts and videos (Choose those appropriate to the grade level and children's interest).

Activities

- Read aloud the mentor text.
- As you read, point to the graphic organizer indicating which stage of the explanation you are reading.
- Repeat with other systems explanations in other mentor texts and videos. Make sure that each text is a system explanation.

LESSON 8. Interrelationships of the Components of a System (Grades 4–5)

Goal: To show students that what makes a system is the interrelationships between its components.

Materials: Three 8 × 5 cards per group of students. Six arrows per group, with one interrelationship (e.g., "can veto bills") written on each (See aforementioned mentor text).

Activities

- Group students and give each group three cards.
- Re-read the system description in the mentor text and discuss how the system works.
- Have student groups draw each component of the system on a separate card, for example, president, Congress, the Supreme Court (They can also download pictures from the Internet).
- Re-read the interaction between components of the system and discuss.
- Give each group the six arrows, each describing one interrelationship, and ask the students to arrange the arrows so that each points from one branch of government to another to show an interrelationship. Students can paste the cards and the arrows to a sheet of paper.
- Ask one or two groups to orally present their results to the whole class.

LESSON 9. Jointly Constructing a Systems Explanation

Goal: To jointly write a systems explanation with students, using the school as the system.

Materials: Large cards with the name of the members of the school community and arrows. Sentence strips to write the identification of the system at the top and the generalization at the bottom.

Activities

- Ask students to name each member of the school community (e.g., principal, teachers, janitors, students) and write them on the component description boxes of the large systems graphic organizer.

- Ask students what each person does and add this description to the component explanation boxes.
- Give each group a set of the large cards (with a member of the community listed on each) and some of the arrows. Have students discuss how the members of the school community relate and then propose how they will lay out the large graphic organizer.
- Ask students to identify the system (e.g., "A school is an institution that imparts learning") and write it at the top in the "Identifying statement" box on the graphic organizer.
- Have students give a generalization and write it in the bottom box (e.g., Schools allow all children the opportunity to learn).

LESSON 10. Write Full Explanations

Goal: To guide students through writing a systems explanation.

Materials: Components of systems that students have studied during the year or in previous grades, including cards with the members of the system and arrows showing relationships. For example, systems could include the rainforest, the desert, the solar system, and the circulatory system. Please note that some texts on systems are not a systems explanation, but a sequential explanation (e.g., how food travels through the digestive system or how air circulates through the respiratory system).

Activities

- Give each group of students (or have students choose) the components of a different system.
- Have students put the components together and present on it. This type of activity can also be done during the school year when those systems are taught, and then reviewed when the explanation unit is taught.
- Have the groups write the section of the explanation on the components and how they relate to one another, including a diagram to illustrate what they have written.
- Have students orally propose the statement of the phenomenon. First, have a few students share with the whole class, then have all students do it within their groups.
- Confer with students to make sure their explanations are accurate.
- Have students propose a generalization to conclude the piece.
- Have selected students orally present their explanations using their diagrams as a guide.

Part II: Language

Explanations share a number of language features with reports, such as technical and abstract vocabulary, action verbs, present tense, passive voice, generalized participants, complex nominal groups, adverbials, and clause complexes. Therefore, after analysis of student work, teachers can decide in which of the areas included in this section students need additional instruction. They can also use similar lessons to focus on the various language features, as suggested for reports. One feature of language that distinguishes explanations from reports is the text connective. In explanations, each component of the explanation sequence is related to the other. Thus, text connectives help to indicate sequence, cause, and condition, depending on the type of explanation.

Denise, a 4th grader, wrote the following piece after the students had learned to write explanations in the context of an electricity unit.

Prompt: Explain how electricity in a circuit can cause a light bulb to light.

The D-cell battery holed's [holds] the
Electricity, the wire's are conected [connected]
to the positive or Negative
end's. Onets [Once] the wire is conectied [connected]
to the end's of ether [either] the positive
or negative, the wire must be
atached [attached] to the tip of the Receiver
A.K.A lite bolb . . . The pathway (A.K.A
The Wire) should be conected [connected] to the
metal jacket. Onets [Once] the path way is
conekted [connected] to the metal jacket
the wire should be cunected [connected] to
the positive or Negative end
then the lite bolb [light bulb] will start to
heat up and lite up! like so.

Verbs

As illustrated by selections from the mentor texts, the verbs (bold) in explanations are mostly action verbs. Passive voice (underlined) is often used because the focus is on the paper or the judges and not the person carrying out the action. In the historical mentor text, the historical background provided at the beginning is in the past tense, but the explanation itself is in the present tense and written with passive voice.

How Paper Is Recycled	*Limiting Power: Checks and Balances*
Recycled paper ***is made from*** used paper. Paper ***is made of*** tiny fibers. Because these fibers eventually **become** weak, paper ***cannot be recycled*** forever. • The paper ***is sorted out*** in the recycling center and ***transported*** to a pulping facility. • The paper ***is soaked*** and ***heated*** in huge vats, becoming pulp. Chemicals in the liquid **separate** the ink from the paper. • The pulp ***is screened*** and ***cleaned*** to remove glue, other debris, and the remaining ink.	Congress **cannot make** laws with the president's signature, and the president **needs** Congress **to pass** the laws he wants. Their powers **balance** each other. And even though the courts **can declare** laws unconstitutional, federal judges ***are appointed*** by the president with the approval of the Senate.

Denise uses action verbs. She does not use passive voice. The real problem with her verbs is the tense because she describes or reports what the elements look like using the present perfect (*the wire is conectied* [connected]) rather than explain how it works in the present, (the wire conducts the electricity). Like with Rachel, writing an explanation after watching an experiment leads Denise to write a mixture of description of what she sees *(the wires are connected)* and a procedure *(the wires should be connected),* rather than *the wires, connected to the positive and the negative sides of the battery, conduct electricity from the battery to the light bulb and back to the battery.* What causes the light bulb to light up is the wires *conducting* electricity, a concept not included in the piece. Teachers need to be clear that experiments are carried out to understand how things work, but when students write an explanation, the focus needs to be on explaining how things work and not what happened in the experiment.

LESSON 11. Verbs

Goal: To teach students to use action verbs, passive voice, and correct verb tense if there are still problems with the purpose.

Materials: A sentence or two from an explanation text written on chart paper and the equivalent sentence if it were a procedure or a description of the diagram, for example, for the explanation text "One end of the filament connects to the side of the metal screw base on the bulb" (*Magnetism and Electricity,* p. 33), a procedure would be written, "Connect one end of the filament to the metal screw base on the bulb" and a description of a diagram would read, "One end of the filament is connected to the metal screw base on the bulb." Mentor texts. Student work.

Activities

- If problems with purpose persist and are revealed through the verb groups, show the students the example sentence from the published explanation and the equivalent as a procedure and description of diagram. Discuss the difference in purpose in the sentences.

- Show students' texts that show similar problems to those in Rachel's text. Have students suggest revisions.
- Deconstruct a mentor text and explain the features of verbs in explanations.
- Choose a student text. Have students indicate the verbs and discuss the features that you are reviewing. Ask the student author and class if any changes are appropriate.
- Repeat with one or two more students' samples.
- Working in groups or pairs, have students look at the verbs in their explanations, review the features discussed, and make any necessary changes.

Generalized Participants

Generalized participants represent the whole category, for example, *paper, pulp, Congress,* and *president.* The explanation is not about a specific president, but the office of the president in general. An explanation of the circulatory system will include things like *heart, vein,* and *artery,* referring to any person and not those specific to a particular person.

Denise does not use generalized participants, but talks about the things that were used in the experiment. She writes about *the wires, the D-cell battery,* and *the light bulb,* but not about wires, batteries, and light bulbs in general to create an electric circuit.

	1	*2*	*3*	*4*	*Uncoached Writing Comments*
Generalized Participants (frogs, volcanoes, Congress)			✓		Uses "the," which makes the writing specific as if she is describing this particular electric cycle rather than telling how any electric cycle works "A D-cell battery holds electricity . . ."

LESSON 12. Generalized Participants

Goal: To help students understand the reason for using generalized participants and revise their writing accordingly.

Materials: A sentence or two from an explanation text written on chart paper and the equivalent sentence if it were a procedural recount. For example, the explanation "*Wires* conduct electricity from the battery to the bulb and back to the battery" was tested but required a different type of writing. To prove this explanation, students and the teacher conducted an experiment. The recount describing the steps of the experiment read, "Once *one wire* was connected to the bulb and the positive side of the battery and *the other* to the negative side of the battery, the light bulb lit up because *the wires* conducted the electricity through the circuit."

Activities

- Show the two sentences. Point at the participants in the text and ask the students what the difference is between the term *wire* in the two texts. The explanation uses the term *wire* in general, while the procedural recount talks about the specific wires used for the experiment.
- Ask the students what the sentence about wires is about. Point out the grammatical features that indicate that one sentence is generalized and the other specific (such as use of plural form and not using "the" the first time the participant is referred to).
- Choose a few student sentences, point to the participants, and discuss whether they refer to the objects in general or to particular ones. Make modifications if necessary.
- Have students work with a partner or in groups to modify the participants, if needed. Help groups with their work, as needed.

Noun Groups

Similar to reports, noun groups in explanations carry a great deal of meaning. For example, in the following samples from the mentor texts, the adjectivals (underlined) add information to the head noun (bold).

Type of Adjectival	*How Paper Is Recycled*	*Limiting Power: Checks and Balances*
Adjectives	*Recycled* **paper** is made from *used* **paper**. **Paper** is made of *tiny* **fibers**. Because *these* **fibers** eventually become *weak*, **paper** cannot be recycled forever. The **paper** is sorted out in the *recycling* **center** and transported to a *pulping* **facility**. The **paper** is soaked and heated in *huge* **vats**, becoming **pulp**.	The Constitution gives *each* **branch** of government the **power** to "check" (stop) certain actions of the other branches. It also balances *each branch's* **powers** with the **powers** of the other branches.

Type of Adjectival	*How Paper Is Recycled*	*Limiting Power: Checks and Balances*
Prepositional phrases	**Chemicals** *in the liquid*	**branch** *of government* **powers** *of the other branches*
Non-finite embedded clauses	The **paper** . . ., [becoming pulp.]	the **power** [*to "check" (stop) certain actions of the other branches.*]
Relative clauses (finite verb)	. . . a **machine** [that spits out the pulp onto a flat moving screen] [where it forms sheets.]	**men** [who wrote the Constitution] One **way** [that they tried to achieve this goal] a **law** [that disagrees with the Constitution] . . . **laws** [he wants]

Most of the adjectivals used are plain adjectives *(huge, each)* and prepositional phrases *(in the liquid, of government)*. Embedded clauses with non-finite or finite verbs also say something about the noun and are found in the more difficult social studies text. Here, the first sentence includes all three types: adjective, prepositional phrase, and embedded clause. Definitions often take the form of an apposition written using commas, dashes, or parenthesis (Derewianka & Jones, 2012). This is seen in the example, "The Constitution gives each branch of government the power to 'check' (stop)" *(Limiting Power: Checks and Balances)*. With 3rd-grade students, it is best just to work with single-word adjectives or prepositional phrases.

As in other genres, children tend to not use many adjectivals. Rachel is no exception.

	1	*2*	*3*	*4*	*Mid-unit Writing Comments*
Adjectivals (*tiny* fibers, *pulping* facility, *strong and lasting* government, the powers *of the different branches*, a law *that disagrees with the Constitution*)		✓			Uses a few adjectivals ("D-cell" "positive" "negative") and appositions with A.K.A. (also known as). "Metal jacket" needs further description.

Besides the lessons suggested here, lessons from teaching noun groups in reports can also be applied to explanations. When doing these lessons, vocabulary and content knowledge should be continually developed.

LESSON 13. Highlighting the Importance of Adjectivals

Goal: To demonstrate to students the power of adjectivals to add essential information in order to help them revise their own writing.

Materials: Paragraph with adjectivals crossed out and the nouns in bold or circled. Samples of student work that could use revision or addition of adjectivals. Projector.

Activities

- Project a paragraph with nouns in bold or circled and adjectivals covered. For example,

  "If the law is challenged in court, the ~~judicial~~ **branch** has the **power** ~~to decide whether it is unconstitutional~~. The ~~court's~~ **power** is a **check** ~~on the power of the other two branches~~." *(Limiting Power: Checks and Balances)*

- Read the paragraph aloud and ask students to try to explain what you just read.
- Uncover the adjectivals and ask, "Can you now tell me what it means?"
- Project student work and have the class identify the nouns (what they are talking about). Ask, "Are there adjectives saying something about those nouns? Do they need adjectives to be more precise?"
- Have students work with their own writing in pairs or groups, identifying nouns and discussing whether they should revise. Confer with individuals or groups as they are doing this work.

> To teach children how to add definitions, Liz Harris (Harris, 2011) included a box at the bottom of the Explanation graphic organizer where students wrote key terms and their definition. Then, she had students choose a couple of terms in their explanations that they thought should be defined. Using the definitions from their graphic organizers, the students added the definitions in their explanations with relational verbs or as an apposition. For example, one student wrote "A tornado forms by a thunder storm [,] called a super cell" (p. 235).

Adverbials

Explanations need adverbials of a variety of types to add specificity (See chapter 3 for more information). Table 7.5 illustrates how the mentor texts use adverbials (underlined), both through words and prepositional phrases. Most of them say something about the verb (bold), but the last example provides detail about an adjective (bold).

Students have encountered these types of adverbials in other genres, such as procedure and recounts. In explanations, they help to reflect whether the students understand the concepts accurately.

Denise had just one type of adverbial that was used in a number of locations, consistent with the repeated structures in her piece.

TABLE 7.5 Types of Adverbials in Mentor Texts

Type of Adverbial	*How Paper Is Recycled*	*Limiting Power: Checks and Balances*
Place (Where?)	The paper **is sorted out** *in the recycling center* and **transported** *to a pulping facility.*	Congress can impeach them and **remove** them *from office.*
Time (When?)	fibers *eventually* **become** weak	
Manner (How? What with?)		It also **balances** each branch's powers *with the powers of the other branches.* . . . federal judges **are appointed** by the president *with the approval of the Senate.*
Extent (How much?)		*too* **powerful**

	1	*2*	*3*	*4*	*Mid-unit Writing Comments*
Adverbials [be recycled *forever* (time), is challenged *in court* (place), balances each branch's powers *with the powers of the other branches* (manner)]		✓			Several adverbials of place such as "to the negative . . ."

LESSON 14. Highlighting the Importance of Adverbials

Goal: To demonstrate to students the power of adverbials to add essential information in order to help them revise their own writing.

Materials: Paragraph with adverbials crossed out and verbs in bold or circled. Samples of student work that could use revision or addition of adverbials. Projector.

Activities

- Project a paragraph with verbs in bold or circled and adverbials covered. For example,

The paper **is sorted out** ~~in the recycling~~ center and **transported** ~~to a pulping~~ facility.

- Read it aloud and ask students to try to explain what you just read.
- Uncover the adverbials and ask, "Can you now tell me what it means?"
- Project student work and have the class identify the verbs (what is happening). Ask, "Are there adverbials adding precise information? Do they need adverbials to be more precise?"
- Have students work with their own writing in pairs or groups, identifying verbs and discussing whether they should revise. Confer with individuals or groups as they are doing this work.
- Note: In chapter 4, Lessons 10–13 include additional ideas for lessons on adjectivals and adverbials.

Clause Complexes

In the upper elementary grades, both the texts that students encounter and those that they compose begin to include more complex constructions (See chapter 3 for a full description). Both mentor texts for explanations included such constructions (See Table 7.6).

TABLE 7.6 Compound and Complex Clauses

Type	*How Paper Is Recycled*	*Limiting Power: Checks and Balances*
	Compound Sentences	
Projection: Idea		Suppose | | the president wants . . . Suppose | | members of the executive or judicial branch try . . .
Additive	The sheets are rolled | | and dried | | and ready for their new life	the president wants one thing | | *and* Congress wants another Congress cannot make laws . . . , | | *and* the president needs Congress . . . Congress can impeach them | | *and* remove them from office
Variation		the president approves | | *or* vetoes them
Concessive		Congress can pass laws, | | *but* the president approves
	Complex Sentences	
Causal non-finite	to remove glue . . . ink. (purpose) to become paper again (result)	

Type	*How Paper Is Recycled*	*Limiting Power: Checks and Balances*
Causal finite	| *Because* these fibers eventually become weak, | paper cannot be recycled (reason)	
Conditional		| *If* the law is challenged in court, | the judicial branch has . . .
Concessive		| *even though* the courts can declare laws unconstitutional, | federal judges are appointed . . .

How Paper Is Recycled is an easier text and has few of these complex constructions. Additive and causal relations are often the first type that children start to write. The more difficult text, *Limiting Power: Checks and Balances,* has greater number and variety of these sentences. The purpose of using these structures is to pack more information and express relations between ideas.

Students have difficulty with clause complexes, and it is hard to tell whether ideas, grammar, or both create the challenges. Denise included a few of these constructions in her writing.

	1	*2*	*3*	*4*	*Mid-unit Writing Comments*
Clause Complexes • Logico-semantic relation appropriate • Accurate conjunction • Missed opportunities		✓			On two occasions, she starts with "Once," signaling a temporal connection. However, she changes the voice in the main clause through the use of a modal. The relation between the two clauses is odd.

Other common problems found in students' writing is the overuse of *and* and *because.* L2 learners sometimes use *when* instead of *as.* Students often string sentences together using *and.* Sometimes *and* is used appropriately to indicate an additive relation between the clauses, but other times it is unnecessary. Still, other times the sentence could be changed to express the relation more accurately. For example, these two sentences written by 4th graders could benefit from changes: (1) *We have two bread. and one is dry and the other is wet.* (2) *and the bread stayed for 5 day and then it grew mold in a plastic bag.* The first *and* can be eliminated. The second *and* in the first sentence indicates an additive relation. The second indicates a temporal relation. The latter could be more clearly expressed with a dependent clause: *After 5 days in a plastic bag, the bread grew mold.* (See Brisk & DeRosa, forthcoming, for a thorough analysis of clause complexes.)

Most times, *because* is appropriately used to indicate reason, even if the reason is not accurate (e.g., *the dampbread decayed faster because it couldn't take the water*). However, some students started their explanations with *because* (e.g., *Because when you stretched the rubber Band it will go Faster.*). The *because* is not necessary and is more typical of oral language. The reason or cause is not explained and only the facts are given.

L2 writers have difficulty with the use of adverbial phrases of time that should start with *as* (e.g., the sentence, "As the corals grow and expand, reefs take on one of three major characteristic structures—fringing, barrier or atoll."). Instead of using *as,* L2 students sometimes use *when,* giving the sentence a different meaning.

Lessons on Formation of Clause Complexes

Students attempt to use clause complex structures as their thinking becomes more complex. It is best to teach clause complexes in connection to students' own work. Because the formation of these structures is connected with expressing themselves accurately, some of these issues might have been already addressed when revising the graphic organizers for accuracy of content. If there are more issues remaining, it is best to review the students' work and decide which of the following lessons are needed.

LESSON 15. Create Clause Complexes (Grades 4–5)

Goals: To match clauses that form a clause complex (sentence) to make sense.
Materials: Clause complexes written in sentence strips and cut up to divide each clause. Include sentences that describe everyday topics as well as sentences from the texts on the topic which students are studying. Have one large set of sentences to work with the whole class and then smaller sets for the students to work on in their groups. Choose sentences from the explanations that will help to reinforce concepts. Example sentences could include the following:

When I am late,	my mother gets angry.
When the circuit is closed,	electricity flows through the filament.

Sentence starters that include the first clause in the clause complex and a conjunction that begins the second clause (e.g., "Congress proposed a bill and . . ."). Worksheet with similar types of sentence starters from concepts addressed in the explanation unit.

Activities

- Put up all of the first clauses from the sentences and have the class read them aloud.
- Show one of the second clauses and ask the students which clause it matches with to form a sentence. Once students choose a first clause to match, have them read the whole sentence and explain its meaning.
- Give students the packets with small sentence strips.
- Have students work in their groups to match the sentences.
- Show students one of the sentence starters that end in a conjunction (e.g., "Congress proposed a bill and . . .").
- Have students complete the sentence.
- Then, change the conjunction (e.g., "but") and have students complete the sentence again. Do the same activity with other sentence starters to work with the whole class.
- Give each group one worksheet with sentence starters and ask them to complete it.
- Have one group share their responses from the worksheet.

LESSON 16. Pack Simple Sentences Into Clause Complexes

Goal: To help students create sentences that combine ideas using clause complexes in order to show relationships between the ideas and to pack the writing.

Materials: Students' drafts with simple sentences underlined that could be turned into a clause complex.

Activities

- Show one of the student examples to the class. Demonstrate how you would combine the ideas.
- Show another student example. Have the students propose a combination.
- Repeat with another example.
- Have the students work in groups to practice with other drafts.

LESSON 17. Revise Students' Sentences

Goal: To help students express complex ideas clearly using clause complexes. (This activity can help review difficult concepts that students are having a hard time expressing.)

Materials: Students' drafts with a few problem sentences underlined. For example, in Denise's piece I would recommend, [Once] the wire is conectied [connected] to the end's of ether [either] the positive or negative, the wire must be atached [attached] to the tip of the Receiver A.K.A lite bolb . . . The explanation for how electricity flows through the circuit would read something like, "Electricity flows from the battery to the receiver or light bulb and back to the battery through the wires connected to the positive and negative side of the battery." Her sentence currently reads more like a procedure describing how to create a circuit (use of the temporal clause "once . . ." + clause signaling the next step).

Activities

- Show one of the student examples to the class. Demonstrate how you would revise the clause.
- Show another student example. Have the students propose revisions.
- Repeat with another example.
- Have the students work in groups revising the sentences you have underlined in the rest of the drafts. If the problem is individual or with just a few students, skip the whole-class lesson and confer with those students.

LESSON 18. Overuse of "And"

Goal: To teach students to eliminate unnecessary use of *and* or to replace it with conjunctions that express the relationship between words or ideas more accurately.

Materials: Projector. Student drafts with excessive or inappropriate use of *and*. For example, the earlier sentence could be used:

We have two bread. and one is dry and the other is wet.
and the bread stayed for 5 day and then it grew mold in a plastic bag.

Activities

- Ask students to circle all the "and"s in their drafts.
- Choose one or two drafts to work on with the whole class.
- Project the text and ask the students how "and" affects the meaning that connects the two clauses. Discuss possible modifications with the class.
- Repeat with other sentences.
- Have the students work in groups to examine the rest of their drafts.
- Walk around to help students and to ensure that they do not eliminate all "and"s, even when they are appropriately used.

Audience and Voice

An explanation will be more or less complex depending on the audience. For example, the following two explanations on how corals are formed differ in the amount of information and the number of steps and technical terms included. The first one is short and very general, accompanied with simple diagrams. The second includes more information, variation, and technical terms. A short excerpt from each illustrates the differences:

> "Coral reefs begin to form when free-swimming coral larvae attach to submerged rocks or other hard surfaces along the edges of islands or continents" (http://oceanservice.noaa.gov/education/kits/corals/coral04_reefs.html).

> "Coral reef formation is only made possible by the cumulative efforts of millions of individual organisms working over very long periods of time. When we consider that the growth rate of the most abundant Caribbean 'hard' coral *(Montastrea annularis)* is only in the range of about 3–9 mm/year, it becomes quite evident that coral reefs are built over decades and centuries—not weeks or months" (www.coral-reef-info.com/coral-reef-formation.html).

Considering the mentor texts included in the two lessons in this chapter, the recycled paper text is written simply, has very few technical terms, and includes only the major events in the process. The text on the balance of powers among the branches of government has more complex concepts, relationships, and language. The voice in an explanation is typically authoritative. The sentences are all declarative and written in the third person, and the language is factual and devoid of judgment. Occasionally modal verbs are used. For example, the mentor text on the branches of government often uses *can* to indicate what the various branches can or cannot do. This text also uses some questions, which is more typical of texts written for children. It is important that students do not feel that they need to always include questions in their own writing. Some texts for children also use the second person to create familiarity with the reader. For example, a causal explanation on sneezing uses the second person: "Sneezing, also called sternutation, is your body's way of removing an irritation from *your* nose" (http://kidshealth.org/PageManager.jsp?lic=1&article_set=10317&cat_id=124).

However, using the third person signals to the students that an event happens with everybody and not just them.

Children tend to include writing features that connect them closer to their audience. For example, they frequently use interpersonal themes (See chapter 3 for details), such as *I think that the damp bread decayed faster. . . .* It is best to encourage students to avoid these features because they place the focus on the writer rather than the topic of the explanation. Students also use the second person to address the audience directly (e.g., *because when you get a magnet and a nale* [nail] *and put the nale on the magnet the nale will become a magnet*).

Knapp and Watkins (2005) noted that children include judgments in their explanations. For example, at the end of the water cycle explanation, a child wrote, "I like rain. Rain is good for you" (p. 129). This would be a more appropriate ending for a personal recount and not for an explanation.

Denise had difficulty with being clear in her purpose and sentence construction, affecting the tenor.

	1	2	3	4	*Mid-unit Writing Comments*
Audience • Choice of topic • Choice of amount of information • Choice of specific information • Choice of specific language to represent processes, participants and their description, and circumstances		✓			The language is simple enough to be appropriate for other children. However, the explanation sequence is not clear enough for children to understand.
Voice • Choice of types of sentences • Person • No need for interpersonal theme		✓			Uses strong modals "must be," "should be." Makes it sound more like a procedure on how to create a circuit. Uses an exclamation at the end. Not common in exclamations, even for children.

LESSON 19. Audience and Voice (Tenor)

Goal: To help students revise their work to achieve an appropriate tenor.

Materials: Student work that includes tenor issues that you want to address in this lesson. Mentor texts that exemplify good models of tenor with similar context of situation as the students' writing.

Activities

The following are typical issues in students' writing that impact the tenor:

- Use of technical terms instead of everyday language
- Level of complexity depending on the audience
- Use of declarative sentences (Some questions may be appropriate when writing for a younger audience)
- Use of third person
- Avoidance of interpersonal themes
- Avoidance of judgment.

Choose the particular tenor issue that you want to address and do the following:

- Read mentor texts and discuss the specific issue in that text.
- Show a sample of student work and ask the class what they notice with respect to the particular tenor issue.
- Ask students to propose revisions.
- Repeat with another sample student text.
- Have students work in groups to revise their texts for the same feature.

Creating a Cohesive Text

Use of appropriate text connectives, avoidance of interpersonal themes, and use of lexical ties help to create a cohesive text. Explanations use different kinds of connectives depending on the type and the audience. Sequential and cyclical explanations use temporal connectives, such as *when, before,* and *after.* For example, in the mentor text, *How a Bill Becomes a Law,* a number of the paragraphs start with *when.* The mentor text about the life cycle of a frog includes several uses of *after.* Some mentor texts for children use bullets for each event in the sequence, as in *How Paper Is Recycled,* or numbers, as in the text on the evolution of reptiles to birds in *How Birds Fly.*

Other explanations also have temporal connections. In addition, causal explanations often include connectives, including *because, therefore,* and *as a result.* Factorial explanations may require enumerative text connectives that add information (e.g., *first factor, second factor*). The mentor text, *How Tornados Are Formed,* uses *first thing* and *second factor* to signal the factors. However, explanations written for children sometimes do not include connectors, as seen in the branches of government mentor text. Unless students' writing requires the text connectives to make the paragraphs clear, it is best not to teach text connectives because students will often overuse them.

An important feature to teach in connection with explanations is lexical ties, especially collocation (words that occur together because they connect with the topic of the explanation) (See chapter 3 for more information on lexical ties).

When a text uses the terms that are related to the topic, then lexical ties are established, helping the reader become aware of the topic of the text. Comparing the noun groups (bold) and verb groups (underlined) of the mentor text and the 4th grader's explanation, we can quickly see that the noun and verb groups in the mentor text all connect with the paper recycling process. In the 4th grader's explanation, the only verb connected with the topic is *decayed.* The verb *fight* would be hardly associated with bread.

How Paper Is Recycled	*4th grader's Explanation on Why Bread Decayed*
The **paper** is *sorted out* in the **recycling center** and *transported* to a **pulping facility.** The **paper** is *soaked* and *heated* in **huge vats**, *becoming* **pulp**. **Chemicals** in the **liquid** *separate* the **ink** from the **paper**.	I *think* that the **dampbread** *decayed* faster because the **water** *couldn't take* the **water** and the **bread** *couldn't fight* it.

Denise appropriately used a number of lexical items related to the electric circuit. However, because there was confusion about the purpose, the text connective was not appropriate.

	1	*2*	*3*	*4*	*Mid-unit Writing Comments*
Text Connectives • Sequential, cyclical, and others: when, before, after • Causal: because, therefore, as a result • Factorial explanations: first factor, second factor Explanations for children use few connectives.		✓			Uses "Once," which changes the purpose. "When" would be more appropriate for a cyclical explanation.
Lexical Ties (Collocation) paper, recycling center, pulping facility, huge vats, pulp			✓		A number of nouns and adjectives connected with the electric circuit.

LESSON 20. Lexical Ties (Collocation)

Goal: To teach students to use technical vocabulary in order to reflect the topic of the explanation. The use of technical terms assists the preciseness of the concepts explained.

Materials: Students' drafts with everyday language with the words that would best be substituted with technical terms underlined. For example, one student explained evaporation as *the warm air toches* [touches] *the water,* rather than *the warm air heats the water.* Another wrote, *The water go up* instead of *rises.* Mentor texts that include the technical terminology. Large sticky notes.

Activities

- Distribute mentor texts among the groups of students.
- Show a draft of student work with the everyday terms underlined.
- Ask students to work in their groups, consulting the mentor texts if needed, to think of terms to replace the underlined words. Ask students to write the replacement words on the sticky notes and bring them up the class copy to put the suggestions above each corresponding word.
- Once all groups have contributed, look at the suggestions for each word, group those that are identical, and read them aloud. If all of the students came up with the same solution, discuss that suggestion's accuracy. If there is more than one suggestion, discuss the differences and how the different words change the meaning.
- Have students look at their own drafts and decide whether their terms also need to be substituted with technical terms.

Resources

- Analysis of student work: Purpose and stages
- Analysis of student work: Language
- Graphic organizers:
  - o Sequential/Causal
  - o Cyclical
  - o Systems
  - o Factorial
- Additional resources that illustrate the genre

Explanation—Analysis of Student Work: Purpose and Stages (Grades 3–5)

Type: **Content Area:** **Medium:** **Intended Audience:**

Key: 1. Needs substantial support; 2. Needs instruction; 3. Needs revision; 4. Meets standard; NA: Not applicable

	1	*2*	*3*	*4*	*Uncoached Writing Comments*	*1*	*2*	*3*	*4*	*Final Writing Comments*
Purpose Sequential: Explain phenomena in a linear sequence. Cycle: In a cyclical way. Causal: One step causes the next. System: How a system works. Factorial: Factors that contribute to an event or outcome.										

(Continued)

	1	2	3	4	*Uncoached Writing Comments*	1	2	3	4	*Final Writing Comments*
Verb Tense Appropriate tense (present, unless the participant does not exist any longer, e.g., dinosaurs) and use of passive voice. Factorial historical (past tense)										
Title (If required by the medium)										
Identifying Statement (In historical explanation it may include background)										
Explanation Sequence (Sequential, cyclical, and causal) Systems: Description, explanation, interaction among components. Factorial: Factors										
Conclusion Optional for sequential, cyclical, and causal Systems: Generalization Factorial: General statement or reinforcement of factors										

Criteria

1. Needs substantial support: The student writer needs extensive help developing that aspect of the genre.
2. There are gaps in the writer's understanding of the specific aspect. The writer has insufficient control. S/he needs instruction and practice.
3. The paper needs revision on one or two instances of the feature. A conference would be sufficient to help the writer meet the standard.
4. The paper reflects what the student should be able to accomplish and write independently given the instruction provided for this grade level (National Center on Education and the Economy, 2004).

Explanation—Analysis of Student Work: Language (Grades 3–5)

Type: **Content Area:** **Medium:** **Intended Audience:**

Key: 1. Needs substantial support; 2. Needs instruction; 3. Needs revision; 4. Meets standard; NA: Not applicable

	1	2	3	4	*Uncoached Writing Comments*	1	2	3	4	*Final Writing Comments*
Verb Groups Action verbs Use of passive voice										

	1	2	3	4	*Uncoached Writing Comments*	1	2	3	4	*Final Writing Comments*
Generalized Participants (frogs, volcanoes, Congress)										
Adjectivals (*tiny* fibers, *pulping* facility, *strong and lasting* government, the powers *of the different branches*, a law *that disagrees with the Constitution*)										
Adverbials [be recycled *forever* (time), is challenged *in court* (place), balances each branch's powers *with the powers of the other branches* (manner)]										
Clause Complexes • Logico-semantic relations are appropriate • Accurate conjunctions • Missed opportunities										
Audience • Choice of topic • Choice of amount of information • Choice of specific information • Choice of specific language to represent processes, participants and their description, and circumstances										
Voice • Choice of types of sentences • Person • No need for interpersonal theme										
Text Connectives • Sequential, cyclical, and others: when, before, after • Causal: because, therefore, as a result • Factorial explanations: first factor, second factor Explanations for children use few connectives.										

(Continued)

	1	2	3	4	*Uncoached Writing Comments*	1	2	3	4	*Final Writing Comments*
Lexical Ties (Collocation) paper, recycling center, pulping facility, huge vats, pulp										

Criteria

1. Needs substantial support: The student writer needs extensive help developing that aspect of the genre.
2. There are gaps in the writer's understanding of the specific aspect. The writer has insufficient control. S/he needs instruction and practice.
3. The paper needs revision on one or two instances of the feature. A conference would be sufficient to help the writer meet the standard.
4. The paper reflects what the student should be able to accomplish and write independently given the instruction provided for this grade level (National Center on Education and the Economy, 2004).

FIGURE 7.1 Graphic Organizer: Sequential/Causal Explanation

Cyclical Explanation

Statement of phenomenon
(states what the phenomenon is)

Explanation Cycle

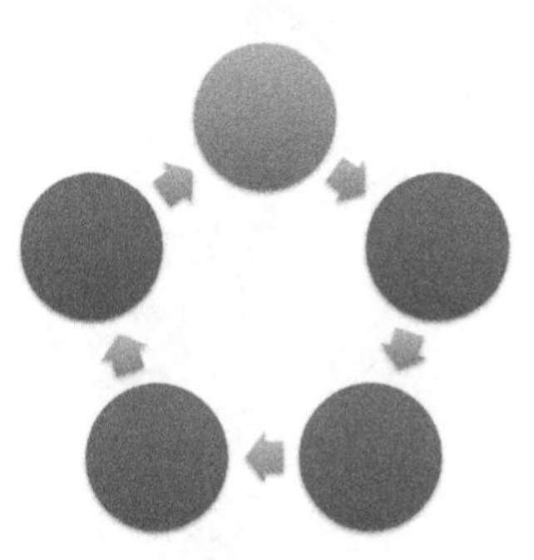

FIGURE 7.2 Graphic Organizer: Cyclical Explanation

Systems Explanations Graphic Organizers

Students fill in the boxes with the appropriate notes and use the arrows to demonstrate the relationships. Then, they cut the boxes and arrows up and rearrange them to show the hierarchy and relationships among and between components. The number of boxes and arrows may change depending on the system.

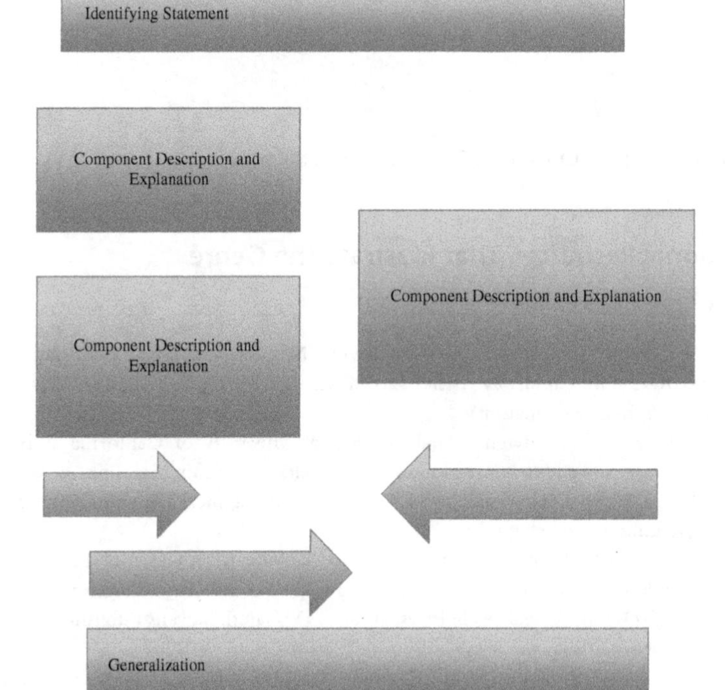

FIGURE 7.3 Graphic Organizer: Systems Explanation

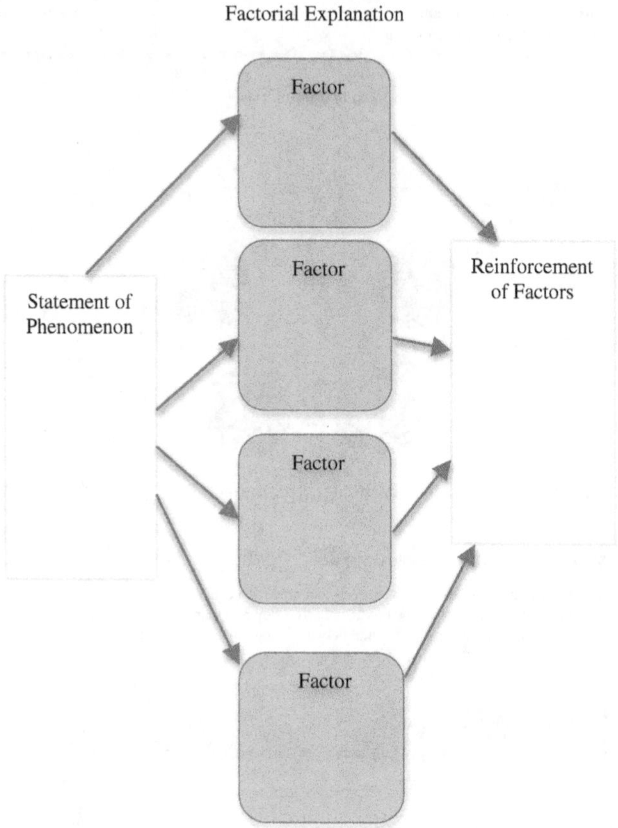

Factorial Explanation

Factor

Factor

Reinforcement of Factors

Statement of Phenomenon

Factor

Factor

FIGURE 7.4 Graphic Organizer: Factorial Explanation

Additional Resources That Illustrate the Genre

Books

Ardley, N. (1995). *How things work*. Pleasantville, NY: Reader's Digest Association.

Bjorklund, R. (2008). *Circulatory system*. Tarrytown, NY: Marshall Cavendish Corporation. (Chapter 2 is an explanation)

FOSS Revision Staff at Lawrence Hall of Science, University of California at Berkeley. (2003). *Magnetism and electricity*. Berkeley, CA: Delta Education. (Examples of sequential, causal, and cycle explanations; includes various biographical and historical recounts. See "Making Static" chapter.)

Frost, H. (2004). *El ciclo del agua: The water cycle*. Mankato, MN: Capstone Press. (Includes an example of a cyclical explanation; bilingual book with basic language)

Hantula, R. (2007). *Rocks and fossils*. Pleasantville, NY: Gareth Stevens Publishing. (Includes both reports and explanations)

Hill, L. (2009). *Gravity*. Chicago, IL: Raintree. (Combines reports, short causal explanations, and biographical recounts)

Hoffman, G. (2008). *Digestive system*. Tarrytown, NY: Marshall Cavendish Corporation. (Chapter 2 is an explanation)

Horenstein, H. (1993). *How are sneakers made?* New York, NY: Simon & Schuster Books for Young Readers. (Example of sequential explanation)

Jones, G. (1995). *My first book of how things are made.* New York, NY: Scholastic Inc. (Demonstrates sequential explanation; easier to read than "How Things Work Encyclopedia")

Kalman, B. (1998). *How birds fly.* New York, NY: Crabtree Publishing Company. (Sequential explanation of how birds fly; includes examples of explanations and reports. "Built for Flight" is a report. Also, "The First Fliers" has examples of identifying statements and historical background.)

Llewellyn, C. (2003). *Starting life: frog.* Oxfordshire, UK: Andromeda Oxford Limited.

Love, C., & Smith, P. (Eds.). (2010). *How things work encyclopedia.* New York, NY: DK Publishing. (Includes examples of explanations and some biographical recounts; contains more difficult language and concepts)

Royston, A. (2003). *My world of science: Conductors and insulators.* Jordan Hill, Oxford, UK: Harcourt Education Ltd. (Includes a cyclical explanation of a simple circuit, p. 12)

Zoefeld, K. W. (2002). *From tadpole to frog.* New York, NY: Scholastic.

Internet Resources

www.ask.com/question/how-do-volcanoes-erupt (How volcanoes erupt; causal explanation)

www.dltk-kids.com/animals/mfroglifecycle.htm (Example of a procedure used to create a frog life cycle)

http://kids.clerk.house.gov/grade-school/lesson.html?intID=17 (How a law is passed; sequential explanation)

http://kids.discovery.com/tell-me/curiosity-corner/science/how-do-electric-circuits-work (Electric circuit; cyclical explanation)

http://kidshealth.org/PageManager.jsp?lic=1&article_set=10317&cat_id=124 (What causes a person to sneeze; causal explanation)

http://library.thinkquest.org/3645/eclipses.html (Solar eclipse; causal explanation)

8

ARGUMENTS

Chapter Map

Pat is reading *Should There be Zoos?: A Persuasive Text* by Tony Stead & Judy Ballester that includes a number of arguments written by a 5th grade class in the Bronx. As he reads, he discusses features of arguments found in the text. After he reads an example where the author compares making kids stay inside to do their homework with keeping animals in cages, he asks,

Teacher: What is he [the author] trying to tell us?
Student: That the animals should have more time outside of their cage.
T: What is Christian [the author] using as an example and who do you think his audience is?
S: The reader.
T: Who is the reader, though? Me? You? Your mom? Who?
S: Everyone.
T: The whole world?
S: –No, I think kids in school.
T: You have to know your audience. The way I talked to the football team last night when they weren't doing well is different from how I talk to you. Very different language . . . Depending on audience you have to use a different example. Christian uses the example of homework and in the beginning he says "we kids . . ." So think about it, he is talking more to the kids.

The purpose of arguments is to persuade the audience to a position or point of view, or to persuade the audience to do something (Butt et al., 2000; Derewianka, 1990). For example, an author could write an argument to persuade someone to believe that smoking is bad or to stop smoking; writing can persuade someone to believe that Italy is the most beautiful country in Europe or to visit Italy. Some classify arguments into two types: *exposition* and *discussion* (Butt et al., 2000; Rose & Martin, 2012). Expositions present only one side of the argument while discussions present both sides of the argument. Derewianka and Jones (2012) propose additional types of arguments including challenges and responses to literature, which can be organized further into personal response, review, interpretation, and critical response. This chapter solely covers expositions, which are more appropriate for the elementary level, and which will be referred to as *arguments* because the term *exposition* is often confused with expository writing, traditionally considered a form of composition that includes arguments, narratives, and descriptions (Harris & Hodges, 1995).

Persuasive genres are difficult but extremely useful in real life and essential in a democratic society (Ferretti & Lewis, 2013). Children "have an intuitive understanding of the importance of argumentative discourse" (Ferretti & Lewis, 2013, p. 113). However, students have great difficulty finding reasons that support the argument and evidence that gives credence to the reasons offered. Although research claims that elementary school children are not ready for persuasive writing, Anderson (2008) argues that they are. She maintains that a lack of exposure to persuasive writing in school is to blame for limited mastery of the genre. With instruction and peer support, elementary school children can become more effective in their persuasive writing (Wollman-Bonilla, 2004). Moreover, the learning features of arguments engage students in academic writing, which they can apply to other genres (Gebhard, Harman, & Seger, 2007).

Children enjoy persuasive writing because it gives them an opportunity to express their opinions. One 5th grader reflected,

> I feel like I like it better because my grades are higher, and persuasive writing is powerful, it can help me get a better education and I can tell people what I think to change their minds.
>
> (Sánchez Ares, 2012, p. 31)

Grade Levels and Content Areas

Arguments are used in all content areas. In ELA, arguments usually relate to students' everyday life (e.g., a group of 3rd graders wrote to their principal requesting lockers). In science, scientific arguments are at the core of scientific inquiry (Zembal-Saul, McNeill, & Hershberger, 2013). For example, 5th graders constructed a scientific argument when they were given a diagram with four houses on different types of terrain and asked to argue which terrain would be the safest place to build a new house.

Historical argumentation is probably the most difficult type of persuasive writing and usually not encountered until high school (Christie & Derewianka, 2008; Coffin, 2006). The purpose of historical arguments is to argue "the case 'for' or 'against' a particular interpretation of the past and foreground the debatable nature of historical knowledge and explanation" (Coffin, 2006, p. 77). These would be very difficult tasks for young learners. Teachers use historical topics as the content to write arguments. For example, 5th-grade teachers had students write letters as if they were colonials trying to convince Europeans to come to America. Similarly, stories can be used as content for arguments. For example, a teacher could have the students argue which was the smartest pig in the story *The Three Little Pigs*. Reading exams often include questions that require students to look for evidence in a text to support a given claim. For example, a prompt on a standardized test read, "Why does reading to the class make Ida feel both happy and scared at the same time? Support your answer with important details from the chapter" (Massachusetts Comprehensive Assessment System, 2009). Using stories to create arguments is different from doing character analysis or thematic interpretation, which are more appropriate for older students (Christie & Derewianka, 2008).

With students in early grades, it may be sufficient just to teach them how to take a stand using oral language and finding evidence from their everyday topics or stories. By 3rd grade, projects, including creating brochures to attract visitors or writing a class letter to the principal, are doable. Essays are better to attempt in

TABLE 8.1 Argument Instruction Across Grades

Type/Grade	*Stages of Arguments*	*K–5 Oral, Games*	*3–5 Oral & Written Brochures, Posters*	*4–5 Oral & Written Essays*
Commonsense arguments	Thesis/Claim	Provided	✓	✓
	Reasons	✓	✓	✓
	Evidence		Provided or ✓	✓
	Conclusion		✓	✓
Using stories as context	Thesis/Claim	Provided	Provided	Provided
	Reasons	Provided or ✓	Provided or ✓	✓
	Evidence	✓	✓	✓
	Conclusion			✓
Using historical context	Thesis/Claim			✓
	Reasons			✓
	Evidence			✓
	Conclusion			✓
Science arguments	Thesis/Claim		Provided	✓
	Reasons		Provided	Provided or ✓
	Evidence		✓	✓
	Conclusion		✓	✓

Key: "Provided": the teacher creates; "✓": the students create upper elementary grades and beyond (See Table 8.1). Upper elementary students can also benefit from the activities recommended for younger learners in preparation to writing argumentative essays.

In the early grades or when initiating students to argumentation through oral activities and games, the teacher should provide the thesis statement and then ask students to provide reasons for the stance. When using literature as the context, the teacher should provide the thesis statement and (often) the reasons, while expecting the students to find the evidence in the text. As students start to write their own arguments, the teacher should allow the students to develop their own thesis statements and reasons, and help only with the evidence for commonsense arguments. In scientific arguments and response to literature writing, the teacher action is reversed, with the teacher helping students with the claims and reasons while the students write the evidence. By 4th and 5th grades, the students are expected to create and progress through all of the stages by themselves.

Arguments Unit

The approach to teaching arguments is organized into activities that do not require the production of written texts, writing in a variety of mediums other than the essay, or essay writing. Scientific arguments are best done orally through 3rd grade. Oral activities can be carried out in the early grades as well as in the later grades before beginning a full argument unit. Beginning in 3rd grade, students can write arguments in the form of PowerPoints, brochures, and posters for the purpose of advertising something or in the form of whole-class letters to make requests. Finally, in 4th and 5th grades, students can be taught to write essays on a variety of everyday topics, using history or literature as the context, and in science class. With each type of activity, new aspects of the genre will be introduced to learners.

Oral Arguments (K–5)

The first set of skills to teach is to take a stand and give reasons for why students support a particular position. Beverly, a 4th-grade teacher, found that children had an easier time persuading a reader *to do something* than persuading a reader *about something.* It is important to practice both types of persuasion and to make the difference clear to students. Finally, lessons to practice oral arguments prepare older students to write. Oral dialogue "is essential for the development of reflective argumentative writing" (Ferretti & Lewis, 2013, p. 114).

LESSON 1. Learning to Give Reasons to Support a Thesis Statement or Claim *to Do* Something (K–5)

Goal: To learn to give reasons to persuade to do something given a thesis statement and an audience.

Materials: Chart paper or smartboard.

Activities

- Brainstorm with students:
  - Who they are trying to persuade
  - What they are trying to persuade them [the audience] to do.
- Write the thesis statement, on the basis of the discussion of what they are trying to persuade their audience to do, on chart paper.
- Have students give reasons that would appeal to that audience and persuade them.
- Write them underneath the thesis statement on the chart paper. For example, after brainstorming, 3rd graders decided that they wanted to ask the principal for lockers. The following is what that class posted on chart paper.

STUDENTS NEED LOCKERS
Reasons that will appeal to the principal
Books stolen School work organized Neat classroom Have a private space

LESSON 2. Learning to Give Reasons to Support a Thesis Statement or Claim *About* Something (K–5)

Goal: To learn to give reasons to persuade about something given a thesis statement and an audience.

Materials: Chart paper or smartboard.

Activities

- For K–1 students:
  - Write a thesis statement on chart paper with two columns below, one titled *yes,* the other *no.*
  - As students come in at the beginning of the day, have them sign their name under either *yes* or *no* depending on their opinion towards the thesis.
  - Call the name of a few students on each side to provide a reason for their selected opinion.
  - Do this activity daily or weekly for a period of time. Have a different claim (thesis statement) each time and have different students give reasons for their stance.
  - You may choose to write the reasons given by the students at the bottom of the columns (Stead, 2002).

Examples: X book is better than Y book; Dogs are better pets than cats	
YES	NO
Why?	Why?

- For Grades 2 and up:
  - o Suggest a thesis statement for the students to consider (e.g., *students need longer breaks, students should be allowed to use cell phones in class*).
  - o Put the following signs around the room: "strongly agree," "agree," "disagree," and "strongly disagree." (See Figure 8.1.)
  - o Have students stand by the sign that matches most closely to their belief, forming a group at each sign. Let students confer.
  - o Have them share the reasons why they took that position.

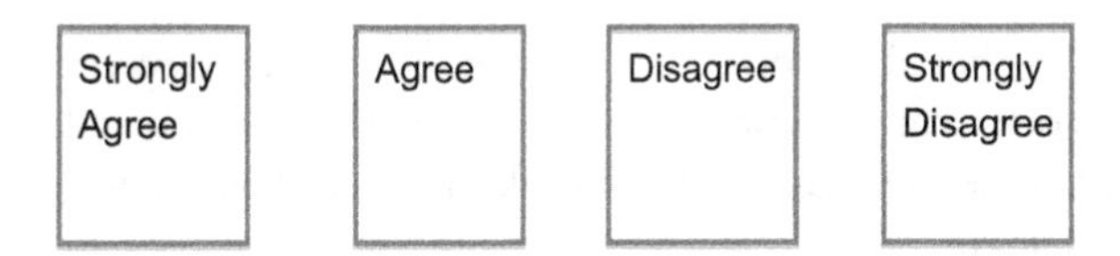

FIGURE 8.1

Thesis statements can be chosen from topics from a content area that students are studying or from a book or article that they are reading. For example, if students are studying about the American Revolution, the thesis could be "American revolutionary forces achieved independence from the British swiftly and easily."

LESSON 3. Taking a Stand in Relation to a Reading

Goal: To learn to take a position in relation to the content of a reading.

Materials: Anticipation guide prepared in relation to a reading. For example, Peggy, a 4th-grade bilingual teacher, passed out the following anticipation guide in Spanish to her students prior to reading *La Moneda de Oro* by Alma Flor Ada:

Anticipation Guide			
	Me	*My Partner and I*	*Author*
1. To be rich means having a lot of money.	Yes ____ No ____	Yes ____ No ____	Yes ____ No ____
2. People who do bad things can't change.	Yes ____ No ____	Yes ____ No ____	Yes ____ No ____
3. It is important to have a lot of money.	Yes ____ No ____	Yes ____ No ____	Yes ____ No ____

(Brisk & Harrington, 2007, p. 124)

Activities

- Have students take a position on the statements related to a reading that you prepared. The statements should reflect important themes inferred from the reading.
- Have students fill in the "Me" column based on their beliefs.
- Working with a partner, have students discuss their choice explaining why they checked *yes* or *no.*
- Have students come to a consensus and fill the second column.
- After reading the selection, have them fill out the "Author" column.

This strategy should be done in connection to the reading curriculum. It helps students practice taking a stand and activates their background knowledge to support reading comprehension (See full description of the strategy in Brisk & Harrington, 2007).

LESSON 4. Role Playing Arguments (adapted from Wagner, 1999)

Goal: To have students practice oral argumentation in specific contexts.
Materials: None needed.

Activities

- Explain the task and facilitate an initial discussion to provide background information for a selected context and inspire students to think about different perspectives.
- Give pairs of students different roles. For example, one student could act as a student, while the other could act as the principal.
- Give students a thesis statement (e.g., *students need lockers, buses need bus monitors, students need longer breaks, students need sweet snacks*).

- Have students act in character and engage in a dialogue with their partner, giving reasons for their stance and disputing the reasons their partner offers.
- Have students switch roles and then give them another thesis statement.
- Have students reflect (or journal) about their role-playing experience and what is was like to argue from different perspectives.

Written Arguments (Grades 3–5)

General Preparation

In preparation to start the unit and on the basis of the school-wide decisions of which genre to teach at which grade level and in connection to which content area, teachers should:

- Determine the content, writing, and language standards
- Choose resources
- Decide how students are going to be grouped
- Decide on writing products: medium, multimodality, authenticity
- Build content knowledge
- Teach students to appropriate academic language
- Plan lessons based on analysis of students' uncoached writing.

There are extensive suggestions about each one of these points in chapter 2. Following are considerations specific to arguments with respect to content and technical language, the CCSS, resources, audience, medium, and prompts for uncoached writing.

It is very important to develop the content in order for students to have appropriate reasons and strong evidence. When planning to write an argument in connection with a scientific experiment, the students should carry out the experiment and discuss the content in anticipation of writing the full persuasive piece. In everyday arguments and those based on historical content, students need to research the topic to find evidence. For example, when students wrote letters as if they were colonials to the British to convince them to join them in the colonies, they first had to research all about the colonies to develop well-supported reasons.

When writing the evidence, students will need technical terms. Thus, as they research the topics, it is important to constantly build the academic language needed to discuss the topic.

Arguments in the CCSS are one of the three text types proposed. From pre-K through 3rd grade, students are expected to express an "opinion" and give reasons. Not until the 4th and 5th grades, though, are they asked to "Provide logically ordered reasons that are supported by facts and details" (CCSS.ELA-Literacy.W.5.1b). "Facts and details" corresponds to "evidence" in the SFL-informed pedagogy. The rest of the standards are generic and may or may not apply to arguments specifically. Some standards apply, but it is not clearly evident by the way in which they are presented. For example, one of the language standards reads,

> CCSS.ELA-Literacy.L.1.5d: Distinguish shades of meaning among verbs differing in manner (e.g., *look, peek, glance, stare, glare, scowl*) and adjectives differing in intensity (e.g., *large, gigantic*) by defining or choosing them or by acting out the meanings.

The strategy described in this standard is used as an instrument of voice expressing the writer's point of view by turning up or down the intensity of meaning. In SFL-informed pedagogy, this is called "grading" (Droga & Humphrey, 2003). The CCSS do not explain why an author would make a particular language or grading choice. There is no mention of audience or voice, key variables to consider when the writer makes choices when composing an argument.

The resources to teach arguments will depend on the medium to be used. To have students write ads, posters, or brochures that are persuasive, teachers can have students watch TV and collect advertisements, posters, or brochures that will illustrate the text structure and language used in these different media. These types of arguments are appropriate for grades 3–5. To learn how to write essays in grades 4 and 5, the following mentor text can be used, as is referred to throughout the chapter to illustrate the stages and language: *Why Dogs Are Better Than Cats* (www.jamesabela.co.uk/exams/dogsvscats.pdf).

The magazine *Time for Kids* has texts that claim to be persuasive. However, they are not always clear or well developed. They should be reviewed carefully before being selected as mentor texts. For other suggestions, check the additional resources at the end of the chapter.

Certain children's literature, although written as fictional narratives, illustrate persuasion through their character's language and, specifically, the use of certain grammatical features to persuade (See list in the additional resources at the end of the chapter). Thus, children's literature is often used to teach argumentation. For example, in the book *Can I Keep Him?*, the mother's language, all in statements, is more authoritative than that of the child, who asks many questions.

> "'Mom, I found this dog sitting all by himself. Can I keep him?'
> 'No, Arnold. Dogs are too noisy. He would bark all the time . . .'"

Similarly, in *Dear Mrs. LaRue,* the point of view from the dog is made stronger by the use of high modality, while that of the vet is made weaker by low modals:

> "I **had to** be taken to the vet/Dr. Wilfrey claims that he **can't** find anything wrong with me, but **I am certain** I have an awful disease. I **must** come home at once."

Kroll (1984) argues that it is likely easier for children to adapt their writing to an audience if the audience is a specific person (e.g., *my cousin, Richard*) rather than a category of persons (e.g., *children*). For this reason, letters written to specific people, such as the principal or a parent, are easier for students to write than letters sent to the editor of a newspaper without having any connection or essays to educators or adults, in general.

The medium will necessitate consideration of the structure and language. For example, an *essay* includes the traditional stages of title, thesis, preview of reasons, reasons with evidence, and reinforcement of the position. An *advertisement* includes the stages in short sentences mixing language and images. Although essays and editorials will be written in the third person, letters can be written in the first and second person, and advertisements and sermons will often include use of the second person.

Prompt for Uncoached Writing: Ask the students to write a piece supporting a statement of something that is of interest to them. Sample statements could include *There should be school rules, Students should have longer breaks, Parents should pick up children from school when they are sick*, and *Cats make better pets than dogs.*

Teachers analyze the writing that emerges from the prompt using the Analysis of Student Work: Purpose and Stages form found in the end-of-chapter materials, to determine what the students can already do and what their challenges are. Teachers can use the Unit Plan (Appendix A) to plot the necessary lessons.

Part I: Purpose and Stages of the Genre

Purpose of Arguments

The purpose of arguments is to persuade the reader to do something or believe something. Children find the first easier than the second. "To do" arguments are more concrete.

Features of Students' Writing

A 4th-grade teacher wrote the question *Should there be school rules?* as a prompt for the uncoached piece. The students decided to write a letter to the teacher to respond and to attempt to persuade her. One of the students wrote the following piece. After the student wrote the letter, she decided to clarify that they were different by adding the word *like* on the margin before each. In addition, she added two hearts, four stars and "Love, [name of the student]" to the top of the second page. She may have felt that she was being too daring with her assertions and wanted to soften the message.

Dear, Mrs. [Name of Teacher],
Yes! I think we sould have
school rules because If
we Did,nt had nd rules we will
be like crazy and we will never
get the part to learn.
Let My give you some Exzapeles
like: Protet you from getting hurt and stol.

Like: follow them you will handel them.
Like: Don,t be crazy or you will be lazy.
Like[1]: Don,t be bad or the teacher will get mad
So if you are gonna be bad I don,t
know what the teacher is gonna say
when se or he is MAD!

So think be-for you do something
or somthing will happen Don,t think it is
the teachers foult it is gonna be yours
falut.

NEVER Ever BE BAD
OR you Will not get a
EDUCATION.
If you make the teachers happy
the whole school is happy
yours truly, [Name of student]

	1	*2*	*3*	*4*	*Uncoached Writing Comments*
Purpose To persuade to do something or to believe something.		✓			Starts with a thesis and preview of reasons, but then it turns into instructions for the students.
Verb Conjugation Present, future, and past tenses in evidence and use of modals.		✓			Present tense, future tense, and use of modality initially; switches to imperative, used to give instructions, present, future.

This student seems to understand the purpose of the genre to persuade, but switches her purpose to give instructions. The topic might have confused her, because school rules are usually written as a protocol or a series of instructions to always be followed (Butt et al., 2000).

Sometimes, students switched genres because the sources that they used for research were written in a different genre. For example, a 4th grader, while trying to write a persuasive essay about protecting endangered species, carried out research on a few animals and ended up writing a report on four endangered species.

LESSON 5. Persuasion in Students' Environment

Goal: To have students identify persuasion in their own lives so that they realize how prevalent the genre is.

Materials: TV, magazine advertisements, brochures, and other media of persuasion found in the community (e.g., students could examine brochures handed out by an animal shelter to convince people to adopt adult cats).

Activities

- Have students watch advertisements on TV or the Internet or look for ads in magazines as homework.
- The following day, discuss the following:
  - The purpose of the advertisements
  - What information was included in each
  - How the ads were trying to persuade their audience
  - Who is the intended audience and what in the advertisement suggests a particular audience.
- Repeat the activities with the other persuasive materials.

LESSON 6. Introduction to the Purpose of Arguments

Goal: To teach students that the purpose of arguments is to persuade the audience to do something or believe something. It is essential to emphasize this purpose first because understanding of the purpose drives the stages and language of the text.

Materials: Travel brochures, magazine advertisements, and additional materials, such as those listed at the end of the chapter in "Additional Resources." Chart paper.

Activities

- Using chart paper or the board, create two columns ("to persuade to do" and "to persuade about").
- Choose one or two of the resources (materials) and read each aloud or, in the case of a video, show it to the students.
- Discuss what the author is trying to do or what the character in the story is trying to do (In the end-of-chapter resources, there is a list of fictional narratives in which a character is trying to persuade another character to do or believe something).

- Write what the author is trying to do for each under one of the columns.
- Distribute the rest of the materials among the student groups and have them decide whether the author or character is trying "to persuade to do" or "to persuade about."
- Have students add their responses to the appropriate columns on the chart paper or board.

Decisions on Audience

Of all the genres, arguments are most impacted by audience (See section on audience in chapter 2). Therefore, students first identify who will be reading their writing. As will be explained throughout the chapter, audience impacts writers' decisions on stages. In addition, audience and voice influence language choices.

Arguments Using Different Media

The specific media chosen will make producing arguments easier or harder. Thus, 3rd-grade teachers, although they taught purpose, stages, and some elements of language, did not have their students produce individual essays. Fifi, a 3rd-grade SEI teacher, had students do a joint construction together as a class. They produced a letter together asking for more time at the school library and sent it to the principal. Students worked in groups to brainstorm reasons and evidence and shared their contributions with the whole class. The teacher then wrote all of their ideas on chart paper. Then, as a class, they chose a few of the reasons and chose the evidence that best supported those reasons. The students worked in English and Spanish, helping each other with the language to be incorporated in the argument. They explored persuasive language to include in the letter. Michelle, another 3rd-grade teacher, had students do short projects after reading *Can I Keep Him?* such as writing a letter to their mothers asking for a pet. Their big project was to write a three-fold brochure convincing people to visit their state or country of origin. Michelle gave the students a worksheet divided into four squares entitled *climate, food/culture, attractions,* and *fun facts.* Students used these worksheets to guide their research and to take notes. She found that initially, without the worksheet, the students were overwhelmed and did not know what information to gather. As a class, they discussed what kind of information would be of interest to people wanting to visit and made recommendations about what to include in the brochure. For example, the class recommended that a Sudanese student omit a sentence listing the various wars that occurred, as that information would not likely persuade someone to visit.

Students in the upper grades can also benefit from attempting different media. For example, Angela, a 5th-grade teacher, carried out an 8-week unit in which students produced a variety of arguments. For science, her students had to invent a machine. Then, the other students in the school voted for their favorite machine. Angela's students wrote advertisements about their science machine inventions and posted them around the school to encourage other students to vote for theirs. In another example, when students complained that there was misbehavior on the school buses, they wrote a letter to the principal arguing for the need for bus monitors. In another class, students read *The True Story of the Three Little Pigs* and wrote letters to the "judge" supporting either the side of the wolf or the pigs. Last, another class brainstormed community issues and wrote essays to persuade community members about double parking, trash collection, the pay scale of the local police, and other issues.

Stages of Arguments

An exposition includes a thesis statement, a preview of the reasons, the reasons supported by evidence, and a reinforcement of the position. Depending on the medium, these stages look different. For example, an essay will include all of these stages, whereas a brochure will include mostly reasons and evidence. The following is a fairly simple text that includes a title, a thesis statement, three reasons, and evidence for each reason. The reasons are not previewed. The conclusion reiterates the positive stance toward dogs.

Stages	*Example*
Title (If required by the medium)	*Why Dogs Are Better Than Cats*
Thesis statement, statement of the position, or claim (including information about the issue)	Dogs are often called "man's best friend" and make ideal pets.
Preview reasons	
Series of reasons, each supported by evidence (In science, math, or response to literature, the evidence is often stated before the reasons)	The most attractive quality of a dog is its faith in its owner and its loyalty. They always greet us when we come home and they will never leave us even in a dire situation. For example there was a sick man and the dog barked and barked until the rescue team arrived. Furthermore dogs are strong animals that will protect us. Houses with dogs are considered much safer than even those with burglar alarms. Not only will they stop thieves, but they will also guard against fire. For example there was a serious fire and a dog managed to pull its owner out. And finally dogs can be trained to help people. Dogs can do a number of things that people can not. For example they can sniff out drugs, find bodies, illicit DVDs and hunt down prisoners. They're also used to help the elderly and disabled.
Reinforcement of statement of position	To sum up, dogs are really friendly, civilized and loyal companions.

Source: www.jamesabela.co.uk/exams/dogsvscats.pdf (Downloaded 8/11/11)

Students need to learn a number of things to successfully compose the stages of an argument:

- *Learning to take a position and give reasons:* Students need to learn to express an opinion about something or persuade the audience to do something. Although it is their own, they need to learn to express it as a general opinion (e.g., *Students should be allowed to have cell phones in the classroom*). Sometimes, the writer is just trying to persuade for himself or herself. For example, a student might write a letter to a parent trying to persuade him or her to buy something. The thesis statement needs to be accompanied with reasons that support the position. There is no need for a fixed number of reasons, which may vary depending on audience.
- *Learning to support reasons with evidence:* Evidence can appeal to the intellect or to emotions (Rog & Kropp, 2004). Writers should chose their evidence depending on the audience. Evidence that appeals to the intellect includes:
    - Facts that can be proven
    - Statistics that offer scientific support
    - Expert opinions or quotations
    - Exhibits, including visual or auditory evidence (pictures, artifacts, recordings).

  Evidence that appeals to emotions includes:

    - Examples that are powerful illustrations of the point of view
    - Anecdotes that illustrate an incident, often part of the writer's personal experience
    - Emotional appeals that include carefully chosen words to sway the reader's emotion in a desired direction.
- *Difference between fact and opinion:* Persuasive writing uses facts to support an author's opinion or point of view (reasons). For example, in the mentor text, being helpful and protective are opinions about dogs. However, the examples of dogs aiding the disabled or pulling their owner from a house on fire are facts (evidence).

Audience impacts all aspects of persuasive genres. With respect to the stages of writing an argument, the following points need to be considered:

- Depending on the knowledge of the topic by the audience, the thesis statement may need to be preceded by background information. For example, the mentor text discussing dogs as pets may first need some background information if the audience included children in cultures that do not have dogs as pets, but rather as working animals. A persuasive piece about girls' rights to education in Afghanistan should include background information on the treatment of women in that country.
- Reasons are also carefully chosen depending on the audience. For example, when students wrote to the principal attempting to persuade him or her to

install lockers, they gave *security* as a reason, which they believed would appeal to an adult. If the audience had been other students, they may have chosen *being fun to decorate.*

- Evidence is chosen given the audience. Certain people may be better convinced with statistics, whereas others may prefer anecdotes and real-life examples. The mentor text seems to be directed to the general public with appealing examples of what dogs can do for their owners.

Features of Students' Writing

Following is the analysis of the sample uncoached piece, with focus on the stages:

Feature	*1*	*2*	*3*	*4*	*Comment*
Title (if required by the medium)					The piece is a letter and doesn't require a title.
Thesis statement or Claim Background (optional) Preview of arguments		✓			Instead of starting directly with the thesis statement, she inserts "Yes" and "I think" at the beginning. Although the prompt was a generalized statement, the student switched to first person, focusing just on her class and not schools in general. Previews: being crazy and not learning
Reasons supported by evidence	✓				Doesn't follow the arguments she previews, instead switches to giving instructions to students as to how to behave.
Reinforcement of statement of position	✓				Concludes with encouraging students to make the teacher happy, unrelated to the initial reasons.

Often, when the prompt is a question, students, instead of writing a thesis statement, write *yes* or *no,* depending on which point of view they choose to argue. The student stated her thesis preceded by an interpersonal theme (underlined): *I think we sould have school rules.* Children do not realize that the use of these interpersonal themes weakens the claim, especially with a phrase with medium intensity as *I think* (Droga & Humphrey, 2003). Because the student switches to giving instructions or advising, she does not provide reasons supported by evidence, failing to reinforce her position.

One great source of difficult for elementary students is to write the thesis statement in the third person, distancing the author from the position. Most academic writing considers the use of the third person more persuasive (Derewianka, 1990). As seen in the uncoached piece, even if the teacher had written the prompt in the third person *(Should there be school rules?),* the student chose to use the first person to focus on her opinion and her classmates *(I think we should have school rules).*

Fourth graders writing persuasive pieces struggled to state convincing evidence (Bermúdez & Prater, 1994). By 6th grade, students showed the ability to make appropriate changes in the content and language of persuasive pieces when writing to different audiences. For example, Martinez, Orellana, Pacheco, and Carbone (2008) show that when students wrote to the principal about the need to do something about the school police, they said the police treated them like criminals. However, when these same students wrote to other students, they wrote that, "They're [the school police] stupid and they bug" (p. 421).

Instruction supports this development. A 5th-grade Spanish-speaking student wrote, *Come live in Jamestown because people are friendly,* using an opinion instead of a proven fact as her evidence. Later, this student revised her piece to read, *Also, we have such great friends. Most important, the young girl named Pocahontas. She is a girl that helps us hunt animals and give us food when we are working very hard. We are also friends with other natives.* Extensive analysis of persuasive pieces, including TV and newspaper advertisements, helped the students to realize what constitutes evidence.

Other issues that students have with respect to the stages are:

- A study of 9-year-olds writing persuasive pieces showed that students had trouble giving sufficient background information (Kroll, 1984).
- Students sometimes have difficulty giving a variety of reasons and repeat the same reason with slightly different wording.
- Students tend to repeat the thesis statement when writing the conclusion.

Lessons To Teach the Stages of Arguments

Before beginning these lessons, it is to be assumed that students will have practiced the activities in the Oral Arguments section earlier in this chapter, either in previous grades or during the year. Before starting the standard process of deconstruction, joint construction, and group/individual construction of the various stages in order to create their own written arguments, students will need a number of lessons to practice giving reasons and evidence.

In scientific and response to reading arguments, giving reasons can be a difficult task. In scientific arguments, the reasons must be accurate, reflecting knowledge of science. The evidence, however, is present in the science experiment. When reading literature, the reasons often have to be inferred from the text whereas the evidence is spelled out in the text. Thus, for science and responses to literature, it is best to teach evidence first and then reasons. For scientific arguments, teachers would begin by carrying out an experiment to collect evidence. For response to literature arguments, students would read the text first. This activity can be done during reading time, using reading strategies to facilitate comprehension.

In commonplace arguments and those using historical contexts, it is easier to state the reasons first. The evidence needs to be researched from a variety of sources. For example, for the thesis statement *People should not smoke,* students can easily come up with the following reasons: *It is bad for people's health* or *People can die of lung cancer.* However, the evidence to support these reasons would be in medical studies that they would need to research. The lessons that follow are ordered for an everyday type of argument, which are the easiest for students and a natural starting point. Arguments in other contexts should follow everyday arguments.

LESSON 7. Deconstruction of Text to Learn About Stages

Goal: To teach the stages of the argument genre so that students learn to organize the text.

Materials: Mentor text. Other texts or videos recommended in "Additional Resources," at the end of the chapter, including magazine advertisements or student work from previous years. Audiovisual equipment. Large version of the argument graphic organizer.

Activities

- Read a few mentor texts and show the videos.
- Using a large version of the graphic organizer, identify the stages and discuss if any are missing.
- Group students and give them a copy of the graphic organizer.
- Have students look at the additional texts to identify the stages of arguments.
- Give each student a few texts and copies of the graphic organizer and have them do the same activity for homework.

LESSON 8. Putting the Argument Puzzle Together

Goal: To learn the stages of an argument with sensitivity to audience so that students understand that the reason and evidence choice vary with audience.

Materials: Prepare the pieces of the puzzles, which consist of:

- Four sheets, each containing a thesis statement written on the top of the sheet with the icon for the audience. The thesis statements should be repeated for each different audience. For example:
  - Students need lockers—icon: principal
  - Students need lockers—icon: group of students
  - Students should take a field trip to the aquarium—icon: principal
  - Students should take a field trip to the aquarium—icon: group of students

- Eight large cards with one reason on each. Two reasons should support each thesis statement.
    - o Eight large cards with one piece of evidence to support each reason. Depending on the class needs, these cards may or may not have the labels "reason" and "evidence" or be of different colors. Without the labels, it could be good practice to have the students figure out the difference between reasons and evidence.

This activity can be done as a large version to work with the whole class, or as a small version to work with each group. Laminating the pieces and putting a fabric hook-and-loop fastener on them can allow the teacher and students to move the pieces around and put them in place, while holding up other pieces to view.

When students appropriately assemble all of the pieces of the puzzle, the four sheets with the thesis statement, reasons, and supporting evidence should read as follows:

1. Students need lockers—icon: principal

REASON: Students carry heavy textbooks around all day, which can be physically strenuous. Access to lockers will prevent stress.

EVIDENCE: "The incidence of back pain in early adolescence approaches that seen in adults. This study identifies 2 factors associated with self-reported back pain in early adolescents that are amenable to change: availability of school lockers and lighter backpacks." (From the article "Back pain and backpacks in school children," www.ncbi.nlm.nih.gov/pubmed/16670549).

REASON: Students can secure their valuable items in personal lockers to prevent theft in the school.

EVIDENCE: Since the beginning of the school year, there have been three thefts of personal belongings in students' backpacks in the school.

2. Students need lockers—icon: group of students

REASON: Lockers provide a space for students to leave all of their things (textbooks, jackets, lunches, athletic equipment) throughout the day. Students do not have to lug as many things around.

EVIDENCE: There have been a lot of complaints from students about carrying all that weight.

REASON: It is fun to decorate the inside of the locker. Locker decorations allow students to express themselves and create a personal space in the school.

EVIDENCE: At my sister's school, students have lockers and they love to be able to decorate them.

3. Students should take a field trip to the aquarium—icon: principal

REASON: A visit to the aquarium can inspire students to take interest in marine animal care and conservations efforts.

EVIDENCE: Story from *The Eagletown Times* (not a real paper or story): "Last Thursday, Ms. Emma Robinson's 3rd-grade class visited the Eagletown aquarium. They have spent the last month studying marine animals and learning about their living conditions. The students took special interest in the threatening changes to the marine environments of the animals and the conservation efforts aimed at slowing and preventing them. Ms. Robinson arranged a conservation-focused field trip for the students. They learned about various efforts and their positive and negative effects.

"Many of the students were inspired by the field trip, and they decided to create an environmental appreciation club at the school. The students spend time volunteering with their families, learning about conservation techniques and efforts, and informing others about them. The new club is thriving thanks to Ms. Robinson's efforts and the trip to the Eagletown aquarium."

REASON: Students need "real-world" exposure to the topics they are studying in class. A visit to the aquarium will provide them with this real-world experience, and they will bring that knowledge back to the classroom.

EVIDENCE: "'Field trips provide students with a window to the real world that they don't get in the classroom, and they can help students understand real-world applications of seemingly abstract topics in math and science,' she [teacher] says. For example, engineers may often use formulas taught in Algebra II, calculus, and chemistry classes" (From the article, "Teachers, Don't Overlook Value of Field Trips," www.usnews.com/education/blogs/high-school-notes/2011/12/12/teachers-dont-overlook-value-of-field-trips).

4. Students should take a field trip to the aquarium—icon: other students

REASON: Students can see the different marine animals they have been learning about in class up close!

EVIDENCE: There was a similar field trip planned and executed a few years ago, and the older sister of one of our current students was one of the students on the trip. She loved seeing the manta rays, and she has been talking about the trip and the rays ever since! She was able to explore the marine animals they had been studying all year.

REASON: Students can spend the day exploring outside of the classroom and have fun!

EVIDENCE: Last year, we made two field trips and they were a lot of fun because we were able to observe our favorite marine animals that we had been learning about! We saw penguins interact with each other, and we watched the aquarium workers feed the sharks. Their teeth were huge, and we were able to buy real shark teeth to bring back to the classroom from the gift shop. We loved seeing everything up close, as we were only separated from the animals by a thin layer of glass.

Activities

- Play the game with the whole class or in small groups.
- For the whole-class version, put up the sheets with the thesis statements and the audience icons.
- Divide the class into a few small groups and give each group an equal amount of reasons and evidence cards.
- If the cards are not labeled or in different colors, then have the students first sort the cards into reasons and evidence. If the cards are labeled or colored, skip this step.
- Have the students choose the two reasons that would go with their particular thesis statement and audience. Have the students come up to the sheet to post the cards in order of significance, leaving space to place the evidence under each reason.
- Have students choose the evidence cards that seem best suited to support each of the reasons given the audience. Have students place the chosen evidence under each reason.
- Read the final product and discuss whether the placement of the reasons and evidence are accurate. Make any changes if necessary.
- Alternatives:
  - Start with a thesis statement and the reasons and ask the students to choose the audience and the evidence.
  - For the small-group version, have each group do the same activities in their groups and then share the results with the class.

Here is an example of a completed sheet (see Figure 8.2) along with a typed display of what the final product should look like:

Students need lockers

Lockers provide a space for you to leave all of your things (textbooks, jackets, lunches, athletic equipment) throughout the day. You do not have to carry as many things around with you.

We have heard a lot of complaints from students about carrying all that weight.

It is fun to decorate the inside of the locker. Locker decorations allow students to express themselves and create a personal space in the school.

At my sister's school students have lockers and they love to be able to decorate them.

FIGURE 8.2

Pat Scialoia, a 5th-grade teacher, had students write essays. First, the class deconstructed a whole mentor text to introduce the stages. He sent students home with additional texts and copies of the graphic organizer to identify the stages. Then, he taught one stage per day, going through the cycle of deconstruction, joint construction of the graphic organizer, student peer revision of the graphic organizer, and individual construction for each stage. He also conferred with the students throughout the unit.

LESSON 9. Development of Thesis Statements

Goal: To teach students to create thesis statements that express an opinion about something or try to persuade someone to do something.

Materials: A few of the examples in different media already used to illustrate both types of persuasion. A strip to write the class thesis statement. Copies of the argument graphic organizer (See end-of-chapter resources). Projector.

Activities

- Remind students of the thesis statements used in oral activities practiced earlier in the year.
- Project a couple of texts and identify the thesis statement for each.
- Discuss the language. Is it a general statement in the third person (e.g., *Students should visit Plymouth Plantation*) or is it specific to a person or group (e.g., *Mrs. Miller should take us to visit the Plymouth Plantation*)? Review various examples in mentor texts.
- Discuss the need for background information with students. Why does the mentor text not include background information? Find examples from the text that include and discuss reasons.
- Brainstorm with the class a thesis statement for the argument to be jointly written by the whole class. For 3rd grade, it would be easier to write a letter requesting something of a member of the school community or to create posters or brochures about visiting the place where students' families came from. The letter requires focus on a specific writer/reader and the brochure can have a common statement, such as *Visit* . . . [name of the country, state, or city]. Fourth- and 5th-grade students should be encouraged to use generalized statements.
- Write the thesis statement on the strip (Figure 8.2). For example:

Schools should offer healthy snacks

FIGURE 8.3

- Give groups or individual students a copy of the argument graphic organizer and have them choose the thesis statement for the argument they want to work on.

- Have a few groups or students share and comment on their ideas.
- Discuss whether the students should add some background information to their thesis statements. If background information is required, what should be added?

LESSON 10. Give a Variety of Reasons

Goal: To encourage students to give multiple reasons to support their thesis statement because it will make their argument stronger.

Materials: There are many examples from the Internet of "reasons to . . ." articles. For example, a travel brochure for Latin America has 10 reasons to travel with the company (www.statravel.co.uk/the-world-brochure.htm; Latin America 2013.pdf, p. 6). Some animal shelters post reasons to adopt an adult cat. Some are simple and just give the reasons (e.g., www.petfinder.com/pet-adoption/cat-adoption/10-reasons-senior-cats-rule/), while others are more lengthy and add information to support the reasons (www.catsontheweb.org/10-reasons.htm). Poster paper.

Activities

- Share a few examples of "reasons to . . ." articles. Focus solely on the reasons in these texts.
- Discuss how the reasons are different in each and how they support the argument.
- Discuss for which audience the reasons would be appealing and why.
- Give the students a thesis statement (e.g., *Five reasons to ban cell phones from the classroom*). Discuss that although thesis statements usually are worded without *five reasons* language, but rather something like, *Cell phones should be banned from classrooms,* starting with the number of reasons is a way to get the attention of the reader and appropriate if listing the reasons and not writing a full essay.
- Brainstorm possible reasons that would support the thesis statement given the audience. Alternatively, the teacher and students can brainstorm without attention to audience and then discuss to which audience or audiences the reasons would be appealing.
- Think about behaviors or beliefs that would be important to promote in a school. Examples could include, *Students should collaborate in class* ("to do" argument) or *Reading is a good habit* ("about" or belief/opinion argument).
- Divide the class into groups. Give each group a different thesis statement. Have the groups come up with 3–5 reasons for their thesis statement.
- Ask groups to share their reasons, revise if necessary, and write them on poster paper.
- Post the list in the classroom, hallway, computer room, or library, depending on where they would be appropriate, in order to persuade others in the school community.

LESSON 11. Development of Reasons for Students' Projects

Goal: To develop reasons for the class project in order to further model how to write reasons and to help students develop reasons for their group/individual projects.

Materials: Resources used for previous lessons, especially those that relate to the class project and students projects. Class graphic organizer with thesis statement. Blank squares of paper to write reasons. Group or individual students' graphic organizers with their thesis statements.

Activities

- Have the large version of the graphic organizer on chart paper with the thesis statement for the class project included (Figure 8.4). Students should have the same graphic organizer as a group or individual with their own thesis statement(s) written.

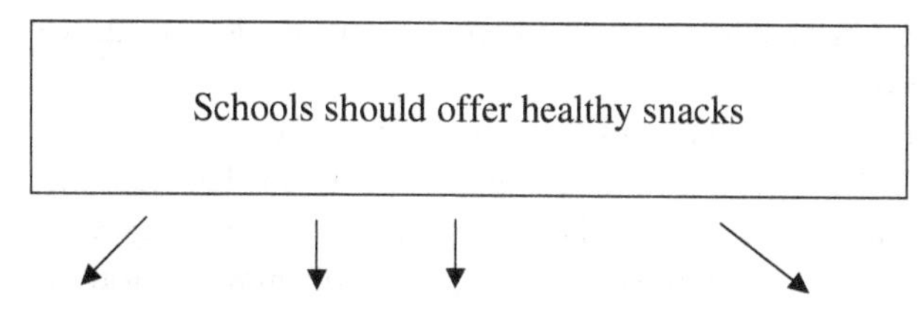

FIGURE 8.4

- Brainstorm with students possible reasons related to the class project and write them on blank squares of paper that will fit under the arrows of the graphic organizer.
- (Optional) Have students in groups read about the topic of the class project and suggest additional reasons or confirm those already suggested.
- Given the audience that the class has chosen, have the students/groups choose the strongest or most appealing reasons. There is no "magic number" of reasons.
- Have students decide the order to present the reasons and place them in the class graphic organizer accordingly.
- Have students work in groups or pairs to choose the reasons to include in their own group or individual arguments. Have them write the reasons on sticky notes and attach them to their own graphic organizers following the same process as before.
- Confer with groups and/or individual students about their reasons. Discuss whether (a) the reasons are related to the thesis statement, (b) each reason is a different point, and (c) the reasons are suitable for their audience.

LESSON 12. Development of Evidence for Students' Projects

Goal: To develop evidence for the class project (further modeling) and to help students develop evidence for their group/individual projects.

Materials: Resources used for previous lessons, especially those that relate to the class project and students projects. Other sources that can provide evidence. Other examples with different types of evidence through multiple forms of media (e.g., this video on an acne cream illustrates a variety of types of evidence, including a TV personality, experts, statistics, and personal examples, www.toptenz.net/top-10-persuasive-tv-ads.php). Class graphic organizer with thesis statement and reasons. Blank squares of paper to write evidence notes. Group or individual students' graphic organizers with their thesis statements and reasons. Projector.

Activities

- Project the mentor text and have students identify the evidence. Discuss the types of evidence.
- Project other mentor texts that have different kinds of evidence and discuss the various types of evidence.
- Show the video and discuss the types of evidence.
- Have the large version of the graphic organizer on chart paper with the thesis statement and reasons for the class project included (Figure 8.5). Students should have their group/individual graphic organizers that they have started creating in previous lessons.

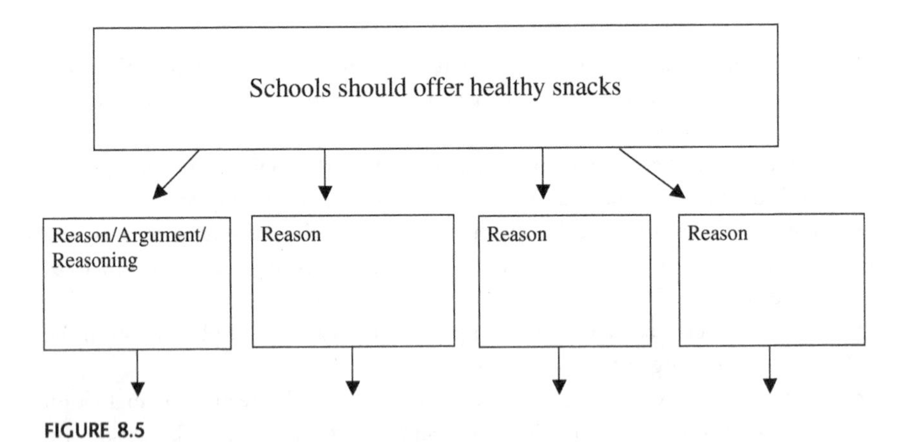

FIGURE 8.5

- Brainstorm with students the potential pieces of evidence related to the class project and write them on the blank square of paper to be put under the arrows in the graphic organizer.

- Have students in groups read about the topic of the class project and suggest additional evidence or confirm those already suggested.
- Given the audience the class has chosen, have students choose the strongest or most appealing evidence. Have them discuss whether the evidence should appeal to the intellect, emotions, or both.
- Have students analyze facts collected in their research to determine which facts will help to persuade the reader. Students should omit facts that do not support their opinion (Stead, 2002).
- Have students decide which pieces of evidence supports which reason and place them in the class graphic organizer accordingly.
- Have students work in groups or pairs to choose the evidence to include in their own group or individual arguments following the same process of brainstorming, researching, checking the audience, and making final decisions. Have students write their evidence on sticky notes and attach them to their graphic organizers.
- Confer with groups and/or individual students about their evidence. Discuss whether the evidence supports their reasons and is suitable for their audience. Have students show where they found the evidence. Make sure there is consistency of point of view when choosing reasons and evidence.

LESSON 13. Development of Reinforcement of Position or Thesis

Goal: To teach students to create a conclusion that connects, but does not repeat, the thesis statement.

Materials: Class graphic organizer and group/individual graphic organizers that have been developed in previous lessons. Projector.

Activities

- Project the mentor text and compare the conclusion with the thesis statement. While the thesis statement says, "Dogs . . . make good pets," the concluding statement reads, "To sum up, dogs are really friendly, civilized and loyal companions." Both sentences present the same idea, but they use different words. Moreover, the conclusion greatly reinforces the thesis statement. Repeat this activity with other mentor texts.
- Review the class graphic organizer created and added to during previous lessons and brainstorm possible conclusions (Figure 8.6). Write them on the board.
- Discuss with the class which conclusion seems to be the strongest reinforcement of the position, always with the audience in mind. Choose one conclusion and add it to the class graphic organizer.

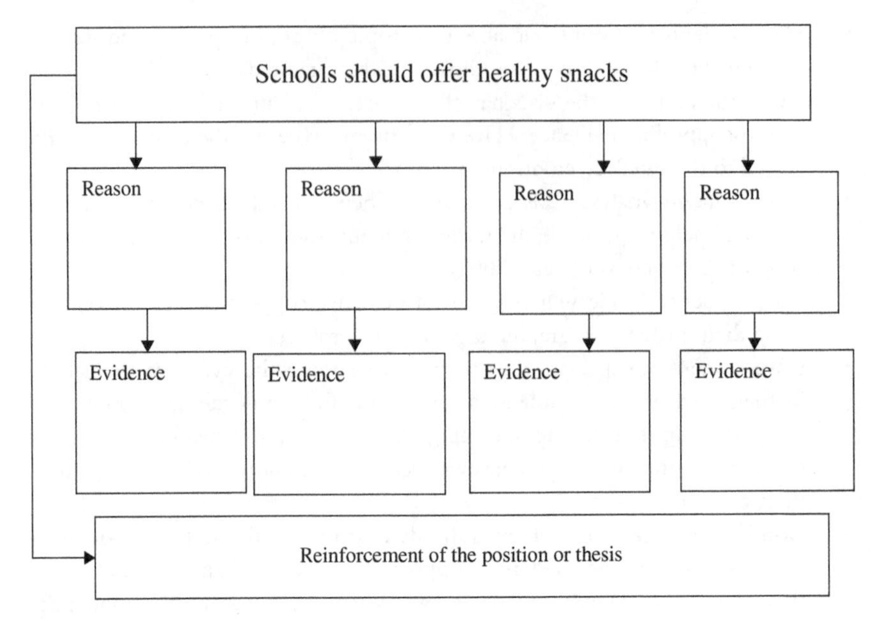

FIGURE 8.6

- Have groups or pairs of students read their group/individual thesis statements.
- Have students brainstorm possible conclusions and choose one to use.
- Continue to confer with groups or individuals, inquiring about the logic used to link the conclusion to the thesis statements in their graphic organizers. By this stage, the teacher should have checked all of the students' graphic organizers.
- Have a few groups or students share with the whole class.

LESSON 14. Produce a Final Essay

Goal: To produce the class essay as a model for the students to simultaneously produce their group/individual essays.

Materials: Class and group/individual graphic organizers. Chart paper. Smartboard or PowerPoint.

Activities

- If background information is needed, use the notes in the graphic organizer to create, in consultation with the whole class, a paragraph with the background information. Then, copy the thesis statement from the graphic organizer.
- Jointly write a preview of the reasons.
- Brainstorm with students how to transfer the notes in the class graphic organizer to create separate paragraphs with reasons and evidence (See suggestions

in chapter 2). While transferring the notes to the full text, bring up selected mechanics of writing, such as indenting to create paragraphs or quoting and citing things that students have copied verbatim from sources or from interviews.

- Following the same process used with the whole class, have students in groups, pairs, or individually write the various components of their arguments.

Part II: Language

Arguments are usually written about general issues, unless the focus is on a particular event or issue (Derewianka, 1990). The language of arguments has to be carefully crafted on the basis of audience and voice. The choices writers make heavily influence the success of their arguments. Therefore, the focus of this section is on how audience and voice influence language choices. An important language element to consider is the choice of specific verbs, nouns, and adverbials that help paint a favorable or unfavorable picture, depending on the perspective that will best support the argument given a particular audience. Additionally, well-developed paragraphs contribute to the clarity of the essay. There are other language features of arguments that will not be covered in the lessons, such as text connectives. These relate to reasoning and were seen in the mentor text *(furthermore, and finally, for this reason)*. Teachers can develop lessons using suggestions for teaching text connectives from other units.

The following 5th-grade student text, written after the class received instruction on the purpose and stages, will be used to illustrate major challenges that students have with language. This is Isabella's first draft. The first two paragraphs are included.

1. *We should't have zoos!*
2. *Why we should have zoos? Zoos are abusive to animals. When a animal dose a confusing trick wrong, the cruel trainer will hit, kicked or shocked the animal very baddly and possably kill the harm less animal. It's horrible what these repulsive trainers are doing- would you like if you were abused? Anmals belong in the wild not in zoo.*

Individual students will need conferencing, as determined by their individual language needs. For example, Isabella constructed some of the future tense incorrectly *(will hit, kicked, or shocked)*. Conferring with her would clarify if she has problems with the formation of the future tense or if she made the mistake because she had *animals get hit, get kicked, get shocked* in her outline.

Generalized Participants

Arguments commonly center on generalized participants, sometimes including beings like *dogs* in the mentor text, but they often include generalized issues, such as pollution, smoking, and school uniforms. Occasionally, arguments can be written to support a specific situation (e.g., *your dog needs obedience school*). Children have difficulty with the use of generalized participants. As seen in the uncoached piece, although the prompt had a generalized participant *(Should schools have rules?)*, the student immediately changed it to a specific topic *(Yes! I think we sould have school rules . . .)*. However, after learning about the purpose and stages of the genre, Isabella mastered the use of generalized participants.

	1	*2*	*3*	*4*	*Uncoached or Mid-unit Writing Comments*
Generalized Participants (dogs, zoos, animals)				✓	The thesis statement is written in first person but that was given to the students. The rest of the piece uses generalized participants: zoos, animals, trainers.

LESSON 15. Generalized Participants

Goal: To help students distinguish when they want to persuade generalized participants, as opposed to an individual or group.

Materials: Student work that illustrates different types of persuasion, some that are appropriate and some that could use revision. Projector.

Activities

- Project an example of student work. Ask the student author, "Are you referring to a specific person or group or to a category, in general (such as kids, teachers, or smoking)?"
- Given the student's answer, read aloud or have the author read aloud and discuss whether the grammar reflects writing to generalized participants or individuals. For example, *students should eat healthy snacks* (third person plural) refers to all kids, but *we should eat healthy snacks* (first person) is limited to the students in that particular class.
- Decide whether the student's draft needs revision and check for consistent language throughout the piece.
- Repeat this activity with a few more student examples.
- Have students look at their writing and discuss in groups to whom they are writing and if their language reflects this and is consistent throughout their writing.

Audience Awareness And Voice (Tenor)

Other aspects of language that play a role in the relationship between writer and audience and express the writer's voice include sentence type use, grammatical person use, modality, evaluative vocabulary, and grading (Table 8.2) (See chapter 3 for more information).

The mentor text illustrates these language choices when writing for a general adult audience (See Table 8.3). The choice of vocabulary supports the point of

TABLE 8.2 Audience and Voice in Relation to Language

Language Feature	*Adult Audience*	*Young Audience*
Language choices to describe reasons and evidence demonstrate awareness of audience.	Reflects interest of adults	Reflects interest of children
Type of sentences	Statements	Can add questions, commands, exclamations
Person	Third person, more authoritative	First and second person, more informal, connecting closer with audience. Except in the case of letters, even to adults, in which they may need to use first and second person
Modality	Can be moderate, not too high (which may show disrespect)	Depends on relationship, it can be more forceful but don't want to sound "bossy"
Evaluative vocabulary	Choice to appeal to audience, careful not to use overly familiar or derogatory language	Appealing to children
Grading (turn intensity up or down)	Convincing, but not too exaggerated	Has more liberty with grading

TABLE 8.3 Audience Awareness and Voice in Mentor Text

Language choices to describe reasons and evidence demonstrate awareness of audience	Use of verbs such as "greet," "never leave us," "protect," "stop thieves," "trained," and "help people," and nouns such as "quality," "loyalty," and "companions," all depicting dogs favorably in the types of qualities an adult appreciates.
Use of technical vocabulary for evidence	"Sniff out drugs," "find illicit DVDs," "hunt down prisoners," "help elderly and disabled"
Types of sentences Statements preferred	All statements
Use of person	Third person
Modality	"Will" (medium), "can" (low)
Evaluative vocabulary To express attitude	"Ideal," "attractive," "strong," "friendly," "civilized," "loyal"
Grading	"Ideal" (turned up)

view. A number of verbs and nouns reflect good qualities of dogs. These are qualities particularly appealing to adults. If the audience were children, then actions such as *play, run,* and *snuggle* might be more appealing. The mentor text is written in statements and in the third person. There are some medium- and low-strength modals. A number of adjectives highlight dogs' qualities whereas others describe critical situations in which dogs were helpful, such as *dire* and *serious.* Both help to make dogs more appealing. Some have the strength turned up, such as *ideal* instead of *good,* the more neutral adjective, and *dire,* rather than *bad.*

Features of students' writing. Isabella's draft exhibits language choices appropriate for children (See following analysis). Isabella understands the power of vocabulary to support her point of view when using such negative verbs in connection to what happens in a zoo. Although *kill* sounds like an exaggeration, it is an acceptable vocabulary choice when children are the audience.

Other language choices appropriate for a young audience are the uses of some questions and exclamations, first and second person, and strong modality. Her choice of words to describe zoos and trainers reflects her strong opinion on the treatment of animals in zoos, whereas animals are *harmless.* The use of *repulsive* is also an exaggeration.

	1	*2*	*3*	*4*	*Mid-unit Writing Comments*
Language choices to describe reasons and evidence demonstrate awareness of audience.				✓	"Hit," "kicked," "shocked," "abuse," and "kill" sets forth her perspective.
Use of technical vocabulary for evidence		✓			Some technical words in the evidence for being abusive, like "shocked."
Types of sentences Statements preferred				✓	Exclamations and questions. The voice seems to consider the audience, other children.
Use of person					Uses first person plural and second person. Most is third person. The mentor text was in third person "Should there be zoos?" Student switched it to "We shouldn't have zoos." However, the students' texts in the book use first person and are addressing kids.
Modality				✓	Uses of "should," strong modality appropriate when a child addresses children. Uses "possably" [possibly], a low modality adverbial to soften the verb "kill," a rather strong assertion. This makes it more believable.
Evaluative vocabulary				✓	"Abusive," "cruel," "repulsive," referring to zoos and trainers. "Confusing," referring to the trick given to the animals, a sign of maliciousness toward the animals. "Harmless," referring to animals
Grading				✓	"Repulsive" (volume up)

Although Isabella seems to be on point with her use of language given her audience, the concern is whether it was planned or intuitive. To test her abilities, she should be given opportunities to write to a different audience to see if she makes different choices and is aware of them.

Some of the other students were not as successful in maintaining a consistent voice. For example, in an argument directed to teachers, some students switched between first and third person. Their choice of words, reflecting their perspective, was sometimes respectful, but also included language that would be appropriate to use only with a close friend.

LESSON 16. Language Choices When Writing to Different Audiences

Goal: To develop student awareness that word choice helps to persuade; language reflects the writer's voice or perspective, but the language may need to change given the audience.

Materials: Mentor text. Additional arguments directed to different audiences. Projector.

Activities

- Re-read aloud the mentor text.
- Ask the students, "Who do think the audience is and why?" Write down their responses and use them to relate to the points you want to make about audience and language.
- Project the mentor text with the nouns, verbs, and adjectives that reflect favorably on dogs underlined.
- Ask the students, "How do you feel about dogs when you read these words? What do you think the author's perspective is on dogs?"
- Now ask about audience, "If the audience were children, what kinds of actions would the author have the dogs do to make them appealing? What adjectives would you use to describe dogs to make them appealing?" Record the student responses.
- Jointly construct a parallel argument about dogs, but using children as the audience and using the students' ideas and responses to inform the construction.

Linda Drueding, a 5th-grade teacher, showed her students a toothpaste commercial for children (www.youtube.com/watch?v=gdcVRueT2cw). Then she discussed the commercial with them, asking the students about the intended audience and what they saw that reinforced that belief. Students talked about images, music, and language.

LESSON 17. Using Grading to Persuade

Goal: To show students how to turn the grading volume up or down to effectively persuade.

Materials: Poem, *The Mosquito's Song* (See "Additional Resources"). Groups of word cards with words that increase or decrease from neutral grading (in bold). Examples include *drenched, soaked,* ***wet,*** *moist, damp; stunning, gorgeous,* ***pretty,*** *nice-looking; petrified, terrified,* ***afraid, scared,*** *upset, worried; pleasant, polite,* ***nice, friendly,*** *amiable, charming;* and *loathsome, revolting,* ***ugly,*** *awful, bad-looking.* Pictures of people showing an emotion, with a range of possible emotions listed. For example, there may be a picture of a sad child with a list that says, *down, sad, unhappy, miserable, bereaved.*

Activities

- Have students look at the pictures and say which of the words from the list best describes the child.
- Discuss (a) why a writer would choose a particular word and grading, (b) that exaggeration can be counter-productive because it can make the argument less believable, and (c) there are times when turning the volume down can help to persuade. For example, in *The Mosquito's Song,* the mosquito makes a better argument by talking about "a *little* drop" and "a *tiny* puncture," turning down the volume to be more persuasive.
- Have students work in groups. Give each group a situation and have them think of a sentence with a reason that requires the grading volume to be either turned up or down to be persuasive. Students should also indicate the audience. For example, for the situation *being late for school,* a student might say to his or her teacher, *I was just a few minutes late,* whereas for the situation *watching TV after bedtime,* a student might say to his or her mother, *it was an extraordinary program that was extremely educational.*
- Have students share and discuss the effectiveness of their language choices given their audience.

LESSON 18. Revision of Student Work for Effective Language

Goal: To help students apply what they have learned in the previous two lessons on language to their own work.

Materials: A paragraph from each student's writing. Have some paragraphs ready to project, others can just be flagged in students' writing. Projector.

Activities

- Project a piece of student writing. For example, Isabella's aforementioned paragraph could be used.
- Ask students to identify the words that the author used to persuade the reader to her point of view. Ask them if the words chosen helped to persuade them.
- Discuss possible alternatives or changes to the words, or decide that they all work well.
- Repeat the activity with a few more selections from other students' writing.

- Working in groups or pairs, have students propose revisions to the rest of their pieces. Confer with groups or individuals as they are doing this work.

LESSON 19. Grammar Choices to Be Effective With Different Audiences

Goal: To show students that the choice of type of sentence, person, and modality depends on audience if the argument is to be persuasive.

Materials: Mentor text, written for adults, uses all statements, third person, medium and low modality, vocabulary that reflects positive attitude towards dogs. *Should There Be Zoos?: A Persuasive Text,* written by and for children (though other persuasive texts written for children can be used), which uses statements, exclamations, questions, first, second, and third person, variety of modality, evaluative vocabulary reflecting the author's point of view, and grading, such as "*ludicrous* idea." Projector. Table 8.3, or something similar, with the features of language and grammar that help develop tenor, written on chart paper. Three large pieces of paper and markers.

Activities

- Re-read the mentor text and then read one of the sections of *Should There Be Zoos?* Ask the students to identify the intended audience for each text.
- Ask students to provide reasons, evidence, or both for their choice.
- Project sections of the texts and have students take turns to come to point out specific language or grammar that indicated the audience and the purpose of persuasion. Remind students of the language features by pointing at the chart paper with the table (Table 8.3).
- Give the class a topic to write a short persuasive piece.
- Divide the class into three groups. Ask one group to write to an adult audience, another to students their age, and the third to younger children.

LESSON 20. Revision of Student Work for Effective Grammar

Goal: To help students apply what they have learned in previous lessons to their own work to demonstrate use of a voice appropriate for their audience.

Materials: A paragraph from each student's writing. Have some paragraphs ready to project, others can just be flagged in students' writing. Projector.

Activities

- Project a piece of student writing. For example, Isabella's aforementioned paragraph could be used.
- Ask students to identify the type of sentence, person, and modality in the piece. Ask students if these features help to persuade them, given that the piece was written for children.

- Discuss possible alternatives or changes to the language features, or have students decide that they all work to persuade the audience.
- Repeat the activity with a few pieces from other students' writing.
- Working in groups or pairs, have students propose revisions to the other pieces. Confer with groups or individual students as they do this work.

Creating a Cohesive Text (Mode)

Earlier in the chapter, the overall cohesion of the text through the development of stages was addressed. When planning to write the whole text, students need to review the stages to determine if the components make sense together. For example, each paragraph in the mentor text presents a reason supported by evidence that dogs make good pets.

There is a further need to ensure that the clauses in individual paragraphs work together, helping the paragraph to flow clearly. Each clause should start with a Theme followed by new information (See chapter 3). The Theme in the following clauses either connects with the original theme or with the new information. For example, in the second paragraph of the mentor text, most of the themes relate to the original "dog" by using pronouns or repeating the word. The pattern is broken only in the fourth sentence when "example" becomes the Theme.

Theme	*New Information*
The most attractive quality of a dog	is its faith in its owner and its loyalty.
They always	greet us when we come home
and they	will never leave us in a dire situation.
For example there	was a very sick man
And the dog	barked and barked until the rescue team arrived.

Features of Students' Writing

Students have great difficulty writing paragraphs that flow. One of the main problems that students have is that they do not always introduce a theme well and, when they do, they overuse pronouns in the theme position, making it unclear what they are talking about. For example, a 5th grader wrote,

> **Moose track** is delisious. **It**'s smooth and mouthwatering. **It** has smooth chocolate and penut buter mixed with vanilla ice cream. **moose track** is so delisious **It** will make you want to eat more and more of it.

The two themes are *Moose track* and *it*. Unless the audience knows what *moose track* is, the reader would not know that it is a type of ice cream. Using *this ice cream* instead of *it* in the third sentence would have made this clear. Further, the second clause could have been merged with the first.

Isabella's second paragraph has some good features and some problems.

Theme	*New Information*
Why **we**	should have zoos?
Zoos	are abusive to **animals**.
When an **animal** dose a confusing trick wrong, the cruel **trainer**	will hit, kicked and shocked the animal very badly
and [the **trainers**] possably	kill the harm less animal.
It	's horrible what **these repulsive trainers** are doing
Would **you**	like if you were abused?
Animals	belong in the wild not in zoo.

The Themes contain topics that are at the heart of her argument, such as *zoos, animals,* and *trainers.* Others relate to the interpersonal function, or the relation between the writer and audience (e.g., *we, you*). If the questions with these themes were eliminated, then the clause, *Zoos are abusive to animals,* her first reason, would become the topic sentence. The second question removes the focus on animals. Sometimes, authors writing to children use this strategy to engage them, but it can also break the flow of the argument.

The pronoun *it* at the start of the fifth sentence relates to the previous new information and would be better expressed with a nominalization, such as, *cruelty to ANIMALS,* language that children at this stage are unlikely to naturally produce. Using the nominalization would eliminate *these repulsive trainers* from the new information position, because it would no longer be new to the reader.

The last clause refers back to the central topic of the whole argument, animals, and the new information relates to the argument, in general, and does not extend the notion of cruelty, the center of this paragraph.

LESSON 21. Review of Paragraphs

Goal: To use the Theme/New Information principle to revise paragraphs to help the information flow.

Materials: A table with two columns, one with the Themes from a paragraph of a published persuasive text that the students have not seen, and the other with the Themes of a paragraph from a student text. Write the examples in two columns on chart paper or project them.

Long before television was invented people	I think we
Books	So they
Many people	So when
Books	and so we

A published argument text, as well as student samples. Large Theme/New Information Worksheet (See end-of-chapter resources) on chart paper or smartboard. Individual worksheets for the groups. Projector.

Activities

- Project the table with the two sets of Themes or show on chart paper and ask the students to identify what each paragraph is about. Ask, "What are the authors arguing about?"
- Discuss what from the columns helped to answer this question, and what made it difficult.
- Do the Theme/New Information analysis of one paragraph of the mentor text on the worksheet, as was illustrated earlier in this chapter using Isabella's paragraph.
- Discuss with the students what they see in the Theme position. Does it help them to understand what the paragraph is about? How does the new information in one clause connect with the Theme in the next?
- Repeat this activity with a few examples of students' work and discuss, similar to Isabella's earlier example.
- Propose possible revisions to the writing.
- Using their individual Theme/New Information Worksheets, have students work on one paragraph in their writing with the help of a partner or group. Confer with individuals or groups while they work.
- If students finish with one paragraph, they can go on to work on additional paragraphs. All students need to work on at least one paragraph. You may assign some paragraphs as homework for additional practice.

Resources

- Analysis of student work: Purpose and stages
- Analysis of student work: Language
- Graphic organizer
- Theme/New information worksheet
- Additional resources that illustrate the genre

Argument—Analysis of Student Work: Purpose and Stages (Grades 3–5)

Content Area: **Medium:** **Intended Audience:**

Key: 1. Needs substantial support; 2. Needs instruction; 3. Needs revision; 4. Meets standard; NA: Not applicable

	1	*2*	*3*	*4*	*Uncoached Writing Comments*	*1*	*2*	*3*	*4*	*Final Writing Comments*
Purpose To persuade to do something or to believe about something										
Verb conjugation Appropriate Tense (present, future, past in evidence, and use of modals)										
Title (If required by the medium)										
Thesis statement or Claim Background information if needed Preview of reasons										
Reasons supported by evidence										
Reinforcement of statement of position										
Cohesive text (Macro and Hyper theme, based on graphic organizer for the genre)										

Criteria

1. Needs substantial support: The student writer needs extensive help developing that aspect of the genre.
2. There are gaps in the writer's understanding of the specific aspect. The writer has insufficient control. S/he needs instruction and practice.
3. The paper needs revision on one or two instances of the feature. A conference would be sufficient to help the writer meet the standard.
4. The paper reflects what the student should be able to accomplish and write independently given the instruction provided for this grade level (National Center on Education and the Economy, 2004).

Argument—Analysis of Student Work: Language (Grades 3–5)

Type: **Content Area:** **Medium:** **Intended Audience:**

Key: 1. Needs substantial support; 2. Needs instruction; 3. Needs revision; 4. Meets standard; NA: Not applicable

	1	*2*	*3*	*4*	*Mid-unit Writing Comments*	*1*	*2*	*3*	*4*	*Final Writing Comments*
Generalized participants (dogs, zoos, animals)										
Language choices to describe reasons and evidence to demonstrate awareness of audience										
Use of technical vocabulary for evidence										
Types of sentences (Statements preferred)										
Use of person Third person, except in letters and sermons where first and second person are used										
Modality Medium and low for adults (more respectful); High modality for adults addressing students.										
Evaluative vocabulary To express attitude										
Grading										
Cohesive paragraphs: Theme/New information										

Criteria

1. Needs substantial support: The student writer needs extensive help developing that aspect of the genre.
2. There are gaps in the writer's understanding of the specific aspect. The writer has insufficient control. S/he needs instruction and practice.
3. The paper needs revision on one or two instances of the feature. A conference would be sufficient to help the writer meet the standard.
4. The paper reflects what the student should be able to accomplish and write independently given the instruction provided for this grade level (National Center on Education and the Economy, 2004).

Graphic Organizer

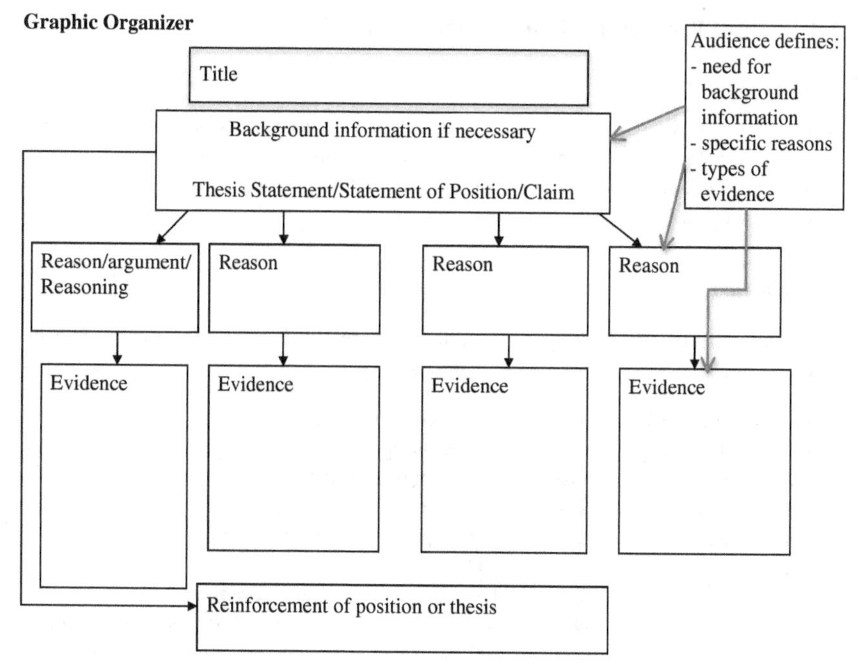

FIGURE 8.7

Theme/New Information Worksheet

Write **Themes and New Information** in one paragraph. Are they connected? Does the information flow? Does the Theme signal what the author is talking about in that paragraph?	
Theme	**New Information**

Additional Resources That Illustrate the Genre

Books

Leavitt, P.B. (2001). "The mosquito's song." In P.B. Janeczco (Ed.), *Dirty laundry pile: Poems in different voices.* New York, NY: HarperCollins. (Persuasive poem)
Stead, T. (2000). *Should there be zoos? A persuasive text.* New York, NY: Mondo Publishing. (Book written by students and their teacher)

Storybooks

There are a number of storybooks that illustrate the language of persuasion by showing characters trying to persuade each other.

Kellogg, S. (1992). *Can I keep him?* New York, NY: Penguin Group (USA) Incorporated. (This book shows persuasion through the dialogue between a child and the mother. The child wants to bring home a series of animals and the mother denies his requests. The two competing sides of the argument are presented by the child and the mother. The strategies used by the characters to persuade can be applied to writers trying to persuade their audience.)
Orloof, K. (2009). *I wanna iguana.* New York, NY: Putnam Juvenile.
Scieszka, J., & Smith, L. (1989). *True story of the three little pigs.* New York, NY: Puffin Books.
Smith, L. (2006). *Glasses: Who needs 'em?* New York, NY: Viking Juvenile. (A story about a child needing glasses and not wanting them. The doctor gives reasonable, and then crazy, reasons to wear glasses. This could be a good example of using facts to support your arguments.)
Teague, M. (2002). *Dear Mrs. LaRue: Letters from obedience school.* New York, NY: Scholastic, Inc. (A dog is sent to obedience school and writes letters trying to persuade his master to come pick him up. It could be interesting to analyze the individual letters and have students write their own letter using some of the issues raised.)
Viorst, J. (1993). *Earrings!* New York, NY: Simon & Schuster. (Story of a girl who wanted pierced ears and earrings, but her parents would not allow her to do so. It could be good to read and then have students write a letter or essay to convince the parents, while critiquing the strategies that the main character used. The only problem with this text is that the Theme is predominantly intended for girls. A similar text may need to be found for boys.)

Examples of How to Create Brochures

www.stocklayouts.com/Downloads/PDF/Preview/TR0110101-Preview.pdf

Internet Resources to Teach About Evidence

www.hhs.helena.k12.mt.us/Teacherlinks/Oconnorj/evidence.html (How to use evidence in persuasive communications)
www.toptenz.net/top-10-persuasive-tv-ads.php (Ten TV commercials with persuasive arguments for products)
www.toucaned.com/Products/PublicHealth/TeensAdultsPosterPamph.html (Brochure about germs; how germs work and how to avoid them)
www.toucaned.com/Products/PublicHealth/ToolKitImages/adult/pamphlets/english/03.jpg
www.youtube.com/watch?v=R9jaOROeYII&feature=PlayList&p=76F12E0A6994189E&index=4&playnext=2&playnext_from=PL (Toyota Tundra commercial)

9

FICTIONAL NARRATIVES

Chapter Map	
Grade Level and Content Areas Fictional Narrative Unit General Preparation Part I: Purpose, Character Development, and Stages of the Genre Purpose of Fictional Narratives Development of Major Characters Sketching the Plot Creating the Text Stages or Plot of the Narrative Skills Needed to Write the Core of the Story Ending Title Resources Types of Fictional Narratives External Attributes, Internal Qualities, and Influence on Plot Analysis Analysis of Student Work Form Worksheet 1: Character Analysis Worksheet 2: Character Development Graphic Organizer Additional Resources That Illustrate the Genre	Deb Nelson and Cheryl O'Connor, two 4th-grade teachers who have a job share, started the unit on fictional narratives by working on character development. Cheryl drew a character on chart paper and explained to the students how they imagined it, noting the external and internal features on the sides of the drawing. Next, students worked on their own characters. In the next couple days, Deb had the students show (through drawing) the kind of person their character was instead of just coming out and saying it. One student had a great example of "before" and "after" work, which Deb put up on the projector and showed to the whole class. His story initially read, *In Indonesia, a big kimodo dragon was feeling lonely so he went into the town to get some friends.* After Deb conferenced with him to distinguish showing and telling, he wrote, *One day in Indonesia, a big kimodo dragon named Jake was so lonely he cried and talked to himself. He read alone and moped around. So he decided to go find a friend.* The other students were then instructed to try showing versus telling to help the audience understand the kind of people (or animals!) they intended their characters to be.

A narrative is a special kind of story that is highly valued in English-speaking cultures. Narratives tell an imaginative story, although sometimes they are based on facts. There are many types of narratives, such as legends, myths, and historical fiction (See "Types of Fictional Narratives" at the end of the chapter). Narratives are structured to be entertaining and to teach cultural values. In narratives, normal events are disrupted and language is used to build up suspense until the plot reaches a crisis point. The basic stages of narratives are orientation, complication, evaluation, and resolution (Labov & Waletsky, 1967; Martin & Rose, 2008). Across different cultures, narratives share a similar organization, but what makes for a complicating event and resolution may differ (Martin & Rose, 2008).

Other story genres may involve a disrupting event that is evaluated, but "the 'point' of narrative is how the protagonists resolve a complication in their lives, once they have evaluated the complicating action with some type of attitude" (Martin & Rose, 2008, p. 67). Thus, the characters play a critical role in narratives and the way in which the characters confront and resolve the crisis teaches the audience about the ways of behaving that are valued in a culture (Rothery & Stenglin, 1997). A narrative may end with a writer's evaluative comment (Butt et al., 2000; Schleppegrell, 2004; Education Department of Western Australia, 1994).

Narratives are a more advanced type of storytelling than personal recounts. Some parents oppose the use of fictional narratives in school because they reflect cultural values. They feel that values should be taught at home, whereas the role of schools is to cover content knowledge such as science, math, and history (Dien, 1994). Children come to school familiar with this genre from home experiences of telling or reading stories. These experiences are reinforced in schools when children read or are read more narratives than other genres. Further, a high percentage of the texts in basal readers are narratives (Kamberelis, 1999).

Although children usually enter school with familiarity of the characteristics and structure of narratives, they may have some difficulty grasping the fictional nature of stories before ages 7 or 8. Pre-school children's early interpretation of a story is that something happened in the past and is unchangeable (Applebee, 1978). By ages 7 or 8, most children are able to differentiate fictional narratives from other non-fiction types of writing and have a well-formed notion of story organization, such as the need for an initial event introducing the characters, the following events, and some kind of final resolution. They also are aware that most narratives are written in the past tense (Kamberelis, 1999). Between the ages of 8 and 14, children progress to writing longer stories, but use the greater length to elaborate and add more detail rather than to impose more structure on their writing (Donovan, 2001; Langer, 1992).

Grade Levels and Content Areas

From a very early age, children have a sense of the narrative genre, but they have difficulty writing stories (McKeough, 2013). Some suggest that "it is the most difficult genre to do well" (Rog & Kropp, 2004, p. 67). Development of characters, taking a third person point of view, creating a problem and a crisis, tracking a number of participants through narrative and dialogue, and building suspense through language and rhetorical devices are features that make narratives challenging to write. In addition, different cultures have different ways of organizing narratives and express different values through them (McCabe & Bliss, 2003), making it difficult for children to acquire new ways of writing narratives.

Research has shown that children can attempt narratives as young as kindergarten age. In the early grades, they are most likely able to include the basic elements of the text structure, including an initiating event, a sequence of events, and a final event. Students also can use basic language features, such as the use of past tense and temporal connectors as well as participants introduced and tracked through appropriate use of reference ties (Kamberelis, 1999). At this young age, students can become familiar with characters' features and the impact on plot through reading and analyzing stories in dialogue with the teacher (Roser, Martinez, Fuhrken, & McDonnold, 2007). To develop all of the features, fictional narratives are best attempted in grades 4 and 5.

A kindergarten teacher carried out a unit on fictional narratives. Although there was variation in students' writing, students started writing pieces closer to personal recount. However, after coaching, they were able to create imaginary stories with problems and resolution. To a large extent, the students copied from the model that the teacher created with the whole class (Brisk & Zisselsberger, 2011). In another class, McPhail (2009) had 1st graders write in a variety of genres. He found that the boys did better in writing when producing fictional narratives, the genre which they preferred overall. Girls, on the other hand, did better in personal recounts (he calls them *personal narratives*) and only 40% achieved their highest scores in fictional narratives. A 2nd-grade teacher had students research animals and then used them as characters for their fictional narratives. She taught them the different stages of the genre. The most successful pieces were from those children who had been read many stories and were using the patterns they learned to create their own narratives. Other students had difficulty with the sequence of events, tracking participants, and creating a crisis. Their characters were, in general, rather flat (Brisk, 2007).

To adapt narratives to different grade levels, consider the following instructional suggestions:

- *Kindergarten:* Read fictional narratives, identify characters, identify external attributes and some internal qualities, and track plot. Oral retelling of narratives stresses the stages of the genre. Have students draw and write or dictate stories without additional coaching.

- *Grades 1–3:* Read fictional narratives; identify characters; identify external attributes and some internal qualities, such as traits and feelings; connect these attributes and qualities to the plot; and have students find the language that reflects external and internal features. Write simple narratives with focus on the stages and basic aspects of language, such as the use of past tense, tracking characters with the appropriate use of pronouns, and connecting text through temporal connectives. Have students write in first or third person. If students write in first person, ensure that they write an imaginary story with a crisis and resolution to make it different from a personal recount.
- *Grades 4–5:* Write narratives with attention to character development and other aspects. Encourage writing in third person.

Writing units are best embedded in content area teaching. Although fictional narratives are typically connected with ELA, research conducted in connection with a content area can be used to inform the topic of a fictional narrative. This research can also help students to overcome the challenge of not knowing what to write about. For example, 4th-grade students created their animal character in their fictional narrative on the basis of the information from their animal reports. The characteristics of the animal were considered when choosing the place where their character lived, what they ate, and other details. Further, children can use their knowledge of natural phenomena, such as volcanoes and hurricanes, to write an adventure.

Historical fiction is a form of fictional narrative that supports the learning of historical content through imaginary stories that use historical figures and events. The use of historical fiction helps students to immerse themselves in the events from a period that they are studying. For example, the book *Baseball Saved Us* explores the internment of Japanese communities during World War II through the experiences of a young boy.

Fictional narratives can also be used to address social issues connected to social studies or science. Although fictional narratives often reinforce cultural norms, they can also challenge cultural practices by showing characters in a variety of roles and actions (Rothery & Stenglin, 1997). For example, *The Name Jar* and *My Name Is Maria Isabel* address the challenges that immigrant children have with their names when they enter school in the United States. There are a number of children's books that explore current environmental problems. For example, *Garbage Collectors* explores the process of dealing with the excessive amounts of garbage disposed in the United States.

Teachers can choose topics that they cover in their social studies and science curricula or others that they think are important but were not covered. It is important that the fictional writing is not the only writing done in connection to the content area curriculum. For example, a teacher had students write a story in which cells were the characters after studying about cells in science. However, she did not ask students to use their knowledge of cells to write explanations or reports, which would have reinforced their scientific knowledge and language. Starting with this kind of fictional narrative writing in an area like science, though, can provide a scaffold to more formal types of scientific writing for students who might be challenged by those genres (Hildebrand, 2001).

Students could be encouraged to turn one of the topics in their persuasive pieces into a fictional narrative. For example, 5th-grade students had written persuasive letters to their principal about the need for bus monitors to make bus rides safer. They could then write a story describing an accident as a result of the lack of bus monitors as a way to make their point.

Fictional Narrative Unit

Fictional narratives are complex. With upper elementary grades, it may take more than six weeks to address character development. It can take longer if students are doing new research in relation to the topic. It is a good genre to do toward the end of the school year because it is a release when students are taking tests, can take advantage of any of the subject area topics already covered during the year, and involves story writing, generally viewed as a fun activity by the students.

There are a number of types of narratives (See the "Types of Fictional Narratives" list at the end of the chapter). Teachers may focus on a type to reinforce what they are covering in their reading program, such as fables, folktales, historical fiction, and others. For example, in the context of studying about Ghana, students explored and wrote trickster tales, which is a type of storytelling from that culture.

General Preparation

In preparation to start the unit and on the basis of the school-wide decisions of which genre to teach at which grade level and in connection to which content area, teachers should:

- Determine the content, writing, and language standards
- Choose resources
- Decide how students are going to be grouped
- Decide on writing products: medium, multimodality, and authenticity
- Build content knowledge
- Teach students to appropriate academic language
- Plan lessons based on analysis of students' uncoached writing.

There are extensive suggestions about each one of these points in chapter 2. Following are considerations specific to narratives with respect to topic, the CCSS, resources, appropriating academic language, and prompts for uncoached writing.

Teachers can use topics that have been explored in other content areas to be the themes of these narratives. This practice will reinforce what students have learned in another content area, save time, and mirror what real novelists do. Authors use this genre to explore an area of interest or to set forth a cause. One teacher went to the webpage of a children's fiction writer and showed her students the research that the writer had done to prepare for the topics in her stories. To make the writing task authentic, the teacher should discuss with students how they can use their fictional narratives to teach their audience something. For example, students could write a story about having an accident when crossing a street with a red light as way to teach safe behaviors when walking home from school. Students could write about the adventures of an astronaut who goes to all of the planets as a way to teach younger classes about the planets in the solar system. Using the topics from content areas reinforces the learning in those areas, increases student interest, and encourages students to write narratives about topics beyond the plots of movies or TV shows that they watch.

In the CCSS, fictional narratives are covered under the narratives category (CCSS.ELA-Literacy W.K-5.3). This is a broad category that covers fictional narratives as well as personal recounts. Thus, the standards are broad and do not distinguish between the features of the two types, except to mention "real or imagined experiences" as the only distinguishing characteristic (CCSS.ELA-Literacy W.3.3). The standards for grades 4 and 5 include some specificity with respect to stages, but they do not specify important features of narratives, such as including a crisis and resolution. Major characters' external attributes and internal qualities are essential aspects of fictional narratives. Moreover, characters are "the driving forces of stories" and, thus, require thoughtful development (Roser et al., 2007, p. 548). The CCSS, in contrast, only generally mentions the introduction of characters, showing the responses of characters to situations, describing characters in depth, and contrasting characters. There is no specification as to what it means to develop a character in depth, how language and rhetorical devices (including responses of characters to situations) accomplish the development of characters, or how the major characters drive the plot.

The CCSS language standards are not genre specific. Thus, features such as writing in the past, choosing first or third person, using language to develop characters, and appropriately using pronouns to track characters throughout the text are not mentioned. The Massachusetts Frameworks, based on the CCSS, recommend that students write in the various types of narratives.

Every classroom usually has a good collection of fictional narratives that are familiar to students. In this chapter, the fable *The Moray Eel and the Little Shrimp* is used as the mentor text to illustrate various aspects of the genre because it is short and has all of the essential features of the genre. For other recommended text, see the "Additional Resources" in the end-of-chapter resources.

Prompt for Uncoached Writing: Write an imaginary story.

Teachers analyze the writing that students produce from the prompt using the Analysis of Student Work: Purpose and Stages form in the end-of-chapter materials to determine what the students can already do and what their challenges are. Teachers can use the Unit Plan (Appendix A) to plot the necessary lessons.

Part I: Purpose, Character Development, and Stages of the Genre

Purpose of Fictional Narratives

The purpose of fictional narratives is to construct a pattern of events with a problematic or unexpected outcome that entertains and instructs. There are elements of suspense and disruption. The suspense builds to the crisis point. The characters are a central element of fictional narratives because they are the participants who experience and evaluate the complication, while often expressing an attitude. The crisis is then finally resolved. Fictional narratives teach ways of behaving that are valued in a culture (Butt et al., 2000; Martin & Rose, 2008) or at a minimum, "invite readers to think deeply about ethics, moral choices, and codes" (Roser et al., 2007, p. 548).

Features of Students' Writing

Students in a 4th-grade SEI class were asked to write an imaginary story in which the main character was a dog. José, a student relatively new to English, wrote:

> *I was loss, I went to a house and started barking. When a woman open the door I rolled around and stick my toung out. The woman took me and took care of me. I finnily had a family. Then I went out side to play fetch and I also got a Dog Biscut. I was the perfect dog for that woman. The End.*

Analyzing this sample, it is clear that José has a general sense of what a narrative is supposed to do. His verbs reflect that he is writing about something that has already passed. However, he has some errors typical of L2 learners, such as not adding *–ed* to regular past verbs and not knowing the irregular form. Thus, when he uses *open* and *stick,* he does not switch to the present tense, but resorts to that verb form because he is still learning how to form the past tense in English.

	1	*2*	*3*	*4*	*Uncoached Writing Comments*
Purpose To construct a pattern of events with a problem, crisis, and resolution.			✓		Has a sense that it is a story that has a problem and a resolution. No intention to teach anything.
Verb Conjugation (Past, except in direct speech)				✓	Didn't put the –**ed** in "open" and wrote "stick," a verb that requires an irregular past form, both typical errors of L2 learners.

Students mostly understand the purpose of stories to entertain, but it is not until approximately age 14 that they become overtly aware that stories can be used to teach something (Langer, 1986). Only after coaching students do they add the purpose of teaching something to their narrative writing. Usually, the teaching element is related to the need to be good to each other and to be friends. For example, one 2nd-grade student wrote a moral at the end of her report because she said her report taught "an important lesson" (Kamberelis, 1999, p. 432). Thus, the purpose of teaching through narratives is not directly obvious to most children.

LESSON 1. Familiarizing Students With the Purpose of Fictional Narratives

Goal: To have students understand the purpose of fictional narratives—to entertain and teach about something.

Materials: Mentor texts, especially those already familiar to the students.

Activities

- Read or remind students of the content in the mentor texts that they have already read.
- Ask students what the purpose is for each of these types of texts. Emphasize both purposes when found, to entertain and to teach.
- Point out the specific cultural values that are stressed by the narrative.
- Compare the purposes expressed in these mentor texts with the purposes of genres that have already been covered.

LESSON 2. Activities That Engage Students With Fictional Narratives

Goal: To engage students with different aspects of the story to encourage them to pay attention to specific information included in the narrative as a way to learn how to include more information about events and characters.
Materials: Depends on the activity chosen from the following list.

Activities

Related to reading stories, teachers can create activities to help students comprehend stories, make connections with characters' features and plot, and stimulate ideas among the students (Roser et al., 2007). Projects could include:

- Introducing *realia,* like maps or objects, that are important in the story.
- Having students dramatize aspects of the story. One kindergarten teacher drew masks of the various characters. The children acted out the story wearing their masks. Another teacher used finger puppets to act out the story.
- Have students visualize the characters who are expressing certain emotions or who have certain traits.
- Draw a story map that looks like a board game with students' collaboration to illustrate the stages of a fictional narrative.

Have students do a short writing project related to some aspect of the story. For example, after reading *The Name Jar,* students could write or tell about the origin of their names. For example, in a 3rd-grade class, a Chinese child wrote his own name in Chinese and then created name cards with his classmates' names in Chinese.

Development of Major Characters

Stories have major and minor characters. The major characters drive the story and hold the readers' interest. These characters need to be well developed to justify their goals, problems, and challenges, and how they end up resolving their problems. Most stories have one principal character, although there is often at least a second important character that needs to be developed, as well. There can be any number of minor characters that do not need much development (Rog & Kropp, 2004). Because "stories are not driven by the plot; the plot is driven by characters" (p. 70), it is important to start writing fictional narratives by creating and describing the main characters. Readers' interest in the characters makes the story interesting and exciting. Readers' understanding of characters helps them to understand the story plot (Roser et al., 2007). Thus, first the students will be taught how to develop characters. Then, they will develop characters for an actual story, think about how characters impact the plot, and start sketching the plot.

There are two steps to the process of character development:

1. Establish the external attributes: age, gender, ethnicity, and physical features; and internal qualities: traits, interests, abilities, values, feelings, goals or motives, and changes over the course of the story.
2. Choose the language, rhetorical devices, and images to express these features.

The following mentor text will be used to illustrate the features of characters in a fictional narrative:

THE MORAY EEL AND THE LITTLE SHRIMP

(From *Fables From the Sea* by Leslie Ann Hayashi, p. 6)

Sunlight drizzled through the water, falling gently upon a rocky reef. A speckled moray eel waited patiently for supper to swim by her cave. With her sharp teeth and speed, she soon caught a small fish. Nearby, a little red-and-white banded shrimp foraged the food. *He's hungry,* the moray thought as she dropped the last bite of her meal in his direction. Grabbing the food with one pincer, the shrimp waved his thanks with another. The moray disappeared back into her home. Months later, the little shrimp recognized the same moray eel rubbing herself carefully against the jagged coral.

"Oh, this terrible itch," moaned the moray eel. The rubbing helped for a while, and then the maddening itch returned. If she scraped any harder, the coral would bite into her soft flesh. Which was worse—the pain or the itch?

The shrimp edged closer. As the poor moray eel twisted in agony, she exposed sharp teeth that could crush a small shrimp instantly. Despite his fear, the tiny shrimp couldn't bear to see the moray eel suffer.

Cautiously approaching the writhing moray, he bowed low. "Perhaps I can help." "How can you help me? You are very little and this itch is very big!" groaned the poor moray eel.

"I can eat the parasites that cause the itch." The shrimp demonstrated by waving and snapping his three sets of pincers.

"Really? You can do that?" the moray asked, astounded. "Why would you do that for me?"

"Once you gave me food. Now you're in great distress and I would like to repay your kindness."

"Well, that's very generous of you."

"I ask only one thing in return."

"What's that, little one?" The moray eel leaned closer toward the shrimp.

"Please don't eat me."

"Oh, I can do more than that. All your meals are on me!" Throwing back her head, the moray laughed, tickled by her own joke.

From that day on, the tiny red-and-white shrimp and the moray eel traveled through the maze of coral caves together. The little shrimp never knew hunger, and the moray eel never had another itch.

An act of kindness, no matter how small, should never be forgotten.

Children's authors use descriptions and illustrations to depict the character's external attributes (See Table 9.1). For example, there are two main characters in the mentor text. They both appear in the images and are described as "A speckled moray eel," "her sharp teeth and speed," "soft flesh," and "a little red-and-white banded shrimp," "He is hungry." These sentences give the physical appearance of the characters, while the pronouns "her" and "he" establish the gender of each character. Age is not important for this story.

The internal qualities are usually expressed more indirectly and are thus harder for children to master (See Table 9.2). The following language and rhetorical resources can be used to express the characters' internal features:

- Verbs (expressing actions and behaviors)
- Adjectivals (adjectives, appositions, prepositional phrases, relative clauses, embedded clauses)
- Similes and metaphors
- Adverbials
- Setting
- Actions from and interactions with other characters
- Dialogue.

TABLE 9.1 External Attributes of the Main Characters

Potential External Attributes	*Name the External Attributes*	*Quote From the Book Illustrating the External Attributes*
	Moray Eel	
Name	—	
Age	—	
Gender	female	*her* sharp teeth
Physical appearance	Speckled, fearsome looking, soft flesh	A speckled moray eel, her sharp teeth, soft flesh
	Shrimp	
Name	—	
Age	—	
Gender	male	*He* is hungry
Physical appearance		a little red-and-white banded shrimp

TABLE 9.2 Internal Qualities of the Two Characters in *The Moray Eel and the Little Shrimp*

Potential Internal Qualities	*Name the Internal Qualities*	*Quote From the Book Illustrating the Internal Qualities*
	Moray Eel	
Traits	thoughtful, not rash, sure of herself	patiently carefully sunlight *drizzled* through the water, falling *gently* upon the rocky reef
	fearsome	sharp teeth, crush instantly
Feelings	in pain; very uncomfortable	maddening, writhing, groaned moaned, twisted in agony
	Incredulous, surprised	astounded How can you help me? Really? You can do that? Why would you do that for me?
Abilities	fast	speed
Values		
Interests		
Goals or motives		
Changes over time	no longer uncomfortable	the moray eel never had another itch.
	Shrimp	
Traits		
Feelings	grateful	waved his thanks Once you gave me food. Now you're in great distress and I would like to repay your kindness.
	hungry	foraged, grabbing
	scared, hesitant	edged, fear, cautiously, perhaps, please bowed low
Interests		
Abilities	pick small things	The shrimp demonstrated by waving and snapping his three sets of pincers
Values	empathetic	couldn't bear to see eel suffer
Goals or motives		
Changes over time	no longer scared, no longer hungry	From that day on, the tiny red-and-white shrimp and the moray eel traveled through the maze of coral caves together. The little shrimp never knew hunger

Sometimes the name or nickname of the character can also reveal its personality. For example, in the book *The Recess Queen,* the mean and controlling girl is nicknamed "Mean Jean" while the sweet one is called "Katie Sue."

In picture books, images can reflect internal qualities, as well. For example, in *The Recess Queen,* the images of Mean Jean with gritting teeth, a frown, and later, a big smile, reflect her personality and demeanor, changing over time.

The left column of Table 9.2 indicates the possible qualities an author may include. The middle column names the qualities the author chose for her two main characters and the third column quotes from the book to indicate the language and rhetorical resources that the author chose to use to reflect those qualities.

Authors do not directly say what the characters are like, but use their writing craft to create the images in the readers' imagination. For example, different types of verbs help to express different qualities of the characters. Some types directly communicate the features, but other verbs indirectly describe, forcing students to infer what the author wants to communicate (Schleppegrell, 2013).

- *Being/having* and *sensing* verbs "tell" the features of the character (e.g., "He's hungry").
- *Saying* and *action* verbs "show" the features indirectly and require students to interpret them. For example, saying verbs that show the state of mind of the eel include "moaned the moray eel" and "groaned the moray eel." Action verbs that describe the eel as happy include "the moray laughed," the shrimp as scared include "he bowed low," and the shrimp as anxious and hungry include "foraged the food" and "grabbing the food."

These characteristics of verbs are not fixed. Sometimes, sensing verbs "show" instead of "tell." For example, "Unhei felt herself blush" (from *The Name Jar*). Students need to infer that she is embarrassed from this description.

In many stories, characters change over time through their experiences and by their interactions with other characters. In the mentor text, the shrimp changes from being afraid of the moray eel to living in a symbiotic relationship. In *The Name Jar,* Unhei changes her mind from wanting to adopt an American name to using her Korean name and teaching everybody how to pronounce it. In *The Recess Queen,* Mean Jean turns from being a mean and domineering girl to a happy and playful one through the influence of Katie Sue.

If students are going to be writing historical fiction, they should take notes when researching the historical figure who will be their main character. These notes should include the person's external and internal features so that they can incorporate them when creating their character.

Features of Students' Writing

When young children read or write fictional narratives, often "they focus primarily on story actions rather than characters' internal reactions and motives" (Roser et al., 2007, p. 550). This is consistent with the idea that young children focus more on plot than on character development. It takes time for children to learn how to develop characters. As they develop more complex stories, they may have difficulty creating equally complex characters (Villaume, 1988).

Children's characters also tend not to be well rounded. Vardell and Burns (1986) report that 3rd graders often created flat characters (i.e., fixed and easily recognizable), while 6th graders created stereotypical characters reflecting traits of a group or type. Roser et al. (2007) found that 2nd and 3rd graders included external attributes, whereas older students also included internal qualities. Internal qualities are most important to develop in relation to the plot (Roser et al., 2007). Students may be able to identify the changes of a character over the course of a story they are reading, but they may have a harder time accomplishing this in their own stories. Beginning in 3rd grade, children began to connect internal qualities with the problem. By 4th grade, their characters are more complex. By 5th grade, "their characters' motivations are made clearer in relation to trouble they experience and they behave consistently unless there is a clear reason to change" (McKeough, 2013, p. 83).

José did not include any external appearance of the dog he described earlier in this chapter. A description of a squalid animal would have reinforced the notion of being lost. He did include one internal quality.

	1	*2*	*3*	*4*	*Uncoached Writing Comments*
Character Development: External Attributes Name, age, gender, physical appearance.	✓				None
Character Development Internal Qualities: Traits, feelings, abilities, values, interests, goals/motives, changes over time.		✓			Showed abilities of the dog ("rolled around and stick my toung out")

Children seem to like characters that are clever and mischievous. They seem to get their clues for developing characters more from movies and TV shows than from books. The following uncoached piece, written by a 4th grader, comes from the movie *Alvin and the Chipmunks,* with descriptions of the characters and events. The scene depicts the human as clueless and the animals as clever. The character traits are named. Because all three characters act in unison, the actions do not necessarily reflect the individual traits.

Once upon a time theyre Were 3 Chipmunks named Alvin, Simon and Theodore they All Could talk. Avin was the Cool Chipmunk, Simon was the smartest and Theodore Was the chubby chipmunk. they all Lived in the city. they went into a Grocery Store where know one noticed them.

When they went into the Grocery Store they saw a Human Holding a Basket full of seeds and nuts. wich were Alvin, Simon, and theodores favorite foods. So Alvin walked forward and said "Lets Go Jump into that Basket and Eat All that food". So they went into the Basket and without Even noticing the Human went with the Chipmunks into the Car and Drove to the Humans House.

While the Human was Driving He was Hungry he noticed all his food was Gone then he saw that theyre were three chimpmunks with Big Belly's.

Students attempted to develop the characters, but it was never consistent nor was it planned. Often, they expressed the internal qualities directly rather than by using language or rhetorical devices. Other times, they expressed the qualities indirectly, but then explicitly named them, as if to ensure that the reader understood what they were trying to express. There were more attempts to develop characters among 4th- and 5th-grade students than 3rd-grade students. The latter group did not demonstrate having a sense that the qualities of the character were important for the story's plot.

1. Expressing External Attributes

Students used adjectivals to describe the character's appearance, for example, *yung Girl named Starlight, big hairy wolf* (Grade 4), *Chubby chipmunk* (Grade 4)

2. Expressing Internal Qualities

- Sometimes, 4th- and 5th-grade students succeeded to describe characters, especially through their actions. For example, a 5th grader showed her character was sad by writing, *They stareded* [started] *crying and crying for a long time.* On other occasions, students showing feelings by naming the feeling, as well. For example, when writing a story about two whales, a 4th grader wrote, *Every time at night my husband comes and asks me the same question "Did the pups come" in my opinion he's over anxious . . .* The husband's actions were enough to indicate anxiety. Quite frequently, students just name the quality (e.g., *her loveable dog, stupid cat*) without including actions to suggest that the dog was loveable or that the cat was stupid.
- Use of saying verbs to denote feeling. Sometimes, students used a verb to denote the feeling *(She yelled why did you took my stff animals),* while earlier in the story the student named the feeling directly *(Elisabith said angrly . . .)* (Grade 4).

- Sometimes, the actions are contradictory, giving completely different impressions of the character. For example, a 3rd grader described a chipmunk going to fetch water and taking a long time because *I spilled the water about 5 times,* giving the impression that the chipmunk was clumsy and not too bright. However, later in the story, the same chipmunk tricks and catches a squirrel that had stolen the chipmunks' nuts, giving the impression that the chipmunk was clever and resourceful.
- Students used similes, but some were awkward. For example, a 4th grader talking about the mother whale in her fictional narrative wrote, *I would start complaining like a criminal in jail for 12 years* or *I'm beat like running from 3 miles.*
- There were some examples of internal qualities used among 3rd-grade students, but they did not always fit the story (e.g., *Repunzel started dancing when she was done painting* to denote she was happy). In that example, nothing that the student described was related to the fact that the character was happy. Another student wrote, *the Fox ran away with a evil grin.* Given in the story the Turkey caught the Fox trying to trick him, thus the fox was unable to eat the turkey, one would expect a disappointed expression instead.
- When there were qualities expressed, students often just named the qualities, for example, *She was Smart and talented. He was king but not very powerful* (Grade 3).
- Some 3rd-grade stories included many characters, making it difficult to identify the main characters. For example, one story started, *There was a Boy named Johny who lived in Texas. He had a Dog named Lighting* (Grade 3). After the first paragraph, the dog was never mentioned again. *Johny* or *the Boy* can be occasionally tracked through a very involved and almost incomprehensible set of events, each involving different characters. None of the actions or descriptions help to develop this character.

3. Character Changes

Students have difficulty changing the internal qualities of a character as a result of what happens in the story. The trend is to have the character go back to his or her original way. The characters start one way, they change because of what happens in the story, but then they go back to who they were at the beginning. For example, the father whale in the fictional narrative was "non-bothering," then he started bothering the mother-to-be, and finally he goes back to being "non-bothering." In another story, Jenna and Elizabeth start as friends, then they fight, and finally they become friends again.

Lessons to Develop Character

Students in grades 1–3 can work on identifying major characters in fictional narratives books, describing as many of the external attributes and internal qualities as they can. The teacher can also show how internal qualities drive the plot. With respect to students' writing, it is best to focus on external features of characters.

In upper elementary grades, students can learn how to develop internal qualities and how these drive the plot. Because it is so difficult for students to develop these qualities, it would be best to start with a few and then build from there. Given that the major characters drive the plot, the lessons in this chapter are designed to help the students work back and forth between developing the characters and sketching the plot. Thus, after developing certain character features, students need to discuss how these features impact the plot and, given the story they want to tell, decide if the major characters' features are appropriate. Because this writing can be very difficult, it is best to illustrate these features through books (mentor texts) and to create fictional narratives as a whole class to reflect the elements included in the lessons. Students should write their own stories as best they can, recognizing that the more subtle aspects of this genre take a long time to develop. It is best not to take the fun out of writing by demanding perfection, especially at a young age.

One type of lesson to help students learn how authors develop characters is the deconstruction of text for external attributes (Lesson 3) and internal qualities (Lesson 4). These lessons can help students improve their reading comprehension and develop skills that they will need in middle school when encountering the response to literature genre called "Character Analysis," common in the ELA curriculum (Christie & Derewianka, 2008).

LESSON 3. Deconstruction of Text to Identify a Character's External Attributes

Goal: To learn how authors express the external attributes of the major characters.
Materials: Mentor text projected on smartboard or written on chart paper. Large version of "Worksheet 1: Character Analysis From a Fictional Narrative—Impact on Plot" in the "External Attributes" section (See the end-of-chapter resources, Figure 9.3) Chart paper. Smartboard.

Worksheet 1: Character Analysis From a Fictional Narrative—Impact on Plot, External Attributes

Character: ________________

Potential External Attributes	*Name the External Attributes*	*Quote From the Book Illustrating the External Attributes*	*Impact on Plot*
Name			
Age			
Other			

- Copies of Worksheet 1 for each group
- Large version of "Worksheet 1: Character Analysis From a Fictional Narrative—Internal Qualities"

Activities

- Read the mentor text and show the illustrations in the text. Ask the students, "Who are the two main characters?"
- For Grades 1–2: Choose one character at a time and ask students to describe the character (or draw the character and then describe). Write the features in the "Name the External Attributes" column. Repeat the activity with the other mentor texts (This can be done throughout the year as you read fictional narratives with students).
- For Grades 3–5, ask students to more specifically name each attribute and write them on the "Name the External Attributes" column of the large worksheet. If an attribute is not mentioned (for example, "age" in the mentor text), discuss why the author did not believe it was important or necessary to include. At this point, students should work on identifying the attribute and where it is reflected in the text. The column "Impact on Plot" will be completed later when working to sketch the plot or stages of the narrative. If students suggest an internal quality instead of an external attribute, write it in the "Internal Qualities" worksheet and tell the students that you will work with them later.
- Then, ask students to come up to the screen or poster, point at the exact language that shows the attribute, and write it in the "Quote From the Book" column. If it is a picture book, have students notice what the images show and note it by putting "image" or "picture" in parenthesis. You can also ask them to name the type of feature, for example, an adjective or dialogue.
- Read another mentor text and repeat the activities. Include a text where the attributes are expressed through visuals. For example, in the book, *The Recess Queen,* the two main characters' external attributes are never expressed in words, but through the illustrations.
- Distribute the copies of the external attributes worksheet.
- Have students, working in groups or pairs, identify the attributes of characters in other texts. Depending on the grade level, the students can either draw the character and talk about the features, or draw and write down the features and quotes from the book.

LESSON 4. Deconstruction of Text to Identify a Character's Internal Qualities

Goal: To learn how authors express the internal qualities of the major characters.
Materials: Mentor text projected on smartboard or written on chart paper.
Large version of the "Worksheet 1: Character Analysis from a Fictional

Narrative—Internal Qualities" (See end-of-chapter resources) on chart paper or a smartboard for each character.

Worksheet 1: Character Analysis From a Fictional Narrative—Internal Qualities

Character: ________________

Internal Qualities: Traits, abilities, feelings, interest, values, and goals

Name the Internal Qualities	*Quote From the Book Illustrating the Internal Qualities*	*Impact on Plot*

- Copies of the worksheet for each group.

Activities

With grades 1–3, work on internal qualities as a response to literature activity:

- Re-read the mentor text. Ask the students:
  - o What are the characters' traits?
  - o How do the characters feel?
  - o Other questions, as needed and appropriate.

Let the students answer what they can. In the mentor text, addressing the characters' feelings may be the easiest to answer.

- As students respond, negotiate the answers with the class and then write them on the worksheet.
- Suggest additional character qualities that students missed, but are important to include.
- Repeat with other books to examine external attributes.

With grades 4–5:

- Using the large version of the worksheet, review the internal qualities and brainstorm examples. For example, ask the students what traits, interests, and abilities might a character have.
- Choose one character from the mentor text at a time and read chunks of the text in which the character is described (directly and indirectly). Ask students to name internal qualities that they glean from the text and write them in the "Name the Internal Qualities" column.

- Ask students to come up to the screen or poster, point at the exact language that shows that internal quality, and write it in the "Quote From the Book" column.
- Repeat the activity with one or two other mentor texts that show external qualities.
- Distribute the copies of the internal qualities worksheet.
- Have students, working in groups or pairs, identify the qualities of characters in other texts. Depending on the grade level, students can draw the character and talk about the features, or draw and write down the features and quotes from the book.

LESSON 5. Practice Developing a Character's External Attributes

Goal: To apply the lessons on analyzing characters for external attributes to have students' develop their own characters.

Materials: Plain paper to draw (all ages). Large version of the "Worksheet 2: Character Development for a Fictional Narrative and Connection With Plot" section on External Attributes (Grades 4–5).

- Copies of the worksheet for each group or individual.

Activities

- Have students choose a character of their own and give the character a name.
- Have students draw the character.
- Have students name the external attributes of their character and label them (younger learners).
- Have students name the attributes of their character and write them in the "Name the External Attributes" column of the worksheet (Grades 4–5).
- Have students present a sentence that would reflect the feature they wrote or labeled and write this in the "Write a Sentence" column.
- If working with 1st–3rd grade students, you may let students write a short fictional narrative with that character as the major character, making sure that they include the external attributes provided in their writing and illustrations.
- Give 4th and 5th graders a copy of the worksheet.
- Have students create characters individually, with the support of a group or pair, following the same process as the whole class activity. As with the deconstruction of text activities, the "Impact to the Plot" will be addressed later.

LESSON 6. Practice Developing a Character's Internal Qualities

Goal: To apply the lessons on analyzing characters for internal qualities to develop their own characters. With early grades, you may skip internal qualities or just develop one character together.

Materials: Chart paper or board. Large version of "Worksheet 2 Character Development for a Fictional Narrative and Connection With Plot" section on Internal Qualities (for Grades 4–5). A choice of characters and their internal qualities. For example:

1. Character: old man, young woman, child
2. Traits: impatient, generous, selfish
3. Feelings: happy, sad, anxious, scared
4. Interests: football, books, video games, tennis, jumping rope

- Copies of Worksheet 2 for each group or individual.

Activities

- Have students, as a whole class, choose a character (1) and a couple of internal qualities (2–4). For example, the class could choose an old man (1), generous (2), and scared (3).
- Then, have students complete "Worksheet 2 Character Development—Internal Qualities" naming the quality that they see and creating sentences to reflect the quality.
- Give students the copies of the worksheet.
- Have students do the same activity in groups choosing from the other items in the lists.
- At this point, you may let students write a short fictional narrative with the chosen character as the major character, making sure that they include the sentences that they developed with internal qualities in their writing and illustrations.

LESSON 7. Changes in the Character Over the Course of the Story

Goal: To teach students that characters are not fixed and can change over the course of the narrative because of the events that occur in a story.
Materials: Worksheets completed from the previous activity.

Activities

- Have students take one of the characters developed (e.g., old man, generous, and scared) and have them describe how one of those features might change as the story develops. For example, the old man who was afraid becomes unafraid.
- Have them do the same activity with one of the characters that they worked on in groups or individually.

Sketching the Plot

The stages of a fictional narrative include title, orientation, sequence of events with problem or complication and crisis, evaluation, resolution, and conclusion. Because the mentor text is a fable, it also includes a moral. When sketching the plot, it is best to focus on the essential components of orientation, problem, crisis, and resolution. The problem is particularly important because "stories are, at their very core, about people and their problems" (McKeough, 2013, p. 78). The title and conclusion can be further developed when the actual writing occurs, as illustrated later in the chapter.

It is also important to show how the characters' features drive the plot (See Table 9.4 at the end of the chapter for a full description). For example, a number of the internal qualities of the shrimp drove the plot in the mentor text. The internal qualities from the mentor text in Table 9.3 have been identified by the type of quality so that teachers can follow along. However, when working with students, it is best to indicate that these qualities can be traits and feelings. Note, though, that students are not asked to specifically indicate if a quality is a trait or feeling because these distinctions are very hard for young children (See "Worksheet 2—Internal Qualities" in the chapter end material).

TABLE 9.3 Internal Qualities of the Shrimp and How They Influence the Plot

Potential Features	*Name Feature*	*Quote From the Book Illustrating the Feature*	*Impact on Plot*
Traits			
Interests			
Abilities	pick small things	The shrimp demonstrated by waving and snapping his three sets of pincers.	Will help solve the problem
Values	empathetic	Couldn't bear to see eel suffer	
Feelings	grateful	Waved his thanks "Once you gave me food. Now you're in great distress and I would like to repay your kindness."	Another factor that led to solving the problem
	hungry	Foraged, grabbing	Caused the other character to help
	scared, hesitant	Edged, fear, cautiously, perhaps, please Bowed low	Added tension to the actions
Goals or motives	help the eel	Perhaps I can help	The shrimp approaches the eel even if afraid
Changes over time	no longer scared, no longer hungry	From that day on, the tiny red-and-white shrimp and the moray eel traveled through the maze of coral caves together. The little shrimp never knew hunger . . .	Provides the ending and the moral

The orientation introduces the central character(s) and other characters (when applicable and appropriate), and when and where the story begins. It may also include information that foreshadows the crisis. For example, the following information is included in the orientation in the mentor text:

Characters: eel, shrimp
When: during the day (sun is shining)
Where: a reef in the sea
Foreshadow: The eel feels sorry for the shrimp and feeds him.

The sequence of events includes the problem and challenges the character faces, building to a crisis, and followed by a resolution. For example, the following information is taken from the mentor text:

Problem: eel's itch
Crisis: eel's dilemma; tolerate the itch or fix it, but risk hurting skin
Resolution: Shrimp offers to eat the parasites that cause the itch.

The sequence of events in most stories tends to be more complicated. For example, the sequence of events in *The Name Jar* includes:

- Problem: American children have difficulty pronouncing *Unhei,* the main character's name.
- First event: Unhei does not want to tell her name to her class.
- Second event: A Korean storekeeper thinks her name is great.
- Third event: Students in her class give her a jar with name cards for her to choose from.
- Fourth event: Grandmother sends her a letter reminding her that her name is beautiful.
- Fifth event: Her friend discovers her real name and its meaning.
- Crisis: The name jar disappears.
- Evaluation: Unhei decides that her name is worth sharing.
- Resolution: Her friend brings home the jar, admitting he had taken it away so that she would keep her name.

Features of Students' Writing

Except for the occasional story that reads more like a personal recount, most of the stories that were written by students in grades 2–5 had some, but not all of the elements of a plot. For example, the chipmunk story included a problem and a crisis, but was rather simple and included few events without much tension. The piece did end, however, with the human character evaluating the situation. But there was no resolution or ending. By 5th grade, "many students include a resolution that fully addresses the problems and complications" (McKeough, 2013, p. 83).

The biggest challenges when creating a plot were:

1. *Absence of a crisis:* The greatest difficulty was building up the events to culminate into a real crisis. For example, a 4th grader wrote about a male whale anxiously asking his pregnant wife if the baby was coming. He bothers her at night while she eats and when she tries to find shelter. Then, he stops bothering her and he finally apologizes. There is no crisis that led to his change in behavior.

   In another example, a 5th grader attempted to write a legend where two clouds are unhappy and crying constantly. Other clouds seek the help of a woman who is dressed as a clown and makes the unhappy clouds laugh, causing the rain to stop. There is a problem and a resolution, but not a crisis. For example, the village could have been flooded from the excessive rain or animals could have been drowning.

2. *Logic of the events:* With the younger students, the sequence of events is often difficult to follow. One 3rd grader wrote a very complicated adventure in which "Johny" encounters a wizard, experiences a hurricane, encounters a "werlock," an old man, a witch, wolves, and Spider Man, and culminates with large group of superheroes who "Destoryed the vemon People." It is unclear whether "the vemon people" refers to all of the "bad" characters in all of the preceding adventures. New characters appear in each event, but then are not seen again. It is not always clear why one event follows the other. Similarly, a 2nd grader had so many events and characters that it was difficult to figure out the number of characters and what exactly was happening to them.

   The 4th and 5th graders' stories were easier to follow, but sometimes the events seemed unexpected. For example, in a story in which four chipmunks barricaded themselves in their house to protect their nuts from a squirrel, they finally let the squirrel in and then "tricked" the squirrel to open the door so that they could ran out. There was no indication that the squirrel was trying to harm them, only that it wanted to get their nuts. Therefore, a reader would think that the last thing the chipmunks would want to do is leave their home at the mercy of the squirrel.

LESSON 8. Deconstruct Text to Identify Basic Plot and How the Characteristics of the Characters Helped to Develop the Plot

Goal: To learn how authors develop a plot driven by the features of the character.

Materials: Mentor text. Large fictional narrative graphic organizer (See the end of the chapter). Large worksheets with the external attributes and internal qualities completed.

Activities

- Re-read the mentor text using the fictional narrative graphic organizer and fill in the key points of the plot.
- Ask the students how the descriptions of the eel being big and fearsome and the shrimp being small are important for the plot. Ask the students if the gender is important for the plot (Note: it would have been important if the author wanted to make a point about power and gender roles, but there is no hint of that in the story). Continue asking questions to complete the remainder of the graphic organizer (See Table 9.4 with a full analysis of external attributes, internal qualities, and impact on the plot at the end of the chapter).

LESSON 9. Joint Construction of Text to Identify External Attributes, Internal Qualities, and Basic Plot

Goal: To apprentice students to create characters and the basic outline of a plot to understand how the two relate to each other.

Materials: Chart paper. Large versions of the worksheets. Large version of the fictional narrative graphic organizer. Smartboard.

Activities

- Review with students the topic that is the focus of the fictional narratives and which specific one will be the whole-class story.
- Decide with the class who the main character for the class story will be (You can also have two characters and do the same activity for each).
- Draw a character on chart paper.
- Using the worksheets, ask the students to name the character and suggest some features for age, gender, and physical appearance to complete the worksheet. Do the same with the internal qualities. Create sentences together and write them down in the "Write a Sentence Reflecting the External Attributes" column of the worksheet (not graphic organizer).
- Orally, create a story together with the class.
- Using the fictional narrative graphic organizer on chart paper or a smartboard, fill in the elements of the orientation and the sequence of events, including a problem, crisis, and resolution. The conclusion can be developed later.
- Discuss how the attributes of the characters are important for the story. Ask if the students would like to make changes or additions to the plot or the characters' attributes for a better match.

LESSON 10. Students Create the External Attributes and Internal Qualities of the Characters and a Sketch of the Plot for a Story

Goal: To have students create the main character(s) and basic outline of a plot to understand how they relate to each other.

Materials: Plain paper to draw. Fictional narrative graphic organizer. Character development worksheets.

Activities

- Working in groups or individually, have students choose the topic of their story.
- Have students choose their main character(s) and have students draw them first.
- Using the worksheets, have students name the character, write some attributes for age, gender, and physical appearance, and some internal features. Then, have students write sentences that reflect those attributes and qualities.
- Working in a group or pair, have students tell their stories orally.
- Give students copies of the fictional narrative graphic organizer and have them fill in the elements of the orientation and the sequence of events, including a problem, crisis, and resolution based on the story they told. Tell the partners or group members to remind the writer if she or he forgot something she or he told orally.
- Discuss with the partners or group members how the attributes of the characters are important for the story. The teacher should walk around and work with individual students or groups to support this discussion and ask the students if they would like to make changes or additions to the plot or the characters' attributes for a better match.

Creating the Text

With the main characters developed and a plot sketched, students are ready to work more in depth on writing their fictional narratives. This process is divided into four sections: writing the orientation, choosing the sequence of events that includes a problem, crisis, and resolution, an ending, and a title. Each section will be illustrated with the mentor text.

Orientation

Structural Elements	*Mentor Text Example* *From* Fables From the Sea *by Leslie Ann Hayashi, p. 6.*
Orientation (who/where/when) Some details that are important later in the story are sometimes included.	Sunlight drizzled through the water, falling gently upon a rocky reef. A speckled moray eel waited patiently for supper to swim by her cave. With her sharp teeth and speed, she soon caught a small fish. Nearby, a little red-and-white banded shrimp foraged the food. *He's hungry,* the moray thought as she dropped the last bite of her meal in his direction. Grabbing the food with one pincer, the shrimp waved his thanks with another. The moray disappeared back into her home.

There are two aspects to consider for an orientation. The first is to decide on the information: who, where, when, and problem foreshadow, which were already established when sketching the plot, but could be reviewed once more. The second aspect is the style. The orientation can be written in different styles. It can simply present the basic information as a narrative, for example, "Once upon a time, a long time ago, many animals lived in Puerto Rico" (from *Why the Coquí Sings*). It can be written through a dialogue, for example, "'I can't find Hannibal anywhere, Mom,' David said. 'I thought he'd be home when we got back from the store.' 'I'm sure Hannibal is all right,' Mom answered. 'Cats know more about storms than people do . . .'" (from *Hurricane*). It can be written through actions, as in the following mentor text. Some authors use a combination of descriptions, actions, and dialogue, as seen in the mentor text:

> Through the school bus window, Unhei looked out at the strange buildings and houses on the way to her new school. It was her first day, she was both nervous and excited. She fingered the little block of wood in her pocket and remembered leaving her grandmother at the airport in Korea. Her grandmother had wiped away Unhei's tears and handed her an ink pad and a small red sating pouch. "Your name is inside," she had said.
>
> (from *The Name Jar*)

Authors sometimes write the *when* and *where* indirectly. For example, in the mentor text, it says, "Sunlight drizzled through the water, falling gently upon a rocky reef," showing that the sunlight happens during the day and in the ocean.

Features of Students' Writing

Children tend to write traditional orientations, beginning with a reference to time, such as *one day, once, long ago,* or *once upon a time,* followed by the introduction of the main character(s). Sometimes, there is a reference to a place. There is usually no foreshadowing, however there are exceptions, such as the uncoached piece presented earlier where the fact that nobody had noticed the chipmunks becomes an important part of the story.

José skipped the orientation altogether.

	1	*2*	*3*	*4*	*Uncoached Writing Comments*
Orientation (who, where, when, what and foregrounding the problem)	✓				none

LESSON 11. How to Write a Captivating Orientation

Goal: To help students write orientations that are interesting and appealing.
Materials: Mentor texts that have different styles of orientation. Large version of the orientation graphic organizer.

Activities

- Read aloud one of the selected orientations, asking the students to point out the *who, when, where,* and *foreshadowing.* Write their responses under each heading of the graphic organizer. For example, using the material of the mentor text, the teacher would write the following student responses:

WHO	*WHEN*	*WHERE*	*FORSHADOW*
Moray eel Shrimp	During the day	A reef in the ocean	Eel throws shrimp leftover food

- Repeat with the other orientations.
- Write three headings: traditional, action, and dialogue. Read the orientation of the mentor text and ask the students which type they think it is. Write the orientation under the appropriate type. Then, with the help of the students, convert the orientation to the other two types. Repeat with the other orientations (See chapter 5 for examples).
- Choose a story for the class to write together. On the orientation graphic organizer, note the *who, when, where,* and *foreshadowing* together with the students.
- Using the information in the graphic organizer, draft with the students the three types of orientations using the same information. Have the class vote for the orientation that they prefer for their class story.
- Have students fill out their graphic organizers (Figure 9.4) for their own story and choose the orientation that they want for their individual story. They can ask for opinions from other students to consider when making their decision.

This lesson can be adapted to different age groups. For young learners, focusing on the elements of the orientation can be sufficient, allowing them to choose the style naturally. Writing a foreshadow may also be difficult for young learners. You can point out these features in mentor texts, but it is not recommended to dwell on them in the joint and individual constructions of text.

LESSON 12. How to Write Indirectly the Where and When (Grades 4–5)

Goal: To learn to express where and when the story took place using descriptions that give a hint as to the *where* and *when*.

Materials: Select mentor texts that indirectly indicate the *where* and *when*. For example, the mentor text starts with "Sunlight drizzled through the water," indicating that it happening during the day. *Too Many Tamales* starts with, "Snow drifted through the streets and now that it was dusk, Christmas trees glittered in the windows," suggesting that it was during the winter around Christmas and in the northern hemisphere.

Activities

- Read aloud one of the selected orientations, asking the students when or where the story happened. Ask the students, "What did the text say that made them think of the time or place?
- Repeat with the other orientations.
- Ask students to suggest three different times when a story can happen (time). Write their responses on the board. Now ask them to think of sentences that would suggest the time without saying it directly. For example, for the time *fall,* students could have written the sentence, *leaves were falling from the trees whirling around in the wind.*
- Repeat this activity with place. For example, for the place *beach,* students could have written the sentence, *while the children built sandcastles, the mother went swimming.*
- Look at the orientation that the class wrote for the class story. Have students suggest to rewrite sections to indirectly indicate the time, place, or both, as needed.
- With students' permission, show one or two of the student's orientations. Ask the class if something could be changed to indirectly indicate the time, place, or both.
- Have students work on their own pieces. Make sure that they understand that changes in language should be made if it would make their story more interesting and better written.

Stages Beyond the Orientation or Plot of the Narrative

The sequence of events in the story unfolds through narrative and dialogue. These events introduce a problem and follow with complications that culminate in a crisis. Then, characters evaluate the situation leading to the resolution.

Structural Elements	*Mentor Text Example* *From* Fables From the Sea *by Leslie Ann Hayashi, p. 6.*
Sequence of Events (including complication, crisis)	Months later, the little shrimp recognized the same moray eel rubbing herself carefully against the jagged coral. "Oh, this terrible itch," moaned the moray eel. The rubbing helped for a while, and then the maddening itch returned. If she scraped any harder, the coral would bite into her soft flesh. Which was worse—the pain or the itch? The shrimp edged closer. As the poor moray eel twisted in agony, she exposed sharp teeth that could crush a small shrimp instantly. Despite his fear, the tiny shrimp couldn't bear to see the moray eel suffer.
Evaluation Evaluation of the preceding events and expecting the following events to be the resolution (Martin & Rose, 2008).	Cautiously approaching the writhing moray, he bowed low. "Perhaps I can help." "How can you help me? You are very little and this itch is very big!" groaned the poor moray eel. "I can eat the parasites that cause the itch." The shrimp demonstrated by waving and snapping his three sets of pincers. "Really? You can do that?" the moray asked, astounded. "Why would you do that for me?" "Once you gave me food. Now you're in great distress and I would like to repay your kindness." "Well, that's very generous of you." "I ask only one ting in return." "What's that, little one?" The moray eel leaned closer toward the shrimp. "Please don't eat me." "Oh, I can do more than that. All your meals are on me!" Throwing back her head, the moray laughed, tickled by her own joke.
Resolution Problem has been resolved.	From that day on, the tiny red-and-white shrimp and the moray eel traveled through the maze of coral caves together. The little shrimp never knew hunger, and the moray eel never had another itch.

Features of Students' Writing

From an early age, children have a general sense of the structure of narratives. Kamberelis (1999) found that K–2 children demonstrated greater knowledge of the text structure features than the more detailed language features. In addition, Kamberelis found that teachers gave a greater amount of specific feedback with respect to the stages of the text when commenting on narratives than other genres that children were exploring. When writing a narrative without instruction, José failed to include events that lead to a climax. He mostly developed the resolution.

Children use the past tense, introduce characters, and track them through their stories. By 2nd grade, students use complex temporal connectives and causal connectives to "represent characters' specific internal states" (Kamberelis, 1999, p. 437). However, there are still a number of aspects that slowly develop with age.

	1	*2*	*3*	*4*	*Uncoached Writing Comments*
Sequence of Events (including complication, crisis)		✓			Starts directly with the problem and goes quickly to the resolution.
Evaluation (optional) Of the preceding events and expecting the following events to be the resolution.					N/A
Resolution Problem has been resolved.			✓		"I finnily found a family" followed by one more event showing a happy dog with a normal life.

Some of the issues students have with respect to the stages are:

1. José's uncoached piece from earlier in the chapter was not very elaborate when describing the events, problems, and crisis. However, with coaching, the stories tend to get more complicated. Students had difficulty developing the crisis and building tension.
2. Resolutions are usually quite simple and quick; more akin to an optional type of ending that restores things to a normal or better state of affairs (Kamberelis, 1999). For example, after writing a very elaborate story with major conflict between the two main characters, the narrative ends with, "*I'm sorry elisabith are We friends. Certainly! And they become friends agien. The End!* Becoming friends is a common type of resolution among children's narrative writing.
3. Kindergarteners initially tend to use the present tense, describing a picture rather than telling a story.

Lessons to Develop the Stages of the Narrative

Mentor texts and the topics developed while learning how to develop characters and sketch the plot should be used as the basis to develop each one of the stages of the narrative: problem, events with complications leading to a crisis, evaluation, and resolution. These lessons include the deconstruction of mentor texts, joint construction of each stage, and students writing the stages for their own stories. Depending on the grade level and the amount of practice needed, the lesson can be carried out over more than one class period.

LESSON 13. Deconstructing the Events, Crisis, and Resolution

Goal: To show students how authors unfold the plot of a narrative.

Materials: Mentor text. Other texts familiar to students that have more events and complications, such as *The Name Jar, Very Last First Time,* or any other previously used. Large version of the graphic organizer (pyramid for the events, crisis, and resolution; see end of the chapter).

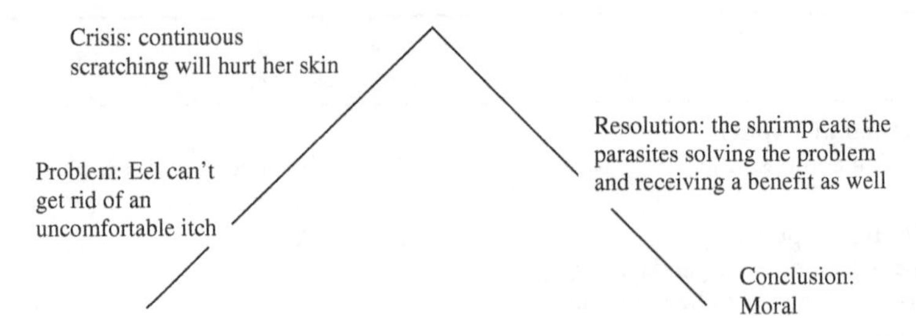

FIGURE 9.1

Activities

- Read the mentor text and discuss the stages: sequence of events, including various complications leading to the crisis, evaluation, and resolution.
- As each stage is discussed, map it on to the graphic organizer (See Figure 9.1). Write the basic concepts to model what the sketch of a plot plan should look like when you try it with students.

Liz MacDonald recalls her experience teaching 2nd graders to write fictional narratives. "My goal in reading *Peter Rabbit* was to have students better understand the elements of a narrative; a genre which they would be expected to write. As I read, I would point out the features of a narrative, including the problem and the solution. I soon discovered that these concepts needed clarification through additional lessons. Upon completion of reading the book, I asked the students to analyze the text by categorizing the different components in a graphic organizer. Identifying the events posed a challenge for a majority of the students. So as all reflective practitioners do, I veered from my plan and inserted additional lessons to scaffold students' understanding of events in a narrative text. I knew that if students' conceptual understanding of an event were not clarified, problems would arise when it was time for them to include events in their narrative piece. One particular lesson that I incorporated was having students order the events of the story of *Peter Rabbit* while viewing an electronic version of the text together on a large screen. The students appeared to have a better understanding of events following the lesson. It was now time for me to move on to teaching students how to gather facts."

Skills Needed to Write the Core of the Story

Before—or while—working on the stages of the fictional narrative, there are a number of skills that would help students enhance their stories. With early grades, it is best to focus on their ability to use the past tense (See chapter 5, lesson 25 for suggestions) and to tell stories in the third person (See chapter 6, lesson 5 for suggestions). Beginning in 3rd grade, dialogue use can be introduced. By 4th and 5th grade, students should be taught how to add tension and how to add information to create an image of time, place, and cultural background of characters. The elements drawn from these lessons can be added to the plot sketch or graphic organizer developed earlier.

One way to keep the reader interested is to build tension. This can be done through time or pressure conveyed through a deadline or some impending event, setbacks to the main character, something revealed to the reader that the character does not know about, anticipation of a major event, and descriptions and actions that reveal tension. The mentor text builds tension by describing the major characters as an eel that is a menacing creature with "sharp teeth," and the shrimp as afraid, thus "cautiously approaching."

LESSON 14. Learning How to Build Tension (Grades 4–5)

Goal: To add an element of tension to students' story plot.
Materials: Graphic organizer with the events in their narratives. Features that build tension listed on chart paper including,

- Deadline or some impending event
- Setbacks to the main character
- Something revealed to the reader that the character does not know about
- Anticipation of a major event
- Descriptions and actions that reveal tension.

Activities

- Read sections of narratives that you have been read with the class before that illustrate the different strategies to build tension. Have students identify the strategies.
- Have a student share the events in his or her graphic organizer and, with the class, discuss an event that the author could add to build tension.
- Repeat with another student's work.
- Have students work in groups or pairs to examine the remaining graphic organizers.
- As the students work, confer with individuals to make sure that their changes or additions make sense.

Authors build characters and change the pace of the narrative by adding dialogue. This type of writing can take up to half of the story (Rog & Kropp, 2004). Children need to understand that the dialogue has a purpose. If dialogue is not controlled or becomes random, excessive, and purposeless, the thread of the narrative can become confusing.

LESSON 15. To Insert Dialogue in the Narrative (Grades 4–5)

Goal: To learn to further build character by using dialogue.

Materials: Mentor texts that are familiar to the students with examples of dialogue that reveal something about the characters. Students' worksheets with external and internal features of their character(s).

Activities

- Read the dialogues of one or two mentor texts aloud.
- Ask the students to describe what the mentor texts reveal of the characters.
- Ask a student to show the picture of his or her character and read some of the features, both external and internal.
- Isolate one external and one internal feature of the character (e.g., *old* and *generous*).
- Working with the whole class, construct a short dialogue revealing both the external and internal features that would fit well in the story. For example, for the external feature, *old,* the dialogue to be added could be,
  - "Do you want to walk with me to the top of the mountain?" asked the young man.
  - "I can't, my heart is not strong any more and it is difficult for me to walk so much," replied Mr. Jones.
- For the internal feature, *generous,* the dialogue to be added could be,
  - "What a beautiful scarf you are wearing!" commented the young woman.
  - "Would you like it? It would make me happy if you accept it," said Laura.
- Repeat this activity with another student.
- As you write the examples, point at the punctuation that accompanies dialogue.
- Have students work in groups to do the same activity with the rest of the stories.
- Have students insert these dialogues when they are writing the stages. Remind them of the needed punctuation.

Fictional narratives create an image of time, place, and cultural background of the characters in which the story occurs. Authors use devices, such as imitating the manner of speech of the time or region. For example, *Mississippi Bridge* takes place in the southern United States and the characters use the dialect of the region in their dialogue. For example, one character says, "Now I ain't gonna tell y'all again" (p. 45). This can be confusing for bilingual learners who are trying to master a more standard dialect.

Dress, food, drinks, names, tools, and vehicles are other devices used. For example, in the book *Too Many Tamales,* the family is cooking tamales for a party. Tamales are typical in Mexico and Central America and among immigrant families from those regions.

LESSON 16. Create an Image of Time, Place, and Cultural Group (Grades 4–5)

Goal: To enhance the plans for students' narratives with images that reflect the time when the story took place, the place where it happened, and the cultural group involved.

Materials: Fictional narrative texts familiar to the students. Students' graphic organizers. List of items that reflect these features, such as dress, food, drinks, names, tools, language, vehicles, or other devices.

Activities

- Tell students that you (the teacher) will identify if the narratives reflect the time where the story took place, the place where it occurred, and the cultural group involved.
- Show them the list of devices. Point out that the list provides examples of some common devices.
- Read a section of the narrative and ask students to identify when the story took place. Ask them to provide reasons for their response.
- Have a student share the plot of his or her narrative. For example, if the students were writing fictional narratives based on a social studies unit about colonial times, you could ask, "What can you do to make the story reflect colonial times?" Possible responses could include the way the people are dressed or the features of their houses or residences.
- Have students work in groups to think about their own writing and plan what they can add to address these features.

LESSON 17. Joint and Individual Construction of Narratives

Goal: To fully develop the plot of a fictional narrative based on the characteristics of the character(s) and the basic plot.

Materials: Student work already developed, that is, character(s) worksheets, basic plot sketch, and additional features, such as dialogue, and sense of time and place. Mountain graphic organizer.

Activities

- Using the sketch of the plot created for the class story, further develop the events using the graphic organizer (Figure 9.5).
- Have students orally tell the story and write down what the students say by using chart paper or projecting it on a screen.
- Have students read aloud what was written and discuss any inconsistencies or missing information.

- Using the sketch that students have created for their narratives, have them further develop the events of their story by using the graphic organizer.
- Have students sit with a partner and tell their story orally.
- Have students add the central part of their plot following their orientation. Younger students can create the plot through visuals, adding or dictating short captions under each picture or drawing.

LESSON 18. Teach Students to Incorporate Accurate Facts

Goal: To show student that even when a story is fiction, some contextual facts are accurate and can be helpful to include.

Materials: Mentor text. Class and student work.

Activities

- Point out or circle the factual elements in the mentor text narratives, such as the behaviors of moray eels hiding in the rocks and coming out only to catch food, and of banded coral shrimp that clean parasites off of eels.
- Have students check or circle the facts in the class fictional narrative. Discuss with the students if these facts are accurate.
- Have the students check or circle the facts in their own fictional narrative. Then, have them check these facts against the research that they had done on the topic. Revise inaccurate facts and add those facts that are missing. For example, one student had a giraffe as her character. In the graphic organizer, she had written South Africa in the "where" box, but failed to write it in the actual story. Fact checking helped her to find this omission. Another student had a penguin as the main character and had him living in the Arctic rather than Antarctica.

Ending

The conclusion of a fictional narrative reveals a lesson learned or changes in the characters from the experience. This occurs at the end of the conflict. Depending on the type of narrative or author choices, there are different ways to end a narrative. Some examples include:

Conclusion Type	*Examples*
Moral	"An act of kindness, no matter how small, should never be forgotten." *(The Moray Eel and the Little Shrimp)*
Quotation from a character	"'That was my last very first—my very last first time—for walking alone on the bottom of the sea,' Eva said." *(Very Last First Time)*
Main character's feelings about what happened	"Then Maria couldn't help herself. She laughed . . ." *(Too Many Tamales)*

Conclusion Type	*Examples*
A summary statement	And to this day Mei Mei talks in Chinese and English whenever she wants. *(I Hate English!)*
Legends end with the impact on the present	"And to this day, the *panettone* of Milano is eaten and enjoyed, especially at Christmas." *(Big Book of Favorite Legends)*

Features of Students' Writing

José's conclusion is quite acceptable, revealing the feelings of the main character.

	1	*2*	*3*	*4*	*Uncoached Writing Comments*
Conclusion (optional) a moral or other type of conclusion depending on the type of fictional narrative.			✓		"I was a perfect dog for that woman."

Students tend to end their narratives by showing that the characters that caused the problem for their main (or another) character changed, for example, *Finally, she did her own work* or *Never again did a fish call KD ugly.* Another common ending is to have characters that start as friends become separated by the conflict, but then have their friendship renewed, for example, *Then they became friends again.* Thus although the characters change during the story, what happens in the story does not really affect the character to make them different from where they started.

LESSON 19. Deconstruction of Text to Learn About Conclusion

Goal: To learn the various ways that authors write conclusions in fictional narratives.

Materials: Mentor texts. Examples of endings on chart paper or ready to project. Handout with examples of endings.

Activities

- Project the endings and distribute a handout of them to help students refer back to examples when they are trying to compose their own conclusions.
- Discuss the different types of conclusions for this genre with the class.
- Give each group of students one mentor text. Have the groups read and discuss the endings and match it with one of the types of conclusion.

LESSON 20. Joint and Individual Construction of the Conclusion

Goal: To have students learn to write the conclusion on the basis of what they have learned in previous lessons.
Materials: Chart paper. Students' notebooks. Projector.

Activities

- Given what students have learned about conclusions, ask students to give suggestions for a good conclusion for the narrative that they worked on as a whole class.
- Negotiate the conclusion with the class as you write the conclusion on chart paper or project it for the class to see.
- In a group or with a partner, have students work on the conclusion in their own work.
- Confer with the students about their conclusions as they work in groups or pairs.

Title. The title usually gives a sense of the topic, as seen in *The Moray Eel and the Little Shrimp.* It can also give a hint that the purpose of the text is a story, such as *My Grandmother's Journey,* and may include features that to make the story sound exciting, for example, *How Many Days to America? A Thanksgiving Story.*

Structural Elements	**Mentor Text Example** From *Fables From the Sea* by Leslie Ann Hayashi, p. 6.
Title	*The Moray Eel and the Little Shrimp*

José used the name of the genre for the title. With coaching on writing fictional narratives, but not necessarily focusing on writing titles, students wrote titles that revealed the character, such as *Max the Bragger,* or something about the story, such as *Blossom's Day of Fall.*

LESSON 21. Title

Goal: To learn to write an engaging title to interest the reader without revealing too much of the story.
Materials: Mentor texts used throughout the unit.

Activities

- Read aloud and discuss the titles of various mentor texts with the students.
- Brainstorm ideas together with the students to show the difference between titles such as *The Frog* and *The Adventures of the Ravenous Amphibian.* Discuss

what the language of the title can show: (a) the topic, (b) the purpose/genre, and (c) how the author makes it interesting and intriguing for the chosen audience.

- Take proposals from the class for the title of the class story. Discuss the three elements of topic, purpose, and engagement features. Decide, with the class, on one title for the class story.
- Have students work in groups to decide titles for their individual pieces.
- Have students share their titles with the class.

Resources

- Types of fictional narratives
- Table 9.4: External attributes and internal qualities of the main characters and impact on plot
- Analysis of student work: Purpose, character analysis, and stages
- Worksheet 1: Character analysis from a fictional narrative—Impact on plot
- Worksheet 2: Character development from a fictional narrative—Connections to plot
- Graphic organizers:
    - Orientation
    - General plot
- Additional resources that illustrate the genre

Types of Fictional Narratives

- *Adventure Stories:* "Features the unknown, uncharted, or unexpected, with elements of danger, excitement, and risk" (Harris & Hodges, p. 5)
- *Ballads:* A narrative poem.
- *Fables:* A short, simple story that teaches a lesson. It usually includes animals that talk and act like people.
- *Fairy Tale:* A story written for, or told to, children that includes elements of magic and magical folk, such as fairies, elves, or goblins.
- *Fantasy:* A highly imaginative story. Its characters, events, and places do not exist, even when believable.
- *Folktales:* A short narrative, handed down through oral tradition, with various tellers and groups modifying it so that it acquires cumulative authorship. Most folktales eventually move from oral tradition to written form.
- *Historical Fiction:* Tells a story that is set in the past. That setting is usually real and drawn from history and often contains actual historical persons, but the main characters tend to be fictional. Writers of stories in this genre, while penning fiction, attempt to capture the manners and social conditions of the persons or time(s) presented in the story, with due attention paid to period detail and fidelity.

- *Legend:* A story about mythical or supernatural beings or events. An unverified story handed down from earlier times, especially one popularly believed to be historical.
- *Modern Fantasy:* Also known as contemporary fantasy, these stories are set in a presumed real world in contemporary times, where magical creatures exist.
- *Mystery:* A literary genre in which the cause (or causes) of a mysterious happening, often a crime, is gradually revealed by the hero or heroine; this is accomplished through a mixture of intelligence, ingenuity, the logical interpretation of evidence, and sometimes sheer luck.
- *Myth:* A traditional story passed down through generations that explains why the world is the way it is. Myths are essentially religious, because they present supernatural events and beings and articulate the values and beliefs of a cultural group.
- *Novels:* A long prose narrative that usually describes fictional characters and events in the form of a sequential story.
- *Novella:* A fictional prose narrative longer than a short story but shorter than a novel.
- *Nursery Tales:* A short rhyme for children that often tells a story.
- *Parable:* A simple short story with the purpose of teaching a moral lesson.
- *Plays:* A form of writing consisting of scripted dialogue between characters, intended to be performed rather than just read.
- *Science Fiction:* Imaginary writing based on current or projected scientific and technological development.
- *Short Stories:* A short story features a small cast of named characters and focuses on a self-contained incident with the intent of evoking a "single effect" or mood.
- *Tall Tale:* A distinctively American type of humorous story characterized by exaggeration. Tall tales and practical jokes have similar kinds of humor. In both, someone gets fooled, to the amusement of the person or persons who know the truth.
- *Trickster Tales:* "A subgenre of folk tales, trouble takes the form of a negative trickster who plagues the hero or a positive trickster who outwits the anti-hero" (McKeough, 2013, p. 77).

Sources: Harris, T. L. & Hodges, R. E. (Eds.). (1995). *The literacy dictionary: The vocabulary of reading and writing.* Newark, DE: International Reading Association; Massachusetts Department of Education (2001, June). *English language arts curriculum framework.* PDF available at Wikipedia http://en.wikipedia.org

TABLE 9.4 External Attributes and Internal Qualities of the Main Characters and Impact on Plot

Potential External Attributes	*Name the External Attributes*	*Quote From the Book Illustrating the External Attributes*	*Impact on Plot*
		Moray eel	
Name	—		
Age	—		
Gender	female	*her* sharp teeth	
Physical appearance	Speckled, fearsome looking Soft flesh	"A speckled moray eel," "her sharp teeth . . . ," "soft flesh"	scared the shrimp
		Shrimp	
Name	—		
Age	—		
Gender	male	"*He* is hungry."	
Physical appearance	small	"a little red-and-white banded shrimp"	Being small makes it logical for him being afraid

Potential Internal Qualities	*Name the Internal Qualities*	*Quote From the Book Illustrating the Internal Qualities*	*Impact on Plot*
		Moray eel	
Traits	thoughtful, not rash, sure of herself	Patiently Carefully Sunlight *drizzled* through the water, falling *gently* upon the rocky reef	
	Fearsome	Sharp teeth, crush instantly	Contrast with the other character
Feelings	in pain; very uncomfortable	Maddening, writhing, groaned Moaned, twisted in agony	Led to the problem and the need to solve it
	Incredulous, surprised	astounded How can you help me? Really? You can do that? Why would you do that for me?	Helps make the actions of the shrimp more important
Abilities	fast	speed	
Values			
Interests			
Goals, motives			
Changes over time	No longer uncomfortable	the moray eel never had another itch	Provides the ending and the moral

(*Continued*)

TABLE 9.4 (Continued)

Potential Internal Qualities	*Name the Internal Qualities*	*Quote From the Book Illustrating the Internal Qualities*	*Impact on Plot*
		Shrimp	
Traits			
Feelings	grateful	Waved his thanks "Once you gave me food. Now you're in great distress and I would like to repay your kindness."	Another factor that led to solving the problem
	hungry	Foraged, grabbing	Caused the other character to help
	Scared, hesitant	Edged, fear, cautiously, perhaps, please Bowed low	Added tension to the actions
Interests			
Abilities	Pick small things	The shrimp demonstrated by waving and snapping his three sets of pincers.	Will help solve the problem
Values	empathetic	Couldn't bear to see eel suffer	
Goals, Motives			
Changes over time	No longer scared, no longer hungry	From that day on, the tiny red-and-white shrimp and the moray eel traveled through the maze of coral caves together. The little shrimp never knew hunger . . .	Provides the ending and the moral

Fictional Narrative—Analysis of Student Work: Purpose, Character Development, and Stages

Content Area: **Medium:** **Intended Audience:**

Key: 1. Needs substantial support; 2. Needs instruction; 3. Needs revision; 4. Meets standard; NA: Not applicable

	1	*2*	*3*	*4*	*Uncoached Writing Comments*	*1*	*2*	*3*	*4*	*Final Writing Comments*
Purpose To construct a pattern of events with a problem, crisis, and resolution.										
Verb Conjugation (past, except in direct speech)										
Title (if required by the medium)										
Character Development: External Attributes Name, age, gender, physical appearance.										

	1	2	3	4	*Uncoached Writing Comments*	1	2	3	4	*Final Writing Comments*
Character Development **Internal Qualities** Traits, feelings, abilities, values, interests, goals/motives, changes over time.										
Orientation Who, where, when, what and foregrounding the problem.										
Sequence of Events (including complication, crisis)										
Evaluation Of the preceding events and expecting the following events to be the resolution.										
Resolution May be followed by a moral or other type of conclusion depending on the type of fictional narrative.										
Cohesive Text (Problem, events, and resolution connect with each other)										

Criteria

1. Needs substantial support: The student writer needs extensive help developing that aspect of the genre.
2. There are gaps in the writer's understanding of the specific aspect. The writer has insufficient control. S/he needs instruction and practice.
3. The paper needs revision on one or two instances of the feature. A conference would be sufficient to help the writer meet the standard.
4. The paper reflects what the student should be able to accomplish and write independently given the instruction provided for this grade level (National Center on Education and the Economy, 2004).

Worksheet 1: Character Analysis from a Fictional Narrative—Impact on Plot. Draw the character based on what the story described or illustrated

External Attributes			
Potential External Attributes	*Name the External Attribute*	*Quote From the Book Illustrating the External Attribute*	*Impact on Plot*
Name			
Age			
Gender			
Physical appearance			

Internal Qualities: *Traits, abilities, feelings, interest, values, and goals*		
Name the Internal Qualities	*Quote From the Book Illustrating the Internal Qualities*	*Impact on Plot*
Changes over time		

The following Language and Rhetorical Resources can be used to reflect attributes and qualities:

Descriptive name	Setting
Verb types	Actions from and interactions with others
Adjectivals (adjectives, prepositional phrases, relative clauses, apposition)	Dialogue
Evaluative words/grading	Introspective thinking
Adverbials	Types of sentences
Similes, metaphors	Use of capitals
	Images

FIGURE 9.2

External Attributes			
Potential External Attributes	*Name the External Attributes*	*Write a Sentence Reflecting the External Attributes*	*Impact on Plot*
Name			
Age			
Gender			
Physical appearance			

Internal Qualities: *Traits, abilities, feelings, interest, values, and goals*		
Name the Internal Qualities	*Write a Sentence Reflecting the Internal Qualities*	*Impact on Plot*
Changes over time		

The following Language and Rhetorical Resources that can be used to reflect attributes and qualities:

Descriptive name	Setting
Verb types	Actions from and interactions with others
Adjectivals (adjectives, prepositional phrases, relative clauses, apposition)	Dialogue
Evaluative words/grading	Introspective thinking
Adverbials	Types of sentences
Similes, metaphors	Use of capitals
	Images

FIGURE 9.3

Fictional Narrative Graphic Organizer

Orientation
Information Graphic Organizer
Who will be in your narrative?
Where they will be when it starts?
When will the beginning happen?
What information foreshadows or gives a hint of what the problem will be?

WHO	*WHEN*	*WHERE*	*FORESHADOW*

Orientation: Write three different orientations (dialogue, action, traditional, or a combination of the three) with the information inserted in the organizer. Then, choose the orientation that you like best.

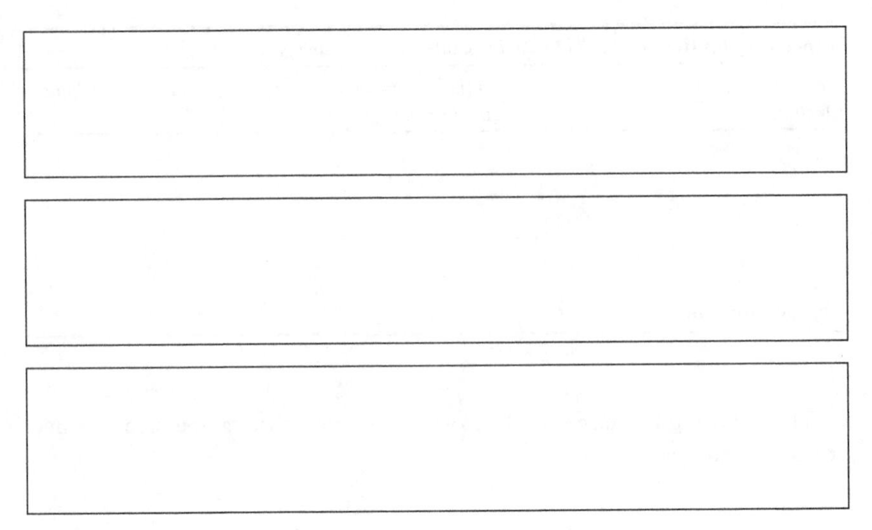

FIGURE 9.4

General Plot of the Fictional Narrative (adapted from Calkins & Cruz, 2006)

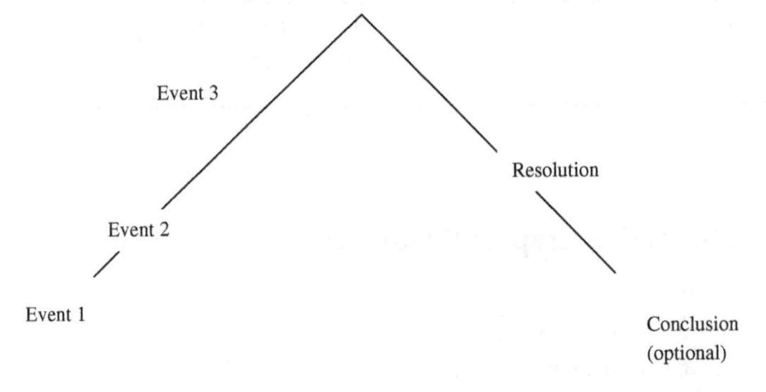

Development of Events (to be repeated for each of the events listed above)

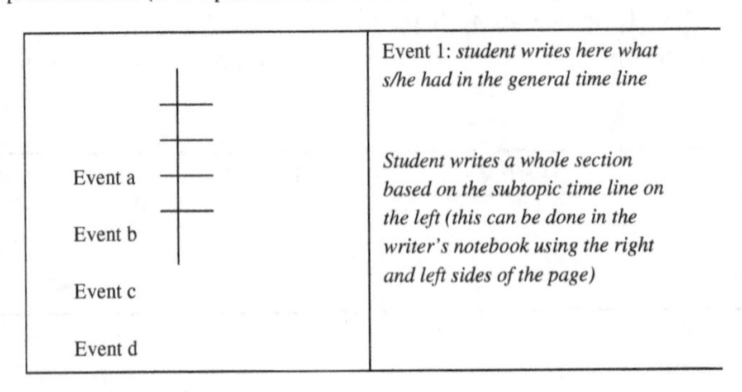

FIGURE 9.5 General Plot of the Fictional Narrative

Additional Resources That Illustrate the Genre

Ada, A.F. (1995). *My name is Maria Isabel.* New York, NY: Aladdin Paperbacks. (also in Spanish)
Andrews, J. (1985). *Very last first time.* Toronto, ONT, Canada: House of Anansi Press.
Bartone, E. (1996). *American too.* New York, NY: Lothrop, Lee, & Shepard Books.
Bourgeouis, P. (1998). *Garbage collectors.* Buffalo, NY: Kids Can Press.
Browne, A. (1998). *Voices in the park.* New York, NY: DK Publishing.
Bunting, E. (1998). *So far from the sea.* New York, NY: Clarion Books.
Cohen, B. (1983). *Molly's pilgrim.* New York, NY: Lothrop, Lee, & Shepard Books.
Cunnane, K. (2006). *For you are a Kenyan child.* New York, NY: Atheneum Books for Young Readers.
dePaola, T. (2007). *Tomie dePaola's big book of favorite legends.* New York, NY: Putnam.
Dorros, A. (1991). *Abuela.* New York, NY: Dutton Children's Books.
Flournoy, V. (1985). *The patchwork quilt.* New York, NY: Penguin Group.
Hayashi, L.A. (2000). *Fables from the sea.* Hong Kong: University of Hawaii Press.
Henkes, K. (1988). *Chester's way.* New York, NY: Greenwillow Books.
Henkes, K. (1989). *Jessica.* New York, NY: Greenwillow Books.
Henkes, K. (1991). *Chrysanthemum.* New York, NY: Greenwillow Books.
Hopkinson, D. (2003). *Girl wonder.* New York, NY: Aladdin Paperbacks.
Ketteman, H. (2000). *Armadillo tattletale.* New York, NY: Scholastic Press.
Kurtz, J. (2000). *Faraway home.* New York, NY: Gulliver Books Harcourt, Inc.
Levine, E. (1989). *I hate English!* New York, NY: Scholastic.
McKay, L. (1998). *Journey home.* New York, NY: Lee & Low Books.
McPhail, D. (2002). *The teddy bear.* New York, NY: Henry Holt & Company.
Mohr, N. (1990). *Felita.* New York, NY: Puffin Books.
O'Neill, A. (2002). *The recess queen.* New York, NY: Scholastic Press.
Poole, A.L. (2000). *The ant and the grasshopper.* New York, NY: Holiday House.
Soto, G. (1993). *Too many tamales.* New York, NY: The Putnam & Grosset Group.
Tarpley, N.A. (2002). *Bippity bop.* New York, NY: Little, Brown, and Company.
Torres, L. (1993). *Subway sparrow.* New York, NY: Farrar, Straus, and Giroux.
Wells, R. (1997). *McDuff moves in.* New York, NY: Hyperion Books for Children.

PART III

Conclusion

Implementing a School-wide Academic Genre-based Writing Curriculum

In the United States reading is the focus of literacy learning. However, writing is an important tool for learning and can be instrumental in improving reading skills. Writing not only helps learners understand and recall material, it is also an essential tool for persuasion and communication. Writing is used to share information, feelings, and happenings. Writing can also help people solve problems (Graham & Harris, 2013).

The purpose of this book is to help fill the void in literacy instruction and move writing from merely responding to texts or prompts to writing that is initiated by the writer's ideas and knowledge. The goal is to familiarize students with academic discourses and to feel the power of language to instruct, recount, inform, and persuade. This is an additive perspective—that is, the purpose of learning the academic discourses is to *add* to the rich repertoires of everyday discourses and languages students bring to school in order to expand their access to a greater range of social contexts than immediate neighborhood, peers, and families. Once children have acquired facility with the genres included in this book they should be given opportunities to choose topics and audiences and to decide which genre or genres will help them accomplish their goals.

Because developing students' writing proficiency takes many years, elementary schools need to plan a coherent writing curriculum to be carried out through these years of schooling. I recommend that schools take the following steps to implement an academic literacy-based writing curriculum:

1. Familiarize staff with the genres as described in this book.
2. Have teachers use the content area curriculum maps and consult the suggestions for which content area and grade levels each genre is appropriate. Teachers at each grade level should
    a. Determine the genres appropriate for that grade
    b. Match each genre with a content area unit.
3. Create a matrix with genres and grade levels to determine if (a) all genres have been covered across the grade levels and (b) there is too much repetition of genres.
4. Modify and finalize the writing plan for the school.

The starting point should be the content area. The focus of this book is on English Language Arts, Social Studies, and Science.

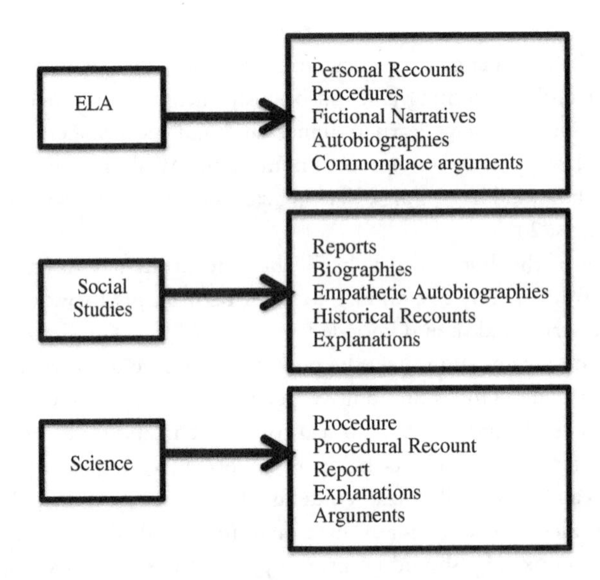

Different genres are more suitable for different content areas and for different grade levels (see Table Conclusion-1). Pre-K through Grade 1 should cover Procedure, Personal Recounts, and Reports. By 2nd grade teachers can add Autobiographies, followed by Biographies in 3rd grade. The hardest genres are Fictional Narratives, Historical Recounts, Explanations, and Arguments, which should be covered in 3rd through 5th grades.

GENRES BY GRADE LEVEL

	Pre-K; K	*1*	*2*	*3*	*4*	*5*
Procedure	✓	✓	✓	✓	Science only	
Personal Recount	✓	✓			✓	
Imaginative Recount					✓	
Procedural Recount		✓	✓	✓	✓	✓
Historical Recount						✓
Autobiography			✓			
Empathetic Autobiography					✓	
Biography				✓		
Report	✓	✓	✓	✓	✓	✓
Sequential Explanation	✓	✓	✓	✓	✓	✓
Causal Explanation				✓	✓	✓
Cyclical Explanation	✓	✓	✓	✓	✓	✓
Systems Explanation					✓	✓
Arguments	Oral Arguments			Oral & Written Arguments		
Fictional Narrative	Identify features of characters when reading			Write fictional narrative		

Pre-K through Grade 1 should plan on writing three genres. It is best to have two rounds for each genre. Thus all three genres can be done in the first half of the year and then repeated again when children have developed their basic writing skills. The other grades can cover between four or five genres in a year depending on the amount of time dedicated to standardized testing. Based on all these considerations each grade level creates a writing calendar matching content and genre units.

Because this book is informed by SFL, a theory that places text in context, the contents can be adapted to the contextual demands of specific educational settings. Professionals using the book to prepare teacher candidates and teachers or using it for planning writing in schools have the flexibility to choose the genres included in Part II to fit their contextual needs. The theoretical and practical information in Part I is useful in any context and can serve as the foundation to adjusting to new contexts.

The plasticity of the content in this book allows practitioners to use it to enhance their existing knowledge of writing and language to create rich school environments where children learn and enjoy writing and sharing their work.

APPENDIX

Unit Plan Template

UNIT	GENRE:	Grade

Unit Preparation [describe your plans for each of these areas]

1. In anticipation and during writing:
   a. Develop content knowledge, including teaching research strategies.
   b. Develop academic language.
2. Content area standards
3. Writing and language standards
4. Resources
5. Students' products
   a. Intended audience.
   b. Whole-class, group, or individual products.
   c. Medium: books, posters, poems, PowerPoints, brochures, etc.

Lessons to Develop the Genre

List and describe briefly all the lessons that you will need to fully develop the genre with respect to

I. PURPOSE
II. STAGES
III. LANGUAGE

You can include lessons suggested in the genre unit (indicate number) or lessons you have developed with experience that are consistent with the theory contained in this book.

Each genre may include as many as 20 lessons depending on the genre and grade level.

For grades K and 1, the unit is divided in two sections. One is done in the early part of the year and involves mostly deconstruction and joint construction of text. The second part is done later in the year when students can start doing their own writing.

	Lesson # in Genre Chapter	*Amount of Time*	*Lesson Content*
1			
2			
3			
4			
5			
6			
7			
8			
Etc.			

REFERENCES

Anderson, D. D. (2008). The elementary persuasive letter: Two cases of situated competence, strategy, and agency. *Research in the Teaching of English, 42*, pp. 270–314.

Applebee, A. N. (1978). *The child's concept of story.* Chicago, IL: Chicago University Press.

August, D., Carlo, M., Dressler, C., & Snow, C. (2005). The critical role of vocabulary development for English language learners. *Learning Disabilities Research and Practice, 20,* 50–57.

Barratt-Pugh, C., & Rohl, M. (2001). Learning in two languages: A bilingual program in Western Australia. *The Reading Teacher, 54*(7), 664–676.

Bermúdez, A. B., & Prater, D. L. (1994). Examining the effects of gender and second language proficiency on Hispanic writers' persuasive discourse. *Bilingual Research Journal, 18*(3 & 4), 47–62.

Bou-Zeinddine, A. (1994). *The effect of pre-writing discussion language, Arabic/English on six adult students' writing in English.* Unpublished doctoral dissertation, Boston University, Boston, MA.

Brisk, M. E. (2007, April). *Enhancing content and language in children's fictional narratives: Tracking the participants.* Paper presented at the American Association of Applied Linguistics conference, Costa Mesa, CA.

Brisk, M. E. (2011). Learning to write in the second language: K–5. In E. Hinkel (Ed.), *Handbook of research in second language teaching and learning* (Vol. 2, pp. 40–56). New York, NY: Routledge.

Brisk, M. E. (2012). Young bilingual writers' control of grammatical person in different genres. *Elementary Education Journal, 112,* 445–468.

Brisk, M. E., & DeRosa, M. (forthcoming). Grades four through eight students attempts at making meaning through complex sentence structures. In L. C. De Oliveira & J. Iddings (Eds.), *Genre pedagogy across the curriculum: Theory and application in U.S. classrooms and contexts.* Sheffield, UK: Equinox.

Brisk, M.E. & Harrington, M. M. (2007). *Literacy and bilingualism: A handbook for all teachers. Second Edition.* Mahwah, NJ: Lawrence Erlbaum Associates.

Brisk, M. E., Hodgson-Drysdale, T., O'Connor, C. (2011). A study of a collaborative instructional project informed by systemic functional linguistic theory: Report writing in elementary grades. *Journal of Education, 191,* 1–12.

Brisk, M. E., Horan, D., & MacDonald, E. (2008). Scaffolding teaching and learning to write: The rhetorical approach. In L. S. Verplaetse & N. Migliacci (Eds.), *Inclusive pedagogy: Research informed practices for linguistically diverse students* (pp. 15–32). Mahwah, N. J.: Lawrence Erlbaum Associates.

Brisk, M. E., & Zisselsberger, M. (2011). "We've let them in on the secret:" Using SFL theory to improve the teaching of writing to bilingual learners. In T. Lucas (Ed.), *Teacher preparation for linguistically diverse classrooms: A resource for teacher educators* (pp. 111–126). New York, NY: Routledge.

Brown, B., & Ryoo, K. (2008). Teaching science as a language: A 'content-first' approach to science teaching. *Journal of Research in Science Teaching, 45,* 529–553.

Bunch, G. C. (2006). Academic English in the 7th grade: Broadening the lens, expanding access. *Journal of English for Academic Purposes, 5,* 284–301.

Bunch, G. C. (2013). Pedagogical language knowledge: Preparing mainstream teachers for English learners in the New Standards era. *Review of Educational Research, 37,* 298–341.

Butt, D., Fahey, R., Feez, S., Spinks, S., & Yallop, C. (2000). *Using functional grammar: An explorer's guide.* Sydney, Australia: National Centre for English Language Teaching and Research: Macquarie University.

Calkins, L., & Cruz, M. C. (2006). *Writing fiction: Big dreams, tall ambitions.* Portsmouth, NH: Heinemann.

Carlisle, J. F., & Beeman, M. M. (2000). The effects of language of instruction on the reading and writing achievement of first-grade Hispanic children. *Scientific Studies of Reading, 4,* 331–353.

Christie, F. (2012). *Language education throughout the school years: A functional perspective.* Chichester, West Sussex: Wiley-Blackwell.

Christie, F., & Derewianka, B. (2008). *School discourse: Learning to write across the years of schooling.* London, England: Continuum.

Cisneros, S. (2002). *Caramelo.* New York, NY: Alfred A. Knopf.

Coffin, C. (2006). *Historical discourse: The language of time, cause and evaluation.* New York, NY: Continuum.

Connor, U. (2002). New directions in contrastive rhetoric. *TESOL Quarterly, 36,* 493–510.

Cummins, J. (1991). Interdependence of first- and second-language proficiency in bilingual children. In E. Bialystok (Ed.), *Language processing in bilingual children* (pp. 70–89). New York, NY: Cambridge University Press.

Daniello, F. (2013). Language in the Common Core: One cannot live on seeds alone. *Journal of Pedagogy, Pluralism, and Practice, 5*(1), 1–17. Retrieved from www.lesley.edu/journal-pedagogy-pluralism-practice/frank-daniello/language-common-core/

Daniello, F., Turgut, G., & Brisk, M. E. (2014). Elementary grade teachers using systemic functional linguistics to inform genre-based writing pedagogy. In L. C. De Oliveira & J. Iddings (Eds.), *Genre pedagogy across the curriculum: Theory and application in U.S. classrooms and contexts* (pp. 183–204). Sheffield, UK: Equinox.

De La Paz, S., & Graham, S. (2002). Explicitly teaching strategies, skills, and knowledge: Writing instruction in middle school classrooms. *Journal of Educational Psychology, 94,* 687–698.

De Oliveira, L. C., & Cheng, D. (2011). Language and the multisemiotic nature of mathematics. *The Reading Matrix, 11*(3), 255–268.

De Oliveira, L. C., & Dodds, K. (2010). Beyond general strategies for English language learners: Language dissection in science. *Electronic Journal of Literacy Through Science, 9,* 1–14. Retrieved from http://ejlts.ucdavis.edu

De Oliveira, L. C., & Iddings, J. (forthcoming). *Genre pedagogy across the curriculum: Theory and application in U.S. classrooms and contexts.* Sheffield, UK: Equinox.

Derewianka, B. (1990). *Exploring how texts work.* Rozelle, NSW, Australia: Primary English Teaching Association.

Derewianka, B. (1998). *A grammar companion: For primary teachers.* Newtown, NSW, Australia: Primary English Teaching Association.

Derewianka, B. (2011). *A new grammar companion for teachers.* Marickville, NSW, Australia: Primary English Teaching Association.

Derewianka, B., & Jones, P. T. (2012). *Teaching language in context.* Melbourne, VIC, Australia: Oxford University Press.

Dewsbury, A. (1994). *Writing resource book.* Portsmouth, NH: Heinemann.

Dien, T. T. (2004). Language and literacy in Vietnamese American communities. In B. Pérez (Ed.), *Sociocultral context of language and literacy* (2nd ed., pp. 137–177). Mahwah, NJ: Lawrence Erlbaum.

Donovan, C. A. (2001). Children's development and control of written story and informational genres: Insights from one elementary school. *Research in Teaching of English, 35,* 452–497.

Droga, L., & Humphrey, S. (2003). *Grammar and meaning: An introduction for primary teachers.* Berry, NSW, Australia: Target Texts.

Edelsky, C. (1986). *Writing in a bilingual program: Había una vez.* Norwood, NJ: Ablex.

Edelsky, C., & Smith, K. (1984). Is that writing—or are those marks just a figment of the curriculum? *Language Arts, 61,* pp. 24–32.

Education Department of Western Australia (1994). *First steps: Writing resource book.* Portsmouth, NH: Heinemann.

Eggins, S. (2004). *An introduction to systemic functional linguistics.* London, UK: Continuum.

Elbow, P., & Belanoff, P. (1989). *A community of writers: A workshop course in writing.* New York, NY: McGraw Hill.

Fang, Z. (1997). A study of changes and development children's written discourse potential. *Linguistics and Education, 9,* 341–367.

Fang, Z., & Schleppegrell, M. J. (2008). *Reading in secondary content areas: A language-based pedagogy.* Ann Arbor: University of Michigan Press.

Ferretti, R. P., & Lewis, W. W. (2013). Best practices in teaching argumentative writing. In S. Graham, C.A. MacArthur & J. Fitzgerald (Eds.), *Best Practices in writing instruction* (2nd ed., pp. 113–140). New York: Guildford Press.

Fitzgerald, J. (2006). Multilingual writing in preschool through 12th grade: The last 15 years. In C. A. MacArthur, S. Graham, and J. Fitzgerald (Eds.), *Handbook of writing research* (pp. 337–354). New York, NY: Guilford.

Fletcher, R., & Portalupi, J. (2001). *Writing workshop: The essential guide.* Portsmouth, NH: Heinemann.

Franklin, E., & Thompson, J. (1994). Describing students' collected works: Understanding American Indian children. *TESOL Quarterly, 28,* 489–506.

Garrett, P., Griffiths, Y., James, C., & Scholfield, P. (1994). Use of mother-tongue in second language classrooms: An experimental investigation of the effects on the attitudes and writing performance of bilingual UK school children. *Multilingual and Multicultural Development, 15,* 371–383.

Gebhard, M., Chen, I., & Britton, B. (2014). "Miss, nominalization is a nominalization": English language learners' use of SFL metalanguage and their literacy practices. *Linguistics and Education, 26,* 106–125.

Gebhard, M., Harman, R., & Seger, W. (2007). Reclaiming recess: Learning the language of persuasion. *Language Arts, 84,* 419–430.

Genessee, F., Paradis, J., & Crago, M. B. (2004). *Dual language development and disorders: A handbook on bilingualism & second language learning.* Baltimore, MD: Paul Brookes.

Gibbons, P. (2002). *Scaffolding language scaffolding learning: Teaching second language learners in the mainstream classroom.* Portsmouth, NH: Heinemann.

Gort, M. (2006). Strategic codeswitching, interliteracy, and other phenomena of emergent bilingual writing: Lessons from first grade dual language classrooms. *Journal of Early Childhood Literacy, 6,* 323–354.

Graham, S. & Harris, K. R. (2013). Designing an effective writing program. In S. Graham, C. A. MacArthur, & Fitzgerald, J. (Eds.), *Best practices in writing instruction. Second edition.* (pp. 3–25). New York: The Guildford Press.

Graves, A. W., Valles, E. C., & Rueda, R. (2000). Variations in interactive writing instruction: A study in four bilingual special education settings. *Learning Disabilities Research & Practice, 15*(1), 1–9.

Graves, D. H. (1983). *Writing: Teachers and children at work.* Portsmouth, NH: Heinemann.

Halliday, M.A.K. (1985). *An introduction to functional grammar.* London, UK: Edward Arnold.

Halliday, M.A.K. (1989). *Spoken and written language.* Oxford, UK: Oxford University Press.

Halliday, M.A.K. (1993). Towards a language-based theory of learning. *Linguistics and Education, 5,* 93–116.

Halliday, M.A.K. (1994). *An introduction to functional grammar* (2nd ed.). Oxford, UK: Oxford University Press.

Halliday, M.A.K. & Matthiessen, C.M.I.M. (2004). *An introduction to functional grammar* (3rd ed.). London, England: Hodder Arnold.

Harris, E. (2011). *Portraits of writing instruction: Using systemic functional linguistics to inform teaching of bilingual and monolingual elementary students.* (Unpublished doctoral dissertation). Boston College, Chestnut Hill, Massachusetts.

Harris, T. L., & Hodges, R. E. (Eds.). (1995). *The literacy dictionary: The vocabulary of reading and writing.* Newark, DE: International Reading Association.

Heath, S. B. (1983). *Way with words: Language, life and work in communities and classrooms.* Cambridge, England: Cambridge University Press.

Hildebrand, G. M. (2001). Re/writing science from the margins. In A. S. Barton & M. D. Osborne (Eds.), *Teaching science in diverse settings: Marginalized discourses and classroom practice* (pp. 161–199). New York, NY: Peter Lang.

Hinds, J. (1987). Reader versus writer responsibility: A new typology. In U. Connor & R. B. Kaplan (Eds.), *Writing across languages: Analysis of L2 text* (pp. 141–152). Reading, MA: Addison-Wesley.

Hinkel, E. (2002). *Second language writers' text.* Mahwah, NJ: Lawrence Erlbaum Associates.

Hodgson-Drysdale, T., & Ballard, E. (2011). Explaining electrical circuits. *Science and Children, 48*(8), 37–41.

Homza, A. (1995). Developing biliteracy in a bilingual first-grade writing workshop. *Dissertation Abstracts International, 53*(12), 2148. (UMI No. 95-33133).

Humphrey, S., Droga, L., Feez, S. (2012). *Grammar and meaning.* Newton, NSW, Australia: Primary English Teaching Association Australia.

Hunt, K. W. (1965). *Grammatical structures written at three grade levels.* Champaign, IL: National Council of Teachers of English.

Huss, R. L. (1995). Young children becoming literate in English as a second language. *TESOL Quarterly, 29*, 767–774.

Hyland, K. (2007). Genre pedagogy: Language, literacy and L2 writing instruction. *Journal of Second Language Writing, 16*, 148–164.

Johnson Dodge, A. (2008). *Around the world cookbook*. New York, NY: DK Publishing.

Kamberelis, G. (1999). Genre development and learning: Children writing stories, science reports, and poems. *Research in the Teaching of English, 33*, 403–463.

Knapp, P., & Watkins, M. (2005). *Genre, text, grammar: Technologies for teaching and assessing writing*. Sydney, NSW, Australia: University of South Wales Press.

Kress, G. (1994). *Learning to write* (2nd ed.). New York, NY: Routledge.

Kress, G., & Van Leeuwen, T. (1996). *Reading images—the grammar of visual design*. London: Routledge.

Kroll, B. M. (1984). Audience adaptation in children's persuasive letters. *Written Communication, 1*, 404–427.

Kroll, B. M., & Lempers, J. D. (1981). Effect of mode of communication on the informational adequacy of children's explanations. *Journal of Genetic Psychology, 138*, 27–35.

Kroll, J. F., & Stewart, E. (1994). Category interference and picture naming: Evidence for asymmetric connections between bilingual memory representations. *Journal of Memory and Language, 33*, 149–174.

Labov, W., & Waletsky, J. (1967). Narrative analysis. In J. Helm (Ed.), *Essays on the verbal and visual arts* (pp. 12–44). Seattle: University of Washington Press.

Laman, T. T., & Van Sluys, K. (2008). Being and becoming: Multilingual writers' practices. *Language Arts, 85*, 265–274.

Langer, J. A. (1986). *Children reading and writing: Structures and strategies*. Norwood, NJ: Ablex.

Langer, J. A. (1992). Reading, writing, and genre development: Making connections. In M. A. Doyle & J. Irwin (Eds.), *Reading and writing connections* (pp. 32–54). Newark, DE: International Reading Association.

Leider, C. M., Proctor, C. P., & Silverman, R. D. (in review). Can written translations index bilingualism and biliteracy in Spanish and English? *Bilingualism, Language, & Cognition*.

Lindholm-Leary, K. (2001). *Dual language education*. Clevendon, UK: Multilingual Matters.

Lipman, D. (n.d.). *Teaching interviewing skills through story games*. Retrieved from www.storydynamics.com/Articles/Education/interviewing.html

Lisle, B., & Mano, S. (1997). Embracing a multicultural rhetoric. In C. Severino, J. C. Guerra, & J. E. Butler (Eds.), *Writing in multicultural settings* (pp. 12–26). New York, NY: The Modern Language Association of America.

Loban, W. (1976). *Language development: Kindergarten through grade twelve*. (Research Rep. 18). Urbana, IL: National Council of Teachers of English.

Lull, H. G. (1929). The speaking and writing abilities of intermediate grade pupils. *Journal of Educational Research,* 20, 73–77.

Marks, G., & Mousley, J. (1990). Mathematics education and genre: Dare we make the process writing mistake again? *Language and Education, 4*(2), 117–130.

Martin, J. R. (2009). Genre and language learning: A social semiotic perspective. *Linguistics and Education, 20*, 10–21.

Martin, J. R., & Rose, D. (2008). *Genre relations: Mapping culture*. Oakville, CT: Equinox.

Martin, J. R., & Rothery, J. (1986). What about functional approach to the writing task can show teachers about 'good writing.' In B. Coutoure (Ed.), *Functional approaches to writing: Research perspectives* (pp. 241–265). Norwood, NJ: Ablex.

Martin, J. R., & White, P.R.R. (2005). *The language of evaluation: Appraisal in English*. New York, NY: Palgrave MacMillan.

Martínez, R. A., Orellana, M. F., Pacheco, M., & Carbone. P. (2008). Found in translation: Connecting translating experiences to academic writing. *Language Arts, 85*, 421–441.

Massachusetts Comprehensive Assessment System. (2009). *2009 MCAS Grade 4 English Language Arts, Question 17.* Retrieved from www.doe.mass.edu/mcas/student/2009/question.aspx?GradeID=4&SubjectCode=ela&QuestionTypeName=Open%20Response&QuestionID=6407

Matalene, C. (1985). Contrastive rhetoric: An American writing teacher in China. *College English, 47*, 789–808.

Matsuda, P. K. (1997). Contrastive rhetoric in context: A dynamic model of L2 writing. *Journal of Second Language Writing, 6*(1), 45–60.

McCabe, A., & Bliss, L. S. (2003). *Patterns of narrative discourse: A multicultural, life span approach*. Boston, MA: Allyn & Bacon.

McKeough, A. (2013). A developmental approach to teaching narrative composition. In S. Graham, C. A. MacArthur, & J. Fitzgerald (Eds.), *Best practices in writing instruction* (2nd ed., pp. 73–112). New York, NY: Guilford.

McPhail, G. (2009). The bad boy and the writing curriculum. In M. Cochran-Smith & S. Lytle (Eds.), *Inquiry as stance: Practitioner research for the next generation* (pp. 193–212). New York, NY: Teachers College Press.

Menyuk, P., & Brisk, M. E. (2005). *Language development and education: Children with varying language experience.* Hampshire, UK: Palgrave MacMillan.

National Center on Education and the Economy. (2004). *Assessment for learning: Using rubrics to improve student writing.* Pittsburg, PA: The University of Pittsburg.

National Governors Association Center for Best Practices & Council of Chief State School Officers. (2010). *Common Core State Standards for English language arts and literacy in history/social studies, science, and technical subjects.* Washington, DC: Authors.

Newkirk, T. (1987). The non-narrative writing of young children. *Research in the Teaching of English, 21*, 121–144.

Páez, M., Tabors, P. O., & López, L. M. (2007). Dual language and literacy development of Spanish-speaking preschool children. *Journal of Applied Developmental Psychology, 28*(2), 85–102.

Pavlak, C. M. (2013). "It is hard fun": Scaffolded biography writing with English learners. *The Reading Teacher, 66*(5), 405–414.

Pérez, B. (2004). *Sociocultural context of language and literacy* (2nd ed.). Mahwah, NJ: Lawrence Erlbaum.

Perry, N., & Drummond, L. (2002). Helping young students become self-regulated researchers and writers. *Reading Teacher, 56*, 298–310.

Recht, D. (1984). Teaching summarization skills. *The Reading Teacher, 37*, 675–677.

Rog, L. J., & Kropp, P. (2004). *The write genre.* Markham, ONT, Canada: Pembroke.

Rose, D., & Martin, J. R. (2012). *Learning to write, reading to learn: Genre, knowledge, and pedagogy in the Sydney School.* London, England: Equinox.

Roser, N., Martinez, M., Fuhrken, C., & McDonnold, K. (2007). Characters as guides to meaning. *The Reading Teacher, 60*, 548–559.

Rothery, J. (1996). Making changes: Developing an educational linguistics. In R. Hasan & G. Williams (Eds.), *Literacy in society* (pp. 86–123). New York, NY: Longman.

Rothery, J., & Stenglin, M. (1997). Entertaining and instructing: Exploring experience through story. In F. Christie & J. R. Martin (Eds.), *Genre and institutions: Social processes in the workplace and school* (pp. 231–263). London, England: Pinter.

Sánchez Ares, Rocio (2012). *SFL Persuasive Writing Instruction: A Case Study for Bilingual Students' Writing Development & Cultural Identity Formation.* Unpublished paper presented at the 2012 Genre conference, Carleton University, June 28, 2012.

Schleppegrell, M. (2004). *The language of schooling: A functional perspective.* Mahwah, NJ: Lawrence Erlbaum Associates.

Schleppegrell, M. (2007). The linguistic challenges of mathematics teaching and learning: A research review. *Reading & Writing Quarterly, 23,* 139–159.

Schleppegrell, M. J. (2013). The role of metalanguage in supporting academic language development. *Language Learning, 63*(s1), 153–170.

Schleppegrell, M., & Achugar, M. (2003). Learning language and learning history: A functional linguistics approach. *TESOL Journal, 12,* 21–27.

Scollon, R., & Scollon, S.B.K. (1981). *Narrative, literacy and face in interethnic communication.* Norwood, NJ: Ablex.

Simpson, J. M. (2004). A look at early childhood writing in English and Spanish in a bilingual school in Ecuador. *Bilingual Education and Bilingualism,* 7(5), 432–448.

Sotomayor, S. (2013). *My beloved world.* New York, NY: Alfred A. Knopf.

Stead, T. (2002). *Is that a fact? Teaching nonfiction writing K–3.* Portland, Maine: Stenhouse.

Templin, M. (1957). *Certain language skills in children: Their development and interrelationships* (Vol. Monograph series No. 26). Minneapolis: University of Minnesota Press.

Thompson, G. (2004). *Introducing functional grammar* (2nd ed.). London, England: Arnold.

Vardell, S. M., & Burris, N. A. (1986). *Learning to write: A developmental/literary perspective.* (ED280073)

Veel, R. (2000). Learning how to mean—Scientifically speaking: Apprenticeship into scientific discourse in the secondary school. In F. Christie & J. R. Martin (Eds.), *Genre and institutions: Social processes in the workplace and school* (pp. 161–195). London, England: Cassell.

Villaume, S.K. (1988). Creating context within text: An investigation of primary-grade children's character introductions in original stories. *Research in the Teaching of English, 22,* 161–182.

Wagner, B. J. (1999). *Building moral communities through educational drama.* Stamford, CT: Ablex.

Walters, J. (2005). *Bilingualism: The sociopragmatic-psycholinguistic interface.* Mahwah, NJ: Lawrence Erlbaum Associates.

Williams, G. (1999). Ontogenesis and grammatics: Functions of metalanguage in pedagogical discourse. In C. Ward & W. Renandya (Eds.), *Language teaching: New insights for the language teacher* (pp. 243–267). Singapore: Seameo Regional Language Center.

Wollman-Bonilla, J. (2004). Principled teaching to(wards) the test?: Persuasive writing in two classrooms. *Language Arts, 81*(6), 502–512.

Zembal-Saul, C., McNeill, K. L., & Hershberger, K. (2013). *What's your evidence? Engaging k-5 students in constructing explanations in science.* New York, N.Y.: Pearson Allyn & Bacon.

Zisselsberger, M. (2011). *The writing development of procedural and persuasive genres: A multiple case study of culturally and linguistically diverse students* (Unpublished doctoral dissertation). Boston College. Chestnut Hill, Massachusetts.

INDEX

Page numbers in *italics* refer to topics within tables and figures.

Printed in Canada